THE JEWISH 1960S

THE JEWISH 1960S

An American Sourcebook

MICHAEL E. STAUB, Editor

BRANDEIS UNIVERSITY PRESS

Waltham, Massachusetts

Published by

University Press of New England

Hanover and London

Brandeis University Press
Published by University Press of New England,
One Court Street, Lebanon, NH 03766
www.upne.com

Printed in the United States of America
5 4 3 2 1

Library of Congress Cataloging-in-Publication Data
The Jewish 1960s : an American sourcebook / Michael E. Staub, editor.
p. cm. — (Brandeis series in American Jewish history, culture, and life)
Includes bibliographical references.
ISBN 1-58465-417-1 (pbk. : alk. paper)
1. Jews—United States—Politics and government—20th century. 2. Nineteen sixties. 3. Social movements—United States. 4. Social movements—Religious aspects—Judaism. 5. Judaism and social problems—United States. 6. Judaism and politics—United States. I. Staub, Michael E. II. Series.
E184.36.P64J42 2004
305.892'4073'09046—dc22 2004008360

BRANDEIS SERIES IN AMERICAN JEWISH HISTORY, CULTURE, AND LIFE

Jonathan D. Sarna, Editor

Sylvia Barack Fishman, Associate Editor

Leon A. Jick, 1992
The Americanization of the Synagogue, 1820–1870

Sylvia Barack Fishman, editor, 1992
Follow My Footprints: Changing Images of Women in American Jewish Fiction

Gerald Tulchinsky, 1993
Taking Root: The Origins of the Canadian Jewish Community

Shalom Goldman, editor, 1993
Hebrew and the Bible in America: The First Two Centuries

Marshall Sklare, 1993
Observing America's Jews

Reena Sigman Friedman, 1994
These Are Our Children: Jewish Orphanages in the United States, 1880–1925

Alan Silverstein, 1994
Alternatives to Assimilation:
The Response of Reform Judaism to American Culture, 1840–1930

Jack Wertheimer, editor, 1995
The American Synagogue: A Sanctuary Transformed

Sylvia Barack Fishman, 1995
A Breath of Life: Feminism in the American Jewish Community

Diane Matza, editor, 1996
Sephardic-American Voices: Two Hundred Years of a Literary Legacy

Joyce Antler, editor, 1997
Talking Back: Images of Jewish Women in American Popular Culture

Jack Wertheimer, 1997
A People Divided: Judaism in Contemporary America

Beth S. Wenger and Jeffrey Shandler, editors, 1998
Encounters with the "Holy Land":
Place, Past and Future in American Jewish Culture

David Kaufman, 1998
Shul with a Pool: The "Synagogue-Center" in American Jewish History

Roberta Rosenberg Farber and Chaim I. Waxman, editors, 1999
Jews in America: A Contemporary Reader

Murray Friedman and Albert D. Chernin, editors, 1999
A Second Exodus: The American Movement to Free Soviet Jews

Stephen J. Whitfield, 1999
In Search of American Jewish Culture

Naomi W. Cohen, 1999
Jacob H. Schiff: A Study in American Jewish Leadership

Barbara Kessel, 2000
Suddenly Jewish: Jews Raised as Gentiles

Jonathan N. Barron and Eric Murphy Selinger, editors, 2000
Jewish American Poetry: Poems, Commentary, and Reflections

Steven T. Rosenthal, 2001
Irreconcilable Differences:
The Waning of the American Jewish Love Affair with Israel

Pamela S. Nadell and Jonathan D. Sarna, editors, 2001
Women and American Judaism: Historical Perspectives

Annelise Orleck, with photographs by Elizabeth Cooke, 2001
The Soviet Jewish Americans

Ilana Abramovitch and Seán Galvin, editors, 2001
Jews of Brooklyn

Ranen Omer-Sherman, 2002
Diaspora and Zionism in American Jewish Literature:
Lazarus, Syrkin, Reznikoff, and Roth

Ori Z. Soltes, 2003
Fixing the World: Jewish American Painters in the Twentieth Century

David Zurawik, 2003
The Jews of Prime Time

Ava F. Kahn and Marc Dollinger, editors, 2003
California Jews

Naomi W. Cohen, 2003
The Americanization of Zionism, 1897–1948

Gary P. Zola, editor, 2003
The Dynamics of American Jewish History: Jacob Rader Marcus's Essays on American Jewry

Judah M. Cohen, 2003
Through the Sands of Time: A History of the Jewish Community of St. Thomas, U.S. Virgin Islands

Seth Farber, 2003
An American Orthodox Dreamer: Rabbi Joseph B. Soloveitchik and Boston's Maimonides School

Amy L. Sales and Leonard Saxe, 2003
"How Goodly Are Thy Tents": Summer Camps as Jewish Socializing Experiences

Sylvia Barack Fishman, 2004
Double or Nothing: Jewish Families and Mixed Marriage

George M. Goodwin and Ellen Smith, 2004
The Jews of Rhode Island

Michael E. Staub, editor, 2004
The Jewish 1960s: An American Sourcebook

For my parents

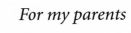

CONTENTS

INTRODUCTION

In the early 1960s, the often lewd stand-up comedian Lenny Bruce had begun delivering one of his more famous satirical routines. In this instance, however, the subversive content had little to do with obscenity. Rather, Bruce extemporized in unexpected ways on the multiple meanings of Jewishness. There was a big difference, Bruce said, between Jewish and goyish (that is, gentile). But it wasn't always what you thought. Not all Jews were Jewish, nor were all non-Jews goyish. It was more complicated. And much simpler.

Bruce offered a helpful primer. "Dig, I'm Jewish," he told audiences. "Count Basie's Jewish. Ray Charles is Jewish. Eddie Cantor's *goyish.* B'Nai Brith is *goyish;* Hadassah, Jewish. Marine Corps—heavy *goyim,* dangerous. Koolaid is *goyish.* All Drake's Cakes are *goyish.* Pumpernickel is Jewish, and, as you know, white bread is very *goyish.* Instant potatoes—*goyish.* Black cherry soda's very Jewish. Macaroons are *very* Jewish—very Jewish cake. Fruit salad is Jewish. Lime jello is *goyish.* Lime soda is very *goyish.* Trailer parks are so *goyish* that Jews won't go near them." And so on.

Several years later, Philip Roth would pay homage to Bruce's routine about Jewish and *goyish* in his classic novel, *Portnoy's Complaint* (1969). Here Alexander Portnoy, Roth's *very* Jewish antihero, kvetched to his own parents: "The very first distinction I learned from you, I'm sure, was not night and day, or hot and cold, but *goyische* and Jewish."

So, you may be wondering, what was Jewish about the 1960s? Why an anthology on the Jewish 1960s? Or let's phrase the question another way: How was this decade different from all other decades? Again, the answer is simple, if also more complicated. If the 1950s were goyish (and they were), then the 1960s were *very* Jewish. Pumpernickel to the white bread that preceded it. Dig?

The Jewish 1960s seeks to introduce a new generation of interested readers to some of the finest essays, speeches, and journalistic accounts by Jewish commentators, spokespersons, prominent rabbis, civil rights and antiwar activists, student radicals, feminists, countercultural leaders, and their neoconservative critics from 1960 through to the early 1970s. Incredibly, and although there exist several excellent anthologies on the sixties, this collection represents the first to acknowledge the decade's significant Jewish dimensions. This fact becomes all the more striking when we recognize that no other American decade during the twentieth century has been so strongly defined by Jewish-led and Jewish-sponsored social activism or so deeply informed and influenced by Jewish culture.

Nor has any decade in the last century had more lasting consequences on the contemporary state of American Jewry. Among other things, this was the era that marked the rise of Jewish pride as well as a Jewish consciousness movement; it witnessed a revitalization of religious communal commitments; and it saw the revival of Jewish particularism as a crucial counterpoint to a liberal-left Jewish universalism. In these and other respects, the very meaning and content of American Jewish identity went through a dramatic shift during the 1960s.

The sources selected for this anthology traverse ideological boundaries as well as religious and secular frames of reference. The selections are not only religious but also religious, not only political but also political, not only intellectual but also intellectual. (And there is also an essay on the legendary southpaw Sandy Koufax.)

The 1960s were an extraordinary time to be Jewish in America. Taken together, a new generation coming of age at that time and an older generation that had come of age before the Second World War composed the most diverse community of Jews the United States had ever seen. This Jewish community was also the most successful. Before the 1960s, Jews had already acquired considerable stature and prominence in virtually every realm of American life; by the end of the 1960s, that level of professional accomplishment became unparalleled. In the fine arts, in theater and film, in music, literature, and criticism, in business and finance, in advertising and public relations, in law and the sciences, in education and in sports, Jews reached a level of achievement that propelled them as a people from the margins to the very center of American life. The upward mobility of second-generation Jews after World War II represented one of the more astonishing rags-to-riches stories in American history.

At the same time, Jews became increasingly mobile in another sense. This involved a mass exodus from the cities to the suburbs. Few moves meant as much, or had so dramatic an impact on American Jewish life. On the one hand, this move enabled Jews finally to transform wholly into white persons in a nation where whiteness remained (and remains) so highly prized. It allowed Jews literally to rebuild their ethnic enclaves amidst the lushness of green lawns, the soft hiss of sprinkler systems, the restfulness of Sunday mornings spent with bagels and lox and the *New York Times*. On weekdays, many Jewish fathers still commuted for work back into the cities while their wives stayed home and their children attended excellent public schools far removed from the decade's social upheavals. In the afternoon, these children attended

Hebrew school, and on High Holy Days, families traveled to new suburban synagogues, only a short drive away.

These comforts of hearth and home provided Jews many things, among them the improbable chance to wax nostalgic over the travails of shtetl life in late-nineteenth-century czarist Russia. It was a quirk of fate even Lenny Bruce could not have conceived. Such was the singular triumph of the smash musical hit *Fiddler on the Roof* (1964), based on the stories of Sholem Aleichem. Here that terrifying moment when Jews were routinely subjected to antisemitic pogroms was backlit with a soft and fuzzy glow. The history became a sentimental and heartwarming saga. For eight record-breaking years, Tevye the Milkman sang (with music by Jerry Bock and lyrics by Sheldon Harnick) to Broadway audiences worlds away from Old World woes:

> If I were a rich man,
> Dai-dle, dee-dle, dai-dle, Dig-guh, dig-guh, dee-dle, dai-dle dum,
> All day long I'd bid-dy, bid-dy bum—
> If I were a wealth-y man.
> Would-n't have to work hard,
> Dai-dle, dee-dle, dai-dle, Dig-guh, dig-guh, dee-dle, dai-dle dum.
> If I were a bid-dy bid-dy rich,
> Dig-guh, dig-guh, dee-dle, dai-dle man. . . .

On the other hand, Jewish suburbia represented much more than kitsch and schmaltz. It also served as a powerful incubator for discontent and alienation. Many young Jews, in particular, experienced life in the suburbs as banal and superficial. The suburban shul was felt to be even worse than this, having morphed into (what some derisively labeled) a bar mitzvah factory whose primary appeal was the lavish recreational facility with its swimming pool and gymnasium. As poet and essayist Judd Teller observed in 1968, the suburban synagogue would have been complete if it could find an occasional moment to ponder matters of faith. And as for the suburban Jew, Teller mockingly commented: "God and faith are not part of his basic vocabulary; he gives them fleeting thought at best and may even be said to be unaligned in the eternal debate between believers and agnostic (there are no atheists in suburbia, or so it appears, because that would mean taking sides)."

Other astute commentators on the American Jewish suburbs of the 1960s offered equally caustic reflections. For example, Conservative rabbi Arthur Hertzberg said of the shallowness of the suburban shul: "Jewish youngsters find that it has too much identification with the caterer and not enough with those Judaic ethics and values that are supposed to give answers to contemporary problems." Little wonder, then, that young Jews frequently regarded their parents' split-level homes in Great Neck or Westchester County (or Shaker

Heights, Ohio, or Brookline, Massachusetts) as suffocating, spiritless abodes. Having moved closer to becoming "biddy biddy rich," Jews had lost their souls, or so it was bitterly proposed. A gilded ghetto, these suburban Jewish worlds were called. It was not meant kindly.

(It must also be added, however parenthetically, that as the fortune of American Jewry rose, not all Jews rose with it. There remained a significant number of poor urban Jews, many of whom were elderly. It was soon argued—and not without cause—that the Jewish federations were neglecting the plight of these Jewish poor. Whether this was due to the fact, as some charged, that the middle-class and liberal federations had feelings of contempt for their downtrodden brethren is open to debate. But there is no doubt that this argument quickly escalated ideological tensions within the Jewish community. As Richard L. Rubenstein put it in the early 1970s, there then existed a "bitter class conflict that lurks beneath the facade of Jewish communal unity." A striking feature of the subsequent rightward drift within the American Jewish community is that formerly liberal commentators justified their conversion to neoconservatism by claiming to speak for these less affluent constituencies.)

The baubles and privileges that came with material success did not directly further Jewish self-discovery or deepen Jewish faith during the sixties. That much is clear. Yet although the effects of having arrived were more paradoxical, they were no less significant. What has been insufficiently acknowledged in standard narratives of American Jewish history is the extraordinary degree to which it was the Jewish youth rebellion that resuscitated the Jewish community. This renewal took many forms, some of which have since floundered, others of which have lasted to the present day. Regardless of the form the Jewish rebels chose, or the precise nature of the many challenges they made to mainstream Jewish professional or religious authority, it is apparent in retrospect that what these young people sought was a more authentic and meaningful Jewish experience. They hungered deeply for *more* Jewishness, not less. And they often blamed their elders for their own ignorance of Jewish tradition. Young Jews quite often harbored suspicions that their elders were ashamed of being Jews and had sought to hide their heritage from them.

This generation of self-styled "New Jews" had a point about their parents, even if their critique lacked tact or empathy. After all, many Jews who had come of age in the prewar era remembered all too well the hostilities and prejudices directed against them in their public schools and on the streets. Attacks from neighborhood thugs shouting antisemitic epithets were a disturbingly common experience for many Jews from that era. During the Second World War, Jews in the military experienced aggressive antisemitism, a cruel reminder that the fight against Nazism was only one piece of a battle American Jews would have to continue to fight when they returned home. Even with the defeat of fascism, the founding of the state of Israel, and the decline of overt forms of discrimination in the United States, Jews continued to feel their doubleness as both insiders and outsiders to American society. Painful memories faded only slowly, if at all. And younger people born in a new and far more tolerant postwar climate expressed amazement (if not disgust) at the hesitations expressed by their parents—to take a risky political position, to speak openly, to stand out in a crowd. "The operative principle on which my generation of American Jews was raised was 'Shah!' [be quiet]," wrote journalist Charles E. Silberman self-critically of his own (older) generation.

This reality left many in that older generation ashamed or afraid to reveal or celebrate their ethnic and religious identities. Admissions quotas, exclusionary rules, and many further forms of antisemitism (both subtle and unsubtle) still existed through the 1950s; many Jews changed their names or otherwise concealed their Jewishness. They would never have gotten hired otherwise. And these attempts to pass as "facsimile WASPs" (to borrow Norman Podhoretz's useful terminology) continued well into the 1960s.

Yet in the 1960s attitudes also began dramatically to change. A small but telling indication may have been the moment when, in the film version of Roth's *Goodbye, Columbus* (1969), the narcissistic Ivy League student Brenda Patimkin (Ali McGraw) informs her boyfriend Neil Klugman (Richard Benjamin) that she has had her nose "fixed." He teases her about it. (Had it been broken?) But it was a young Barbra Streisand who had already best articulated the new Jewish consciousness. "Is a nose with a deviation a crime against the nation?" she quipped in *Funny Girl* (1968). Here was an early stirring of Jewish pride, reflected also in the mainstream, and it signaled more profound and positive changes still to come.

The emergence of a new—and energetic and creative—Jewish youth movement is crucial to an understanding of the Jewish 1960s. As mentioned, it was far from monolithic, but rather quite internally diverse. Many young Jews dropped out of Jewish life altogether, searching for alternate religions, striving for altered states, or experimenting with a variety of non-Jewish (and often non-Western) meaning-making systems. Others rejected religion altogether; secularism certainly remained ascendant among Jewish university students. Still this rejection of Judaism cannot be taken necessarily as a rejection of Judaic values. To the contrary, and especially among the movement of Jewish youth who identified with—and pioneered—the political goals of the "New Left," an expression of Jewishness certainly found its way into these young people's passionate desire to do good deeds—through the fervent involvement in the African American civil rights struggle, through their participation in the many protests to end the war in Vietnam, and in a broad array of initiatives to combat socioeconomic injustice. Given the priority that Judaism and Jewish heritage place upon ethical behavior, it is no surprise that a striking percentage of university students affiliated with the New Left came from Jewish backgrounds.

After the Six-Day War in 1967, many Jewish student activists underwent a sharp political reassessment. "Two weeks ago, Israel was they; now Israel is we." "I had not known how deeply Jewish I was." These became unofficial catchphrases for younger and older Jews alike. For the phrases summed up just about everything. After the military attack by the Arab nations against Israel, and the stunning and sudden victory of the Israeli military, many Jewish youth in particular decided that their activism needed to devote far more attention specifically to the survival of the Jewish people.

Numerous young Jews now redirected their energies from universal concerns to the particular issues that confronted the Jewish community. Radical Jews organized and demonstrated on behalf of Soviet Jewry. They debated with Jewish philanthropies so that increased resources be provided to improve Jewish education and reduce "Jewish illiteracy." They established dozens of new Jewish student newspapers on college campuses across the United States. They put together their own news agency, the Jewish Students Press Service, as a clearinghouse for radical Jewish articles and alternative information. (It still exists to this day.)

Some of these young people also now rededicated themselves to more Jewishly spiritual pursuits. They formed communal living arrangements where religious study would be the center of daily existence. Called *havurot,* or religious fellowships, these settings provided young Jews with homes where they could explore how best to re-create Judaism both in a more participatory and in a more egalitarian (and nonsexist) way than in the traditional synagogue.

The radical Jewish movement and the Jewish counterculture, and the renewal of Jewish identification that these fostered, contributed greatly as well to the emergence of a Jewish women's liberation movement. Jewish women's liberation, in turn, provided much of the impetus and inspiration (by the early 1970s) for a Jewish gay and lesbian movement. Here again a key goal was equal recognition in synagogue life, in the community, and within the family. And as we look back on the 1960s with decades of hindsight, there can be little dispute that these efforts by the Jewish counterculture, Jewish feminists, and Jewish gay and lesbian activists served mightily to revitalize the mainstream Jewish community. Indeed, it is inconceivable what might have happened to Jewish communal life if not for the efforts of these movements for social change, religious reawakening, and gender and sexual justice.

At first there was tremendous resistance to these changes. Many in the professional Jewish organizations were not willing to relinquish their own prerogative to initiate and institute change to a ragtag bunch of college students and their allies. But young people were in no mood to be patient. Young Jews accused their parents of indulging in "checkbook Zionism" when they donated to the United Jewish Appeal but cared nothing about the state of Israel in a more heartfelt way. Young people labeled their elders "Uncle Jakes" because they acted like the equivalent of an "Uncle Tom" in the African American community. And they damned their parents for their "Bagels & Lox Judaism" because they practiced a fake religion that was content to put a Christmas tree beside the menorah.

In short, this was more than a Jewish generation gap. This was a Jewish generation chasm. Young people laughed to different jokes, appreciated different movies, read different books, and listened to different music than their elders. No *Fiddler on the Roof* for Jewish hippies! Instead, the most celebrated songwriter for this generation (with apologies to Rebbe Shlomo Carlebach) was the Minnesotan Bob Dylan. Was Dylan a *Jewish* songwriter? Can "Masters of War" (from Dylan's first album in 1963) in any way be seen as reflective of a prophetic Jewish tradition? Dylan wrote:

Come you masters of war
You that build all the guns
You that build the death planes
You that build the big bombs
You that hide behind walls
You that hide behind desks
I just want you to know
I can see through your masks

You that never done nothin'
But build to destroy
You play with my world
Like it's your little toy
You put a gun in my hand
And you hide from my eyes
And you turn and run farther
When the fast bullets fly. . . .

Indeed, one point that this anthology seeks to make is precisely that the limits of Jewishness cannot be set. The necessary difficulty of deciding how to distinguish between what should and what does not count as Jewishness informs many of the selections included in *The Jewish 1960s.* The anthology pitches the largest tent possible. This appeared to be the only way to represent adequately the decade's multiple performances of (and resultant contests over) Jewishness, as well as the best means to demonstrate how Jewishness came to alter so greatly in its content in the course of the decade. Therefore, you will find the voices of the most influential rabbis of the era, such as Arthur Hertzberg, Abraham Joshua Heschel, Arthur Lelyveld, Richard Rubenstein, Seymour Siegel, and quite a few more. You will read excerpts from many of the leading Jewish periodicals from the time, reflecting all religious denominations and many political directions, such as the Labor Zionist journals *Midstream* and *Jewish Frontier, Conservative Judaism, CCAR Journal, The Reconstructionist, Jewish Press,* and several others. And you will find selections reprinted from journals put out by the most important professional Jewish organizations, like the *Congress Bi-Weekly,* published by the American Jewish Congress, and the American Jewish Committee's *Commentary,* as well as pieces that originally appeared in independent Jewish venues like *Sh'ma* and *Jewish Currents.* No anthology on the Jewish 1960s would be complete without these.

However, I decided also that it was necessary to include a range of further perspectives that might not, at least at first glance, seem properly to belong in an anthology like this one. There are excerpts from newspapers published by the Jewish student press movement of the late 1960s; these certainly belong here. But I have also chosen to include statements by anarchist youth leader Abbie Hoffman as well as poet and self-designated Buddhist Jew Allen Ginsberg. (Ginsberg once declared: "America, I'm putting my queer shoulder to the wheel," and spoke also for many other queer Jews when he did so.) There are articles by Norman Mailer and Susan Sontag even though neither makes mention of his or her own Jewishness. Still, I would suggest, these essays are reflective of sentiments held by many American Jews at that time. And an essay by political philosopher Michael Walzer opens the anthology, even though (and again) there is no reference by the author to his Jewish identity. And yet, I believe that Walzer's views are *very* Jewish—both in the Lenny Bruce meaning of the phrase "very Jewish" and in the ways Walzer expresses the feelings of so many young Jews toward the growing movement for African American civil rights at that time.

"If we blow into the narrow end of the shofar, we will be heard far," Cynthia Ozick eloquently wrote in 1970 during a visit to Israel. "But if we choose to be Mankind rather than Jewish and blow into the wider part, we will not be heard at all; for us America will have been in vain." This anthology attempts to heed an important piece of Ozick's advice because it so deliberately narrows its scope solely to represent (and reprint) the words of American Jews during the 1960s. But a larger purpose of the anthology is to challenge Ozick's perspective as well; for the selections gathered together in this anthology also illustrate by example that the either/or position Ozick proposes was *not* the view of so many Jews at that time. This simple but crucial truth tends to be forgotten. In the 1960s, it was possible to speak—and speak loudly and passionately—as Jews *and* as Humankind. Nor was this seen to diminish what it meant to be Jewish. Quite the contrary. Whether this still remains true or possible today for Jews in a new century with new hopes and (especially) with new fears is another question entirely. Although, to return to Lenny Bruce's satirical observation, it might simply be that we are once again living through goyish times. All the more cause to recollect the way we once were.

THE JEWISH 1960S

1

Going South

Why did so many American Jews—both young and old, secular and observant—choose to play such a profound and prominent role in the Deep South's divisive (and frequently dangerous) civil rights debacles of the early 1960s? What did the African American civil rights movement have to do *specifically* with the evolution of Jewish identity during this era? How did the movement influence and alter what it meant to be a Jew in America? To what extent, if any, is it accurate to conclude that it was a sense of their own Jewishness that motivated these activists to abandon the relative safety of their northern white privilege and travel south to participate in Freedom Rides, prayer pilgrimages, voter registration drives, demonstrations, and marches?

The essays collected in this first chapter provide only partial responses to these broad and complex questions. No brief collection of essays can do more than that. However, these essays do offer considerable insight—social and cultural, psychological and historical—into a range of significant themes highly relevant to the Jewish 1960s. There is, for instance, and perhaps surprisingly, a vivid and unnerving reminder of Nazi Germany for many activists as they travel through a segregated South. At the same time, and distressingly, the activists must cope with southern Jews who resist and resent mightily this unwelcome intrusion by northern coreligionists into local matters. Having achieved a separate peace with their (white) gentile neighbors, southern Jews are hardly anxious to become aligned with desegregation. These essays also underscore the extent to which Jews believed in a special bond between blacks and Jews, due mainly to a shared history of oppression and slavery. And yet these selections indicate, however subtly, some of the incipient underlying tensions that very shortly would explode this seeming alliance.

Michael Walzer, a graduate student at Harvard University, begins the story in early 1960. It is February, and four African American freshmen at a college in Greensboro, North Carolina, enter a downtown Woolworth's. They sit at the lunch counter and attempt to order. They are told that they cannot be served because "We don't serve colored here." But they refuse to leave. The following day, the four students return with more classmates and again demand service at Woolworth's lunch counter. They are again refused. And they return day after day for a week until more than a thousand students march through Greensboro to demand the right to order coffee at Woolworth's lunch counter. Walzer provides a vivid and enduring portrait of this new social movement for racial justice and equality. And yet, he makes not one reference to his own Jewishness.

In 1961, the Freedom Rides begin. African Americans and whites travel south by bus to challenge the segregation of interstate bus facilities. That May, a bus is attacked by a mob in Alabama; it is firebombed, and the Freedom Riders are surrounded and brutally beaten. The following year, Betty Alschuler recounts her experience riding a bus as part of an interracial mission that journeyed from Chicago to Georgia. She reflects mightily—and with poignant ambivalence—on the difficult place of Jews both as insiders *and* outsiders to this southern (and typically Christian) struggle for African American civil rights. And Albert Vorspan, director of the Commission on Social Action of Reform Judaism, offers his cogent impressions on the prominent role northern Jews played in the Freedom Rides.

In May 1963, the focus of the southern crisis moves to Birmingham, Alabama, where Dr. Martin Luther King, Jr., is leading silent marches to demand equal access to public facilities. Demonstrators are attacked by vicious police dogs and blasted with fire hoses. At the same moment, the Rabbinical Assembly (Conservative) is meeting in the peace and quiet of the Catskills; distressed at their own inactivity, the rabbis pass a proposal that calls for a delegation to travel immediately to Birmingham to show solidarity with Dr. King. Nineteen rabbis volunteer, including Richard Rubenstein, whose account of his experiences remains a classic statement from the era.

Finally, two years later, in March 1965, another Conservative rabbi, Seymour Siegel, joins a far larger group of rabbis from all the major denominations to participate in a march from Selma to Montgomery, Alabama. Organized by the Student Nonviolent Coordinating Committee (SNCC), and led by Dr. King, the march aims to protest the racist murder of a SNCC worker during a voter registration drive. Two prior attempts to complete the march have been blocked by police and white supremacists. Siegel describes the events surrounding the third march. After crossing a bridge, the marchers face a barricade of state troopers. And although Dr. King decides to turn back and avoid pointless bloodshed, one marcher, James Reeb, a white Unitarian Universalist minister, is nonetheless attacked and fatally beaten by a mob.

A Cup of Coffee and a Seat

MICHAEL WALZER

Durham, North Carolina, is probably a town like many others; I doubt that ordinarily I would have found it unfamiliar. I saw it, however, only at night and carried away only two memories. The first is of a drug store with its lunch counter closed, where I did not get a cup of coffee. The second is of a policeman to whom I showed an address, who did not give me directions. The address was that of a Negro church where Martin Luther King was speaking at 8:00 that evening, February 16. The policeman said he had never heard of the street. Later I learned it was the main street in the Negro section of town.

Two days later I was in Raleigh, a half hour by bus from Durham. Raleigh is a handsome town; its main street, dominated by the state capitol, is wide and spacious; the store fronts are plain, not gaudy. In front of four of those stores some twenty Negro students were picketing. As a Northerner I expected, and felt, the tenseness of the city. The day before there had been a fight on the picket lines and a Negro boy had been hit with a tire chain. What I found there, by talking to Negro students and visiting their colleges, was a spirit and a method of action which made such incidents . . . incidental. Dangerous they were—and are—but they are not the key to the sitdowns. For the Negro students, like the earlier Montgomery bus boycotters, are engaged in a new kind of political activity, at once unconventional and non-violent.

Late in the afternoon of Monday, February 1, four freshmen from the Agricultural and Technical College, an all-Negro school in Greensboro, North Carolina, walked into a downtown Woolworth's, purchased a few small articles and then sat down at the lunch counter. Not one of them had ever sat there before. They each asked for a cup of coffee and were told that they would not be served. This was the customary policy of the store: "We don't serve colored here." Yet the students refused to leave; they remained seated, and ignored, until 5:30 when the store closed. The next morning at 10:30 the freshmen reappeared with sixteen friends and resumed their sitdown. Again they were not served. Again they did not leave until 5:30. During the seven hours they studied or talked quietly. The counter in front of them was not covered with the usual cups and saucers but with books, notebooks, sliderules. Several policemen came in and walked up and down the aisle that ran the length of the lunch counter, staring at the sitdowners. There was no disturbance; nor were the students intimidated.

On the third day the Negroes occupied virtually all the forty seats at the Woolworth's counter. Describing that day one student wrote:

> After attending a mass meeting in Harrison Auditorium, I was . . . inspired to go down to Woolworth's and just sit, hoping to be served. . . . by luck I was able to get a ride with six other fellows. We rode down to the parking lot and there left the car, after which we walked to Woolworth's, read a passage from the Bible and waited for the doors to open. The doors opened and in we went. I almost ran, because I was determined to get a seat and I was very much interested in being the first to sit down. I sat down and there was a waitress standing directly in front of me, so I asked her if I might have a cup of black coffee and two donuts please. She looked at me and moved to another area of the counter.

The number of sitdowners continued to increase, spilling over into other chain stores. A few white sympathizers joined in—an act of considerable bravery in the South. Finally the lunch counter was closed. The students agreed to a two-week "truce"; the manager agreed to negotiate. At this writing, a full month later, the counter remains closed.

Sitdown in the South has a very literal meaning. In the past, the variety and five and dime stores have freely invited Negroes to every counter but the lunch counter. There they were not permitted to sit down on any of the long row of stools, but were served standing up at a far end. Negroes were often hired to cook the food or wash dishes, hard jobs and especially in restaurants of this sort. But the counter was a color line: on the side with seats only whites sat.

As in the buses, sitting down together at a lunch counter symbolizes a kind of equality which Southern whites have not been prepared to admit. Nor have Southern Negroes, until very recently, been prepared to demand it. Now the sitdowns have made clear the immediate and central issue in the integration battle. "We don't want brotherhood," a Negro student told me when I visited Durham, "we just want a cup of coffee—sitting down." This was a demand for an end to the ordinary, unrecorded, day-to-day indignity of Negro life in the South—an indignity more demoralizing, perhaps, than the terror of lynching or murder has ever been. The A&T students were "tired of humiliation." The method which they found in their "tiredness" was so dramatically effective that in the week following their demonstration, sitdowns were staged in half a dozen North Carolina towns and within two weeks had spread to more than twelve cities in four states: Virginia, Tennessee and the Carolinas. The sitdowns spread unpredictably; it is obvious that there was no central organization. Yet it is not entirely fair to call the movement spontaneous. "*In a way,*" one student said, "*we have been planning it all our lives.*"

Everywhere the pattern was more or less the same. The Negro students, well-dressed and quiet, came into the stores—always the local branches of national chains—and sat down at the lunch counters. They were jeered at more frequently as news of the demonstrations spread, but did not reply. There were occasional fights. The counters were closed or roped off after a day, sometimes after only an hour; signs were posted saying "Closed for repairs," or "Closed in the interest of public safety." At this point in many of the towns a mayor's committee hastened to arrange some sort of negotiations. For a moment the students were confused: they could not continue their sitdowns once the counters were closed, yet they had a deeply ingrained distrust of Southern negotiation. "If we negotiate," the editor of a Negro college paper told me, "my grandchildren will still be worrying about that cup of coffee."

Now, in the last few days of February, action has been resumed; picketing, boycott, mass marches are the new methods of the students. Their activity continues to be orderly, disciplined, non-violent. Yet the number of incidents, usually provoked by white hecklers, has increased; several students have been attacked and beaten up; many more have been arrested. Negro high-school students have imitated their older brothers, but in larger numbers and without the same organization or discipline. And in the meantime, the movement has spread to the deep South; sitdown demonstrations have taken place in South Carolina and Alabama.

II

I asked every student I met what the first day of the sitdowns had been like on his campus. The answer was always the same: "It was like a fever. Everyone wanted to go. We were so happy." In Durham students were still pouring into town after the original sitdowners had closed the counters and started home. The two groups met with cheers, many of the students raised two fingers in the air for victory. The news from Greensboro was spread rapidly by the press and radio; more effectively, it spread along the basketball circuit. Most of the schools involved in the early weeks were athletic rivals; basketball games were occasions for the transfer of enthusiasm. A&T played five games in two weeks and students at each of the five schools were shortly involved in sitdowns.

Organization on each new campus was amazingly rapid, accompanied by the usual bickering over leadership positions ("Everyone wanted to be on a committee"), but fundamentally shaped by a keen sense of solidarity. The student council was usually at the center of what was invariably called, with no self-consciousness, the Student Movement. Sometimes command was assumed by the campus NAACP, sometimes by an *ad hoc* committee. Few students talked about anything else; the seemingly endless discussions of tactics among the leaders and within the committees were repeated in the dorms, in the canteen, in the local (illegal) beer hall. Even in the last it seemed to dominate the more usual topics: basketball and girls.

After the counters had been shut in Durham and negotiations begun with a "human relations committee" appointed by the mayor, a sign appeared on the door of the student council office at North Carolina College: *"Please stand by for further instructions concerning movement. (signed) Leaders."*

The office really looked like a room from which a movement was being run. A bulletin board extended the length of one wall. Newspaper articles about sitdowns throughout the state were posted, along with various notices, instructions and a few recently received CORE pamphlets. Piled high on the desk of one of the council officers were schedules filled out by more than 500 students, listing their free hours so that the sitdowners could be relieved and a minimum of classes missed. The office was almost never empty; students came in to hear the latest news, do a little work, or jubilantly read their clippings.

When I reached the council office at Shaw University in Raleigh it was even busier. The students at Shaw and at nearby St. Augustine's College had been the first to begin picketing once the lunch counters had closed. I visited the office on the sixth day of picketing. Two old desks stood at either end of a rectangular room; chairs lined the longer sides. At one of the desks a girl sat, checking the pickets in and out and arranging transportation into town. The students sat around, waiting for their rides, the boys restless, the girls more quiet.

The placards they would carry stood on a ledge along the wall: *"Do we eat today?" "How do we get invited to lunch?" "Temporarily closed. Why? Just a cup of coffee. Shame!" "Let's be Just for a change. No traditions attached."* At about ten o'clock the first carload of pickets, four girls and three boys, drove downtown. Before they left they received instructions which I heard repeated many times that day: "Walk in a single file. Don't bunch up. Don't talk. We'll get relief out." It was pouring outside; it rained all day and well into the night.

At the other desk sat a boy from Jamaica, small, smart, a member of the Intelligence Committee which was running things at Shaw. He was there all day. "We say we don't cut classes," a student told me, "our teachers say we don't cut classes; but we cut classes." On the desk in front of the Jamaican boy were a few old textbooks, left there by student pickets. Among them I found a copy of Big Bill Haywood's *Autobiography*, with the bookmark near the end. The Jamaican boy knew about Haywood, but wouldn't talk to me about him. He spent the day—when he wasn't on the phone—reading an Ibsen play.

Posted on a wall over one of the desks was a giant placard headed "Shaw University—St. Augustine College Student Movement." The placard was covered with a detailed diagram of the movement's organization, which looked as if it had been copied out of a textbook on bureaucracy. At the center was the Intelligence Committee; straight lines pointing downward connected it with the student councils of the two cooperating colleges; lines radiated upwards to various subsidiary committees: transportation, negotiation, etc.

Every night since the sitdowns started, the Intelligence Committee had called mass meetings at both Shaw and St. Augustine's. Together the two schools have about one thousand students; Shaw, slightly larger, is a Baptist school, St. Augustine's Episcopalian. The meetings have been marvelously well attended. But the night I was there the rain was pouring down outside, and only about 200 students assembled in the Shaw auditorium; there were seats for twice as many. The leaders were immediately afraid that student enthusiasm was waning and sent runners to the library and dorms. Meanwhile the meeting began, with a prayer from the floor and the singing of a hymn. The president of the student council called it "our national anthem"; the hymn had as its appropriate refrain: "March on, march on, until victory is won."

There was a leak in the roof of the auditorium and throughout the meeting, during singing and speech making, I could hear the water sloshing about in a giant bucket perched precariously upon two seats about halfway to the back of the room.

In the middle of a report on the size of the picket lines that day, the entire basketball team shuffled sheepishly into the hall; they were dragged along by the captain of one of the picketing groups. He rushed to the front of the auditorium and began denouncing the players for practicing during mass meetings. One of the players, obviously no militant at all, tried to defend the team; "We can't disrupt the whole basketball schedule," he said, "for just one movement." But he was shouted down and the student who had dragged him in took the floor again to display a remarkable talent for oratory. There had not been enough men on the lines that day, he said. (In general the girls were more ardent about picketing than the boys.) Several girls had been pushed, one had been slapped, by white men. That would never have happened had enough male students been walking. There could be no excuses; the girls needed protection, and—after all—the boys might meet their future wives "in the movement."

III

The students in Greensboro called their demonstration a "passive sitdown demand." What was most impressive about it, however, was the number of students it involved in *activity.* None of the leaders I spoke to were interested in test cases; nor was there any general agreement to stop the sitdowns or the picketing once the question of integration at the lunch counters was taken up by the courts. That the legal work of the NAACP was important, everyone agreed; but this, I was told over and over again, was more important. Everyone seemed to feel a deep need finally to act in the name of all the theories of equality. Once the sitdowns had begun, marching into Woolworth's or picketing outside became obvious, necessary, inevitable activities.

After a week or more of comparative neutrality, the police also began to act, supported by an interpretation of the trespassing law provided by the attorney-general of North Carolina. In that "liberal" state where race relations—so the newspapers but not the Negro students said—were "good," state officials, like the store managers, had at first declined to take the students seriously. They had no real contact with Negro students and were hardly capable of understanding their new temper. During the first week the Greensboro newspaper periodically announced that the sitdowners were losing both numbers and staying power. Someone compared their activity to college panty raids; it was all a prank. But as the movement began to spread, the astonished whites took a harder line. On Thursday of the second week, 43 students were arrested in Raleigh, charged with trespassing on private property. The story of those arrests reveals better than anything I know the nature of the student movement. It was told to me by a boy at Shaw University in a slow deliberate drawl with an undertone of pure joy.

On Wednesday, the Shaw–St. Augustine students had shut down the lunch counters at four stores on Fayetteville Street, a few blocks from the state house. The following day a small group of more ambitious students started out to Cameron Village, a suburban shopping center. There they were told that the entire center, including streets and sidewalks, was private property. They telephoned to the student council office and someone consulted a Negro lawyer in Raleigh. He told them that the streets and sidewalks were public; he thought the police interpretation of the trespassing law should be tested. Fifteen more students drove out to the center. They were window-shopping when the vice-president of Cameron Village Inc. appeared on the scene with a single policeman. The students were officially notified that they were trespassing and given two minutes to leave. At the end of the two minutes—the vice-president looking at his watch—the policeman arrested one of the students. Apparently he thought that would be sufficient, for it would provide a test case. *But the other students refused to leave; they crowded around the policeman and demanded that they too be arrested.* One by one they were asked to leave and given two minutes. They waited their turns. When five had been arrested the policeman phoned for a paddy wagon. Eighteen students were under arrest when it arrived. Later twenty-five more came out to Cameron Village to "windowshop." When the news of the first arrests reached campus, there had been a rush for cars. "Everyone wanted to be arrested."

Two weeks later when the now famous forty-three came up for trial, so many of their fellow-students jammed into the courtroom, that the judge postponed the case. The fire chief said that the crowd constituted a fire hazard. Perhaps it did. But the remarkable solidarity of the Negroes constituted a far greater danger to white supremacy. In Tennessee where some eighty sitdowners were fined for "disorderly conduct," thousands of Negroes gathered on the courthouse steps singing hymns and the national anthem. Inside, the sitdowners insisted that they would all go to jail rather than pay the fines.

The fact that many of the Negro colleges were state supported has provided an obvious opportunity for North Carolina politicians to bluster and threaten. At first it was only the college presidents who were under attack; later students were threatened with expulsion. The attorney-general of the state—now a candidate for governor—is widely quoted among Negro students as having said, "If these administrators can't control the kids, we'll get administrators who can." The result of such threats has been that students have sometimes had to fight on two fronts; both in the stores and on the campus—and the fight has become both complicated and confusing. When I left Durham negotiations were in progress between a committee appointed by the mayor, which could not speak definitely for the chain store managers, and a committee appointed by the president of North Carolina College, on which the sitdowners were not represented. Having closed the lunch counters downtown, the students returned to campus and began circulating a petition against their president's committee.

IV

At North Carolina College, Durham, three young men led the student movement. They were described to me by the editor of the campus paper as the righteous man, the prudent man and the proud man. The righteous man most fully embodied the spirit of the movement. He was a veteran and had spent two years in Japan. That was the only time in his life, he told me, when he had lived like a free man. When it was time to come home, the white boys were happy and he was afraid. Now he led the younger students with a quiet determination; he was the only one of the leaders I met who clearly possessed charisma. "We won't stop, regardless . . ." And he took the strongest position I heard on the confusing problem of negotiations. "If I have to negotiate for a cup of coffee, I won't pay for it. I won't negotiate across the table and then again across the counter."

The most remarkable thing about these students is their self-confidence. They have grown up in a South which is no longer a terror for them, but still a continual source of insult and indignity. They have been in the army or spent time in the North—summers at church camps, a year working in New York, a visit to relatives. They have developed thin skins; segregation is no longer tolerable to them. They have unlearned, perhaps they never learned, those habits of inferiority which have cursed Negro life in the South for a century. They have felt every insult—as an insult. They could not understand the "complacency" or the "fearfulness" of their parents. Students told me many times that their parents had been "brainwashed." "When the insurance man comes to the door," one boy said, "he asks, 'Is Thomas there?' I tell him my father's name is Mister Brown. But my father answers to Thomas and says yes, sir."

Less than twenty years ago, in the early forties, a Negro soldier was shot and killed by a Durham bus driver when he refused to move to the back of the bus. The bus driver was acquitted by an all-white jury. I learned this from a white man, a German refugee who taught philosophy to the Negro students of North Carolina College. Not one of the students mentioned the murder. Instead they told one story after another about more minor but to them terribly important incidents in the buses, in stores, on the job. The stories usually ended with some version of: "I ran out of that store. I almost cried . . ." One student told how he had held a door open for a white woman who refused to come through. "I slammed the door. I stopped being courteous."

The schools I visited had one-third to one-half Northern students, most of them from Pennsylvania, New York and New Jersey. But it was the Southern students who were supplying the fervor which kept the movement going. And among the Southern students it was especially the girls—perhaps because they are less mobile, more likely to stay south. The Northerners were often too blasé or too cynical to play a major part in the fight for integration. The Southerners were more militant (and more religious), committed to a long and grueling struggle. None of them seemed to expect anything else. It probably is hard to be a Negro in the South and grow up naive. So their every act seems to have something of calculation in it: on the buses in Durham I noticed older Negroes moving as if by habit towards the back, while the Negro college students sat as far front as possible. And this surely was an act of will; one boy told me that after being insulted once, he had not ridden a bus for two years.

At a mass meeting of more than 1500 Negro adults in Durham a young woman from a Methodist church sang a hymn whose refrain (I may not have it exactly) was: "Give me Jesus, you can have all this world." The words did not seem appropriate at a meeting whose purpose was so emphatically to win a place for the Negro *in* this world. Yet it revealed the tone of the meeting almost as surely as did the chant begun by Martin Luther King: We just want to be free. A religion which seizes upon, dramatizes and even explains the suffering of the Negro people is joined here to an essentially political movement to end that suffering. Out of that combination, I believe, comes the stamina, the endurance so necessary for passive, non-violent resistance. The new self-confidence of the young people, however, is as important, and among them I found occasional discontent with "camp-fire religion." One boy told me that for King passive resistance might be a faith, but for him it was only a strategy. Another boy, smiling, said that he expected God to help the student movement, but meanwhile the students "would help the hell out of God." Though the press has played up the role of divinity students in the sitdowns, I discovered that most of the leaders on the campus were sociology, psychology, economics and physics majors. And yet for all of them, religion is a habit whose forms are fortifying and strengthening. Prayers and hymns are normal features of student meetings.

Several students I spoke with had read Gandhi, more had read about him. But I rarely felt Gandhi present among these Negroes as a significant or potent symbol. It was the Montgomery bus boycott, coming in their early manhood, that had been the decisive event. On the other hand, I have never encountered students so "up" on the law; many of them could literally recite every important court decision since school integration was ordered. Passive resistance and endless legal action were the two political forms with which they were familiar. I was a little surprised to find virtually nothing special—nothing Southern, nothing Negro—in their views of the presidential candidates. A few said they would not vote; a few said they would never again vote Democratic. Many more engaged me in discussions as to the relative merits of Kennedy and Stevenson. Presidential politics seemed to them a universe apart from sitdown, picketing, student solidarity.

For the Negro student these new forms of political activity were a kind of self-testing and proving. Each new sitdown, each day of picketing, each disciplined march, each mass meeting was cause for pride and exhilaration. White students who were willing to participate were welcomed. But I attended two long meetings between Negro and white students at neighboring colleges (most of the students had never met before) and I never heard a Negro ask, or even hint, that whites should join their picket lines. It will be better for *them,* and for us, I was told, if they come unasked. The boy who said this was the same one who had told me that what he wanted was not brotherhood, but a cup of coffee. He was right of course, it is not necessary to feel fraternal towards the man you sit beside at a Woolworth's lunch counter. But what about the man you walk beside in a picket line? For it is there, I believe, on the line, that real equality is finally being won.

Notes from the American Revolution—1962

BETTY ALSCHULER

I have returned from a war—a revolutionary war fought without firearms, without generals, without front lines. For ammunition, the smoldering spirit of the black people of America, like a gusher of oil, is breaking out of the shale with all the fury of pent-up human emotion. Non-violence is violence. Non-violence amid southern hospitality is the more violent. Every revolution has its style, and this one carries the paradoxes of superficial manners and death to an exquisite extreme.

Along with 40 ministers from Chicago—some dark, some white—I went to Albany, Georgia, on a prayer pilgrimage in August, 1962. The front lines of the war are found as soon as black and white gather. As the door of the bus closed us in together, we knew the depth of our fear. A Jew, as I am, heading south, led by a Christian minister on a Christian mission, has a crowd of memories. My head was teeming: "And the Egyptians dealt ill with us," "And a stranger shalt thou not oppress for ye know the heart of a stranger seeing ye were strangers in the land of Egypt."

CURIOUS BUT FRIGHTENED

I felt a common cause with these good men and women who had been moved to mid-wife freedom in the south, but the gulf that separated us is also wide. Their spirit of confession and atonement for their own sins was a deep part of their journey—their own guilt. Jail could be a catharsis for their spirit. Not for mine. I had no intention of going to jail, but I wanted to understand the nature of the struggle first hand, and by my presence to lend support to the side of freedom.

I was curious, but I was also frightened, and I knew that I was bringing with me my own fear of the dark, the unconscious melancholy shadows which attach themselves to dark people whether we will it or not. I could be overwhelmed by this too. I could come out on the wrong side of the war. I could say with the White South: Stay away from me, black person, you are my fear and I will put you down; I will disgrace you, because you are the self I cannot bear. You are the filth in me and only because you are there (black, filthy and sexual) on your side of town, in your place, can I be pure and clean. Only if I keep you down can I maintain my own image. O Father Freud, you have taught me well and I go to a Holy War to fight my segregated self. I see myself on both sides of the battle. I think the black people know this and I think they will say it some day. Whether we have helped them or not, taught them or not, loved them or not, they will hate us.

ENEMY TERRITORY, U.S.A. 1962

All night on the bus. Hot, humorless dawn, Evansville, Indiana and then across the Ohio River. Enemy territory, United States, 1962. In front of the bus station, Marionsville, Kentucky, a tough, teenage white boy stands. We can see his sullen face reflected in the glass door. His back is turned toward us. At his feet is the rolled up morning paper and a pile of jagged rocks. I dress him in a Nazi uniform. The others in the bus think he is there by accident. They are new to war, but I know he has been waiting for us. We get out of the bus and move quietly into the small restaurant across from the bus station. The white, fearful face of the waitress says she will not serve us, and she needs her job, doesn't she? We leave quietly. And the bus rides further south.

We change places on the bus, and moving toward the back is a seat next to the window. I inquire of the Negro man if the seat has been spoken for, and he smiles and stands to give me room to sit down. He *remains* standing. He remains *standing*. America, the Beautiful! It takes a few seconds to catch on that I have to invite him to sit down next to me, again. He is an ordained minister who has studied at Northwestern, but he was brought up in the south. He is seated next to me and he reads. He is curious about me, but he reads. I must always speak to him first. He is over polite. I can't believe how black his skin is. Will I ever believe it? In soft liquid speech he tells me that it is dangerous to sit this way in the south. When we ride through the towns, some one may throw a rock through the window if they see a white woman in the back of the bus with him. I think of the Israelis on the borders of the Arab world, their feet on their ancient earth. Whose country am I in? I am a threat to him for whom I come. (Of course, I do not move.)

THE BLACK HOUR OF FATIGUE

The country is hilly and the soil is changing color, redder now. The Unitarian is glad there is a Jew with the party. He feels less like an outsider. The Catholics are glad; they feel less like outsiders, too. The Negro is glad there is a Jew; we have been slaves. The Protestants are glad, I don't know why. Across Kentucky and Tennessee, and night falls as we move into Georgia.

As soon as the sun goes down, it is 1:00 A.M. The clock has come to that black hour of fatigue, and stays there for weeks. In the murky light of the bus there is talk of prayer. The Reverend Mr. Still, tall, gray haired, strong, knows that the ways of prayer differ for us all and finds a common ground for us. He teaches us a kind of concentration, a projection into the situation which we are to meet. He introduces us to Police Chief Pritchett, whose humanity and ours are now involved with each other and in touch with each other. Mayor Asa Kelly, Dr. Anderson, the local leader of the Albany movement, a chiropractor. I can't meet him in my mind. Is this prayer? What is prayer? This concentration helps and we know it. I praise the unknown God in my own way. I think about the women of Israel who left Egypt and went into the desert, trusting their men, but still fearful for the safety of their children. My daughter rides with me and I am most afraid for her. She is young, vigorous, ignorant, and brave. She has fewer memories. She is very blond and beautiful.

Americus, Georgia. Is the town all asleep or are the blinds drawn shut in fear? The stars shine in the summer sky but give no light. We say blessings in the ways of the three faiths and we wait in the dark. The driver is cross. We have made a wrong turn in the road.

The police are waiting for us at the first gas station in Albany where we must stop in order to find our way to the Andersons' house, headquarters of the local battle. The police are courteous. They escort us to the Negro section of town and we pull up to a stop. Darkness, voice of the police telling the driver the safest place for his bus, and we are directed to Church for dinner and a room assignment.

TROOPS ARMED WITH BIBLES

The church women have cooked enormous amounts of food and they are tired, but they stand smiling and waving their cardboard fans back and forth to keep the flies away. We eat, get a room assignment and drive off into the dark again. Dogs bark out the darkness. We stop on a dark street. Dogs bark, a rooster crows three times. Our hostess is a tiny dark woman. Her house, which she risks her life to share, is tiny and dark and hot—full of a bizarre collection of objects which once belonged somewhere else. Her manners are beautiful. She would do anything for us. We have come from far away to fight by her side. We wash with cold water. She puts a large bed-pan beside our bed, which we know we won't be able to use. Who is responsible for plumbing in America? Who says we will run the pipes here and not there? Who says there will be street lights here and not there, sidewalks here and not there. Darkness, dirt, odor. I have a soiling dream and know my own fear. White people of Albany, Georgia, you do not need to dream of excrement. You flaunt it for the world to look at. You sleep pure in your white beds but your shame is the town we are in.

In the morning, Dr. King addresses the meeting. I can't remember what he says, but I felt his power. This is charisma. No person is untouched. He is a leader of men, but remote, unlikable. Would I have liked Moses? I am afraid of this great man. Moses gave God's laws; obedience was to the Torah. Charisma, however, speaks to the dependency of all of us, to our childish primitivism, and I am on guard. There seems to be no plan. We are used to having plans. We are in suspense. We are in a church which has been threatened. We are troops armed with Bibles, a book which has been used before. God has been used for terror. This is a Holy War and a race war and something deep inside of me (what is it?) says I cannot be used this way.

JEWISH MEMORIES INTRUDE

Freedom songs sung by beautiful rich colored voices. Clapping, rhythmic melody. "We are Climbing Jacob's Ladder," Gospel songs. But I am not a soldier of the cross. I close my mouth, for I can't sing this. As I do, I think some part of me is shut off from this war. I can't be wholehearted about it. How can I fight a war which does not engage my whole self? Because I am Jewish? I do not know.

A white woman describes the jail. She has been in many jails. She is too proud of this. She loves her martyrdom. I feel personal panic at the thought of being locked up, stripped of possessions by police, trapped behind bars in a dirty place. I respect my own panic. It is a warning. This is not my way. I wonder if I am a coward. But I know I have to withstand the passion of this group. The symbolic act of going to jail has been a way for some, but it has also increased the power of the police. The white community in Albany has irresponsibly given over their power to Chief Pritchett. He makes the decisions. He protects both sides. He is bold and intelligent, but O, America, what a travesty of your dream!

Dr. King disappears. I do not like this. Moses? The plan, when it is finally divulged, has obviously been carefully drawn up. The cars are waiting. The route of the prayer march is carefully explained. It is not fully explained that we will not all be jailed together. There is no lawyer present. I see my daughter and our rabbis caught up in the passion of the moment and I do not like it. I have already been told that the Jews in Albany "have all the power and all the money." Terrible memories harass me and I wonder if I will ever see any human movement without the memories of my people's murder. I can't separate the longing for freedom of an enslaved people from our own enslavement, but I can't be pulled with it, into what? Dr. King quoted Martin Buber. The Thou of the Negro has been made an It in the south. Yes, but Prayer, too, can become an It and God can be made an It. My God is a God I cannot know, but I know his law. In a Negro freedom meeting, I feel the need of the Law, for the welling up of the years of repression, the surging of the spirit, can turn into a terrible destruction.

Perhaps I sit too close to the scenery and, as in a theatre, the illusion is lost. A singer says "Let's quiet them down."

"THIS IS NOT A JEWISH PROBLEM"

When the ministers and rabbis march off to pray in front of the city hall, the town is waiting. The police are waiting. Traffic had been blocked. There are no cars moving. The sidewalks are crowded. It is much too quiet for so many people, but when the arrest is made, a cheer goes up from the crowd. I am walking, a white American still free. I am told to keep moving by the police and I am tempted to cheer, too, cheering the courage of those who silently obeyed the order to walk into the jail. But, as the two silent columns file into the alley, I realize the crowd is cheering their own bigoted victory and the skill of their police chief, hollering a bully's holler when his victim falls. America, 1962, cheers as men are jailed. What kind of law and order is this?

Two rabbis arguing, in the basement of the Bethel AME church, on a steaming August day, as to whether or not it is appropriate to wear a *tallis* on the march. The Orthodox rabbi says it is. The Reform rabbi says it isn't for him because he would not use one normally when he prays with his congregation and, therefore, he would not wish to wear one on the march. He, normally, marches? Gets arrested? The dispute is settled amicably though it had been heated. No *tallis* is worn.

My daughter and I speak with two members of the Jewish Congregation in Albany. Two men of dignity and status. My daughter tries to convince them that integration is a must. I listen. We hear frightened men, confused men, say "This is not a Jewish problem. This is not for outsiders. We have been good to the Negro. See the air-conditioned school. We are afraid for our children. We are good friends with the Christian here. Go away and don't bother us. The courts will settle this the American way." They are charming, gallant, well-assimilated southerners who know the art of speaking to women. They tell us that the pressure on their town has made the moderate stand impossible, and that they must be silent.

CAN THEY BE REACHED?

I see these gentlemen, Jews, under their southern manners, trapped. If the Klan marches, and they are gathering, if violence breaks, they know they will get it. They can take little initiative. My sympathy goes to them, even though their speeches are absurd. Who is an outsider in the age of spacecraft? We are all stuck on the little planet together. What is this north and south? There is air-conditioning for the Negro children, but when they graduate from the school their learning is pathetically inadequate. The Jewish townsmen even mention the woman who worked for them for thirty years and is like one of the family. A woman can only be a maid in Albany. There are only a very few factory jobs open to the young women, for very small pay. I want to ask my friends how they thought a Negro woman in Albany would marry and raise a normal family, but I don't. Fear and blindness have immobilized them. They cannot stop to ask questions. They speak with all the self-righteousness of people who suspect they are in error, but would lose everything if they confess.

The Jewish men, speaking with pride of the thousands of dollars their town has poured into the police force, are so absolutely ridiculous that one is speechless before them. Can they be reached? Should they be reached, or should we ask only for mercy, and hope that the course of events around them will not sweep them up in its eddy. I cannot agree with them as they ask us to rely on the courts of Albany to solve the problem. I know there is a backlog of a thousand cases, when young people, white and black, are languishing in their jails with no way to get out, with no lawyer to help them.

One young white girl, picked up on a vagrancy charge because she was found in a Negro bar, has been in for seven weeks, no family or friend to help and no money for bail. The courts in Albany are a joke, and Justice is mocked. My Jewish friends are still silent.

"For He has not made us like the people of other lands, nor set us level with the clans of earth, nor fixed our share to equal theirs, our lot to match their crowd and clamor." Who can help the southern Jews to see that if their status—political, economic, social—becomes their over-riding concern, their future is in jeopardy as surely as if they stood boldly for integration?

PENTAGON OF THE ALBANY MOVEMENT

After our conversation with the Fathers of the Albany synagogue, my daughter and I walk back through the town to the Bethel AME Church, too quiet now. The church is silent and empty. Dinner is waiting for us at the Union Baptist Church several miles away.

There are no buses running in Albany. The Negroes have put them out of business. Taxi drivers lose their licenses if they cross the color line. No white cab would come for us, and no Negro driver could pick two white people up on the wrong side of the main street. We realize we need the Negro integrationists for our food, lodging and transportation. By telephone and word of mouth, our goings and comings are watched over and cared for. The driver might be so weary he swayed over the wheel of his car, the car itself so in need of repair it cannot always respond, but the spirit so moves these people that, through the fatigue, poverty and confusion, their plans are carried through. We are in good hands.

Andersons', the headquarters for this phase of the war, will probably never boast a monument, a cannon, or even a flag, but a 10 x 12 room in the back of the house is the Pentagon of the Albany movement. Women are cooking and ironing in the background as the two telephones ring and the three typewriters click all day and all night. Where is the mass meeting tonight? What time you all want me to registra? CBS wants a report. The rabbi's wife is sending bail money. King is muck. Tell him to get out of our town. Tell Freddy, who is out cutting the grass, to get down to the city jail with a message. Where's Andy? Where's King?

TAKE HEED—AMERICA

While I am on a phone watch, a radio station from the north calls in for a report. What can any one tell? There are seventy people in the city jail tonight because they want to pray in public. Perhaps a war correspondent can report certain news, but the truth of Albany, 1962, is only that white supremacy is finished. The truth must be faced in the U.N., in Africa and in Chicago. Mayor Daley, Tshombe, Laurie Pritchett, King and Khrushchev all have the same problems to work out. There is power, fear, repression, and boundless passion on all sides. If the student spirit, the insights to be wrested from the histories of all revolutionary change, and the basic truth that we are all God's children can possibly be welded together, there is hope for the future. If either the immature passions of the Negro people, or the repressive fears of the White man dominate, we shall all go down in a conflagration.

Take heed, America—look to your segregated souls and cities. Your north and your south are in danger. No community is without responsibility. No armaments can protect your children from this battle, no space flight flee this truth. Policemen run the town, and the law of the land is flaunted with pride. The Klan is gathering. Peril is at our doorstep.

The Freedom Rides

ALBERT VORSPAN

The Freedom Rides, which held the headlines and the attention of the world for several months, have given way to new and different emphases in the ongoing fight for civil rights in America. Now seems to be a good time to assess the Freedom Ride technique and to measure its results. While there have been strong differences of opinion among civil rights workers themselves as to the efficacy of the Freedom Ride technique, it seems to me there can be little question that the Rides did (1) dramatize in an extraordinary way the unfinished business of racial equality in America, and (2) compel more vigorous Governmental action, culminating in the clear ruling of the Interstate Commerce Commission that segregation in interstate commerce must be halted forthwith.

For a variety of reasons, the Freedom Rides touched the Jewish community in a deep and special way. Perhaps no other phase of the civil rights struggle, since the historic desegregation decision of 1954, has had so emotional an impact on the Jewish community as did the Freedom Rides. In the first place, a fairly high percentage of the Freedom Riders were Jewish college students from the North. In addition, a number of rabbis participated in highly-publicized interfaith and interracial Freedom Rides into the deep South. Of these, two rabbis were arrested in Tallahassee and another two in Jackson, Mississippi, for challenging segregated facilities. Not only were they identified in the press as rabbis but, naturally, their statements explaining their participation were based on Jewish ideals. Indeed, one Long Island rabbi explained his motivation not only in terms of his interpretation of Judaism but also, very movingly, in terms of his personal experience as a young man in Nazi Germany.

By and large, Northern Jews responded with high enthusiasm to the Freedom Rides and to Jewish participation in them. Some of the congregations lavished honors and tributes upon the rabbis who took the Freedom Rides. While a few members loudly disapproved of their own rabbi's conduct in joining the Rides ("He should have asked us first; after all, he's *our* rabbi"), the prevailing response of congregants was that of pride. Some of the congregations raised funds to cover bail and bond. Others got up substantial contributions to CORE in support of Freedom Rides. Many Jewish groups invited Freedom Riders to address them; a few Freedom Riders spoke in Northern synagogues from the pulpit. CORE quickly developed a closer working relationship with local Jewish groups than some of the long-established civil rights groups had ever been able to achieve. It was quite clear that the Freedom Rides seized the imagination of Jews in the North, many of whom feel chronically guilty about their failure to "do anything" about racial segregation in the South. The Freedom Rides gave them, as to all Northern liberals, an outlet for frustration and a kind of vicarious involvement in a great moral drama.

But the reactions of Southern Jews were altogether different. Negative reactions, ranging from disquiet to disgust, were virtually unanimous among Southern Jews. It was not surprising that many Southern Jews opposed the Freedom Rides. Indeed, a small but noisy segment of the Southern Jewish community has opposed every anti-segregation move since, and including, the Supreme Court decision of 1954. What was remarkable was that the Freedom Rides were largely disapproved also by many of the liberal Jewish leaders in the South whose own commitments to equality were unquestioned and who have themselves worked ceaselessly, if quietly, for Negro rights and desegregation.

Said a Jewish communal leader from Georgia, who has often stuck his own neck out in defense of integration: "Look, there's no question we've got to speed up the fight against segregation. The world won't hold still for 'moderation.' But I have grave questions about the Freedom Rides. I belong to the Southern Regional Council and most of them share my questions. In the first place, there is a natural resentment of Northerners breezing in here—to hit and run. The sit-ins were very successful here because they were local kids and they stuck to it until they won. But people put the Freedom Riders down as grandstand players who preferred to make a big noise down here to doing something about segregation in Chicago and New York and Philadelphia where they came from."

A Jewish businessman in upstate Florida put his reaction this way: "I'm for integration but I'm strongly opposed to the Freedom Rides. I know that Northerners would automatically believe the second part of that statement and think I'm lying about the first. Well, let 'em. It happens that the Negro leaders in my community come to me for both advice and financial help. When the colored kids were arrested during the sit-ins in my town, I put up the bail money. And I'd do it again. Because in the last analysis we are going to have to do the job ourselves, locally, colored and white, and I can tell you it does us no good whatever when a bunch of bright-eyed Yankees come waltzing down here in a bus, come out to the bus station to make a circus play, only to find to their obvious disappointment that we had long since desegregated the bus station."

A Mississippi rabbi put it even more sharply: "These Freedom Rides are doing no good. Especially the ill-advised rabbis. Do you know how much anguish and courage it takes for us rabbis in the Deep South who break our backs and risk plenty every time we speak out, working practically underground, to fight for decency, against the wishes of our own congregants most of the time? Do you think we are helped by these rabbinic carpetbaggers? I would still disapprove but I would at least respect my colleagues if they did what some of the Quakers and some of the Episcopalians have done—and that is to go to jail for their whole sentence as witness to their commitment. But I have no respect for those who got their pictures in the papers, had somebody put up their bond, and hightailed it back to California and New York as heroes to hit the lecture circuit."

These conflicting views have collided sharply at national conventions of Jewish organizations concerned with civil rights. Indeed, it has been obvious that the words "Freedom Riders" have become highly charged symbols, almost red flags, which have blinded both antagonists and protagonists to the realities of what should be done next in the civil rights battle. At one large national Jewish convention, a controversy over the words "Freedom Riders" in a civil rights resolution so preoccupied the delegates (who voted finally to eliminate the reference) that few seemed to notice the important substantive part of the resolution and its far-reaching action provisions. So much have these words become symbolic of deep feelings, often unrelated to substance, that one synagogue leader actually threatened his national congregational body that he would take his congregation out of the organization if a resolution mentioning "Freedom Riders" was so much as considered at a convention. As is usual with such threats, it was a dud.

The Freedom Rides undoubtedly achieved important results. But it is equally obvious that there is room for honest disagreement among men of good will as to whether or not this is the best kind of technique to achieve the ideal of equality. As for the Jewish community, the Freedom Rides did deepen divisions and engender resentments between North and South. This is both unfortunate and unavoidable. It should not, however, obscure the all-important truth that the Jewish community of the South has been making definite, though undramatic, progress toward the acceptance of responsibility for participation in the desegregation process. An increasing number of Jewish leaders, lay and rabbinic, have been taking positions of leadership in the desegregation of southern communities. Jews had no inconsiderable part in the successful transitions of such communities as Dallas, Memphis, and Atlanta. Increasingly, Southern Jewish Community Relations Councils are assuming responsibility, and together with other liberal forces in the community, working toward an open, democratic community. The Southern Jewish community has a long way to go but it has come a long way from the silent, sullen, fearful group which seven years ago wanted nothing to do with the flaming issue of segregation.

Despite the temporary misunderstandings and the deep feelings which boiled to the surface in recent months, there is reason to hope—and pray—that American Jewry, North and South alike, can move ahead together to help vindicate that dream of equality which Judaism first gave to the world and upon which American democracy must stake its future.

The Rabbis Visit Birmingham

RICHARD L. RUBENSTEIN

Rabbinical conventions serve to renew old friendships and contacts. They also help to create new anxieties about one's age, status and abilities. Usually the conventions run their predictable course and peter out in time for the rabbis to return to their *shabbat* pulpits. This year, the convention of the Rabbinical Assembly (Conservative) was different.

On Tuesday, May 7, the convention met to consider a proposal by Rabbi Harold Schulweis of Oakland, California that an Institute for Righteous Acts be established whose purpose would be to document altruistic deeds done by non-Jews to save Jews during the Hitler holocaust. The proposal touched an understandably sore nerve. In the midst of the debate, one rabbi queried why we were concentrating our energies on what had happened twenty years ago.

"Are there no righteous acts to be recorded today?" he inquired. "Are there no righteous acts even of righteous Arabs which we could document?" he demanded in all seriousness. Then, almost as an afterthought, the rabbi asked whether the Rabbinical Assembly was doing the right thing by meeting altogether rather than adjourning to Birmingham, Alabama, to aid Dr. Martin Luther King and his followers in their struggle for human rights.

It is difficult to assess how much of this gentleman's comments was rhetoric and how much genuine concern. He was not one of the nineteen rabbis who actually left the convention to go to Birmingham. His words did catch fire. The convention was determined to do something about the problems of contemporary America, though there remains very good reason for continuing to be concerned about the wounds of twenty years ago. Within a very short time, nineteen rabbis volunteered to leave immediately for Birmingham, $1,500 was raised out of pocket by the convention to defray travel expenses, and Rev. A. D. King (Martin Luther's brother) was called. He said the rabbis would be welcome.

In the past few years, many clergymen have taken part in the struggle for human rights in the South. They have done so as individuals. These personal testimonials have been important and inspiring. The nineteen rabbis were the first clergymen to go as representatives of their entire clerical group. They were empowered by resolution "to speak and to act on behalf of human rights and dignity." In all our contacts, we stressed that we came as representatives of almost 800 Conservative Rabbis who serve over 1,500,000 congregants. This turned out to be of great importance. One of the greatest anxieties expressed by the Negro leaders was the anxiety lest they be isolated. When Dr. Martin Luther King met with us, he explained that his movement was religious in character and leadership. He complained that he had received very little support from the official religious bodies or their leaders. At the rallies we attended, news dispatches were read telling those deepest in the struggle of the reaction of the world to their fight. Student demonstrations in London, declarations of solidarity in Birmingham, England and press support from any quarter had an electrifying effect on the Birmingham group's morale. Our presence was taken as an important symbol of mutual concern and solidarity.

DILEMMA OF THE SOUTHERN JEWS

We arrived in Birmingham at 3:30 A.M. Wednesday, May 8. We were met by two groups, representatives of Dr. King's Southern Christian Leadership Conference and leaders of the Jewish community. It is not difficult to understand the agonizing anxieties of the Jewish community when they learned that nineteen "foreign" rabbis were to descend upon them. In order not to involve or embarrass them more than was necessary, we had not informed them of our coming. Of course, our very presence involved them, willy-nilly. Although we had lost a night's sleep, the leaders of our group (Rabbi Everett Gendler of Princeton, N.J. and Rabbi Sidney Shanken of Cranford, N.J.) met with the leaders of the Jewish community until five in the morning. The next evening our entire group met with them. Our meetings brought to light an aspect of the freedom conflict which has received little attention in the national press. The small Southern Jewish community is tragically caught in the struggle for Negro rights in a highly precarious and difficult way.

Almost from the moment we arrived, we learned a new nomenclature. We learned that in Birmingham there were "merchants" and "businessmen," that "businessmen" were part of the power structure and "merchants" were not. The businessmen controlled the banks, primary industry, and utilities. The merchants controlled the stores. Businessmen were Gentiles; merchants were largely Jews. The first thrust of the Negro struggle had necessarily been directed against the merchants. The initial demands of the Negro groups involved unrestricted use of lunch counters and fitting rooms as well as better employment opportunities in the stores. No matter how much the merchants wanted to give in (and this varied greatly with the individual merchant), they could move no farther nor faster than the business and political power structures would permit. One of the roots of Negro anti-Semitism in the South consists of the fact that their initial struggle has frequently brought them face to face with Jewish merchants who had to say no to them. The businessmen were far better able to hide behind the nameless, faceless anonymity of the corporations they dominated.

Since our departure from Birmingham, the arch-segregationists have called for a boycott of the "Quisling" merchants who "gave in to the Negroes." To the untrained northern ear, this seems simply the retaliation of the arch-segregationists against the white moderates. It takes only a few hours in Birmingham to realize the poisonously anti-Semitic character of the segregationist's boycott appeal. Whether the agreement between the responsible whites and the Negroes stands or falls, the Jewish community is bound to be hurt badly, because it is caught in the crossfire.

The objective of the Jewish leaders was to dissuade us from any public action or, failing that, to secure our agreement to consult with them before taking action which might endanger them. I personally felt that there was much justice in their request, though we were caught in a tragic conflict between our commitment to human rights, which served the best interests of all Americans in the long run, and the local and short run interests of the Jewish community of Birmingham. We could not ignore our responsibility to the local community, although, if Dr. King requested a demonstration, there would have been no honorable way for us to have refused. We promised to consult with the local people before taking any action, if time permitted. We urged the leaders of the Jewish community to use their good offices to end the demonstrations, thus making any further demonstrations unnecessary. Without revealing confidential information, I can honestly write that the leadership of the Jewish community proceeded to act with great dignity and in a way that no Jew could be ashamed of.

COMPLEX MOTIVES BRING RABBIS TO BIRMINGHAM

On the way down to Birmingham, a number of us asked ourselves why we were going and what we could accomplish when we arrived. None of us was very certain of the answers. I wish I could report that we all knew exactly what we were doing and that we were motivated by the urge to advance human rights. That isn't the way things happened. I can only speak for myself, but I have the feeling that my motives were not much more mixed than those of many of my companions. There was an element of curiosity in my going. I had been in Berlin the week of the border closing in August 1961 and I had never forgotten the excitement. I learned a great deal about contemporary Germany by being on the spot in a crisis area. As a writer, I wanted to go to Birmingham to get a good story. I had done that sort of thing before. Of course, in the back of my mind, I was not unaware of the fact that the mission would receive wide approval in my home community. I liked that.

Some of my motives were terribly complex. Nobody moves into a trouble area unless he has reason for not caring whether his head gets smashed in or not. This is a very fine way to avoid the problems of life, especially the inner problems. I wish I were able to say that I have finally arrived at that stage in life where I could regard all of my inner problems as solved. I haven't, and I suspect that I never shall. This means that when the unseen and ofttimes unintuited pain gets too great, I'll always be under the temptation to be a hero. Heroes are people who court danger when the going inside themselves gets rough.

There were other, better, reasons for going to Birmingham. I've been a little sick and tired of the recent refrain that "Jews were passively compliant in their own downfall under Hitler," which some of our slickest magazines have been feeding us. I wanted to be an actor in events rather than a spectator or commentator. Though my motives were mixed, when I found myself confronted with the actual agony of Birmingham, I achieved an increasingly clear understanding of why I had come and what we could, as a group of rabbis, accomplish.

I was genuinely surprised to learn how very much our visit really mattered to the Negroes engaged in the struggle. When we entered their churches, we were greeted as "our rabbis," as if we were a precious possession. We marched down the aisles amid standing and cheering congregations. I quickly sensed what was happening. The basic religious metaphor, repeated by the Negroes over and over again, was the metaphor of Moses and the children of Israel. He had led them out of slavery into freedom. Dr. King was their Moses and they were the children of God struggling to be free. There were almost no Christological references in either their preaching or their singing. This was Mosaic religion. The children of God were seeking the promised land of freedom. Inner problems such as how to resolve the conflict between what one wants to do and what one is compelled to do did not mean very much to these people. No mention of the problem of the inner psychological man was made in the congregations we visited. Every participant had the good fortune I no longer possessed of being able to identify his personal anguish with some visible, tangible goal of the group. That is why their religious symbols all dwelled on the experience of Moses and the children of Israel.

EXAMPLE OF ISRAEL IS STRONG MOTIVATIONAL FORCE

The normal contacts of Negroes and Jews have not been very happy. Both groups are victims of a system they cannot control. Jews are barred from positions of significance within the economic power structure. As a result, too many of them are forced to live off Negroes as marginal merchants or landlords. This is not the best way for two peoples to attain mutual respect and understanding. The roles are inherently anxiety-producing. Negro anti-

Semitism is an understandable reaction to Jewish marginality. Very seldom do victims of a system recognize their mutual concerns. When I returned from Birmingham to Pittsburgh, a number of people asked me why I had gone to all that trouble "for the *schwartzers.*" They could not understand that freedom and human dignity are indivisible.

On the Negro side, the Jews make an ideal target. All of their understandable aggressions and resentments at the white community can be directed with far greater safety towards Jews than towards Gentiles. This places additional pressures on the Jewish community to seek safety by identifying with the non-Jewish whites. In spite of these pressures, many Southern Jewish leaders have played important roles in the struggle for human rights in their communities.

The Negro community saw the rabbis in a way in which they had seldom seen Jews. By our very presence we were handing down a kind of "apostolic" succession to them. We were saying that the flesh and blood children of Israel were behind them in their struggle, that we had gone from slavery to freedom, and we knew they would. The convention behind the symbolism of solidarity was heightened by our willingness to incur risks of physical harm to bear witness to our convictions.

The Negro freedom movement would die without music. But the songs they sing are no longer spirituals, the expression of a rejected slave heritage. They sing powerful freedom songs which are among the finest folk songs current in America today. Why they are not better known among folk song enthusiasts, I do not know. A high point of our visits to the churches was the teaching by Rabbi Seymour Friedman of *Hineh ma tov uma naim shevet ahim gam yahad* (Behold how good and how pleasant it is for brethren to dwell together in unity, Ps. 133.1) to the congregations. It was exciting and impressive to see 2500 members of a congregation locking arms and singing *Hineh ma tov* as if they were around a *kibbutz* campfire. There was a deep scriptural affinity between their songs of freedom and the biblical verse they were taught. A great deal more was communicated by music than could possibly have been done by words alone.

Modern Israel offered another kind of inspiration. At one church rally for teenagers, the preacher urged the youngsters to read Leon Uris' *Exodus* and learn how the Jewish people had endured every degradation only to win their land and their dignity. The example of Israel was all the more significant because of our presence.

BIRMINGHAM AN ENFORCED DICTATORSHIP

There was no exaggeration in the stories of police brutality. I walked through the deserted streets of Birmingham Wednesday and Thursday, May 7 and 8, and experienced the same sort of terror I had felt two years earlier as I walked through the dark and dreary streets of East Berlin. The same police, the same dogs, the same battle helmets and the same guns intruded upon my sense of security in Birmingham as they had in East Berlin. The analogy is tragically apt. The men from nowhere, the radicals outside society, had triumphed for the moment over the forces of compromise and social order in Birmingham, as they had in Hitler's Germany and elsewhere in Europe. As I walked through the streets, I saw hundreds of arch-segregationist Alabama Highway Police who had been sent by Gov. Wallace "to maintain law and order." They were tense, violent, and frightened men. Their presence was provocative. They were really in Birmingham to create violence rather than to suppress it. Negro leaders have commented that they had little quarrel with the local Birmingham police, but that they wanted the segregationist highway police removed. These men were largely "rednecks," lower middle class petty officials with little but the sense of whiteness to give them a feeling of identity. They were pathetically dependent upon the myth of Negro inferiority for their own human dignity. Were that lost, they would face the most awesome of all psychological problems—the problem of self-confrontation. They were prepared to assault and to murder rather than give up the Negro as the standard whereby they could be assured of their own worth.

This was fascism in everything but name. The radicals outside of society, having no stake or investment in adjudicating conflicting community interests, were prepared to wreck the negotiations and impose their will by force. The logic of their strategy, if successful, can only lead to the military or paramilitary dictatorship of the whites over the Negroes. Nor would the Negroes be the only ones whose freedom would be lost by the continuation of enforced segregation. The white community would have to be kept under continued surveillance, lest some of its members seek opportunities for reconciliation between the communities. This has already happened. Birmingham has less of a government than an enforced dictatorship led by Commissioner of Public Safety Eugene "Bull" Connor, a former sports announcer. He is typical of the marginal men whom the chaos of segregation has vomited into positions of leadership. When a merchant took down offensive segregationist signs such as "Colored Dressing Room" without actually desegregating, Connor and his men swiftly found costly "fire violations" which closed the store until expensive repairs had been made. In one case, a store was forced to purchase a nine thousand dollar elevator before it could reopen. Clearly Connor's tyranny affected the whites as much as the Negroes.

The whites finally found Connor so intolerable that a new form of government was voted with a new, somewhat more moderate Mayor, Albert Boutwell, and a city council. Thus the arch segregationists have been repudiated by the whites as well as the Negroes. However, the lack of a clear mandate has not deterred Connor, as it never deterred European fascists. His forces have appealed to the arch-segregationist Alabama Supreme Court. The question of whether a viable agreement can finally end Birmingham's turmoil largely rests on whether the Boutwell government can be legally empowered to take over.

The new government will not entirely solve matters. Should the segregationist leaders insist upon wrecking the agreement of the moderates, they can do so. They can boycott and bomb and tyrannize until Birmingham is absolutely divided into two hostile, unreconciled communities living together in hatred and violence. The pattern will spread and the future of America will not be very bright.

AMERICA'S LAST CHANCE

All the rabbis who participated in the visit came away absolutely convinced that Dr. Martin Luther King is leading America's fight rather than just the Negro's fight. If he fails, the Negro community will turn towards more violent and embittered men. America will be increasingly rent by malice as it has never been before. The Negroes cannot be stopped. Children who are not yet ten years old are prepared to go to jail and they know precisely why. They have turned their backs on their Uncle Toms and they will have their rights and their dignity, no matter who opposes them. The question is no longer whether the Negro revolt will succeed. The only remaining question is how bloody the revolt will become before it succeeds. Although I did not really know why I went to Birmingham, before I was there twenty-four hours I learned that I was fighting for America's last chance. And, I was proud that I could participate. Either we can create decently and honorably a community in which all of us have the rights and opportunities which were promised us at this nation's founding, or none of us will have them.

There are over twenty million Negroes in the United States. Within the lifetime of most of us there will be over forty million. That is almost as many people as are in Italy. No group that large can permanently be submerged unless it submerges itself. Until now, the worst chains worn by the Negroes have been their own. By accepting the white man's degrading image as valid, they have kept themselves in a prison without walls, the hardest kind of prison from which to escape. They've opened the last prison, the prison they themselves have built and now nothing can stop them. Either every American will be free or the day of reckoning will be as bloody and as terrible as James Baldwin has suggested. Nor ought Jews to think that the "*schwartzers*'" problem doesn't concern them. It does. Whichever way Jews turn, there will be great risk. The risk is unavoidable. If Jews turn their back on this struggle, they will not diminish their peril. They will only diminish their dignity and their sense of personal and social morality.

FREEDOM WILL BE ONLY A BEGINNING

I am glad I did not have to demonstrate, because I was scared. Of course I would have demonstrated had Dr. King asked. If we had been concerned with our comforts, I would have remained in the bourgeois ease of the impeccably traditional Pioneer Country Club. I also have no doubt that, had we demonstrated, there would have been bloodshed, even if all we did was to pray in public. The "redneck" State Police would have delighted to bash in the heads of a few of those "Jew Nigger-lovers." Yet, as I flew northward to Pittsburgh, I realized the final irony of our visit. I admired the Negroes, especially their youngsters, because they had something I didn't have—a cause. Life was simple for them. If only they could sit at the lunch counter, enter the dressing room, or enter the voting machine, they would have achieved their goal of freedom. I had stood prepared to suffer possible physical injury for their goal, but on returning home, I realized that their problems would only begin when their freedom had been won. It was a matter of little consequence that had prompted Jean-Paul Sartre to say "We are condemned to be free." As long as the Negro community can fight for visible, tangible goals, it can focus all the pain and ambiguity of life on the fact that the goals remain unachieved. Happy men are they who dwell under the illusion that freedom is an end rather than a beginning. Of course, the best of the Negro leaders were keenly aware of this problem. I wonder, however, whether they have speculated on the fact that, were their community not effectively disenfranchised, the clergy would not provide its leadership, that the Negro freedom movement would be more nakedly political and power-minded, and that most of the religious elements would speedily disappear.

Once the fight for Negro freedom is won, the Negro problem will begin in earnest. When each human being has the right and opportunity to move as far as his abilities will carry him, the ironies and the ambiguities of life do not disappear. On the contrary, they are then felt more deeply and with greater suffering. By fighting for Negro rights, I was in part fighting for the time when the pain the Negro feels will be his own rather than the pain others inflict upon him. But that is as it should be. The good society will not be a society without suffering; it will be a community in which each man is free to come to terms with his own pain rather than to inflict or endure the pain of others.

Pilgrimage to Selma

SEYMOUR SIEGEL

"Welcome to Selma—the City of 100% Human Interest." These words of greeting appear on a huge billboard standing near the now-famous bridge leading into Selma, Alabama.

The white residents may still believe that these words are true. But the world now knows that Selma, like other localities in the Deep South, has shown little human interest in the disenfranchised half of its population—the half with black skins.

The tragic plot that unraveled itself is well known. Selma's dreary streets have been on millions of television screens. Its ridiculous sheriff and his bully-boy possemen have dominated the front pages of newspapers across the nation and the world. In the ironical way history has of choosing its crucial battlegrounds, this ugly, sullen town in the Alabama Black Belt has taken its place beside Montgomery, Birmingham, and Philadelphia, Mississippi, as a landmark in the struggle for Negro freedom and human dignity.

A sense of elation, mixed with foreboding and not a little fear, filled my heart and the hearts of my colleagues as we set out on the first leg of the journey to Selma. On the plane to Atlanta there were many clergymen and theological students representing the whole spectrum of religious life in this country. Rabbi Gershon Levi, an officer of the Rabbinical Assembly and the rabbi of the Jamaica Jewish Center, and I arrived in Atlanta in the small hours of the morning to find scores of other clergymen milling around the airport trying to arrange transportation to Selma.

We were directed to the office of the Southern Christian Leadership Conference—the organization of Dr. Martin Luther King. It was here that we first encountered "The Movement"—as the civil rights effort is called. In the modest office located in a somewhat run-down Negro neighborhood we found other Selma pilgrims. Several young Negroes—hardly out of their teens—were in charge. Religious books were displayed everywhere and short prayer services were held periodically. The quiet courage and the know-how which comes with experience were most impressive. These youngsters are for the most part products of the worst schools in the nation. They have known systematic humiliation, which is the lot of the Negro both North and South. Yet the power of the ideal of freedom and the practical experience of leadership have brought out their native intelligence and filled them with eloquent dignity.

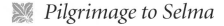

The next morning, we boarded a chartered bus to take us to Selma. The mood on the bus was serious—though the assembled clergymen could not forgo the opportunity of using the occasion to catch up on the latest happenings in the various theological schools and religious denominations. Though the bus was watched by several cars filled with highway police, the five-hour journey from Atlanta was accomplished without incident. Crossing the bridge, graced by the ludicrous sign of welcome, we were in Selma!

The town is undistinguished in every way. Its buildings are old and ugly. As we walked to the Negro neighborhood we were watched by sullen whites. Some hollered out crude and obscene epithets. Others seemed to laugh compulsively, like people at a loss to do anything else. A few looked puzzled. I heard one woman say under her breath, "They must be crazy." On the main street were several large stores bearing unmistakably Jewish names. And everywhere were the upholders of the law—beefy state troopers, natty in their razor-sharp creased trousers; sheriff's men, and local policemen.

The Negro neighborhood, recognizable by its unpaved streets, is dominated by a large church and a housing project, built with federal funds. The church is literally and figuratively the center of the community. Not only were the meetings held there, but first-aid stations, commissaries and makeshift communications posts were located there.

Near the Browns Chapel were thousands of people—local Negroes, civil-rights workers and clergymen. In addition to the other four members of the Rabbinical Assembly delegation there were about a dozen rabbis present. (I am speaking only of Tuesday, March 9, the day of the abortive march across the bridge. Many others came later.) There were bishops, professors, deans of seminaries, and administrative heads of large denominations, and among the clergymen, of course, was the soon to be martyred Rev. James Reeb of Boston, Massachusetts.

We heard that a federal judge had issued an injunction against marching. Meetings had been held in the church where the practical and theoretical aspects of the problem of defying the law were discussed. We were told that one of the most effective speeches was by a Negro minister who recalled that Queen Esther had been requested by Mordecai to see the king on behalf of her people. When she protested that it was against the law to do so, Mordecai insisted that now was the time and no delay could be risked. "We are like Queen Esther," said the Negro preacher, "and we want to see the king."

After Dr. King emerged from conference with associates the march was formed. At the beginning the religious leaders were asked to walk at the head of the line, to be followed by the Negro demonstrators. The strategy was that since the troopers would be hesitant about attacking whites, the other demonstrators would be protected. However, when it was realized that the result would be a segregated line, the formation was changed and the Negroes were interspersed among the whites. And so the march began—four abreast, stretching for at least a mile.

The marchers did not know, of course, that Dr. King had made a tentative agreement with the authorities to turn back after crossing the bridge. The marchers were solemn, breaking the tension by singing freedom anthems. (Several Negro youngsters wore *yarmulkes* they had acquired from the Rabbinical Assembly delegation to Birmingham two years ago.) The troopers stood by as we marched through the town nearing the bridge. There was a sense that history was being made. The tension contributed to this feeling. So did the self-conscious joining of white and black hands. Even the hostile whites, impassive and uncommunicative, seemed to realize that something important was happening.

What followed is now history. The march went across the bridge. There it encountered the majesty of Alabama law. The assembled were led in prayer by Dr. King. Newsmen and television cameras recorded the cadenced eloquence of the prayers beseeching the Almighty to aid the cause of freedom and to open the hearts of Sheriff Clark and his men to the power of love and compassion. A gasp went up from the marchers when the order to turn back was given. For many, it was a sigh of relief. There was, thank God, to be no violence.

The mood of the marchers as they returned to the church was a mixture of relief and resolution. The local whites continued to watch impassively. Dr. King—perhaps protesting too much—explained that the events of the afternoon had been a victory. Of course, neither he nor anyone else could have known that the full impact of the day's activities was to be felt only later on when one of the assembled clergymen would be murdered.

History—contrary to popular belief—rarely repeats itself entirely. Yet there is an instructive parallel between "The Movement" and the Zionist struggle for a Jewish homeland. The young workers from SCLC and SNCC and CORE resemble the *chalutzim* in many ways. They—like their Jewish counterparts—court danger daily and have abandoned the enticements of bourgeois comfort to respond to the call of duty. But there is a further parallel. Dr. King represents responsible, moderate and courageous leadership. He is sober-minded and, above all, non-violent. In this he resembles the leadership of the Hagana in the 40s. But he is under constant pressure not only from the Sternist-type extremists represented by the late Malcolm X, but also from other groups who chafe under the restraints imposed by non-violence and moderation. Like the Irgunists, they are pushing for more desperate and dramatic acts against the constituted authorities. So far, he has managed to channel the Negro protest away from violence. For this, the whole country—North and South—owes him an enormous debt of gratitude. One shudders to contemplate what might have happened in Selma had some Negro fired a gun.

After the speeches, about 5:30 in the afternoon, Rabbi Levi and I were driven back to Montgomery by a Negro couple from Selma. Our drivers proudly showed us their registration numbers, which were necessary in order to fill out a voter registration form. They had been gruffly rebuffed many times. Sheriff Clark had them thrown in jail. But they were determined to register. They represented the vanguard of the forces which will radically change the South.

Most of our fellow clergymen began leaving Selma about the same time. Some, however, remained because they had a later plane or bus. Others wanted to get something to eat before starting back home. One of these was the Rev. James Reeb. . . .

A few days later, the President of the United States, who had been the object of bitter criticism among the Selma marchers because of his reluctance to use federal force, stood before the Congress of the United States and the whole nation clothed in the grandeur of his office. In his Southern drawl, he was to repeat the words we had heard so often in Alabama and in other places where civil rights workers congregated—"We shall overcome." Like the Selma marchers, like James Reeb, like the many anonymous heroes of the civil-rights movement, the President took his symbolic place on the barricade facing the Sheriff Clarks and the Governor Wallaces. But behind him now stood the awesome power of the United States and of an aroused public. And now there was every prospect that we would, indeed, overcome.

2

At Home (Almost) in America

The essays in this chapter cover a relatively brief period of time—the less than two years from the winter of 1963 to the fall of 1965—but they nonetheless offer a decidedly broad range of suggestive reactions to a widespread sense that Jews were beginning truly to feel that they were "settling in" in America. To be sure, this was experienced by the vast majority of American Jews as a very good thing, indeed. Given the horrors of the not-so-distant past, it was a tremendous relief. And why not? Why not feel good about a great democratic nation that respects cultural differences, constitutionally affirms the separation of church and state, upholds civil liberties, and permits ethnic groups to foster group pride and awareness? Why not look around at so many realms of public and professional life and celebrate the bold achievements of Jews—in politics, in math and science, in the entertainment industry, in sports, in the universities, and in the business world? In the postwar era, the old barriers to advancement had crumbled fast, and Jews were really making it, to borrow the title of the memoir by *Commentary* editor Norman Podhoretz (published in 1967). Which is to say as well that this new sense of comfort was experienced with no small degree of ironic reflection and genuine ambivalence. For some astute commentators began to turn the question around: Should Jews really ever feel secure and at home in America?

The chapter opens with two commemorative essays for President John F. Kennedy after his assassination in Dallas on November 22, 1963. At first (and possibly even second) glance, they might appear to say little that is especially "Jewish." Yet this may be precisely the point. There was no need to underscore why American Jews in particular had wept for Kennedy; they joined all decent and law-abiding American citizens when they did so. Still, as the essay by Shad Polier, a vice president of the American Jewish Congress and chairman of its Commission on Law and Social Action, implies, John Kennedy's greatness resulted from his embrace of a liberal tradition also dearly cherished by American Jews. With more foreboding, and rather less optimism, the editorial mourning Kennedy in the Labor Zionist *Jewish Frontier* emphasizes the potential for xenophobic extremism that still continued to be nurtured on American soil.

Arthur Hertzberg's trenchant essay from 1964 takes a dissenting position on the Americanization of the Jews. An influential historian and Conservative rabbi, Hertzberg boldly challenges whether the openness of American life has really proven beneficial to the survival of the Jewish people. Repeatedly, Hertzberg affirms that Jews are becoming "just like everybody else" in America, but he offers the dire prediction that this might well lead to the ultimate demise of Jews in the diaspora. Turning to examples from European history and citing as well the rise in intermarriage and the decline in religious education among American Jewish youth, Hertzberg paints a bleak picture. In the end, he suggests that Israel—and not the United States—be recognized as the genuine home for all Jewish people, and he tentatively promotes aliyah, especially for the younger generation.

This discussion of aliyah surfaced again, and with much contentious debate, among the young participants at the Fourth Dialogue in Israel, sponsored by the American Jewish Congress and held in Tel Aviv and Jerusalem in July 1965. The organizing goal of the conference (with Shad Polier presiding) was to bring together the postwar generation in the United States and the post-independence generation in Israel. Sparks flew, although not necessarily along predictable lines. For instance, not all the American youth dismissed the idea of aliyah; not all the Israeli participants defended it. But other heady concerns—such as the inherent meaning of Jewish identity, and how (or how not) to demonstrate one's own "Jewishness" in America—also emerged. In this light, the contributions of the secular liberal civil rights activist Paul Cowan appear to have been especially incendiary.

The chapter concludes with a brief look at the events of October 6, 1965. As it happens, it was Yom Kippur, the holiest of Jewish High Holy Days. It was also the first day of the World Series between the Minnesota Twins and the Los Angeles Dodgers. On that day, the celebrated left-handed star for the Dodgers, Sandy Koufax, said that he intended to go to synagogue and would not pitch as scheduled. (As the story goes, when Don Drysdale, another exceptional pitcher, took the place of Koufax in the rotation—and got badly beaten—he reportedly joked with his manager afterward: "Hey Skip. Bet you wish I was Jewish today, too.") But when Koufax returned to win two games in the series, including the final victory, it was like an American (Jewish) dream come true. Observant—*and* a winner! As the editorial from the *Jewish News* of Detroit, Michigan, proudly notes, maybe there were a few larger lessons to be learned from this great Koufax story.

Kennedy's Impact on American Freedom

SHAD POLIER

In the less than three years in which John F. Kennedy was President of the United States he so greatly contributed to mankind's hopes for peace and human dignity that his assassination left not only our own nation but the whole world bereft and numbed. Our country was uniquely blessed that in President Kennedy we had a man who gave to us that rare combination of culture, intellect, vision and statesmanship. Our tragedy is that he was lost to us in his young manhood. Yet in the brief period of his leadership he exerted a persuasive influence upon the course of American life. In instance after instance he lifted us to higher plateaus and fixed our eyes ever more clearly upon the goal of a fuller realization of the American dream of freedom and equality.

President Kennedy's death, however, warns us that there are forces in our nation which, unless checked, can transform our dream into a deadly nightmare. These are the forces of hatred and hostility, of bigotry and bitterness, of fear and fury, of cruelty and callousness. They are the ingredients of the witches' brew whose latest victim was the President of the United States, and whose recent victims include Medgar Evers, also slain by a sniper, and the Negro children who perished in the bombing of a Birmingham church.

In a very short time we shall be tested in our resolve to live in the spirit in which President Kennedy died. It is for us to see that the emancipation of the Negro and the freedom of all Americans shall be advanced by enactment into law of an effective civil rights bill. Such a measure, more than any monument, would be a fitting memorial to a man who by word and deed used his high office not only to oppose discrimination against the Negro but to accord to him equal status.

In his brief term of office President Kennedy appointed many Negroes to places of high honor and responsibility, named hundreds more to positions of importance, and earnestly pressed the task of eliminating discrimination within the vast civil service, including its offices in the deep South. By these acts he did more than strike a blow for equality. He helped shatter the image of Negro inferiority.

President Kennedy welcomed the Revolution of our times, the massive and determined effort of the Negro, both in the South and in the North, to achieve equality now. His warm greeting to those who participated in the March on

Washington was no isolated phenomenon. In person and through his representatives in the Executive branches of the Government, he strove unceasingly to encourage both the North and South to accept the inevitability, and to understand the righteousness, of the Negro's strides toward freedom. [. . .]

This is not to say that the President, in every instance, went as far or as quickly as the Negro community or civil rights organizations wished and hoped he would go. It was a disappointment that his Executive Order regarding housing built with Federal aid was so limited in scope and that the civil rights bill introduced by him did not include a provision for a fair employment practice commission. That there were these and other disappointments in the field of civil rights does not, however, detract from the realization that they reflected no lack of concern but, rather, a difference in judgment as to what could be achieved and what should not be risked lest more be lost.

An example of the courage and integrity of President Kennedy was his statement at the press conference two days after the Supreme Court had held unconstitutional the recital of the Regents Prayer in the New York Public Schools. President Kennedy did not limit himself to saying that the decision should be supported because the Constitution, as interpreted by the Supreme Court, is the supreme law of the land. He went on to observe that:

> I would think that it would be a welcome reminder to every American family that we can pray a good deal more at home, we can attend our churches with a good deal more fidelity, and we can make the true meaning of prayer much more important in the lives of our children. That power is very much open to us. And I would hope that, as a result of this decision, all American parents will intensify their efforts at home.

It is to be remembered that a week later, at the annual meeting of the Governors' Conference, a resolution was adopted—with only Governor Rockefeller abstaining—deploring and attacking this historic decision. Also to be recalled is the bitter attack upon the Court for which Catholic Church leaders and organs were the principal spokesmen. That less than a year later an even more sweeping decision by the Court in the prayer and Bible-reading cases evoked so different a response must to a considerable measure be attributed to the leadership displayed by President Kennedy in June 1962. It is not without irony that the man whose election as President marked a triumph over religious bigotry should have thus so forthrightly championed separation of Church and State.

President Kennedy firmly opposed, on Constitutional grounds, any use of Federal funds to aid parochial schools at the elementary and secondary school levels. In this instance, too, his position was at complete variance with that of the Catholic Church. Indeed, the opposition of the latter was to account for the votes in the Rules Committee which kept the Administration's bill from ever reaching the floor of the House. [...]

This brief chronicle of some of the contributions of John F. Kennedy to civil rights and civil liberties is fraught with reminders of all that remains to be done. Each of us must experience a sense of personal responsibility as we reflect how much greater the task will be now that he is not here to lead, to counsel, to cheer, to guide and to encourage us. Yet his example will be with us, and each of us must be thankful that he lived with us even for so short a time.

The Pity of It An Editorial

JEWISH FRONTIER

In the weeks that have elapsed since the assassination of President Kennedy the national sense of loss has not lightened. The country, recovering from its first shock, has resumed its normal activities as is inevitable but the questions posed by the horror in Texas remain urgent and unanswered. The commission of inquiry headed by Chief Justice Warren will no doubt cast whatever light is possible on the attendant circumstances of the death of John F. Kennedy and will, we trust, allay all suspicions as to the identity of his murderer—suspicions still voiced in the capitals of friendly Western nations. But even if all required judicial processes will confirm the case of the Texas police against Lee Oswald and will establish, as seems likely, that he alone was the killer, we cannot escape the realization that there were others in Texas and other parts of the South who were ready to pull the trigger. That a self-styled "Marxist," warped and half-demented, was the assassin should not obscure the fact that the vocabulary of terrorism has become endemic in some parts of the United States. Not only solitary crackpots but organized bigots, particularly of the extreme Right, have created a climate in which violence breeds and proliferates. One of the most ominous sounds in the land in the past weeks was the applause with which some schoolchildren in New Orleans and Dallas greeted the announcement of the President's murder. A moral climate which makes such a reaction possible indicates how deeply the hate-propaganda of the extreme white segregationists has permeated its adherents. The frank applause of the children was the barometer of the extent of the corruption. The children's candor was damning evidence of the kind of conditioning they received in the adult world they respected. No doubt these youngsters have since learned that honest joy must not always be honestly expressed. If greater discretion will be the only lesson taught by the tragedy in Texas then there is much to fear. One member of a White Citizen's Council resigned publicly after Kennedy's death, apparently in a belated appreciation of where the course on which he had embarked led. And a few courageous voices in the South have been raised in protest against the supposedly "respectable" connivers in violence. The mobs who screamed at small children going to school, who spat at Adlai Stevenson, and who pasted inflammatory placards on their streets, raised from their midst the assassins who bombed children and gunned down all whom they opposed—from an obscure fighter for civil rights to the President of the

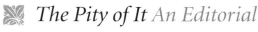

United States. But too many in Texas and elsewhere are still more concerned with their public image than with remedying palpable evils.

There will always be the mad and the envious to whom all excellence is a challenge to be destroyed. For such sick souls a radiant figure like that of John F. Kennedy, dowered with good looks, ability, wealth and success, becomes a natural target for hostility. However, the lone psychotic is primarily a security problem. His actions, no matter how fearful their consequences, can only be dealt with by society in terms of therapy and prevention. He is the accident which precipitates the tragedy, and society must guard itself against him in whatever way can be devised.

More frightening because more fundamental is the systematic encouragement of violence by extremists of the Right. It is no secret that the first assumption in all quarters after the President's death was that he had been the victim of a Rightist cabal. Nor is it a secret that Adlai Stevenson, after his reception in Texas, urged the President to cancel his proposed journey to Dallas. That the actual shooting was done by an Oswald does not alter the significance of such assumptions and warnings for they gauge the temper of a group not merely of an individual. No matter how sharply one may disagree with Marxism as a social system, there is nothing in its tenets which preaches terrorism. The same cannot be said for the reactionary fanatics and neo-Nazis who drill secretly in uniform.

Fortunately for the United States and the world, President Johnson has entered upon his office with resolution and courage. He has pledged himself to continue the enlightened social policies of the man he succeeds. Perhaps in the present mood of the country Congress will enact the legislation initiated by John F. Kennedy. The most enduring memorial to the late martyred President would be the prompt passage of the Civil Rights Bill for which he fought.

America is Galut

ARTHUR HERTZBERG

The modern Jewish community, from its synagogues to its defense agencies and charitable funds, has been based on the belief that a definition of Jewish identity could be found which would make it possible for that identity to last, and not erode, within a democratic order. Two further notions are involved in this proposition: first, that it is somehow wrong and undemocratic even to attempt to be a Jew today on foundations which have no analogues in the rest of society, and, second, that any such attempt is doomed to failure, because the majority of the Jewish community will find it unacceptable. In turn, therefore, Jews have helped to devise or popularize such theories of democratic identity as cultural pluralism and the tri-faith image of America. These notions have been used to defend the idea that the Jew could be himself in America in the way everybody else was being himself. In its own view of itself, the leadership of American Jewry's major bodies, the Establishment, has therefore been engaged with extraordinary energy and great pathos in saving and perpetuating Jewry and Judaism by providing us with explanations of ourselves through which we could be, comfortably, both Americans and Jews.

Such is the theory of the Establishment—but what of its practice? The norms that it sets for Jews are quite easy to identify. A "good" Jew today, by its standards, is one who is involved with powerful emotion in the future of the State of Israel and the destiny of all other Jews all over the world; in religion, he is expected to belong to a synagogue and to provide his children with some Jewish education, but he does not need either to believe in the Jewish God or to follow the precepts of the tradition; in charity, he is supposed to major in the support of specifically Jewish causes at home and, abroad, in helping Jewish refugees and, above all, the State of Israel; it is presumed without question that he will oppose vehemently the intermarriage of his children and be only someone mollified by the accession of someone born a non-Jew to his Jewish family by conversion. These are the *mitzvot*—the commandments—enjoined by the Jewish Establishment. Consonant with its theory, by obeying them, the Jew in America supposedly behaves "just like everybody else."

The nub of the issue is that this is patently not true. These norms are, each in specific, not really equivalent to the parallels supposedly to be found in the behavior of other minorities. Taken together, these *mitzvot* fashion a unique *Gestalt.*

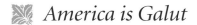

Without entering into sterile arguments about political theory, it is clear that the American Jewish community is expected by its leaders to be more involved in Israel (sometimes, even negatively) than, for example, the American Irish are in Ireland. The Jewish emotions which are expressed by giving children a "religious" education or in battling against their marrying out, are often emotions held by non-believers. Such people are expressing the momentum of an identity and historic experience which cannot be comprehended in conventional Western confessional terms. There is a level of concern among believing Catholics and Protestants for their co-religionists, including those in other countries, but we expect non-believing American Jews to give more to, care more about, and be more actively involved in Jews elsewhere than such an American norm commands. It is, for instance, well known that Jews continue to raise more, in absolute figures, for their overseas causes than either the Protestants or the Catholics of America. Relatively, this means a per capita ratio of about 15 to 1, and any lessening of the imbalance is an immediate cause of worry and complaint.

In theory, therefore, the Establishment has talked the language of being "just like everybody else"; in practice it has behaved uniquely, and it has demanded such behavior of those who would heed it. This discontinuity between theory and practice has inevitably troubled the organized Jewish community. Because the problem is really too painful to confront, since it involves the making of choices which the community would rather avoid, it has been easier for the Jewish Establishment to substitute public relations for serious thought. The dilemma however refuses to disappear, especially since the situation from which it arises refuses to stabilize.

On the evidence of their own children, all of the uniquenesses which mark the "good Jews" of the Jewish Establishment are eroding in the generation that has now come to maturity. Their politics are indeed becoming just like everybody else's, which means that there has been a perceptible lessening of any specific passion about other Jews. To a considerable degree indeed, the equivalent generation in Israel, in its own need for a sense of national normalcy, and therefore for playing down its relationship to a unique irridenta, has been encouraging this development. In religion, the rate of affiliation even in this, the "third generation," still seems high, but there is universal agreement among all observers that personal conduct is even less influenced among them by Jewish norms. Recent studies by a number of national and local Jewish charitable bodies (quite revealingly, almost all have remained unpublished) prove beyond doubt that the "third generation" is ever more tending to give to general rather than to specifically Jewish causes, and to give not by Jewish standards but by the rather more minimal ones current in the general American environment. The rate of intermarriage among those presently marrying is at least one in seven, and rising. It is still the lowest rate of any white community in America, but it shows every sign of approaching the estate of being "just like everybody else's."

The next generation is settling down in America, to behave like a university trained segment of the big city bourgeoisie, indeed to be a major component of it. What shocks the Jewish Establishment in this image is the fear that it must see itself, on this evidence, not as a solution to the question of Jewish life in a democracy, but as a way station on a slow, seemingly inevitable road to evaporation. [. . .]

What has all this to do with the concept of exile? In the classic Jewish tradition exile meant, in the first instance, the notion that the Jew was outside of society and of history, waiting for his return to his own land. Meanwhile he suffered the pain of living in an environment hostile to him and uncongenial to his very nature. The American Jewish Establishment has denied the idea of the Return, and it has vehemently maintained that democracy is congenial to Jewish existence. Nonetheless, it is abundantly clear that what has made this outlook work for a generation or so, as Jewish inner content has been evaporated, is an immediate memory of suffering at the hands of the gentile world and the momentum of many centuries of Jewish faith. It is very nearly true that everything else said in the name of the Establishment is a tactically useful gambit, in protection of this emotion. But this memory and this momentum have lessened markedly. Indeed, the very words (as opposed to feelings) of the Establishment have helped it lessen. And so a new nuance of the pain of the Exile is now being experienced, or rather, it is being re-experienced in America.

It is this: the Jew cannot settle down in freedom to be himself, "just like everybody else." When in his own inner consciousness he begins to approach a real feeling of at-homeness within the larger society, what remains of his Jewish identity is too little and too personalized to sustain a community. It inevitably follows that there is only one possible mode for the survival of a Jewish community in a free society. It can live only by emphasizing what is unique to itself and by convincing its children that that uniqueness is worth having.

The Jewish Establishment has, so far, been unable to devise a policy based on this premise. In part the reason has been a fear that has consistently colored modern Jewish thought for the last two centuries. It is the idea that a democratic order is not really hospitable to a radical deviation from the norms that are usual within its society. In particular, this fear has been all the stronger because such deviants as the Quakers, with their history of pacifism, are at least Christians, and therefore they are not, historically, the object of the peculiar hatred which is anti-Semitism. The protective coloration of likeness has appeared to the Establishment to be an indispensable tool with which to create safety for the Jew; to emphasize difference has seemed to be a form of courting danger. This means, of course, that the Jewish Establishment has accepted a version of democracy which defines it, at least in relation to the Jew, as a form of liberal totalitarianism.

A second, perhaps even more fundamental, bar to a consistent policy of apartness, has been the loss of religious faith. Insofar as the Jewish Establishment has attempted to argue within democracy for what is uniquely Jewish, it has tended to argue that there are "Jewish values," which represent one nuance of the highest ideals common to the Western tradition. This is completely unconvincing. If that is all there really is to the Jewish spirit, why should anyone feel compelled to express what amounts to conventional liberalism in terms of an inherited group or ethnic identity? A serious and continuing Jewish apartness can be sustained in a free society only in the passion of religious commitment. This, however, means something radically different than our contemporary Jewish "religion," which is itself a form of institutional assimilation to the prevailing American modes; it is even a bridge to the disappearance of the individual Jew. Nothing less than a radical commitment to a religious imperative can make Jews again want to be "a peculiar people."

It is possible that in the next generation, or in the one thereafter, Jews in America will indeed be sufficiently rooted in the experience of freedom not to be afraid to announce a radical difference from the majority. One cannot be too hopeful, because what has appeared before in other places during the 19th century in the third and fourth generations of freedom, were personalized sensibilities and sensitivities. Jacob Wasserman and Franz Kafka are, indeed, paradigms of a third kind of *Galut:* the apartness that remains for a post-Jewish Jew in post-Christian Christendom.

The greater danger to Jewish survival is that there are no signs of a religious renewal, as distinguished from institutions or even theology. Apartness may, therefore, be the only way in which a serious Jewish community can continue, but that apartness must have content. For such content we can only wait. Or we can tire of waiting, and of its quiet dangers to our own Jewish identities, and start thinking seriously, for the first time since adolescence, of *aliyah:* at very least, the *aliyah* of our children.

The Fourth Dialogue in Israel
The Challenge of Jewish Youth

AMERICAN JEWISH CONGRESS

PRESIDING:
Shad Polier, *Chairman, Governing Council, American Jewish Congress*
and
Shlomo Avineri, *Political Science Lecturer, Hebrew University*

PANELISTS:
Paul Cowan, *B.A., Harvard University*
Jane Satlow Gerber, *B.A., Wellesley College*
Benjamin Kedar, *Student in History, Hebrew University*

[. . .]

Mr. Paul Cowan: This hasn't yet become a dialogue: people are just making speeches about what they think. So let me say, too, what I think.

I begin by declaring that I personally feel a very strong loyalty towards Israel, and if there should ever be a crisis, there is no question in my mind that I would work or fight to help Israel as much as I could. But I must note that we are not a homogeneous people: there are many different sorts of Jews both here and in America. We can assert that we should be one people; we can make all the qualifications we wish. Our diversity, however, is a fact.

It is also a fact that even the Americans who are here, different as we are in points of view, don't represent a real cross-section of American Jewry. I personally know many American Jews who feel no particular loyalty towards Israel, people who, for one reason or another, would agree that Nasser's brand of socialism is better than Israel's brand of socialism. This condition of diversity is demonstrated further by the circumstance that David Berger and Joseph Solomon probably have far more in common than David and I, they being religious in outlook and I not being particularly religious. On the other hand, Muki Tzur and I, it seems to me, have a great deal to talk about—or, at least, we have had a great deal to talk about over the past two days, basing our discussions on political rather than religious matters. I am open to any qualification on that statement, but so far it appears to be true.

In America there is a large number of Jews who do seem to be political, who do translate, for whatever reason—because they are American or because they are Jewish—what would have, a generation or two ago, been religious values into some kind of ethical or political action. Now, David talked about the moral duty to come to Israel. For a person who is interested in political ethical work rather than in religious ethical life, there is also a moral duty. I myself feel that I have a very strong moral duty to work at various things at home, for example, the civil rights movement. (I would say, incidentally, that the fact that students work in the civil rights movement has made it as strong as it is.) I speak only for myself, but it seems to me that a commitment to the civil rights movement is a greater moral duty than coming to Israel merely because one is a Jew—as the Israelis assert.

I can imagine where Israel would have a strong appeal for certain Jewish youth. For example, I passed through Beersheba about three years ago and there were many things that I learned there. There were many relationships, for example, between North Africans and Europeans, and between people of different cultures, from which I derived a great deal. There were also many government programs which proved very instructive for me, and which might entice me to work in Israel, because they provide a deeper channel than I might find in America. It is certainly true that for me, Beersheba, because of its smallness, because of its immediate problems, is a far more manageable place than New York City. For example, the scientific research that was going on in the desert was very important to me. In New York City, scientific research isn't that important to me: I don't feel it as a significant part of my life. In any case, that is the kind of appeal that would bring me to Israel—a descriptive appeal of how this country challenges its problems. But that kind of appeal would have to be made to me as a particular kind of Jew; it can't be made to me as a Jew in general.

There is another question that I have. People have been talking about assimilation. For a person such as myself, for whom Judaism is primarily ethical and political, what does assimilation mean? In the United States, it seems to me that assimilation, for many of us young people, means assimilation into a crude, nationalistic culture, which, to be sure, does exist in various places in the country—in Scarsdale and Bar Harbor, as well as Miami Beach—and from all of which I must dissent. Therefore, the many Negroes, the many Christians who share my dissent, share a great deal with me—perhaps more than the people who actually do live in Scarsdale. *That* is my own way of resisting assimilation. [. . .]

Mrs. Jane Satlow Gerber: [. . .] One of the problems which the Israelis face in speaking to us is that the vast majority of American Jewish college youth has not gone beyond the most superficial commitment to their Judaism;

that the ideological substratum is no longer there which will create a bridge between us.

I would ask Paul Cowan what he means by ethical and political Judaism. To me it is not really clear as to what is the political Judaism that he is building his life's work upon.

Mr. Cowan *(interjecting):* I agree that it's an abstraction to talk about ethical and political Judaism, and I regret using those terms. I certainly agree that the same kind of ideological qualities exist among many people of different backgrounds, who get into the civil rights movement. On the other hand, for me at least, there is a Jewish factor operating. There was something particular about being brought up as a Jew, about having my mother remind me of Eastern Europe, about World War II, about the Holocaust, about having gone to a prep school where anti-Semitism was rather thick. All this gave me a special sort of sympathy for oppressed people; this led me to work in the civil rights movement. I have no idea whether that's true of other Jews.

There was also something, I think, in my being Jewish that gave me a real appreciation of variety, of cosmopolitanism, of pluralism. Being Jewish gave me a feeling that the deepest thing I, as a Jew, had to defend was the right of every man to speak his mind and the right of every other man to listen to whoever spoke his mind. Now for me—I can only speak personally—that came partly from being a Jew. It might also have developed if I were a Christian; it might not develop in other Jews. Does that answer your question? [. . .]

Mr. Benjamin Kedar *(Hebrew):* I must, I am afraid, open on a negative note. I do not think there is as yet any real dialogue between Israeli and American youth. The Hebrew University, as you may know, recently completed a survey that documented the appalling lack of understanding between the two. This unhappy fact, of course, is also borne out by the polarity of opinion which seems to be taking shape here on this rostrum. I, myself, have previously taken part in any number of debates between Israeli and American Jews. I am very sorry to say that even at the best of times these occasions gave rise to mutual ridicule and belittling of each other's positions. Sometimes things got worse, and it was a matter of open hostility.

What are the roots of this unfortunate situation? The lack of understanding derives, I think, from the fact that neither of the two parties recognizes the legitimate existence of the other; the Israelis do not recognize the legitimacy of the American community, and the American Jew will not accept Israel as a truly Jewish society. We Israelis were educated to regard the Diaspora as being an unhealthy condition. To a large extent, the average Israeli subscribes to the opinion that any Diaspora Jew who does not come to

Israel is really a traitor. Mr. Yadlin, in effect, illustrated this position when he said yesterday that an Orthodox Jew cannot lead a full religious life unless he lives in Israel. This, of course, is the famous Ben-Gurion attitude, which created so much controversy not long ago.

Now, I, too, feel that one cannot live fully as a Jew anywhere else but in Israel. Still, we must see these matters in proper perspective, if we are to have complete and true communication; we must, both of us, abandon our stock positions. For Israelis, of course, the stumbling block is an acceptance of the Diaspora. Can we recognize the viability of Jewish existence abroad? To my mind, a compromise is called for. We should, on the one hand, recognize legitimate Jewish existence abroad; this however, must be arrived at without jettisoning Zionist ideology.

It has been suggested that there are now two ways of Jewish life—our way, the Zionist way, and the American way. I readily grant that both are legitimate alternatives for a Jewish way of life. That does not, however, mean that both are of equal importance and significance. For me—and I believe for most Israelis—our way seems better. Our Jewish way of life is total and is not dependent on the tolerance of the majority. American Jewry is constantly being confronted by the pressures of the larger society. To be a Jew in America therefore means to make a choice. If an American Jew chooses to pursue his Jewish destiny in America, we must respect his preference. But even though I do not count myself among those who try to pressure American Jews into coming here by threats and intimidation, nevertheless, I should be happy if American Jewry were more committed to *aliya.* Still, as I indicated, I do not feel that American Jews are enjoying a false existence.

Before I conclude, I would like to take issue with what the Minister of Education said last night, about Israel being a *Jewish* State. This is not true. Israel is a State of Jews. Its society is not monolithic—there is a religious Jewry here, and also a non-religious Jewry—and we cannot therefore define Israel in terms that would exclude any Jew.

Now, a last remark: I cannot take seriously the claim that the civil rights movement is a true outlet for Jewish activity. I admit that such activity is indeed rooted deeply in the Jewish consciousness, as the participation of Jews in revolutionary movements over the last fifty years has demonstrated. The question, however, is: does this also contribute to the Jewishness of those Jews who participate in the particular movements? Experience, I believe, has shown us otherwise. [. . .]

Sandy Koufax, an American Hero

DETROIT JEWISH NEWS

The World Series, which concluded last week with a victory for the Dodgers, once again has an important moral lesson for Americans. In our sports arenas we have proven that it is possible for people of all faiths, of all races, to meet on equal ground.

It is not because Sandy Koufax is an observant Jew that there is so much interest in the events that marked the contest between the Minnesota and California teams. It is because working side by side with Koufax, and facing them in opposition, were ball players who were black and white, who worship in synagogues and in churches.

This is the great lesson on the baseball diamond, as it will henceforth be on the football fields, in basketball, in hockey and in other sports.

This accounts for the American spirit of good will, for our demand for fair play and mutual respect in dealing with our neighbors and fellow citizens.

It is heartening to know that Jews are not limiting themselves to book lore—much as we would like to see many more become knowledgeable—but are also devoting themselves to wholesome sports. And because of it we are proud that Sandy Koufax stems from our ranks and is so respectful in relation to his ancestry.

3

Living with the Holocaust

There is a widespread perception about periodization that lingers today in discussions about the history of the Holocaust in American life. It is the notion that the topic of the Shoah really only burst into public view after the Six-Day War in June 1967 between Israel and the Arab nations. The assumption remains that during the pre-1967 era, Americans—including American Jews—demonstrated a generalized indifference to (or avoidance of) this anguishing subject.

An aim of this chapter is to offer testimony that disputes this perception. Indeed, talk about the Shoah began immediately in 1945, and though it subsided in the early fifties, it returned again in the later fifties; more centrally for our purposes, by the first years of the 1960s, there was no reluctance to discuss the history and memory of the Holocaust. On the contrary, and as the angered essays by Lucy S. Dawidowicz and Marie Syrkin illustrate by example, there was little compunction about going public—not only to offer information about the Holocaust, but also to discredit inaccurate distortions of it. And strikingly, in these instances at least, the recipients of their full-scale assaults were other Jews.

The opening piece by Dawidowicz addresses screenwriter Rod Serling's 1960 television drama about the destruction of the Warsaw Ghetto. Broadcast as part of the widely acclaimed CBS series *Playhouse 90*, Serling's *In the Presence of Mine Enemies* is a travesty, Dawidowicz argues. And although she does not quite say so directly, Dawidowicz also implies that Serling (a Reform Jew) was so eager to appease a gentile audience (and a corporate bottom line) that he did not hesitate to dispense with both historical accuracy and human decency in the process. Dawidowicz's is an absolutely scathing critique.

Marie Syrkin's rebuttal to political philosopher Hannah Arendt's best-selling book, *Eichmann in Jerusalem: A Report on the Banality of Evil* (1963) is no less devastating. Arendt famously contended that European Jews had been passive (and often even complicitous) before the onslaught of German Nazism; Arendt further asserted that even leading Nazis like Adolf Eichmann had merely operated as bureaucrats who furthered the Final Solution more as a result of their sense of duty than due to any deep conviction or overt antisemitism. Syrkin, editor of the Labor Zionist *Jewish Frontier,* reveals her evident rage at these analyses as she works to demolish both Arendt and her text; by the end, Syrkin's attack begins to feel quite personal.

Yet another goal of this chapter is to highlight, however broadly, the uneven evolution of post-Holocaust theological and cultural discussion in the second half of the decade. Despite what we may think about the Holocaust today, there was little or no consensus in the later 1960s about what it ought to mean, or what its legacies might be. The focus here is on a symposium held on March 26, 1967; on that day, *Judaism,* a publication of the American Jewish Congress, convened an annual meeting of its board of editors. Chaired by Steven S. Schwarzschild, the journal's editor, the invited panelists included Emil L. Fackenheim, a professor of philosophy at the University of Toronto, and George Steiner, a well-known literary critic. While a great deal was said that remains noteworthy, it is nonetheless the statement by Emil Fackenheim that has subsequently achieved truly historic status. Here it was still several weeks before the Six-Day War when Fackenheim introduced (what he termed) a 614th commandment, that is, "the authentic Jew of today is forbidden to hand Hitler yet another, posthumous victory." The repercussions of this concept remain powerful.

The closing selections in this chapter are both by internationally renowned Jewish intellectuals, each of whom—as it happens—chose to journey to Israel soon after the Six-Day War. In the case of Abraham Joshua Heschel, a professor at Jewish Theological Seminary, the visit to Israel after the war was also his first. The visit prompted him to write *Israel: An Echo of Eternity;* a brief, but emotionally intense, excerpt from this book is included here. And finally, there are the reflections of literary critic Alfred Kazin. Writing in 1970, Kazin reflects rather mournfully on his earliest memories of the knowledge of a Nazi plan to destroy the Jewish people. The year was 1943. And Kazin mulls as well his uncomfortable gut feeling that the modern world has not learned much—and certainly not enough—from the enormity of the catastrophe that was the Shoah.

Boy Meets Girl in Warsaw Ghetto

LUCY S. DAWIDOWICZ

Rod Serling's *In the Presence of Mine Enemies*, is, as far as I know, the first television play about the Warsaw ghetto. It was presented last May by "Playhouse 90" on the CBS network.

Serling created seven characters: four Jews—Rabbi Adam Heller, his grown son Paul and daughter Rachel, and Emanuel, a neighbor; two Germans—Captain Richter and Sergeant Lott; a Polish peddler, Joseph Chinik. The rabbi is a kind of priest-type who abhors violence, equating German atrocities against Jews with the Jewish desire to fight back, preaching "Love your enemies." The daughter, at nineteen constantly reminiscing about her childhood, remains passive even after she has been raped by the German officer. Paul, the son, is the Jew who takes up arms against the Germans. He is kill-crazy, contemptuous of his father and his religion, all his humanity concentrated only on his sister. His own father twice equates him with the Nazis. Finally, there is the neighbor Emanuel, the scared, hysterical Jew, looking for escape, forever building hiding places.

As for the non-Jews, first the Pole. He is the rabbi's friend, who daily comes into the ghetto with food. Later he sacrifices himself for the Jews, by telling the Germans that he, not Paul, murdered the Nazi officer. With this sacrifice he prevents mass-murder reprisals against the Jews. Of the two Germans, Captain Richter is the villain, a Prussian officer who hits a rabbi, rapes his daughter and preaches extermination of the Jews. But Sergeant Lott—he is young, handsome, nineteen like Rachel the beautiful Jewess, whom he loves and whose rape makes him want to atone for Germany's sins. Indeed, knowing the ghetto will be utterly destroyed, he comes to rescue Rachel. And off she goes, her father the rabbi's blessing upon her and her unborn child.

As the young lovers flee, Paul takes his rifle, the rabbi his Bible. Together father and son join the ghetto fighters, the picture fading out to the sound of gunfire.

There was not one single moment in the entire play, as I watched it and later read the script, that did not offend or outrage with its falseness and fraudulence. This ghetto was no ghetto, this rabbi no rabbi, these Jews no Jews, these Germans no Germans, and this Pole no Pole. Where were the tragedy and glory of the Warsaw ghetto?

Here are the bare facts about the Warsaw ghetto. The Germans walled off an area in the heart of the city, about a mile by two and a half. The Poles were evacuated from there and 360,000 Jews moved into the area which could house 160,000. Later more Jews were brought into the Warsaw ghetto, until there were nearly half a million.

Until the summer of 1942 the Jews in the Warsaw ghetto were allowed to live, if they could survive starvation, epidemics and indiscriminate terror. In 1941 alone, about 45,000 died—10 per cent of the population. A vast network of Jewish self-help institutions (communal kitchens, schools, cooperative workshops, medical aid) sustained thousands of others.

Deportations to the gas chambers at Treblinka began in July 1942. The Nazis advertised the move as "resettlement" for work in the Eastern provinces, offering bread and marmalade as travel relations. Thousands volunteered. Before long the Jews learned the destination of the trains, though it was hard to believe. Terror and police brutality continued to provide deportees. By the end of September only some 65,000 Jews were left in the Warsaw ghetto. But within a month the remaining Jews had planned resistance.

In January 1943, when German detachments entered the ghetto to begin its final liquidation, they were greeted with salvos. They retreated. Three months later, on April 19, 1943, the eve of Passover, they returned—2,000 elite troops under General Juergen Stroop, a detachment of engineers, tanks and a battery of light artillery. Their opponents—several hundred young men and woman, 22 units of the Jewish Fighter Organization, armed with revolvers (some the grudging gift of the Polish underground, some dearly paid for) and ghetto-produced grenades. Stroop expected to complete the ghetto's liquidation in three days, but it took four weeks. The Germans gassed, dynamited and burned the ghetto, house by house, shelter by shelter. They flooded the sewers and unleashed savage police dogs. Only a remnant of Jews survived.

The Warsaw ghetto Jews were the first people anywhere in Europe to rise against the German occupation. While fighting their unequal battle, they appealed to the world for help, but there was no response. Without friends or allies, isolated behind ghetto walls, they were sustained only by their desperate desire to die resisting.

But Serling knew little of all this and showed none of it.

First some small things. The play opens on a room, with many Jews standing in orderly rows as a German officer reads off names. Those called step out of line. I was baffled as to what was going on. But Serling had a German explain: "We call them in here to pick out the ones who are to die today."

This scene was supposed to be a "selection." But what really was a selection? The Germans would cordon off a street, a section, and drive everyone into one open area. There, under heavy police and SS surveillance, they would select the Jews for life or death, according to the color of one's identification card (some colors were good and others bad), or one's appearance, or a Nazi's whim.

Serling doesn't know what the ghetto was; his characters move freely in and out, above or below ground. On the spur of the moment, Paul scurries through the sewers out of the ghetto, into SS headquarters, strangles the Nazi captain, and is back home in no time.

Then the rabbi. Serling's rabbi is an Orthodox Polish rabbi. Yet he accepts wine from a Pole (the Jewish law is very explicit: Wine is forbidden to Jews if non-Jews have had any part in making it or have even touched it). He plays chess with the Pole (a devout Jew was expected to spend his time studying the Torah, not in jesting, levity and frivolity). He keeps a volume of Spinoza with his holy books (Spinoza was excommunicated 300 years ago and his reinstatement as a Jew is quite unlikely). This rabbi read Freud, Spengler and Nietzsche (see above on chess). This rabbi recited poetry—not the Psalms (ditto). This rabbi let his daughter at the age of nine go to a dance with a boy. (?) He allowed his own child to go to carnivals with the Polish peddler (Jewish law declares that children should study the Torah all day and not be disrupted from their studies "even for the purpose of building the Temple"). This rabbi says *sholem aleichem* for goodbye (it means "hello"). After both Germans beat him, he calls them "my children."

The rabbi is not even a caricature. No rabbi in the Warsaw ghetto or anywhere except TV would have called the Germans his children, any more than he would have called ravenous beasts his children. Many Orthodox Jews did at first oppose Jewish armed resistance. They believed they must accept God's will and die for *Kiddush ha-Shem* (Sanctification of the Name, martyrdom for Judaism) like the Jews during the Crusades and the Chmielnicki massacres of 1648. But once these Orthodox Jews realized the Nazis intended to liquidate the ghetto and its inhabitants, even those who did not think it in the Jewish tradition to fight back gave their full support to the Jewish Fighter Organization. I cannot imagine a Jew, rabbi or not, so shorn of human feeling as to equate a Jewish resistant with a Nazi. But Serling must have thought the equation true; his characterization of Paul was sufficiently unpleasant.

About the Pole. Jews still talk about the Poles and their role during the war. Yes, there were decent Poles who risked their lives to help Jews hide from the Nazis—a few hundred, perhaps a few thousand. But there were tens of thousands who sold Jews protection at outrageous prices, who turned them in for a half-pound of sugar, who helped the Nazis hasten them to the gas chambers. The Poles were not like the Danes, the Dutch, the French, Belgians or Italians. Only the Ukrainians outdid them in helping Germans wipe out the Jews. But Serling has created a Pole who not only helped, but who sacrificed himself for

Jews, who on the screen became the foil for the cowardly Jew who is taken screaming from his hiding place. Yet even this fictitious Pole is not good enough for Serling. He must have the good German to rescue Rachel, the beautiful Jewess.

A friend of mine who was a courier for the Jewish Fighter Organization outside the ghetto reads the memoir literature of Jewish survivors. She told me she read somewhere about a German who helped a Jewish woman escape; she thinks it is the only incident. Perhaps there was another, perhaps there were even a hundred. Is this the story of the Warsaw ghetto? I watched the young German explain to the rabbi: "We are not beasts. Some of us like to read. . . . We respond to beauty. Some of us have not forgotten how to love." I remembered a closing passage in the autobiography of the man who put millions of Jews to death in Auschwitz: "Let the public continue to regard me as a bloodthirsty beast, the cruel sadist, and the mass murderer; for the masses could never imagine the commandant of Auschwitz in any other light. They could never understand that he, too, had a heart and that he was not evil."

Why did Serling so abuse the history of the Warsaw ghetto? Was he smoothing over his monumental ignorance of his subject with slickness, loud music and name stars? Clearly he did not strive for authenticity. It would have been easy enough to correct the obvious mistakes of fact. Serling did not even take the trouble for that. But his conception is also altogether inauthentic. He intended to glorify the Jews in the Warsaw ghetto, but he defamed them. This came about because he was not really writing about the Warsaw ghetto or the German annihilation of six million Jews. His message was L-O-V-E. Love cleanses, love purifies, love redeems. Love makes the world go round. It puts the Warsaw ghetto on a national network; it sells gas and cigarettes. It's the poor man's idea of psychoanalysis and the marginal Jew's idea of Christianity.

The Warsaw ghetto uprising has become the symbol of the Jewish catastrophe in World War II. Six million Jews were killed and Jewish life in Eastern Europe—the seat of Jewish creativity—wiped out. The horror and tragedy are unmatched in history's annals. Among Jews the Catastrophe takes its place alongside the destruction of the Second Temple. It is part of Jewish history, the specific experience of Jews at a time when Western Christian culture was said to have reached its height. It is a unique experience with a particular meaning not just for Jews, but for Christians.

But Serling shunned the specific and the unique. He does not think the Jewish experience significant for itself. Everything must be brought down to the Common Denominator, universalized and generalized into lifeless shadows of good and bad, love and hate, boy and girl.

In the Presence of Mine Enemies received high praise from critics and public alike. An unbelievably large number of Jews acclaimed it. Only those who had themselves experienced Nazism or who knew Jewish life in Eastern Europe were pained and horrified.

Serling's intention to evoke the grandeur of the theme may have been enough to stimulate a positive response to the play. His intent rather than his accomplishment inspired pride and sympathy. Then, too, there was gratitude for 90 minutes devoted to a painful tragedy. The subject itself probably generated among many viewers deep feelings which they attributed mistakenly to the play's "truthfulness."

These responses were possible because of the distance in time and spirit that we have traversed. We have traveled very far in the seventeen years since we perceived the end of Jews in Europe. We were horrified and compassionate then. Do we remember? We have turned away from the horror and our memory of it; today we don't remember even our own anguish.

We are even prepared to believe retroactively in a soap-opera version of the life and death of the Warsaw ghetto.

Hannah Arendt The Clothes of the Empress

MARIE SYRKIN

The debate sparked by Hannah Arendt's *Eichman in Jerusalem** is almost as disturbing as the book itself. A good many qualified reviewers in various journals have attacked not only Miss Arendt's views but the scholarship on which her conclusions are presumably based. Numerous vital errors and misstatements of fact have been pointed out by her critics. Her champions, however, have in no instance bothered to take cognizance of such factual objections. The readers outraged by Justice Musmanno's harsh review in *The New York Times Book Review* made no attempt to argue on the basis of the factual material adduced by the Justice; instead, they excoriated his failure to grasp the author's deep insights. The poet Robert Lowell, for example, while admitting that he was not "a suitable authority" to make a "point by point refutation," was impressed by "so much detail, profundity and intuition." (N.Y. *Times,* June 23, 1963.) Dwight Macdonald confined himself to discussing Miss Arendt's theory of totalitarianism. *The New Yorker,* which devoted five issues to Miss Arendt's report of the trial, ignored, with one exception, all communications, many of which expressed not merely disagreement, but cited flagrant and major errors. Nor has Miss Arendt deigned, thus far, to refute particulars. This astonishing indifference to charges of gross inaccuracies and omissions of pertinent data—charges which, if sustained, seriously undermine the author's main theses—is a perplexing feature of the discussion. It can only be explained on the assumption that Miss Arendt is considered exempt from the criteria of reliability usually applied to any work which pretends to be objective scholarship rather than tendentious exposition. If so, it is a dubious kind of honor to accord an intellectual as widely praised as Miss Arendt.

The New Yorker (July 20, 1963) in an unprecedented display of emotion mourned editorially the 'breakdown" of communication which made possible the misunderstanding of a "historian, philosopher, and humanist" of Miss Arendt's caliber. In the interests of clarification, *The New Yorker* helpfully offered a resume of Miss Arendt's ideas: "She recorded the behavior of individuals and of nations, and found within her story a moral for Germans, for citizens

**Eichmann in Jerusalem: A Report on the Banality of Evil,* by Hannah Arendt. The Viking Press, New York, 275 pp., $5.50.

of other Western countries, and for Jews—in descending order of responsibility: It is evil to assent actively or passively to evil, as its instrument, its observer, or as its victim." This capsule formulation has its uses, for in the widespread discussion of the book it is precisely the "evil" of the *victim* that is at issue—whether in descending or ascending order of responsibility. And for many readers even the "order" is beclouded.

Bruno Bettelheim, who agrees with Arendt in the main, granted in a laudatory review (*The New Republic,* June 15, 1963) that "Arendt at times creates an ambiguity in her evaluation of guilt. Thus on cursory reading she seems to plead that Eichmann was a victim and that Jewish leaders were heavy with guilt." But a characteristic of the debate is that it is not "the cursory readers" who have made the most devastating indictments of the author's method. It is the scholars, the specialists in contemporary Jewish history.

In a moving letter to Miss Arendt, who is his old friend, the great Jewish scholar and historian, Gershom Scholem, writes in German from Jerusalem (*Mitteilungs Blatt,* August 16, 1963): "Your book revolves around two centers, the Jews and their behavior during the catastrophe, and Eichmann and his responsibility. I have considered the problem of the Jews for many years and have studied no small measure of the literature on the subject. It is clear to me, as to every thoughtful contemporary of these events, how bitterly serious, complex and not readily reducible this problem is. . . . The question that you have raised is a genuine one. Why then, since we know this, does your book leave one with a feeling of shame and bitterness not in regard to what is reported but in regard to the reporter? . . . The answer, insofar as I have one and which because I value you so highly I must give . . . lies in the heartless, sometimes downright mean-spirited [*hämische*] tone with which you treat a matter at the very center of our lives." After making various specific objections, he writes: "In the camps men were degraded and, as you yourself say, brought to cooperating in their own destruction, the execution of their fellows and the like. Is therefore the boundary between victims and persecutors wiped out? What perversity!" In her presentation of the question he finds no "considered judgment" but often "overstatement degenerating into demogogy."

Miss Arendt's answer (in the same issue of *M. B.*) indicates her view of the controversy. She thinks that Scholem's independence of judgment has been warped by the "American-Jewish" campaign of "misrepresentation." To the man whose standing as original thinker and scholar is no less than her own, she writes: "I cannot believe that you read the book uninfluenced by so-called public opinion, manipulated in this case, you would have misunderstood the following . . ." and she lists the by-now familiar areas of misunderstanding: her charges applied only to "Jewish functionaries"; she never said Eichmann was a Zionist, and she did not mock Zionism. It was all irony. And she adds, "What confuses you is that my arguments and my way of thinking are unpredictable [*nicht vorgesehen*]. Or in other words that I am independent."

The question of Miss Arendt's bewildering originality I shall here leave aside, but the "irony" missed by Scholem and so many other readers is more to the point since it is the most frequent defense offered against jarring citations from her work. Her references to Zionism can serve as an example. Of Eichmann she writes that he read Herzl and was converted "immediately and forever to Zionism." She refers to the Nazi expulsions, which preceded extermination, as the "pro-Zionist" stage of the Nazi movement, and she describes one of Eichmann's concentration schemes for his captives as "(a Jewish homeland, a gathering in of the exiles of the Diaspora)." *If this be irony, at whom is it directed?* One does not have to be a Zionist to be shocked, or to "misunderstand" the author's intent. [. . .]

Why should there be these difficulties? *Eichmann in Jerusalem* is neither *Finnegan's Wake* nor *The Waste Land.* Miss Arendt is more given to categorical pronouncements than the seven types of ambiguity. What then caused the "breakdown"? One reason lies in the author's macabre humor, so tasteless in context; another in her bland omission and distortion of relevant data; but the chief reason is that her accusation of the Jews, far from being ironic or even subtle, is explicit and unequivocal, and is not at all limited to "Jewish functionaries." She writes: "But the whole truth was that there existed Jewish community organizations and Jewish party and welfare associations on both the local and international level. Wherever Jews lived, there were recognized Jewish leaders, and these leaders, almost without exception, cooperated in one way or another, for one reason or another, with the Nazis. The whole truth was that if the Jewish people had really been unorganized and leaderless there would have been chaos and plenty of misery but the total number of victims would hardly have been between five and six million." This "whole truth" illumines a lot of territory—Europe, America, Palestine (the "local and international level") and every aspect of Jewish life.

II

The author's theme, the "banality of evil," is developed in her account of how Jews behaved and what Eichmann did. Everyman, given the conditions, is capable of unspeakable evil and she tries to demonstrate that Eichmann is everyman. He is "terrifyingly normal," a conscientious little cog in the Nazi murder machine. Every time she is faced by evidence of his murderous initiative she explains that her subject is merely overconscientious. Yet the author's philosophic understanding of the banality of evil, so steadfast in regard to Eichmann, deserts her when she surveys the host of his victims. In arraigning their guilt she becomes hortatory instead of all-comprehending. And it is this difference which brings into question the paradox of her position: To kill millions is banal; any one of us could do it under the pressures of a totalitarian state. But to be among the sufferers is somehow culpable; any one of us would have faced death more valiantly, else what point is there to the author's accusations?

To sustain her twin theses—the normality of Eichmann and the moral aberrations of the Jews—Miss Arendt, basing herself largely on Raul Hilberg's *The Destruction of the European Jews,* recapitulates the familiar events of the Nazi holocaust. *En passant,* she snipes industriously at Zionism, Israel, Ben-Gurion's "show trial," the witnesses, the prosecuting attorney, and the justice of the Judges. At the end of the script the only one who comes out better than when he came in is the defendant. The victim comes out worst.

The legerdemain with which Miss Arendt shuffles evidence to sustain her image of Eichmann as an obedient underling, neither a fanatic nor an anti-Semite, is impressive to any one who has examined the sources she uses. Eichmann found himself on trial in Jerusalem not because he was a chance Nazi captured indiscriminately by vengeful Israelis but because he was head of the Department of Jewish Affairs, the man in charge of rounding up all European Jews for their extermination. It was Eichmann who reported to Himmler in August, 1944, on the success of his program and gave the figure as six million killed. Eichmann's celebrated admission, "I will jump into my grave laughing because the fact that I have the death of five million Jews on my conscience gives me extraordinary satisfaction" is briskly explained by Miss Arendt as "sheer rodomontade." Everyman is merely boasting here, for as we all know "bragging is a common vice." He boasts too when he "pretended" to have invented the ghetto system or the plan to ship all Jews to Madagascar. When he threatened angrily "to drop France" from his program because the French were not delivering Jews fast enough to him—a statement which the Jerusalem Court viewed as evidence of his authority—he was again boasting. Miss Arendt is equally skeptical of Rudolf Höss, commandant of Auschwitz, who testified to Eichmann's ingenuity in introducing Cyclon B, the gas used in the gas chambers, and of the Lutheran Minister Heinrich Grüber who had tried to help the Jews and who characterized Eichmann as "a block of ice." [. . .]

Nor does Miss Arendt's transformation of this hyperactive agent of the Nazi terror into an automaton jibe with Eichmann's view of himself. In the Sassen Papers (Buenos Aires, 1957), accepted as authentic by both prosecution and defense, he stated: "Had I been just a recipient of orders, then I could have been a simpleton. . . . When I reached the conclusion that it was necessary to do to the Jews what we did, I worked with the fanaticism a man expects from himself as a devoted national-socialist." That he changed his tune in Jerusalem is not surprising. Harder to understand is the omniscient confidence with which Miss Arendt brushes aside the historical record.

III

Miss Arendt's second thesis—that of Jewish collaboration—is expounded in as arbitrary a style as the first, but with one significant difference. In her account the author has achieved the miracle of humanizing Eichmann, the mass-murderer who is not a "monster," and only the informed reader can take issue with her. But the Jews in their extremity are dehumanized, and again it is only the informed reader who is fully in a position to disagree.

Writing of the Jewish Councils Miss Arendt declares: "To a Jew this role of the Jewish leaders in the destruction of their own people is undoubtedly the darkest chapter of the whole dark story." (She credits Hilberg with revealing it.) No. For a Jew, and, one trusts, a non-Jew, the "darkest chapter" is the Nazi murder of six million.

The Jewish Councils, established by Nazi decree in 1939, had to conduct community affairs and transmit Nazi orders. Some kind of organization had to exist among the imprisoned Jewries of the ghettos for the distribution of food, sanitation, and even education. It is clear from all accounts that the ghettos became isolated worlds whose inhabitants clung to the illusion that some would survive until liberation. The Jewish Councils, forced to assume responsibility, had the agonizing task of fulfilling German orders and at the same time of trying to shield the ghetto from Nazi savagery. According to Hilberg, "the Jewish Councils, in the exercise of their historic function, continued until the end to make desperate attempts to alleviate the suffering and to stop the mass dying in the ghettos"—a statement which might seem to qualify Miss Arendt's somber vision of Jewish functionaries engrossed in writing deportation orders.

To indicate how the Jewish Councils relished their authority, Miss Arendt comments as follows on the first announcement issued by the Budapest Council: "We still can sense how they enjoyed their new power—'The Central Jewish council is granted the right of absolute disposal over all Jewish spiritual and material wealth and over all Jewish manpower.'" But she does not bother to relate the circumstances (reported on the same page by the same Hilberg) which explain this announcement. Eichmann had arrived in Budapest to form a *Judenrat.* To enlist the unwitting cooperation of the Jews in their eventual destruction he assured them that they had nothing to fear unless they refused and that "after the war the Germans would be *gutmutig* [amiable] again." The

Budapest council members asked for compliance because they honestly believed that obedience would save Jewish lives. When they discovered the truth, the "Jewish leaders" (Hilberg) implored the Allies to bomb the railway junctions. So much for their "enjoyment."

Eichmann's elaborate deception was typical of the Nazi technique. Every first hand account of the ghettos describes the ingenuity with which the Germans kept their victims from discovering their doom. The ghettos not only segregated the Jews but divided them into manageable groups before whom the Nazis held out the promise of "resettlement" in the East. In the Warsaw Ghetto people who reported voluntarily to the transfer center were given bread and marmalade as an indication of Nazi kindliness. Postal cards, supposedly from previous deportees, kept arriving to prove that the writers were alive and working. To combat doubts the Nazis showed motion pictures of the comfortable life in the "work camps." The trickery was maintained till the very entrance into the gas chambers: men and women undressed voluntarily in the belief that they were entering a shower bath.

When, despite Nazi adroitness, the truth began to filter back to the ghettos from the extermination centers, many rejected the information as atrocity propaganda. They could not believe the humanly unbelievable. By the time the realization of the truth was inescapable, the majority of survivors was too reduced by hunger, disease and incarceration for even a gesture of opposition to the Nazi machine.

Emanuel Ringelblum (*Notes from the Warsaw Ghetto*), the archivist of the ghetto, asks in the diary discovered after his death: "A very interesting question is that of the passivity of the Jewish masses who expire with no more than a slight sigh. Why are they all so quiet? Why does the father die, and the mother, and each of the children, without a single protest?" He answers: "the fear of mass reprisals" and the "physical passivity" of those dying of hunger.

In the recently discovered Kaplan Diary, we read (July 30, 1943): "Amid all the tragedy of sudden expulsion, one minor detail is perhaps the most tragic of all: people come to the transfer point voluntarily, saying, Take me from the quagmire of the ghetto. I will die anyhow."

Ringelblum, Kaplan and other firsthand reporters vehemently denounced individual members of the Councils. One of the most abject episodes in the Kaplan Diary is his account of a terrified Council member huddling with his wife in his office, afraid that the Germans will seize her the moment she steps from his side. Yet these searing portraits can be accepted not as libels but as authentic descriptions of ghetto life, and the reason is that the diarists present complete not partial pictures. One never forgets that the cowering council member is as much a victim of the Nazi terror as the fellow victim whose name he inscribes. Those who refused to fulfill German orders were immediately shot (Paul Eppstein, Theresienstadt) or deported. (See Isaiah Trunk's Yiddish account, *Tzukunft*, Vol. 68.) Yet in the face of all the evidence, in her answer to Professor Scholem who reminds her of her statements in regard to the helplessness of the individual before total terror, Miss Arendt writes: "These people were not under the direct pressure of terror but only of indirect." How indirect is shooting?

Two questions are involved in the evaluation of the Councils. The first is moral. Regardless of the effect of their actions, how did they behave? No single answer can be given. Some men were noble, like Adam Czerniakow who killed himself to alarm the world; some were weaklings who tried to save their own families and themselves; most honestly believed that they protected the ghettos from immediate and complete annihilation through the sequence established by the Nazis, and that each deferral promised survival for some.

The second question—would more Jews have survived if there had been no Councils or other forms of organization, as Miss Arendt states—requires only a reference to history. It has already been shown (Hilberg, Robinson, and particularly Lionel Abel in *Partisan Review*, Summer, 1963) that in Russia where no Jewish Councils had been set up, the unorganized Soviet Jews were massacred by the advancing Nazis at an even more rapid rate than in Poland. 900,000 Soviet Jews were murdered by the *Einsatzgruppen* in the first months of the Nazi-Soviet war. Lionel Abel asks pointedly: why does the author ignore such massive evidence which invalidates her thesis? Where the Jewish Councils did function, they were impotent. The most that can be said is that in some instances they determined the place in the death march. They could alter no one's fate, not even their own.

Of the most degraded group, the Jewish commandos in the extermination centers, Miss Arendt writes: "The well-known fact that the actual work of killing in the extermination centers was usually in the hands of Jewish commandos had been fairly and squarely established by witnesses for the prosecution." Not at all. After a review of the entire testimony, Dr. Robinson has pointed out that "not a single witness made such a statement," and that no other evidence to this effect exists. S.S. men did the killing. Jewish commandos were compelled to work on corpses. So much for "fairly and squarely."

In a sense the whole discussion of Jewish Councils is diversionary. No cabal to hush up disclosures as to their failings exists—as Miss Arendt implies. Public trials of individual Council members have taken place repeatedly in Israel. (The trial of Hirsh Barenblat of Bendzin is now in progress in Tel Aviv.) The indignation aroused by Miss Arendt stems from her charge of total Jewish collaboration: leaders, parties, organizations, and associations on the "local and international level" constitute the people.

IV

To sustain her charge of total collaboration Miss Arendt manages to transform every positive attempt to save Jews from the Nazis into something suspect. [. . .]

All the desperate abortive ransom negotiations, conducted by such noble figures as Gisi Fleischmann in Slovakia as well as Joel Brand in Hungary, appear in Miss Arendt's text as a chipper, self-seeking collaboration between privileged "Zionists" and the Nazis. Just as the author obscures the distinction between persecutor and victim, she merges killer and savior. All are involved in a symbiosis of guilt. She ignores the constant struggle to organize spiritual and physical resistance long before the Warsaw Ghetto's last stand: the underground classes and lectures to maintain morale; the unceasing attempts of girls and boys posing as Aryans to link the severed ghettos by bringing information and smuggling in a pistol or two; the reverse effort of volunteers outside Europe to breach the ghetto walls and to establish contact with the immured Jewries. An awareness of these attempts is certainly relevant to an understanding of the role of Jewish "leaders" and "parties." This part of the record is not to be found in the Nazi documents on which Hilberg mainly based his study. The extensive Yiddish and Hebrew documentary literature of the period—which Miss Arendt apparently did not consult—does provide the material. There is a problem in scholarship here, and the admirers of Miss Arendt ought to confront it.

Her explanation of the few occasions when Jewries were saved are as willful as her reasons for their destruction. The 8000 Jews of Denmark escaped because they were in the midst of a brave, friendly population located on the coast opposite Sweden; the Danes ferried the Jews across nightly. The courage of the Danes and the accident of geography, not the quality of their "leaders," proved the salvation of the Danish Jews.

To explain the comparative failure of the Nazi extermination program in Italy Miss Arendt makes one of the most sweeping declarations in a book notable for brushing aside obtrusive facts: "The Germans, yielding, as usual, when they met resistance . . ." (page 162). Is this characterization of the Nazi terror to be taken seriously? The Germans were more circumspect in Italy because they were dealing with an ally, not a conquered country.

These are only a few instances of the author's technique. As history, *Eichmann in Jerusalem* is shockingly inaccurate and insofar as her thesis depends on the objective marshaling of evidence it is on shaky ground. Far from being the "quiet, moral, rational" document commended by *The New Yorker*, the book is a tract in which the author manipulates the material with a high-handed assurance.

Nevertheless, those who admire her "insight"—the common nexus of guilt which supposedly binds Nazi and Jew, sinner and sufferer—and those who are deeply offended by it, are both entitled to a *specific refutation* of the bill of particulars which critic after critic has rendered against the work. As a responsible writer, Miss Arendt should offer it. The cry of lèse-majesté is not an adequate rebuttal.

Jewish Values in the Post-Holocaust Future
A Symposium

STEVEN S. SCHWARZSCHILD, EMIL L. FACKENHEIM, AND GEORGE STEINER

STEVEN S. SCHWARZCHILD

We meet in order to try to explore together a problem which we believe to be important for Judaism, for the Jewish people, and therefore for the world. Permit me to attempt a definition and explanation of the problem that we have set for ourselves in the phrase, "Jewish values in the post-Holocaust future."

In the face of new facts language always fails. The catastrophe that overwhelmed European Jewry, and therewith the people of Israel as a whole, during the reign of Nazism was and will forever remain an absolute *novum*—the enactment of absolute human and historical evil. We speak of it as "the Holocaust." But there have been other holocausts, and they were nothing like this. In such a linguistic perplexity Jews usually, and rightly, turn to Hebrew as the one language that is in accord with their spirit and with the reality of their experiences. Thus we try the word *sho'ah*. But there have been other *sho'ot*, and they cannot compare quantitatively or qualitatively, in very principle, with the human bestiality and immorality that exercised themselves upon us. Thus it turns out at the very beginning of our conversation, as I doubt not its further course will prove over and over again, that because the Jewish experience of the 30's and 40's was truly *sui generis*, all speaking about it and its consequences will be thoroughly inadequate. Perhaps silence would be the only proper posture toward it.

But this would be too simple. The Holocaust is so agonizing, even *ex post facto*, precisely because it is the ultimate paradox. It imposes silence even while it demands speech. George Steiner's latest book, which deals largely with this problematic, expresses the paradox in its very title, *Language and Silence*. We have to try to live in the world and with the people that went through and, in one way or another, participated in that great purgatory. And human living means language. But surely henceforth—and this is the first premise of our conversation this afternoon—human language, and all that it implies in understanding, values and aims, must be fundamentally different from what it was before. We hold that, in the perspective of what our eyes have seen, the world, history, and the role of Israel in these must be totally reevaluated by Jews as well as by non-Jews. Our understanding of them, and therefore the words which we use for them, must be completely revised.

We are saying that a new age has begun. Christians think that the watershed of human history occurred on Calvary. The French Revolution wanted to start counting the years anew beginning with 1789. There was a whole generation of European intellectuals who thought, and some still dare think, that the First World War changed the face of the earth. Jews, to the contrary, have always insisted on measuring time in such a way as to proclaim their belief that God's original will for man has been and still to this day is continuously operative. I doubt that even now we would be prepared to sacrifice the unity of history any more than the unity of God Himself. But we must confess that the unity of history is different from what we may previously have thought it to be. We know not what it is. We are deeply puzzled as to how to redirect it. To try to find the beginnings of answers to this question is, perhaps, our chief concern here.

The post-Holocaust world is fundamentally different from the previous world. Many of the sensitive writers, Jewish and Gentile, have been saying this, with varying degrees of success, for two decades. Some few thinkers have tried to tackle the implications of this recognition, however gingerly. Many Jews, in Israel and the Diaspora, have acted on it almost instinctively. But religious thinkers have overwhelmingly shied away from this truth. As far as Christian thinkers are concerned, the astounding and—at least to me—almost as frightening fact as the Holocaust itself is the influential sector of opinion which asserts a new and unbounded—of all things!—optimism about man and history. With very few exceptions, Jewish religious thinkers have tended to avoid the issue altogether. The most favorable interpretation of this latter fact that I can think of is that the few survivors of the disaster are trying to save themselves.

But the questions imperiously demand a hearing. In 1949 I put them something like this to an audience of Jewish D.P.s and survivors in the center of Europe: What new knowledge of God has risen out of the chimneys of Auschwitz? What do we know now about man that we did not know before he created Maidanek? By what values shall we try to live that have been seared into our flesh in Bergen-Belsen? What new Jewish actions have been commanded by the loudspeakers in Buchenwald? What new words have been pressed on our lips by the whips and boots of Theresienstadt? In short, what will the world of tomorrow have to look like which we now know to be, to be able to be, and to have been what Rousset called l'univers concentrationnaire?

To conclude the explication of our title phrase, we want to concentrate on the "future." We do not primarily want to ask how we and the world have in fact been affected by what has happened, nor what our present condition is as a result (though these are, of course, indispensable and important preliminary questions). We *are* asking, and asking in all seriousness: Knowing what we do, having become what we are, seeing the world as it is—by what values are we to act among ourselves and in relationship to the world at large in our future? We hold—and this is the second premise of our conversation—that this future of ours is perforce a future different from all other futures that have ever been, in that it is, as they were not, a "post-Holocaust future." Specifically, we put these three questions, in a very tentative and optional fashion, to the four main participants in the conversation: 1) What seems to you to be the present condition of the human world in the perspective of the Holocaust? 2) What do you hold to be the demands made upon us and upon the world by having to live after the Holocaust has taken place? 3) In this light, what do you think will have to be the world in the future?

These questions can also be phrased in terms of the time and place in which we happen to be assembled. Today is Purim. This is a day preeminently suited to the consideration of the role of a tried and saved Israel in the world and in God's providence. By a rather rare coincidence, in 1967 it is also the Christian Easter. I venture to suggest, without wishing to spell it out, that the coincidence of Purim and Easter could lead to more useful and perceptive reflections on the role of Christianity in the tragic Jewish theodicy than the more frequent coincidence of Passover and Easter. Furthermore, a few short blocks from where we are meeting in New York City, a "be-in" is taking place right now in Central Park, with colored balloons, gift candies, guitars, young people with long hair and somewhat unconventional clothes. I, for one, want to ask what our relationship is and ought to be to the world of established institutions and beliefs in which the Holocaust took place—and what is and should it be to the new, rebellious, youthful, alienated world that, in large measure, like the remnant of Israel itself, has fallen heir to its poisoned wells?

Our [. . .] panelists come from very various backgrounds and disciplines. But they have this in common: they are profoundly concerned and literate Jews, and in their lives and work they have given testimony to their sensitivity to the historic centrality of the Holocaust. We shall begin our proceedings with opening statements by the members of the panel.

EMIL L. FACKENHEIM

Our topic today has two presuppositions, which, I take it, we are not going to question but will simply take for granted. First, there is a unique and unprecedented crisis in this period of Jewish history which needs to be faced by all Jews, from the Orthodox at one extreme to the secularists at the other. (Thus I take it that we are not going to discuss the various forms of Judaism and Jewishness as though nothing has happened.) Second, whatever our response to the present crisis, it will be, in any case, a stubborn persistence in our Jewishness, not an attempt to abandon it or escape from it. (Thus I take it that we shall leave dialogues with Jews who do not want to be Jews for another day.)

How shall we understand the crisis of this period in Jewish history? We shall, I think, be misled if we think in the style of the social sciences which try to grasp the particular in terms of the universal. We shall then, at best, understand the present Jewish crisis only in terms of the universal Western or human crisis, thus failing to grasp its uniqueness; at worst we shall abuse such an understanding as a means of escaping into the condition of contemporary-man-in-general. Instead of relying on the sociological mind, we must rely on the historical mind, which moves from the particular to the universal. But the historical mind, too, has its limitations. Thus no contemporary Jewish historian at the time of the destruction of the First or the Second Temple could have fully understood the world-historical significance of that event, if only because, in the midst of the crisis, he was not yet on the other side of it. We, too, are in the midst of the contemporary crisis, and hence unable fully to understand it. As for our attitude toward the future, this cannot be one of understanding or prediction, but only one of commitment and, possibly, faith.

How shall we achieve such fragmentary understanding of our present crisis as is possible while we are still in the midst of it? A crisis as yet unended can only be understood in terms of contradictions as yet unresolved. Jewish existence today is permeated by three main contradictions:

1) The American Jew of today is a "universalist," if only because he has come closer to the full achievement of equal status in society than any other Jew in the history of the Diaspora; yet this development coincides with the resurrection of Jewish "particularism" in the rebirth of a Jewish nation.

2) The Jew of today is committed to modern "secularism," as the source of his emancipation; yet his future survival as Jew depends on past religious resources. Hence even the most Orthodox Jew of today is a secularist insofar as, and to the extent that, he participates in the political and social processes of society. And even the most secularist Jew is religious insofar as, and to the extent that, he must fall back on the religious past in his struggle for a Jewish future.

3) Finally—and this is by far the most radical contradiction, and one which threatens to engulf the other two—the Jew in two of the three main present centers of Jewry, America and Israel, is at home in the modern world, for he has found a freedom and autonomy impossible in the pre-modern world. Yet he is but twenty-five years removed from a catastrophe unequaled in all of Jewish history—a catastrophe which in its distinctive characterizations is modern in nature.

These are the three main contradictions. Merely to state them is to show how false it would be for us to see our present Jewish crisis as nothing more than an illustration of the general Western or human crisis. I will add to the general point nothing more than the mere listing of two specific examples. First, we may have a problem with "secularity," like our Christian neighbors. But our problem is not theirs, if only because for us—who have "celebrated" the secular city since the French Revolution—the time for such celebrating is past since the Holocaust. Second, while we have our problems with academically inspired atheism and agnosticism, they are central at best only for Jews who want to be men-in-general. For the authentic Jew who faces up to his singled-out Jewish condition—even for the authentic agnostic or atheistic Jew—a merely academically inspired doubt in God must seem sophomoric when he, after Auschwitz, must grapple with despair.

We must, then, take care lest we move perversely in responding to our present crisis. We must first face up and respond to our Jewish singled-out condition. Only thus and then can we hope to enter authentically into an understanding of and relation with other manifestations of a present crisis which is doubtless universal.

In groping for authentic responses to our present Jewish crisis, we do well to begin with responses which have already occurred. I believe that there are two such responses: first, a commitment to Jewish survival; second, a commitment to Jewish unity.

I confess I used to be highly critical of Jewish philosophies which seemed to advocate no more than survival for survival's sake. I have changed my mind. I now believe that, in this present, unbelievable age, even a mere collective commitment to Jewish group survival for its own sake is a momentous response, with the greatest implications. I am convinced that future historians will understand it, not, as our present detractors would have it, as the tribal response mechanism of a fossil, but rather as a profound, albeit as yet fragmentary, act of faith, in an age of crisis to which the response might well have been either flight in total disarray or complete despair.

The second response we have already found is a commitment to Jewish unity. This, to be sure, is incomplete and must probably remain incomplete. Yet it is nonetheless real. Thus the American Council for Judaism is an anachronism, as is, I venture to say, an Israeli nationalism which would cut off all ties with the Diaspora. No less anachronistic is a Jewish secularism so blind in its worship of the modern secular world as wholly to spurn the religious resources of the Jewish past; likewise, an Orthodoxy so untouched by the modern secular world as to have remained in a pre-modern ghetto.

Such, then, are the responses to the present crisis in Jewish history which we have already found, in principle however inadequately in practice. And their implications are even now altogether momentous. Whether aware of what we have decided or not, we have made the collective decision to endure the contradiction of present Jewish existence. We have collectively rejected the option, either of "checking out" of Jewish existence altogether or of so avoiding the present contradictions as to shatter Jewish existence into fragments.

But the question now is whether we can go beyond so fragmentary a commitment. In the present situation, this question becomes: can we confront the Holocaust, and yet not despair? Not accidentally has it taken twenty years for us to face this question, and it is not certain that we can face it yet. The contradiction is too staggering, and every authentic escape is barred. We are bidden to turn present and future life into death, as the price of remembering death at Auschwitz. And we are forbidden to affirm present and future life, as the price of forgetting Auschwitz.

We have lived in this contradiction for twenty years without being able to face it. Unless I am mistaken, we are now beginning to face it, however fragmentarily and inconclusively. And from this beginning confrontation there emerges what I will boldly term a 614th commandment: *the authentic Jew of today is forbidden to hand Hitler yet another, posthumous victory.* (This formulation is terribly inadequate, yet I am forced to use it until one more adequate is found. First, although no anti-Orthodox implication is intended, as though the 613 commandments stood necessarily in need of change, we must face the fact that something radically new has happened. Second, although the commandment should be positive rather than negative, we must face the fact that Hitler did win at least one victory—the murder of six million Jews. Third, although the very name of Hitler should be erased rather than remembered, we cannot disguise the uniqueness of his evil under a comfortable generality, such as persecution-in-general, tyranny-in-general, or even the-demonic-in-general.)

I think the authentic Jew of today is beginning to hear the 614th commandment. And he hears it whether, as agnostic, he hears no more, or whether, as believer, he hears the voice of the *metzaveh* (the commander) in the *mitzvah* (the commandment). Moreover, it may well be the case that the authentic Jewish agnostic and the authentic Jewish believer are closer today than at any previous time.

To be sure, the agnostic hears no more than the *mitzvah.* Yet if he is Jewishly authentic, he cannot but face the fragmentariness of his hearing. He cannot, like agnostics and atheists all around him, regard this *mitzvah* as the product of self-sufficient human reason, realizing itself in an ever-advancing history of autonomous human enlightenment. The 614th commandment must be, to him, an abrupt and absolute *given,* revealed in the midst of total catastrophe.

On the other hand, the believer, who hears the voice of the *metzaveh* in the *mitzvah,* can hardly hear anything more than the *mitzvah.* The reasons which made Martin Buber speak of an eclipse of God are still compelling. And if, nevertheless, a bond between Israel and the God of Israel can be experienced in the abyss, this can hardly be more than the *mitzvah* itself.

The implications of even so slender a bond are momentous. If the 614th commandment is binding upon the authentic Jew, then we are, first, commanded to survive as Jews, lest the Jewish people perish. We are commanded, second, to remember in our very guts and bones the martyrs of the Holocaust, lest their memory perish. We are forbidden, thirdly, to deny or despair of God, however much we may have to contend with Him or with belief in Him, lest Judaism perish. We are forbidden, finally, to despair of the world as the place which is to become the kingdom of God, lest we help make it a meaningless place in which God is dead or irrelevant and everything is permitted. To abandon any of these imperatives, in response to Hitler's victory at Auschwitz, would be to hand him yet other, posthumous victories. [. . .]

GEORGE STEINER

I am honestly not certain that there is much to add. I imagine that the point is that no Jew, including all of us up here, can speak well for any other Jew. The Diaspora and the lack of dogmatic eschatology make of Judaism a multiplicity of personal choices. I cannot really understand the formulation of the subject too thoroughly: I am not sure I know what I would want to say about the values of Judaism after the Holocaust, but I do feel I would like to say something about the values of one particular Jew.

Yet, at the same time, there is a cohesion of all Jews, a very curious mutual recognition in the moment of meeting. Jewishness, as distinct from Judaism, is an almost physical code of antennae, which reach out across national and linguistic barriers and even through the mask of assimilation. Anyone who has traveled in the world knows the curious, haunting swiftness with which, however you are dressed, however, you behave, the other Jew in the community finds you out. I believe I would know a Chinese Jew were I to meet him in the crowd in Canton.

Why? There are tricks of the eye and step that are possibly the remembrance burned into the skin of the long hunt. We have been on the run a long, long time. But the principle of recognition, recognizance, of knowing again, of locating ourselves in the secret mirror of the man we meet, that may lie deeper. We touch here on that most unpleasant and important of subjects—the matter of race, about which American Jews, it seems to me, very often exhibit a very understandable gingerliness. That question is presently moving into a new and problematic light. In the present state of inquiry into the structure and stabilities of the genetic code, only a very foolhardy man would be dogmatic about racial differences and characteristics or about the way in which social habituations penetrate psychosomatic patterns. It is conceivable—I say no more than that it is conceivable—that when Jews meet, be they Unitarian or Williamsburg, Cantonese or Moroccan, they know each other as do animals of a cognate species. Simply because one's enemies say certain things, they need not be lies. That is the fascination of the truth. Hence, I think that our question is a two-fold one: the values of one particular Jew; and the values of belonging, whether we would or not, to that somewhat mysterious community of historical, racial awareness which we call Jewishness.

I believe that the most coherent position towards one's own identity results from an attempt to bring these two questions into living reciprocity. To do this, I would like to try for myself simply to rephrase the issue. I am not very sanguine nor well informed about the values of Judaism after Auschwitz. But I do have strong feelings about the value of being a Jew after Auschwitz. We are survivors of a very careful program of total elimination, compounded of direct action, Nazism, about which in this room there is no need to say anything whatever, and of indifference, about which there will be a need to say a great deal more, because this is one of the chapters hardly written about, hardly discussed, except by the specialists. One thinks of the fifty above-quota visas offered in this country in 1937, when 100,000 children could have been saved. One thinks of the position of England, the country where I make my home. One thinks of the frontiers closed in France. And it is my conviction that had Hitler not made a foolish military move, had Hitler stopped, let us say, after Czechoslovakia and said: "I really stick to my promise now. That's enough. I won't invade, I won't attack; you let me do internally what I wish"—then the ski slopes of Garmisch would be full of tourists to this day, a few miles away from the concentration camps. In other words, Nazism is not a unique demonism; it almost carried out what the world by and large was prepared to see carried out. The historians support this in detail, for in the beginning the Nazis watched closely whether there would be reflexes, whether there would be counter-moves; and it was only when it appeared that the world did not give a damn, that the Nazis began implementing the full plan. Thus we are survivors, not only of one particular doctrinal bestiality, but also of a very widespread, let us call it at its most courteous, indifference. Men are always accomplices to whatever leaves them indifferent.

If we are survivors, survivors bear scars, but they also have privileges. I imagine that Lazarus had license to make bad jokes, to pick his nose at dinner, and to be occasionally tactless after his wondrous return to the living. Interestingly, we know almost nothing about his behavior afterwards. This is surely a much more interesting problem than his resurrection; and I daresay that three days in a Galilean tomb was less of death than two nights in the ditch at Babi Yar or three days in the cesspool at Treblinka.

Outside Israel, the Jew continues to be a guest among men, more or less welcome, more or less accepted, but a guest nevertheless. To say that I believe this to be the case also in America—and I have said it—is to invite not only misunderstanding but obvious malaise and unhappiness for both parties in the conversation, so I will therefore limit myself to only one point. To say that a large Gentile community, which is also today almost the most nationalist on earth in many of its aspects is different from all other such communities in history is to say that history makes a quantum jump; is to say that there are fundamental ontological, metaphysical discontinuities, and that it cannot happen here or there for some fundamental metaphysical reason. I plead guilty to not believing this. I do not think history makes quantum jumps. I think that where there are powerful categories of similitude, history has recognizable patterns and dangers.

This is entirely my own belief, and I do not want to press it upon you. But Auschwitz has made the Jew a guest with certain privileges of indelicacy, of irritancy, of subversion. I think he must try to make creative the malaise which his hosts will experience, whatever his behavior. That malaise remains, behave he as deferentially and as urbanely as he may. And if this is so, let us make this malaise creative, productive, fruitful. I think we must do this by the simplest injunction (usually ascribed to Nietzsche, but actually, forgive the small pedantry, a quote from Pindar): "Labor to become what you are." I think we must refuse to be other than what we are. That is to say, we must not accept the fiction, and it is a fiction, of assured permanent residence, of acceptance, of entrance into the Gentile nation. We must not accept it if the price is nationalism, national patriotism, in any militant sense. The Jew must, I think, rejoice in the distrust of his nationalist host and say: "Yes, I am potentially disloyal to any policy that I believe evil or inhuman. 'My country right or wrong' is a slogan for barbarism. My city is that of man; my citizenship, that of human possibility. I am not a tree, to exult in rootedness"—rootedness, I must say, is a word that always jars me in the mouth of a Jew—"but a man, endowed with the marvel of legs, with the knowledge that there are many languages in which fathers can teach their children, and that frontiers are a cruel myth which have again and again been closed to me for my destruction." Now, for the Jew of genius it has long been true that exile is home. Marx, of course, lies buried in Hampstead and Freud in Golders Green; if I remember rightly, the ashes of Einstein were scattered in New Jersey. We are not a people for cemeteries and plots of ground. Even in death Moses was a delightfully displaced person. What was the fate of the exceptional has, I think through the Holocaust, become our common privilege. A Jew who is a nationalist in a Gentile community is aping his own destroyers. Quite simply, men have made us guests among them; let us teach them, so far as our example may, to be guests of each other. For if they do not learn it, civilization as we know it may go to violent destruction.

Here is where I think the peculiar uniqueness of our task lies, because I wonder whether any nation in history, any people, race or tribe, has a greater obligation to live and teach this lesson of common humanity, this refusal to consider a passport as anything but a contract, renegotiable at all times, in the light of conscience, than the Jews, who *may* have launched upon history and ourselves the murderous boomerang of arrogance and nationalistic fervor. For it is in Judaism that we find claims which the Hellenic world did not put forth. We know today that Nazism subtly mimed the millenary claims and the myth of singular election in the Judaism of the Pentateuch. In a way that I do not think we have yet fully understood, there was between the Nazis, the core of the Nazis, and the Jews a kind of hideous relationship of parody. When I am reminded, as we have just been, of Judah Halevi's statement that Jewish history is the core of universal history, it reminds me of nothing more than the Chinese claims of the Middle Kingdom as being alone human; and there are other claims that go back as far. So, to the extent that we may be responsible for having spoken of being a people exalted, a people divinely elect against others, certainly during the time of Joshua and the Judges, to that extent the boomerang sought us out and nearly destroyed us totally. Perhaps the instruction of that is that we must never again accept those claims and those nationalisms.

The value of being a Jew after the Holocaust is a tremendous one. I think it is extremely appropriate that we should be meeting on Purim, a day of pleasure, of noise and rejoicing, because the value of being a Jew after the Holocaust is the value of being a man who has experienced to the uttermost the bestiality of man. We have very few surprises ahead of us. We know in our charred marrow what men can become when they yield their reason to a flag and put their feet in boots. The value of being a Jew is to try to make truth one's locale and free inquiry one's native tongue. I suspect it is the deep conflict between this aim and the anguishing political and strategic necessities of the day which accounts for the grave malaise in Israel. To be a Jew is to rejoice in the links stronger than any political loyalty, which may connect us with the most audacious that is being thought and said, which connects us with the linguistics of Noam Chomsky and the anthropology of Claude Lévi-Strauss, with the physics of Rabi and the music of Schoenberg, the poetics of Kafka and the mathematics of Kantor. And though I would yield, of course, to Professor Popkin's deep knowledge of the richness of the Orthodox community in Amsterdam, I will not let him expel Spinoza; he is one we want to keep.

When moored—please, not anchored—in the uncertain haven of a nationalist community (and what Gentile communities are not deeply nationalist?), this is a citizenship which we must try to make ours—a citizenship of protest.

Let me conclude quite simply. I think we all carry with us, each of us, from childhood on, some totemic or talismanic figure. Mine is a man called Marc Bloch, probably the greatest medieval historian ever, the man who, with Tawney, founded the modern way of thinking about agricultural and economic history in France. Marc Bloch escaped in the debacle in 1940, got to England, and came to a college in my own University, where, having escaped with his life, he was warned not to go back under any circumstances. Marc Bloch there wrote a small book called *Etrange Défaite* ("Strange Defeat"), the deepest book written on the collapse of France in 1940, merciless and pitiless. It was the work of a man who had thought it through and saw the rottenness and the horror of France and of the nation that had been his. He left the manuscript with Sir Dennis Brogan and went back into France. He joined the underground in a gay and amused way, skeptical even then about his colleagues and their naivetés and how they were running affairs. He was captured and tortured a long time, and he did not say a word. He was taken out near Grenoble to be shot with other hostages. Among those who were about to be killed with him, Bloch saw a boy of only fourteen or fifteen, an FFI courier who had been picked up by the Germans. He saw that the child was terribly afraid, and he asked the Germans for permission that they be shot together. Marc Bloch took the child by the hand, and the last thing he was heard to say—this has been authenticated by witnesses—was: "Now, you must listen to me. It will not hurt very much." They went out together, and he was speaking to the boy right to the end.

The values of that moment, the historian's training, the gift of humanity—these belong to all men, not alone to the Jews. But the Jew, I think, may have the uncomfortable obligation and privilege of practicing them right now pretty constantly and at whatever price of discomfort. [. . .]

Disaster

ABRAHAM JOSHUA HESCHEL

1945 . . . A new conception: The world is a slaughterhouse. Hope is obscene. It is sinful to remain sane.

Six million lives gone. Wherever we dwell, we live in a graveyard. Only one way out, the way to the inferno.

1945 . . . Is this what is left of us: chimneys in the extermination camps?

What shall come after the holocaust: nights of despair, no dawn, never, but shrieks in perpetuity? Anguish forever, no relief, life is gall, history a scourge? Has the world lost its soul? Have civilization and humanity nothing in common?

Has Auschwitz annihilated our future as well?

Three out of four Jews in Europe—dead. Two out of five of us anywhere in the world—dead. Will the spirit of those who survived be reduced to ashes? The Allied Armies which freed the concentration camps came upon tens of thousands of emaciated bodies, skeletons, dry bones. "Son of man, can these bones live?" Judaism was reduced to dry bones, faith in God was on trial. Will this people, crushed, battered, crippled, decimated, impaled, find strength to survive?

What should have been our answer to Auschwitz? Should this people, called to be a witness to the God of mercy and compassion, persist in its witness and cling to Job's words: "Even if He slay me yet will I trust in Him" (Job 13:15), or should this people follow the advice of Job's wife, "Curse God and die!" (Job 2:9), immerse itself into the anonymity of a hundred nations all over the world, and disappear once and for all?

Our people's faith in God at this moment in history did not falter. At this moment in history Isaac was indeed sacrificed, his blood shed. We all died in Auschwitz, yet our faith survived. We knew that to repudiate God would be to continue the holocaust.

We have once lived in a civilized world, rich in trust and expectation. Then we all died, were condemned to dwell in hell. Now we are living in hell. Our present life is our afterlife. . . .

We did not blaspheme, we built. Our people did not sally forth in flight from God. On the contrary, at that moment in history we saw the beginning of a new awakening, the emergence of a new concern for a Living God theology.

Escape from Judaism giving place increasingly to a new attachment, to a rediscovery of our legacy.

How would the world have looked at the Jewish people if the survivors of the concentration camps had gone the path of complete assimilation? Flight from God? From Judaism?

What would be the face of Western history today if the end of twentieth-century Jewish life would have been Bergen-Belsen, Dachau, Auschwitz? The State of Israel is not an atonement. It would be blasphemy to regard it as a compensation. However, the existence of Israel reborn makes life less unendurable. It is a slight hinderer of hindrances to believing in God.

We are tired of expulsions, of pogroms; we have had enough of extermination camps. We are tired of apologizing for our existence. If I should go to Poland or Germany, every stone, every tree would remind me of contempt, hatred, murder, of children killed, of mothers burned alive, of human beings asphyxiated.

When I go to Israel every stone and every tree is a reminder of hard labor and glory, of prophets and psalmists, of loyalty and holiness. The Jews go to Israel not only for physical security for themselves and their children; they go to Israel for renewal, for the experience of resurrection.

Is the State of Israel God's humble answer to Auschwitz? A sign of God's repentance for men's crime of Auschwitz?

No act is as holy as the act of saving human life. The Holy Land, having offered a haven to more than two million Jews—many of whom would not have been alive had they remained in Poland, Russia, Germany, and other countries—has attained a new sanctity.

So many lives of people whose bodies were injured and whose souls were crushed found a new life and a new spirit in the land. The State of Israel, as it were, sought to respond to the prophet's exhortation: "Strengthen the weak hands, and make firm the feeble knees" (Isaiah 35:3).

In 1937, the period of Nazi persecution and expulsion of the Jews from Germany, I concluded a book about Don Isaac Abravanel, who lived during the time of the expulsion of the Jews from Spain in 1492, with the following words:

> The Jews, who had played a leading role in the politics, economics and social affairs of their country left (had to leave) their Spanish homeland. The conquest of the New World was achieved without them. Had they remained on the Iberian peninsula they would surely have participated in the deeds of the Conquistadores. When the latter came to Haiti they found 1,1000,000 inhabitants; twenty years later only 1,000 remained.

In 1492 the Jews, who were desperate, had no inkling what an act of grace was involved in their misery. Driven out of Spain, they had no part in the atrocities soon to be carried out in the New World.

And yet, there is no answer to Auschwitz. . . . to try to answer is to commit a supreme blasphemy. Israel enables us to bear the agony of Auschwitz without radical despair, to sense a ray of God's radiance in the jungles of history.

Living with the Holocaust

ALFRED KAZIN

When war broke out in 1939 I was still a "socialist" of sorts, and for reasons that pertained to 1917 rather than 1939, I was tritely opposed to America's getting into the war. I had grown up in an entirely Jewish milieu, but as a writer was just beginning to live in and to know the larger American scene. I was bored by the self-conscious ethnocentrism in which I had grown up and found no illumination in Judaism; Zionism meant to me only my highly theoretical interest in the kibbutz as a possible nucleus of socialist community. I felt newly married to the world outside all-Jewish Brownsville and to the promise of modern American literature, which I was hungrily absorbing shelf by shelf. The Soviet-Nazi pact horrified me. But since I was not a Communist with mind glued to the Soviet Union but a literary radical with a great many apolitical notions about the better future toward which we were all heading, I was not destroyed by the Nazi-Soviet alliance as I thought of it, and even felt liberated; it made unnecessary certain intellectual fancies about Russia.

Then bit by bit, without recognizing how many pre-war illusions I had left behind me, I felt myself, as a writer of "Jewish origin," part of the life and death struggle of millions. I was staggered by the destruction of so many values and moral concerns that I had taken for granted. I found that I relied—almost for sanity—on a conscious relationship to the whole Jewish past. When I was growing up, that past had seemed to dwell in me. But now it seemed to be outside me, was being played out on the screen of world history. I could virtually *see* it being destroyed.

Not merely did I become conscious in a distinctly new way of sympathies that I had always had. I felt peculiarly related to any example, every bit of personal history, any distinct *name* rescued from the otherwise all too unknown and unseen millions of Jews undergoing their unprecedented ordeal in Europe. One day in 1943 I felt a thrill of the deepest pride when I found in a corner of the *New York Times* the last message of Shmuel Ziegelboim, who in the Polish exile government in London represented the General Jewish Workers' Bund. He had taken his life in May, 1943 in order to call attention to the destruction of Polish Jewry and had addressed this letter to the President of Poland and Premier Sikorski:

I take the liberty of addressing to you my last words, and through you to the Polish government and the Polish people of the Allied states—to the conscience of the world.

From the latest information received from Poland, it is evident that the Germans, with the most ruthless cruelty, are now murdering the few remaining Jews in Poland. Behind the ghetto's walls the last act of a tragedy unprecedented in history is being performed. The responsibility for this crime of murdering the entire Jewish population of Poland falls in the first instance on the perpetrators, but indirectly it is also a burden on the whole of humanity, the people and the governments of the Allied states which thus far have made no effort toward concrete action for the purpose of curtailing this crime.

By the passive observation of the murder of defenseless millions, and of the maltreatment of children, women and old men, these countries have become the criminals' accomplices. I must also state that although the Polish government has in a high degree contributed to the enlistment of world opinion, it has yet done so insufficiently. From some 3,500,000 Polish Jews and about 700,000 other Jews deported to Poland from other countries—according to official statistics provided by the underground Bund organization—there remained in April of this year only 300,000, and this remaining murder goes on.

I cannot be silent—I cannot live—while remnants of the Jewish people of Poland, of whom I am a representative, are perishing. My comrades in the Warsaw ghetto took weapons in their hands on that last heroic impulse. It was not my destiny to die there together with them, but I belong to them, and in their mass graves. By my death I wish to express my strongest protest against the inactivity with which the world is looking on and permitting the extermination of my people.

I know how little human life is worth today; but as I was unable to do anything during my life, perhaps by my death I shall contribute to breaking down the indifference of those who may now—at the last moment—rescue from certain annihilation the few Polish Jews who are still alive. My life belongs to the Jewish people of Poland and I therefore give it to them. I wish that this remaining handful of the original several millions of Polish Jews could live to see the liberation of a new world of freedom, and the justice of true socialism. I believe that such a Poland will arise and that such a world will come.

I trust that the President and the Prime Minister will direct my words to all those for whom they are destined, and that the Polish government will immediately take appropriate action in the fields of diplomacy. I bid my farewell herewith to everybody and everything dear to me and loved by me.

S. Ziegelboim

The *Times* article concluded: "That was the letter. It suggests that Shmuel Ziegelboim will have accomplished as much in dying as he did in living."

Reading Ziegelboim's letter on a New York morning, I had the distinct sensation of being addressed by him personally, of having known him all my life. I was disgusted by the glibness with which some reporter had added: "possibly Shmuel Ziegelboim will have accomplished as much in dying as he did in living." And though it was Ziegelboim's connection with the Bund and the old democratic socialist movement that made him so especially dear to me, I also knew, in 1943, that "this remaining handful of the original several millions of Polish Jews" would, if they lived, not in Poland see "the justice of true socialism." "True socialism" was like the Jewish God to me—familiar but not real.

I published an impassioned article in *The New Republic*—I was then literary editor—on Ziegelboim, his death, his message to the world. I said that the tragedy of the peace, when it came, would be the political "realism" that would try to conceal the void in ourselves created by the destruction of the Jews. Ziegelboim's letter went generally unnoticed; my article stimulated some equally emotional notes from writers lamenting the cruelty of the times. Even my colleagues at *The New Republic,* humane and liberal, showed an easy sense of resignation about the "Jewish tragedy" that isolated me in my own thoughts, made me feel obsessive to myself as a Jew.

I had never, to my knowledge, suffered any disadvantage in being a Jew; my being a Jew seemed to interest the various writers and editors who had helped me along, and who had encouraged me to write on Jewish writers and "Jewish" themes. But the "Jewish tragedy," as people sighingly called it, suddenly brought home to me, as nothing in my upbringing had done, the fact that the Jews were an anomaly in the affairs of the world, that to many the massacres were an affront to the life of reason and a threat to normal living. Just as there seemed to be no place for the Jews in the "New Europe," so there seemed to be no accounting for the "Jewish tragedy." The historic existence of Jews seemed to make no sense except to Jews (and not to all of them by any means). And indeed the murder of millions of Jews made so little sense even to those who could grieve for them that the immediate horror for me, who guessed the full extent of the Holocaust as anyone attentive to the Nazi movement since the thirties could have guessed it, was that most people we knew—including many Jews—could not absorb this "tragedy"; could not even respond to it, did not want to take it into themselves. One was aware that all traditional frameworks for explaining were gone, that there was equally no help in modern thought for living with it.

Was it because "humankind cannot bear very much reality," as Eliot was writing about something surely more trivial than the Holocaust, or was it more likely that the Holocaust was not "real" to many people—not even to some of the people who suffered it? [. . .]

On many sides, indeed, for Jews as well as non-Jews, the Holocaust—as it came finally to be known, in a symbol that does not always help us to *see* what happened—was so inexplicable as to be virtually inadmissible. To Jews like myself, brought up on the idea that "history" has been our ruling hope as well as proof of our continued existence—the most striking reaction in oneself was a kind of terror that the organized killing of millions of innocent people could be shrugged off *mentally* by anyone at all—and that, on a higher level, people would make so little effort to think about "the Holocaust." There seemed to be no place in many distinguished minds for this, though there was mind enough to investigate the subtlest mysteries of physical matter. There was no room for the Jews, and no room in many minds for the fate of the Jews. The "six million" were an intrusion on common sense, on ordinary civility, on the pleasures of the mind. If there was a mystery, it was simply something one was stuck with, that one *lived* by affirming one's "Jewish origins," by not betraying oneself "psychologically." And indeed many remarkable people have done that and only that—have sought not to be lacking in "honor" toward themselves as Jews.

This obligation to one's Jewish "identity" has never been my problem. It was not being a Jew in society that troubled me—it was the mystery of Jewishness, the further mystery of why so much evil was directed against it, the mysteriousness of so many Jewish expectations. It was the exceptionality of Jewish history and Jewish fate that at once spellbound and baffled me. The Holocaust was "unaccountable," yet in some way it was intrinsic to Hitler's war. The most "irrational" side of the war was somehow at the heart of it. [. . .]

The war has been over for twenty-five years, and those years have not added to our understanding of the Holocaust, even to our compassion—far from it. In the last few years even the old belief in Jewish exceptionality has diminished for Jews as they become deghettoized, more aware of the destruction visited on other peoples, more purely political-minded. There has been the most obvious erosion of the sacredness connected with Jewish experience. One may agree with Emil Fackenheim that Auschwitz is unique, that it cannot be compared with Dresden and Hiroshima. Nevertheless—and this seems to me the real experience of the Holocaust *now*—the people who suffered at Dresden and Hiroshima, who suffer in Vietnam, are not likely to see Auschwitz as unique in a world where Jews particularly have learned to rely on their own power rather than on God—and in which so many post-Christians do not see Jewish history as spiritually relevant.

For me the Holocaust is present now as it was in Hitler's time. I should like to think that it will be present forever to the mind of humanity. But the fact is that the de-spiritualization of Jewish experience, even the fact that Israel's proudest boast is that it is a *state,* a state like any other, works against the sanction long given by outsiders to the long cherished belief (among Jews) of Jewish exceptionality. The covenant, handed down from Sinai in letters of fire, could still be read in the darkest ages by those who resented the Jews as the ghost at the Christian feast. But in the cruel open light of our planet, of modern revolutions and counter-revolutions in which genocide has indeed turned out to be a weapon against many peoples, it is impossible for many a young Jew today to see the Holocaust as exceptional or the Jews as even a unique historical entity. The devastating politicization of contemporary culture is no doubt one effect of World War II, which as Kurt Vonnegut says, "certainly made everyone very tough." We are living with the effects of the Holocaust, in a world of blinding "realism," exactly as one might have predicted in 1943 when the death cry of the European Jews went unheard.

It is my impression that every new generation now believes less and less in the uniqueness of Auschwitz, in extra-national reasons for the existence of Israel, in Jews as offering a spiritual message to mankind. This has been the second and unexpectedly cruel experience of living with the Holocaust. What we experienced first, and will feel to the end of our lives, was the guilt of "looking on." Today we are accused, from every source, of seeming to claim too much for Jewish martyrdom in the past and for Israel's total legitimacy now. In 1970 we are by no means, even to ourselves, "the heart of the world," the "light of the world," the "salt of the earth," or what an Israel government document during the 1967 war called "God's people." In this respect our material success in America, our uniformly middle-class status, make our reputed Biblical "mission" to the world as strange to us as it does to many post-Christians—who in any event look on many of us as post-Biblical and hardened cynics like themselves. [. . .]

There are many signs that in America we are drawing to the end of the age of liberal tolerance, of what we glibly called the "Judeo-Christian" tradition—which, exactly that, helped to create a climate of respect, if not always of understanding. But in the ever-harsher, more secular, more purely political and violently torn America into which we are moving, Jews may seem as incomprehensible as they are in China. As the world refuses more and more to recognize the "chosenness" that has in fact been the basis of Jewish existence unadmitted by many "modern" Jews, the problem will become the need to define ourselves religiously. If the problem of adjusting ourselves to the "Jewish problem" were purely political, it would have been solved long ago. Certainly

Jews have done all that human beings can do for the sake of ideology, and at the moment they are exercising many unexpected kinds of power. But the problem is a religious problem for us, a problem of re-defining ourselves again in this speciously universalist climate where so many hostile nations and ideologies are trying to define us out of existence.

4

Black-Jewish Relations

The 1960s witnessed a serious rupture in the historic relationship between American Jews and African Americans. Naming the reasons for this break—and suggesting what might be done to repair it—also became cause for great controversy. While there is a valuable literature on African American perspectives toward the subject of blacks and Jews, this chapter focuses solely on Jewish responses to black-Jewish relations during the decade. In so doing, it seeks to suggest how diverse and internally contradictory those Jewish responses often were.

For some Jewish commentators, the imminent demise of a black-Jewish alliance was taken as a natural, even inevitable, consequence of the rapidly rising social and economic status of Jews, who could scarcely by this time claim that they remained an overtly oppressed people in the United States. Blacks and Jews might once have spoken together about their respective histories of enslavement and subjugation, but to continue to do so only underscored the painful fact that blacks often remained on the bottom rung of society, while Jews quite clearly did not. The loss of a shared predicament might be a matter to mourn, but it was nonetheless nothing for which Jews in particular bore a special responsibility. To the contrary, or so this argument continued, Jews had done more to assist African Americans toward equality than any other white ethnic group. With African Americans urging white people to get out of many civil rights organizations, and with the new militant call for Black Power, there was little left for Jews to do. And yet wrapped in this argument, there were also at times expressions of an unsubtle chauvinism, that while Jews could rise on their merits, by contrast African Americans never did, and so sought special privileges. Whether or not blacks ought to receive such privileges thus too became a disputatious issue.

For other commentators the rupture between blacks and Jews had more than anything else to do with the ugly eruptions of antisemitism in black America. Many argued that the source of this problem was the strong role Christianity had long played in African American life; thus, blacks had merely absorbed the anti-Jewishness of Christian tradition. (And the tragic paradox here was that black antisemitism was spreading just as white Christian America was abandoning its own anti-Jewish prejudices.) Meanwhile, still other spokespersons speculated that black antisemitism might primarily be the result of the prominent (and far from happy) role that Jewish shopkeepers frequently played in poor and urban black neighborhoods. Small wonder, these commentators proposed, that black rage aimed at white America lashed out at these most visible of white people, that is, Jewish merchants in the ghetto.

At the same time, the most progressive of Jewish leaders (many—though far from all—of whom were affiliated with Reform Judaism) tended to interpret matters in quite a different light. Black antisemitism was not epidemic, nor was the death of a black-Jewish alliance a foregone conclusion. Rather, American Jews had grown increasingly complacent to the point where they were essentially similar to any other white ethnic group. Jews no longer wished to believe that their Jewishness carried with it any particular moral or social obligations. And so Jews increasingly tended to rationalize those obligations away. Plus (and this was the best kept of all secrets) Jews had never especially liked or trusted African Americans in the first place. Certainly they did not want their own children to go to school with them. In short, if there was prejudice in black-Jewish relations, it moved in both directions.

A brief summary cannot do justice to this topic. And the several selections in this chapter do not offer more than an introduction to the full range of Jewish responses to black-Jewish relations in the 1960s. It is crucial therefore to keep in mind that the rupture that emerged was not solely between blacks and Jews; it was also between (urban, lower-middle-class, and often more religiously observant) Jews and (suburban, upper-middle-class, and often more acculturated) Jews. As race relations worsened in the course of the decade, class divisions *within* the Jewish community were also exacerbated.

At the March on Washington in August 1963, Martin Luther King, Jr., delivered his "I have a dream" speech. That same day, Joachim Prinz, a longtime ally of Dr. King's and the president of the American Jewish Congress, also delivered a strong argument for the continued commitment of all Americans—not least of all, American Jews—to the cause of African American civil rights. Prinz's speech is reprinted here. And that Prinz chose to cite his own experiences as a rabbi in Nazi Germany seems highly germane in this context.

In the fall of 1963, the board of education in New York City proposed that all New York public schools move toward full integration. To accomplish this goal, the board decided to "pair" elementary schools in neighboring communities as a means to achieve racial balance. Labeled the Princeton Plan because it had been first tried in Princeton, New Jersey, in the fifties, two of the first schools to be paired in New York were in adjacent neighborhoods in Queens:

Jackson Heights (which was primarily white—and Jewish) and Corona (which was overwhelming African American and Hispanic). The plan met with stiff opposition from white parents. The essay by Myron Fenster, a rabbi in Jackson Heights, offers a fascinating inside look at the movement to curtail school integration. And, as it happened, the white parents would ultimately defeat the school integration plan.

White resistance to African American civil rights is precisely the topic of Albert Vorspan's biting satire on white liberalism. Although his essay is not directed only at American Jews, it is difficult not to read into several of his "ways out for tired liberals" a fairly unambiguous critique of the reticence of Jews to get (and stay) involved. And while the language of Abraham Joshua Heschel does not resemble Vorspan's, he is no less appalled by those Jews who sought to abandon the fight against racism. For, as Heschel pointedly writes, racism is nothing more nor less than satanism.

The 1960s was the decade of symposia. In late 1966, the Labor Zionist magazine *Midstream* published a symposium called "Negro-Jewish Relations in America," which was also subsequently published in book form. The selections reprinted here by literary critic Leslie Fiedler, historian and rabbi Arthur Hertzberg, and writer Paul Jacobs are especially cogent, if hardly in agreement with one another or with perspectives expressed elsewhere in this chapter.

In early April 1968, Dr. Martin Luther King, Jr., was assassinated in Memphis, Tennessee. His death sent shock waves throughout the nation, and there were spontaneous and destructive riots in several cities. In introducing the next issue of *Dissent* magazine (which he edited), the critic Irving Howe captured well the anguish felt by so many after King's death.

The chapter concludes with the dissenting opinion of Bernard Weinberger, an Orthodox rabbi based in Williamsburg, Brooklyn, and the president of the Rabbinical Alliance of America. So far as Weinberger is concerned, the time for Jewish involvement in black civil rights is over. Put plainly, the black-Jewish alliance is finished—and it should stay that way.

“America Must Not Remain Silent . . .”

JOACHIM PRINZ

Following is the address delivered by Rabbi Joachim Prinz, president of the American Jewish Congress, at the March on Washington, Lincoln Memorial, August 28, 1963:

I speak to you as an American Jew.

As Americans we share the profound concern of millions of people about the shame and disgrace of inequality and injustice which make a mockery of the great American idea.

As Jews we bring to this great demonstration, in which thousands of us proudly participate, a twofold experience—one of the spirit and one of our history.

In the realm of the spirit, our fathers taught us thousands of years ago that when God created man, He created him as everybody’s neighbor. Neighbor is not a geographic term. It is a moral concept. It means our collective responsibility for the preservation of man’s dignity and integrity.

From our Jewish historic experience of three and a half thousand years we say:

Our ancient history began with slavery and the yearning for freedom. During the Middle Ages my people lived for a thousand years in the ghettos of Europe. Our modern history begins with a proclamation of emancipation.

It is for these reasons that it is not merely sympathy and compassion for the black people of America that motivates us. It is above all and beyond all such sympathies and emotions a sense of complete identification and solidarity born of our own painful historic experience.

When I was the rabbi of the Jewish community in Berlin under the Hitler regime, I learned many things. The most important thing that I learned under those tragic circumstances was that bigotry and hatred are not the most urgent problem. The most urgent, the most disgraceful, the most shameful and the most tragic problem is silence.

A great people which had created a great civilization had become a nation of silent onlookers. They remained silent in the face of hate, in the face of brutality and in the face of mass murder.

America must not become a nation of onlookers. America must not remain silent. Not merely black America, but all of America. It must speak up and act, from the President down to the humblest of us, and not for the sake of the Negro, not for the sake of the black community but for the sake of the image, the idea and the aspiration of America itself.

Our children, yours and mine in every school across the land, each morning pledge allegiance to the flag of the United States and to the republic for which it stands. They, the children, speak fervently and innocently of this land as the land of "liberty and justice for all."

The time, I believe, has come to work together—for it is not enough to hope together, and it is not enough to pray together—to work together that this children's oath, pronounced every morning from Maine to California, from North to South, may become a glorious, unshakable reality in a morally renewed and united America.

The Princeton Plan Comes to Jackson Heights

MYRON M. FENSTER

If I had to choose the least likely place where a furious hassle would develop over a proposed 35% Negro enrollment in a school, and where children asked to go an extra 4 or 5 blocks would cause their parents to become involved in an unbelievable imbroglio—I would have selected Jackson Heights in the borough of Queens in New York City which has now been my residence for almost a decade. But I would have been wrong.

In recent years, the borough of Queens has been undergoing an explosion of new apartment buildings; each neighborhood within it has grown by tens of thousands. Jackson Heights, one of these communities closest to Manhattan, has about as much character as any area where one apartment house has been built on top of another. What once was a garden community with a country club atmosphere has given way to the new buildings which consumed every available lot, and half a dozen moving vans can be seen on any Friday, moving families in or out—in from the Bronx or Manhattan's West Side, out to the greener areas of Nassau and Suffolk counties. That movement continues unabated.

The odd thing is that even now no one really knows or cares where Jackson Heights begins or ends—that is on all sides except one. To the North and South it merges indistinguishably into Woodside and Elmhurst and technically even LaGuardia Airport is part of Jackson Heights. But anybody who has ever lived in the community knows that along its eastern perimeter runs Junction Boulevard, the line that divides it from the Negro community of Corona. And it is to this area that in recent months, all eyes have turned, for this contiguousness with Corona has caused the hand of accidental fate to be placed on Jackson Heights in a prospective move to decrease de facto segregation in the schools of New York City.

By September of 1963, after a sweltering summer of Negro discontent, after the March on Washington was already history and the taste of a dignified victory was sweet in the mouth of America's Negroes, talk about fully integrating two public schools in this area began. The previous June, State Education Commissioner James E. Allen had called for an end of racial imbalance in the schools of New York, defining imbalance as any school having more than 50% Negroes. Corona's school is 97% Negro.

Suddenly, Jackson Heights was face to face with its most recent, and as far as anyone can recall its first, crisis. For when the hand of fate touched this white community with its post-war influx of Jewish families, no one would have predicted the reaction, least of all those of us who were supposedly its leaders and thought we knew our people and their reactions.

My own awareness of this local crisis could not have begun more casually. In Israel, where I had been spending the year, Bull Connor's hoses and dogs in Birmingham were given a featured spot on the front pages. But both Birmingham and Jackson Heights were far away. And then, on my first Sunday home, I was called by a friend who told of a meeting that night in a South Ridge rumpus room. It had to do with "that school integration business."

I went to the meeting. My own son was scheduled to begin attending the kindergarten of the "white" school. But deciding to go was easier than finding the meeting. South Ridge, and its adjoining North Ridge, are two huge cooperatives comprising some 30 six-story apartment buildings. When I found the right rumpus room, P.S. 149, a large 25-year-old building on 93rd Street, was close by. A few blocks away is Junction Boulevard.

Fifty feet from the rumpus room I knew I was in the right place. The crowd spilled out into the street and buzzed around in small agitated groups. Some policemen stood by, casually twirling their night sticks. Inside, the room was sweltering from overcrowding. Rumpus rooms were not constructed for meetings like this, with a few hundred people sitting and as many ringing the room and jostling for a good position. A bespectacled and earnest man was conducting the meeting. He was in the process of making a statement on why the plan was illegal and should be opposed, how equality and integration were not the issues, since both schools in question had long ago been integrated. He was also calling for the dismissal of the PTA of P.S. 149, the school attended by 87% white children, for these parents had, according to him, actually gone out of their way to institute a plan for eliminating the existing segregation in the overwhelmingly Negro Corona school. "By what right, by whose authority," he demanded, "have they begun to make plans without our approval? They have forfeited their right to our confidence!"

After his statement, he called for questions and comments, and then the storm of emotion which had thus far been contained erupted. Shouting became the order, as speakers were repeatedly interrupted, especially if they indicated approval of the integration plan. One parent vehemently suggested that he would fight to the end to see to it that his child would not be bussed into Harlem—though nobody suggested bussing children to Harlem. I began to look around, concern now coupled to curiosity, to see who these people were. Some of them looked faintly familiar, others I knew well. There was my neighbor, whose son played with mine, and she was apparently rooting with the opponents. There was a girl who sang in our Synagogue choir, also among the opponents. In front of me was a woman (whose high heels apparently were killing her, for she had one of her shoes off) who gave out with her own brand of the Bronx cheer whenever someone displeased her, which was quite often. "Sure, he can talk big," she would say to no one in particular, "his kids go to a private school." And when one young bearded speaker began to talk on a note of approval, identifying himself as a teacher, she bellowed, "How'd ya like that beatnik to teach your kid? Sit down ya' bum!"

The "anti's" seemed to be in the majority. That is not to say that they or anyone knew clearly what it was they were against. At this time, it was not yet the Princeton Plan which had been suggested, but what seemed to send most of the speakers into a frenzy was a suggestion that their children would have to cross Junction Boulevard to go to the "Negro" school.

The speakers mostly invoked the neighborhood school, and defended it with fervor. They summoned all the rhetoric of democratic individualism to prove that it was right to send their children to the nearest school. All denied feeling any prejudice against Negroes. Finally, one young man stood up: "I happen to be a Jew and so I know something about prejudice. I think we should go out of our way to help the Negroes instead of fighting them." But a few moments later, another speaker countered, "If the Negroes want to get ahead why don't they work hard the way we Jews did? Where I went to school there were only Jews and we did all right. Nobody gave us anything. Why can't they get ahead the same way?"

Something was wrong. I hadn't remembered it this way. My one defense to questioning friends abroad was that the South lived in the past. Yet, here were the people whom I thought of as "liberal," who lived in a neighborhood where the candy store, the bakery, the delicatessen, the butcher shop, were all closed on Rosh Hashanah and where the *New York Post* sold briskly on the newsstands. "Liberals" were not supposed to act this way.

But suppositions were beside the point. The majority of these, mostly young people, a large number of whom were Jews, seemed to be saying that they didn't want any new plans to start with *them*. They wanted things as usual and would defend their right to preserve their largely segregated school on the white side of Junction Boulevard. Walking home after the meeting that night, I was shaken. I could see that we were in for a long period of tension without a compromise solution. For that night, and later as well, we saw the raw emotions that gave rise to extremism. The form of that extremism was different here than in Birmingham, but watching parents spew their views with hate is not a comforting sight anywhere. [. . .]

By this time, I believed that no minister could simply sit in the midst of this crisis and say nothing, hoping it would vanish by itself. With two of my rabbinical friends we proceeded to the rumpus room meeting. I felt quite good about having them along with me, but we went as individuals and not as a "rabbinic group."

In the course of my remarks that evening, I urged, apparently without convincing anybody, that I could not see how this plan was a violation of the neighborhood school concept. After all, the schools are only 5 blocks apart. I also made the point, which I still think to be true, that most of the people in the cooperatives are not bigots, for if they were, they wouldn't have moved onto the fringe of a Negro area. There are certain fears the white community has that would have to be understood. Some of them might even be legitimate. But they could all be overcome. I concluded that while deeply ashamed of what we had seen thus far, I was sure that reason would ultimately prevail.

When I sat down I felt hopeful that my remarks had had some effect, for at least there had been a respectful silence. But any delusions were rapidly shattered in the next few moments. When I had entered the hall, a young Negro minister with his jacket off, shirt open and sleeves rolled up, was in the process of talking. He had to shout at times in order to keep his voice above the undercurrent of talk. It seemed to me that he was pressing too hard, for his voice took on a belligerent tone which blunted its effectiveness. I think he sensed that he was not successfully communicating and this only increased his determination. He was attempting to describe what it is like for a Negro to grow up in New York, that the hurts and slights are different than down South, but very real nonetheless. His words were concluded to a round of applause by some and jeers by the rest. Following him, a Negro woman educator tried to point out the benefits of a fully integrated education, citing the spur to achievement that would result and some of the other psychological data uncovered by the Supreme Court decision that demonstrated the inferiority of segregated education. The logic was faultless. But the Supreme Court was remote and Corona was real.

After the formal speeches, the floor was thrown open to questions. Before very much could happen, an extremely agitated young man came forward, a person whom I had never seen before, and who, I was later told, was not from the community. He pointed a finger at Rev. Galamison and shouted, "Aren't you the Rev. Galamison that writes for the Communist magazine?" He went to name some obscure periodical that I had never heard of before. In a moment the whole place was in an uproar.

Rev. Galamison was visibly upset, but refused to speak saying he "wouldn't dignify that smear with an answer." The tension hung heavily in the air; no one knew just what to do. Rev. Galamison was at that time unknown to most of us—it was still some months before the school boycott led by him in February of this year. Instinct dictated that it was necessary to relieve the terrible indignity of the moment. I walked over and introduced myself. He smiled weakly and within the next few moments what had remained of the meeting had broken up. Its end was quickened by a fire marshal who came to complain of overcrowding, but I think everyone was relieved to leave the tension behind. [. . .]

I decided to devote my sermon on Kol Nidre night to the theme of intergroup tensions. Atonement to the Negro community for past wrongs seemed to me an appropriate call of the season. What the mail indicated was that if the Negro has not been treated fairly that is his problem and not ours. We ought not to perpetuate bigotry—we also ought not to be the first actively to help alleviate it. "Would the Negroes help us if we needed their help?" an anonymous correspondent wrote. "Where were the Negroes during the Hitler regime?" someone else wanted to know after starting his unsigned letter with . . . "*Yold*, don't be a fool and get yourself involved in something that is not your business. The Negro would be the first to remind you that charity begins at home. Let's not be the first on line for anything." The only hostile comment I have received from a member of our Congregation, however, more than made up for all those who never wrote. It is worth reproducing in its entirety to demonstrate the depth of emotion that the issue has generated. Incidentally, at this writing, I have yet to meet the author, who remains a name on the rolls of our membership list.

". . . Your opinion expressed before the local School Board tonight regarding the Princeton Plan was not the opinion of the Jewish Community of Jackson Heights. There is no doubt in my mind that you were influenced by a few Communist members of your congregation. [. . .] Either you represent the Jewish people or get out of Jackson Heights . . ." [. . .]

On the whole I must say the Board of Directors and the people generally have been encouraging. That is not to say that they agree. But that they respect my right to say what I believe has been a source of satisfaction.

My impression is that the congregants feel differently about "color problems" than do their rabbis. It may have to do with a different perspective. Until now the discussions have almost always proceeded on a theoretical basis, especially in the North, and there has been a minimum of tension. But many of the people in my congregation still think of the Negroes as *schvartze*—especially among the older generation. And while some rabbis have taken dramatic and necessary steps, their main work, as I see it, will be to convince the people they face each week that if they are to live with the new Negro that is emerging, a new white will also have to come into being. It is not going to be an easy task. I think rabbis now have to make the point that they hold the opinions they do, not "because he's a rabbi, it's expected," but because they mean it for themselves and their families. Most synagogues have moved out of mixed neighborhoods. Many rabbis have moved personally. In such an atmosphere it is difficult to ask the congregants to take the first step.

Slowly, after initial hesitations and an attitude of, "this is what we would like but we also would like parent cooperation" (in other words, an attitude inviting noisy protest), the Board of Education settled on the Princeton Plan for P.S. 149 and P.S. 92. Each school would have its own kindergarten, while P.S. 92, the Corona school, would house the first and second grades, and P.S. 149 in the white neighborhood would house grades 3 through 6. Oddly enough, the geographical setup is strikingly similar to that of the original plan as it was put into effect in Princeton, New Jersey, some 16 years ago—two very close schools with different racial compositions that are "paired" into one in order to achieve a better system of integration.

The somewhat amazing fact in the proposed plan for Jackson Heights, given its reactions so far, is that the District Superintendent estimates that bussing of any kind will be necessary for only about 30 children, out of a total of 1600 that would be involved. Only these thirty will be more than 10 blocks away from P.S. 92. Further, it is expected by the Superintendent that after the two schools have been rezoned into one, the Negro population in each will not exceed 35%. The physical facilities of both schools will be improved and a teacher-enriched program will be instituted. A $200,000 renovation is envisioned for the 50-year-old "Negro" school, including a complete electrical rewiring of the building and remodeling of the classrooms.

In addition a teacher for corrective reading, a librarian, a guidance counselor, a social worker, and a psychiatrist are promised under the new arrangement for the old school. There will be no more than 28 children in a regular class rather than upwards of 35 as often prevails now; and a five (rather than the current four) hour day is promised for future first graders. A full principal and supervisory staff will be placed in each of the schools and altogether the impression is given by the harried Board that they will spare no effort to make a show case of the two schools to discourage the critics. Still, all of this has not even made a dent on the vociferous pickets of the Board who some weeks ago circled in protest, chanting poetically and in unison, "Princeton Plan in the Garbage Can."

It was with some envy that I read of the original plan as it was formulated in the more staid academic community of Princeton. There is so little that is radical about it, that one of its original proponents said, "We need to be apologetic about it because it was so simple. I didn't think the Plan was so terribly wonderful at the time."

On the surface it still isn't. It provides for mixing the population of the paired schools and the creation of one school for the upper and one for the lower grades, the pooling of facilities, services and everything else. Indeed, when it was instituted in Princeton long before the 1954 Supreme Court ruling, it was accomplished without violence or even protest. Of course, Princeton has a large representation of university people, professionals and educated housewives.

The protesting parents claim to be infatuated with the neighborhood school. They don't want their children to cross Junction Boulevard, a major thoroughfare, into an area they are not sure of. "There is no discrimination," they say, "anymore than when we do not go walking around Harlem at night. Of course, Ralph Bunche, Jackie Robinson and Martin Luther King are fine people, but they don't live in Corona. Besides, it has nothing to do with the Negroes. I want to send my child to the school closest to us."

Their opponents remind them that Corona is not Harlem and that it has neat if modest one-family homes that are well-kept. The idea of pillage on the streets is precisely the stereotype that has to be overcome and will be only by a plan of this type.

Still a third opinion sees the basic inadequacy of both these schools in the light of our changing times. Both are old and some people believe fairly inadequate educationally.

The Board of Education, faced with boycotts, pressures, the tides of emotion and history is now committed to the implementation of the Princeton Plan. Many Negro leaders have already announced that the sixty schools scheduled for the pairing procedure still represent inadequate integration. There are hundreds of parents in the community ready to make an effort to bring the Princeton Plan successfully to Jackson Heights and Corona. Yet, at this writing, the prospects are uncertain. [. . .]

Some people believe that opposition to integration sentiment has already died down. Others claim it is just beginning to build up.

By September we should know whether we can implement the Princeton Plan constructively or whether it will throw the community for a loss.

Ten Ways Out for Tired Liberals

ALBERT VORSPAN

A college student was once asked what he would like to get out of college. "Me," he replied. This story is appropriate to the mood of a rising number of white liberals—including many Jews—in their response to the unceasing demands of the racial crisis in American life. These whites are battle-weary, irritated, tense, guilty, frightened and they nurse feelings of rejection and anxiety. What they would like to get out of the civil rights struggle is . . . themselves. And they are succeeding. Would you, too, like to get out of the nerve-wracking pressure chamber of the Racial Revolution? There are escape hatches. The following are recommended as highly effective "outs," tried and tested in communities throughout the country. These "outs" are respectable, effective and popular. Indeed, they are quickly becoming the clichés of white resistance.

Out #1—"Why Can't Negroes Pull Themselves Up By Their Own Bootstraps The Way We Did?"

This "out" requires skipping lightly over the obvious differences between the Jewish and Negro situations. Acknowledge that the Negro has his troubles, but don't admit that the American Negro has been crippled by white society—a society which today demands he get out on the track and compete with white runners. Forget that Jews brought to America a rich cultural heritage, that when they faced anti-Jewish discrimination, some changed their noses and/or their names. Ignore the fact that Negroes have learned many things, but they have not yet learned how to get out of their black skins. If these elementary facts can be conveniently overlooked, or at least disparaged ("Oh, I know they've been segregated and all that, but . . ."), Out #1 should be all you need to assure a graceful exit.

Out #2—"I Believe In Human Rights, But Negroes Are Just Going Too Fast And Pushing Too Hard."

Don't weaken this one by conceding that Negroes have to run as fast and as hard as they can if they are to stand still. As a matter of fact, Negroes haven't succeeded very well even in staying where they were. Are our big cities more segregated today than they were ten years ago? Are our suburbs white nooses around the necks of our black belt inner cities, and our schools getting more segregated all the time? Is it true that some 800,000 white pupils, for example, have left the New York City public school system over the past decade and that they have been replaced in large measure by Negroes and Puerto Ricans? Never mind. Never mind that desegregation in the South is moving at so glacial a pace that only 1 percent of the Negro school children of the deep south have been integrated ten years after the Supreme Court decision; that Negro unemployment is twice that of whites; that for Negroes this is the depression of the 1930s all over again; that half of the youngsters out of work and out of school are Negro; that almost half of American Negroes are trapped in a cycle of poverty which, like wealth, is inherited from generation to generation! Some wise guy may ask you: "Negroes are pushing too fast for *whom?* Too fast for *what?*" If this happens, switch quickly to

Out #3—"I'm For Civil Rights, But I Will Not Go For The Breaking Of The Law And Civil Disobedience."

This one is a trump card and should be played with strength. No sensible person can deny that some demonstrations have been ill-advised, some have undoubtedly been harmful to the civil rights cause, and there will be other unwise and impulsive adventures in the future. Don't fall into the trap of referring to the current struggles as a revolution because no revolution has ever been pretty and manicured . . . not the American Revolution, nor the French Revolution nor the birth of the State of Israel. The important thing is to denounce the demonstration and bloody riots in Harlem—a blockbuster of an example. Do not try to imagine the depths of despair from which they spring nor to understand this fact. When the Negro does not irritate our conscience through demonstrations, *we don't know he exists.* He is invisible, living on the wrong side of the tracks and the wrong side of the color line. If he refuses to be invisible, to be quiet, to accommodate himself to your desire for social peace, if he *will* be noticed, this is a definite threat to your peace of mind. Did Jews condemn violations of the Nazi Nuremberg laws? Did Jews protest the illegal immigration of Jewish refugees into Palestine? Never bring up such comparisons. If you extend the same standards to Negro demonstrators, you blow your advantage. This "out" has a good moralistic ring. It demonstrates that you are an independent fellow who calls the shots frankly as you see them. While putting you on record *for* Negro rights and *for* law and order, the beauty of it is that it also takes you right "out" of the battle.

Out #4—"Civil Rights, Yes, But Forced Integration, No!"

This is a sweetheart of an "out." It touches all the bases—civil rights, freedom of conscience and a robust opposition to any semblance of coercion. It hits like a hammer, but at all costs avoid being forced to define your terms. What is "forced integration" anyway? Is prohibiting discrimination in hotels and restaurants "forced integration"? Is forbidding discrimination in employment "forced integration"? The force of the government *is* behind these, true, but if it is force we oppose, let's knock out compulsory education, income tax, the military draft and traffic rules. By all means, don't paint yourself into a corner and begin suggesting how non-discrimination and civil rights can be achieved *without* the force of law. You will wreck the whole "out" because it can't be done. The history of America is testimony to the futility of depending solely upon long-range education, voluntary suasion and "changing men's hearts" in the pursuit of human rights. But don't get into this. Just purse your lips and proclaim: "Nobody is going to tell *me* who I should . . ."

Out #5—"They Don't Want Our Help Anymore!"

You can get a lot of mileage out of this. Certainly you can quote some of the wilder and more demagogic statements of Negro extremists. You can cite examples of white men who have been eased out of the civil rights leadership though they have devoted their lives to the struggle for equality. In referring to Negroes, talk about "them" in a grand sweep. Don't be specific about Negro leaders, because Roy Wilkins, James Farmer, Martin Luther King, Whitney Young, Bayard Rustin and every other important Negro leader acknowledge that the Negro Revolution cannot possibly be won by Negroes alone. They realize that Negroes represent only 10 percent of the population, and that the civil rights movement must necessarily be joined to a fight for massive social and economic measures to eliminate poverty, wipe out slums, improve medical care and achieve full employment. Such an undertaking—nothing less than the remaking of American society—requires a coalition of Negroes and white liberal, labor, Jewish and other progressive forces in American life. But these facts should in no way muffle the note of hurt pique about what "they" are saying and doing.

Out #6—"After All We've Done For Them,
Negroes Are Anti-Semitic Anyway."

This argument is, of course, only good by and to Jews because non-Jews who are anti-Negro tend to be anti-Jewish, too, and they might see Negro anti-Semitism as a sign of redemption.

For Jews, this argument has real appeal because Jews *have* done a great deal for civil rights, including help in the organization and progress of the NAACP, passage of civil rights legislation, foundation funds for Negro education, voting for liberal candidates and many similar contributions. Play up this side of the coin and maybe the discussion will not get around to looking at the other side of the coin at all. That has to do with the flight of Jews from racial problems of the city to the white sanctuary of suburbia; the fact that the sole and inherently unhappy contact which most slum Negroes have with Jews is as landlord, pawnshop owner, liquor store owner and loan shark; the sullen and often ugly resistance of Jewish neighborhoods in New York City and elsewhere to school integration plans and other devices to achieve equality; the almost total lack of peer-to-peer contact between Jews and Negroes; the frequent exploitation of Negro maids. A 1964 study of racial attitudes in Chicago found Jews highly prejudiced against Negroes and Puerto Ricans, "more prejudiced than non-Jews were against Jews."

But, nonetheless, there *is* Negro anti-Semitism and it is probably rising. Attacks by Negroes against the Chasidim in Brooklyn have happened—and they were brutal and unprovoked, and so were the attacks against Jewish merchants in Harlem. These examples should be waved aloft like a bloody shirt, because what Jew can fail to be incensed or shaken by these developments? It is sure to evoke an historical visceral response. You might even be able, depending upon the vulnerability of your listener, to raise the specter of an "American Mau Mau." In general, stick to emotions and fearful images, because the facts are that Negro anti-Semitism is not very high, as proved by the *Newsweek* poll, that it is largely subsumed in a general distrust of whites, and that responsible Negro leadership condemns it at every turn.

The thing to do is to play on the ingratitude of the Negro who, shockingly, looks upon the Jew as part of the white power structure and the benevolent community establishment which, North and South, has robbed him of his dignity and his manhood. If Negroes don't like us, they can fend for themselves. Whatever this attitude lacks in logic, charity and Jewish principles, it more than compensates in its susceptibility to human weakness and wounded pride. For greater results, couple with Out #5.

Out #7—"Rights Must Be Earned, Not Handed Out On A Silver Platter."

This "out" lacks something in sophistication and should be used advisedly, but it does conjure up the spirit of rugged individualism and pioneer sturdiness which Americans honor so warmly in the breach. Of course, we do not withhold the right to vote from stupid and corrupt "rednecks" of Mississippi, but we do expect a Negro college professor there to "earn" his right. We do not deny access to our hotels and restaurants to pimps and addicts and adulterers and illiterates and field workers for the Cosa Nostra, but it is true that these worthies have earned their rights by having achieved whiteness which, after all, only a fraction of the world population has thus far accomplished.

A note of caution on this "out." *Don't try it on an American Negro.*

Out #8—"Where Were They When 6,000,000 Jews Were Being Killed By Hitler?"

Rather nasty, but contains an element of surprise. Who knows where American Negroes were in the 30s since, until recently, they were invisible in American life?

During the war, of course, many were in the armed forces, helping to destroy Nazism, though they had to do this under rules of segregation more akin to the spirit of Nuremberg than of the United States Constitution. But the nice thing about this "out" is the implication that, if American Negroes really cared, they could have stayed the hand of the Nazi murderers. Another implication is that, despite the irritations which Negroes face, this is really minor compared to what Jews have known.

In resorting to Out #8, it is necessary to gloss over the situation of the Negro in America. For, though America has never used gas ovens, we have—for 300 years—visited spiritual and psychological death upon generations of black men. Negro youngsters in the slums, we now know, are frequently lost in the race of life before they even get to the first grade, their self-image distorted, their self-esteem destroyed, their incentive for learning blasted, their spirit shriveled by poverty and by the narrow world of their experience. And yet most of white America acknowledges no more responsibility for that than did the good, fat burghers of Germany for what was happening in the smoking crematoria in their countryside.

Out #9—"It's Not A Matter Of Integration At All; It's A Matter Of Education."

This "out" should not be advanced as a hypothesis; it would be pronounced as a latter-day revelation from Sinai. Contend that strengthening the quality of Negro schools is the only goal that is important, not "moving kids around on a chessboard." But do not drop your voice lest some zealot inquire: "Isn't that separate but equal?" If that does happen, switch your argument ever so slightly so that it goes: "It's not a matter of integration at all; it's a matter of economics." Concede anything, dodge and weave, but do not grant that integration is the moral essence of the entire issue. Because, after all, everybody knows that racial integration was a popular banner when it meant kids in Little Rock, or James Meredith at the University of Mississippi or the terrible things that happened in Birmingham. But *now* when they talk integration they're talking about *your* plant, *your* block, *your* school, *your* job and *your* serenity. As everybody knows, such things are reckless, create severe tension and "simply cannot be accomplished overnight."

Out #10—"Integration Is A Fine Ideal, But It Just Causes A Strain For Both Colored And White Kids."

Telling because true. There is a strain. It is a difficult ordeal for both races. But don't discuss the alternatives because they are all unpleasant, including the failure of American democracy, the alienation of the rest of mankind, the decay of our cities, the continued sense of racial superiority by white Americans, the toll of psychological damage, waste of human resources and the price of welfare subsistence for the blacks. Integration is the key to whether or not America can fulfill its own vision of equality and effectuate a multi-racial and open society. And the strain of adjustment to a better, larger society is the kind of creative tension which leads to growth in human relations and enlargement of the human spirit. Integration is the key to whether or not Americans can learn not only to accept but to *cherish* differences, thus joining a world of diversity, of dynamism, of variegated color and of teeth-rattling change. Integration is the challenge of living and working with all people. Don't try the old chestnut that Negroes don't want integration; they do. If they win it, that will be because equality is an aspect of their humanity and is not our gift to bestow or withhold. But you keep out of it. Mind your own business. "Am I my brother's keeper?" doesn't mention black brothers.

These are among the best and most visible "outs." You may find others in the heat of argument. By selecting those best fitted to your own needs, you may build yourself a sturdy case for washing your hands of the entire untidy problem. By all means, don't use them *all;* you certainly don't want to appear to be a bigot. You needn't feel guilty about using these "outs" judiciously because they have become quite fashionable as the sound of the turtle is increasingly heard in the land—the snap of heads pulling back into their shells.

To keep you from getting confused, avoid reading the Bible, stay away from synagogue, don't talk to any Negroes except your maid (and these days you can't even be sure of *her*), and reserve your passions for your private world. Find peace of mind and ease of sleep . . . these are the advantages which the dead have always had over the living.

Religion and Race

ABRAHAM JOSHUA HESCHEL

At the first conference on religion and race, the main participants were Pharaoh and Moses. Moses' words were: "Thus says the Lord, the God of Israel, let My people go that they may celebrate a feast to Me." While Pharaoh retorted: "Who is the Lord, that I should heed this voice and let Israel go? I do not know the Lord, and moreover I will not let Israel go."

The outcome of that summit meeting has not come to an end. Pharaoh is not ready to capitulate. The exodus began, but is far from having been completed. In fact, it was easier for the children of Israel to cross the Red Sea than for a Negro to cross certain university campuses.

Let us dodge no issues. Let us yield no inch to bigotry, let us make no compromise with callousness.

In the words of William Lloyd Garrison, "I will be as harsh as truth, and as uncompromising as justice. On this subject [slavery] I do not wish to think, to speak, or to write with moderation. I am in earnest—I will not equivocate—I will not excuse—I will not retreat a single inch—and I will be heard."

Religion and race. How can the two be uttered together? To act in the spirit of religion is to unite what lies apart, to remember that humanity as a whole is God's beloved child. To act in the spirit of race is to sunder, to slash, to dismember the flesh of living humanity. Is this the way to honor a father: to torture his child? How can we hear the word "race" and feel no self-reproach?

Race as a *normative* legal or political concept is capable of expanding to formidable dimensions. A mere thought, it extends to become a way of thinking, a highway of insolence, as well as a standard of values, overriding truth, justice, beauty. As a standard of values and behavior, race operates as a comprehensive doctrine, as racism. And racism is worse than idolatry. *Racism is satanism*, unmitigated evil. [. . .]

How many disasters do we have to go through in order to realize that all of humanity has a stake in the liberty of one person; whenever one person is offended, we are all hurt. What begins as inequality of some inevitably ends as inequality of all. [. . .]

My heart is sick when I think of the anguish and the sighs, of the quiet tears shed in the nights in the overcrowded dwellings in the slums of our great cities, of the pangs of despair, of the cup of humiliation that is running over.

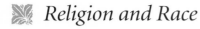

The crime of murder is tangible and punishable by law. The sin of insult is imponderable, invisible. When blood is shed, human eyes see red; when a heart is crushed, it is only God who shares the pain. [. . .]

It is not within the power of God to forgive the sins committed toward men. We must first ask for forgiveness of those whom our society has wronged before asking for the forgiveness of God.

Daily we patronize institutions which are visible manifestations of arrogance toward those whose skin differs from ours. Daily we cooperate with people who are guilty of active discrimination.

How long will *I* continue to be tolerant of, even a participant in, acts of embarrassing and humiliating human beings, in restaurants, hotels, buses, or parks, employment agencies, public schools and universities? One ought rather be shamed than put others to shame. [. . .]

Let us cease to be apologetic, cautious, timid. Racial tension and strife is both sin and punishment. *The Negro's plight,* the blighted areas in the large cities, are they not the fruit of our sins?

By negligence and silence we have all become accessory before the God of mercy to the injustice committed against the Negroes by men of our nation. Our derelictions are many. We have failed to demand, to insist, to challenge, to chastise.

In the words of Thomas Jefferson, "I tremble for my country when I reflect that God is just." [. . .]

Racism is an evil of tremendous power, but God's will transcends all powers. Surrender to despair is surrender to evil. It is important to feel anxiety, it is sinful to wallow in despair.

What we need is a total mobilization of heart, intelligence, and wealth for the purpose of love and justice. God is in search of man, waiting, hoping for man to do His will. [. . .]

This world, this society, can be redeemed. God has a stake in our moral predicament. I cannot believe that God will be defeated.

What we face is a human emergency. It will require much devotion, wisdom, and divine grace to eliminate that massive sense of inferiority, the creeping bitterness. It will require a high quality of imaginative sympathy, sustained cooperation both in thought and in action, by individuals as well as by institutions, to weed out memories of frustration, roots of resentment.

We must act even when inclination and vested interests would militate against equality. Human self-interest is often our Nemesis! It is the audacity of faith that redeems us. To have faith is to be ahead of one's normal thoughts, to transcend confused motivations, to lift oneself by one's bootstraps. Mere knowledge or belief is too feeble to be a cure of man's hostility to man, of man's tendency to fratricide. The only remedy is *personal sacrifice:* to abandon, to reject what seems dear and even plausible for the sake of the greater truth;

to do more than one is ready to understand for the sake of God. Required is a breakthrough, a *leap of action.* It is the deed that will purify the heart. It is the deed that will sanctify the mind. The deed is the test, the trial, and the risk.

The plight of the Negro must become our most important concern. Seen in the light of our religious tradition, *the Negro problem is God's gift to America,* the test of our integrity, a magnificent spiritual opportunity. [. . .]

Daily we should take account and ask: What have I done today *to alleviate the anguish, to mitigate the evil, to prevent humiliation?*

Let there be a grain of prophet in every man!

Negro-Jewish Relations in America
A Symposium

LESLIE A. FIEDLER, ARTHUR HERTZBERG,

AND PAUL JACOBS

LESLIE A. FIEDLER

[. . .] The Negro [. . .] tends to regard the Jew either as a Colored Man who is deviously passing as White; or a goddamned White Man pretending, for reasons hard to fathom, to the fate of the excluded Colored Man. The Jew, meanwhile, is struggling with the vestigial sense of being a third thing, neither-either, however one says it; and he therefore thinks of himself (his kind of awareness driving him compulsively from feeling to thinking) of being free to "pass" in either direction, in a world which oddly insists that he identify himself with one group of strangers or another, Hamitic or Japhetic. And he knows that historically segments of his people have done both (some first pretending to be White, then becoming prisoners of their pretense; some following the opposite strategy): that in Israel, for instance, it is possible to observe these two groups, "Black Jews" and "White Jews," in open conflict. He is, therefore, baffled as well as resentful when he discovers himself denominated "White" without choice and made the victim in a Black-White race riot; just as he was once baffled as well as resentful to discover himself linked without choice to Negroes in being excluded from White clubs and hotels and restaurants. And he is doubly baffled and resentful when the Negro switches from hating him as White to despising him in a mode imitated from those earlier-arrived North European Americans, who thought themselves so much Whiter than he.

How can the Jew not help seeing Negro anti-Semitism as a kind of culture-climbing, an illegitimate attempt to emulate WASP style—and, inevitably, a belated and misguided attempt; since the WASPs are abandoning the racist attitudes to which the Negro aspires at the very moment he is assimilating them. Even Hitler, certain more ignorant or frantic Negroes tend to think of as just another White Man—rather more efficient than most, though not quite efficient enough in eliminating his Jew-enemies—and thus they have not felt shamed out of their anti-Semitism by the rise and fall of Nazism, or their WASP opposite numbers (who cannot help feeling Hitler in some sense one of them) have tended to be. It is especially unassimilated, unassimilable Jews, Jews who do not even seem to want to look like all other Americans, who stir the fury of Negro hoods—say, Hasidim with their beards, *peyes* and gabardines.

At the deepest mythological level, is it not the Jewish religion, finally, as well as the Jewish ethnic inheritance which bugs the Negroes? Certainly this would be understandable enough; for insofar as they are Christians, fundamentalist, evangelical Protestants, do they not inherit the simple-minded anti-Jewish mythology of the Gospels (which Catholics long had the good grace to keep out of the hands of subliterates) with its simple-minded melodrama of "our" Christ killed by "the Jews"? And do not Negroes in particular possess the additional sentimental myth of Simon the Cyrenean—kindly Negro by the wayside—who helped Jesus bear his cross as the Jews hooted and howled for his blood? And insofar as they are becoming Muslim (Why could not the first attempt of the ill-fated founder of that movement to establish a Black Judaism have succeeded?), are they not obsessed by the legendary notion of the "Evil Jacob," Israel the Usurper—as well as the myth of Isaac before him doing poor Ishmael out of his heritage? And as Muslims, do not they (along with the members of other non-Mohammedan Afro organizations) identify themselves with an Arab-African anti-Jewish political mythology, which leads them to consider Jews, in America as well as Israel, even wickeder than the rest of the depraved "hoojis"? Are not both Christianity and Islam, finally, being offshoots of a more primitive Judaism, subject to spasms of a kind of collective sibling rivalry, which passes over on occasion into fratricidal strife? And is not the *shul*-goer or temple-attending Jew caught once more in the old bind between the Christian Negro for whom he is not (spiritually) White enough—not sufficiently washed in the Blood of the Lamb—and the Muslim Negro for whom he is not (mythologically) Black enough—not far enough removed from the White Man's God? [. . .]

Jewish writers, from Mailer to Nat Hentoff, may try to escape the mythological hang-up by redefining themselves as imaginary or "White Negroes" (the very term was, of course, invented by a Jew)—just as their more political brethren have tried to assimilate to a world which mythologically rejects them by linking arms with Negroes in protests and demonstrations. But though young Jews have an affinity not only for protest but for folksongs, jazz and marijuana (how much more readily they assimilate to pot than to the paleface medicine of whiskey), the whole syndrome, they have trouble making it across the legendary line—remain always in danger of being told that they cannot *really* commit themselves to the Movement, cannot *really* make authentic jazz, cannot *really* sing the blues. The point is that other mythological demands are being made on them—to play the false liberal, or "Mr. Goldberg" or, ultimately, the super-ego in one or another currently unfashionable form.

So much—for the moment—about the Negro or Negroizing mythologies of the Jew; though I suppose a word at least demands to be said about the "Black Socialism" (the term antedates its adoption by actual Blacks), that presumably revolutionary anti-Semitism which poor Negroes have inherited from White workers, *lumpen* proletarians, peasants and "red-necks." This view (to which Leo Frank was once a victim) sees the Jew as rich, powerful, devious, behind the scenes if not at the centers of power—a Boss, in short. But this view tends to become less and less influential as the leading elements of the Negro Movement become prosperous or mobile and educated enough to afford overt anti-Semitism. It is real enough, to be sure, but is it not finally a vestige, as old-fashioned, which is to say, as peripheral in the current situation as the remnants among the aging Jewish bourgeoisie of the simple-minded anti-Negroism appropriate to our social-climbing days: the contempt of the still insecure Jewish housewife for the *schwarze* who cleaned for her, or the Jewish marginal small businessman for his Negro janitor, or the underpaid Jewish salesman for his Negro installment customer? Do we not enjoy rehashing such elementary prejudices, long after we have made it in a way which renders them irrelevant, precisely because they are no longer urgent; and leaving them we would have to confront relationships much more difficult to analyze or confess?

Almost as familiar, and therefore quite as ritually satisfying to discuss yet one more time are certain good old Freudian notions—long since lapsed into semi-popular mythology—about the Negro: the projection onto the Negro male, for instance, of the sadist nightmares about his own women dreamed by the white male etc. etc. These have always been rather confused as far as Jews in America are concerned, by the fact that Jews themselves have played similar mythological-sexual roles in WASP erotic fantasies: and in Norman Mailer's last novel one can see enacted in the form of comic melodrama a kind of contest between his (half) Jewish hero and a particularly potent Spade to see which one will possess the blond all-American *shikse*—which, mythologically speaking, amounts, I suppose, to an argument about which one of us she is dreaming these days. More interesting, and more dangerous to broach, are questions about the role of homosexual rather than heterosexual fantasies in the earlier stages of the Civil Rights Movement. I am not referring to the fact that there has been a strange confluence of the Homosexual Rebellion (the emergence of queer America from underground to the daylight world) and the Negro Movement; but rather to the influence on that Movement of the old anti-female dream of a pure love between males, colored and white, so crucial to our classic literature in the United States. I myself can report having heard several times in various forms from young civil rights workers the cry, so authentically American it was hard at first to believe: "Oh, Christ, things were great when just us buddies black and white were fighting it out together; but these White chicks are just down here to get laid." [. . .]

So naturally a new mythology is being invented, appropriate to that new solution; though like all new myths this one, too, contains within it one very old, indeed, the myth of the Jewish Daughter, Hadassah (renamed Esther, which is to say, Ashtoreth) dancing naked for our salvation before the Gentile King. I sat the other day eavesdropping on the conversation of a group of very young white girls—most of them pretty, blonde daughters of Jews with black boyfriends, discussions what they would do when the first race riots broke out in Buffalo. And one of them suggested that they march between the two opposed packs, Black and White, carrying signs which read: MAKE LOVE NOT WAR. It was elegant and vain as the loveliest dream; and I am old and cynical enough, after all, to know it; as I know how much there is dark and desperate even in their young love, and as I realize how much in marriage itself (for some few of them *will* marry their Negro boyfriends, I am sure) is a problem rather than a solution. To make matters worse, I had just been reading in the *East Village Other* a statement by a Negro poet, who not so long before had been able to write that he had "married a Jewish Lady to escape Bohemia," that Jewish girls only married Negroes in order to emasculate them. And I was aware that it was his paranoid and sinister mythology which operated in the tensions that made headlines day after day; but I knew that the counter-mythology of those young girls had power to move men, too. I, at least, prefer to live in its hope rather than the Negro poet's despair, convinced of its superiority to all the weary mythologies of mere politics. The disillusionment it will inevitably breed at least still lies ahead, and (if I am lucky) I may not live so long.

ARTHUR HERTZBERG

The relations between Jews and Negroes are deteriorating. There is now the seed of conflict and, perhaps, even of tragedy.

The confrontation between Jews and Negroes is created, in the first place, by some hard sociological facts. In every big city in America the Negro ghetto, from Harlem to Watts, is inhabiting an area which was last occupied by Jews. Many of the white landlords, and, perhaps most of the shopkeepers who remain in such neighborhoods, are left over from the earlier days. In the Negro ghetto the conflict between landlord and tenant, between seller and buyer, between creditor and borrower is, therefore, very often between Negro and Jew. For example, some 750 stores were destroyed in the Watts riot a year ago; it is reliably estimated that five hundred were owned by Jews.

On the average, Jewish landlords and shopkeepers are perhaps kinder to Negroes than the rest; or perhaps there is no difference. There is reason to believe that the roughest treatment meted out to the poorest elements in the black ghettos comes not from white but from Negro shopkeepers and landlords. All this does not matter to the teenager who feels that he must steal a bicycle, because he cannot possibly imagine ever being able to buy one. "I want what you've got," means to him that he wants what the owner of the bicycle store has, and that owner is most often named Greenberg or Cohen.

In the second place, as both James Baldwin and Nathan Glazer have seen, Negroes and Jews require quite different things from American society. The battle of the Jews for their equality in America has been waged under the slogan of a career open freely to talent. Jews did not ask any advantages to repay them for centuries of persecution. The structure of the Jewish family outlasted the ages, and the Jewish tradition of learning remained strong. Sam Levinson has recently exaggerated when he proclaimed that the home of his immigrant parents had "everything except money," but it did provide such moral and intellectual foundations that the Jewish individual needed nothing more than a partially open society to make it possible for him to advance rapidly. For the Negro, the problem is in reverse. Slavery disintegrated the family and subjection permitted very little learning to penetrate. Most Negro individuals in America today need opportunities which are weighted in their favor to give them a fair start.

The conflict between these two outlooks can only become sharper. With some variations all minorities in America have used the same path of ascent: the governmental bureaucracies and the service occupations. Both fields could be entered by individuals far more easily than the dominant power structure of banks, insurance companies, steel mills and the like. A child of a minority can enter the bureaucracy because his people vote, and he can get into the service occupations because there one is essentially in business for himself. The Negro is now bidding for these places, and the bid must increase as more Negroes attain higher education. It is inevitable that the first Negroes to appear in considerable numbers will not, on the average, place as high on competitive examinations as their white peers, precisely because they will have begun from a disadvantaged starting point. Inevitably, however, they will demand access to the roles in society for which they have prepared themselves, and they will regard any barriers, no matter how seemingly reasonable, as white self-protective devices. As Negroes fight ever harder to enter the higher levels of the bureaucracies, the staffs of hospitals, or the university faculties, they will be encountering a rather large proportion of Jews, who made it out of their ghetto a generation before through these very avenues. [. . .]

The notion that there are "true interests of the movement for Negro civil rights" which anti-Semitism does not really serve is true, but only in the ultimate, moral sense. The true interests of the Negro at this moment are, from his point of view, in going as far and as fast as he possibly can, and he has now realized that the only way to go there is not through gradualism and "popular front" alliances but through making the Negro ghetto too explosive to ignore—and, alas, an all too available way of doing this is to use Jew-hatred. In such a situation there can only be power bargainings between groups and communities. Jews must resist, through all the influence and power at their disposal, and they must engage in the quest for accommodation, at a cost acceptable to them.

In the light of these reflections it seems to me that all of the other questions raised for this discussion fall by the wayside. The Jewish establishments have made more liberal declarations about Negroes than any other, but that makes no difference to a revolutionary situation. The issues between Jews and Negroes are not misunderstandings between the two groups but hard questions about power and position. It is ridiculous to pretend that at this moment in American history, the texture of Jewish and Negro experiences are similar. The Jews are the most vulnerable of the haves, and the Negroes the most unfortunate of the have-nots. They may have some rhetoric in common; they are together the heirs of moral imperatives; but the real question is what love and justice mean, concretely: how many Jewish school principals are commanded by the joint Negro-Jewish commitment to morality, and Jewish memories of persecution, to go sell shoes, so less well-trained Negroes can hold their jobs. This is a problem not for the writers of liberal resolutions. If it is to be solved it must be dealt with by an odd team: Talmudists, who apply moral norms to concrete problems, and power-brokers.

PAUL JACOBS

The six Negro women and I sat, talking, in an apartment in the Nickerson Garden public housing project in the heart of Watts. Outside, the kids were screaming at play and the bells of an ice cream truck kept playing the same tune, maddeningly, over and over again. The women were all friendly, for I had been brought there by someone they trusted.

They were talking about the "Jewboys," about how they get cheated, especially by one man, whom they always call "Leon the Jewboy." They explained that on the 1st and 15th of each month, "Leon the Jewboy" drives a truck into the housing project, takes out a rack filled with clothes and rolls it from door to door trying to sell them merchandise on credit. "Jewboys" weren't the same as white people to them, and when I asked them how they tell the difference, one woman patiently explained it to me, as if I was a slow-witted but nice child:

"The white man don't have time to be knockin' on no door, and that Jew, that's his stick—(as I heard her use the word "stick," I realized that here is cross-culturalization at its best or worst—a Yiddish word being used in an anti-Jewish context)—he's been doin' it for years, that's why he controls most of the money. Now I know a Jew isn't a white man and besides he talks like a Jew—"

Another woman interrupted. "He'll tell you, you don't have to pay me but a dollar or whatever you got, you just give it to me and I'll come back—"

"Uh Huh," said the first woman, "the white folks don't do *that.*"

"You can pay him two dollars a month and he'll come back for the next twenty years," chimed in still another, as they all broke out laughing.

They vied with each other in telling me stories of how they'd been cheated, and there was even an element of bitter admiration in their description of how the "Jewboys" take advantage of their foolishness and ignorance. I asked if they ever saw any Jews in the project except the salesmen. There was a pause while they thought, and then someone said, rather incredulously, "For what? For what would they come down here? They come down here they're gonna make them some money, you know. The 'Jewboy' always done that. I remember my father used to tell about when he'd go into a store to buy a suit, and he'd put the suit on and the Jew catched it in the back and holds it and says it fits real good. And when you get home two folks can wear that coat."

They burst out laughing again, and continued regaling me and each other with stories of how they've been "taken by the Jew." They never say "Jewish," either, but always refer to "the Jew" or the "Jewboy." I asked whether any of the white storekeepers in the area cheat, too.

"They all cheat," is the answer I got. "They have to cheat 'cause we don't have nowhere else to go. If I know you don't have nowhere else to go, I'll charge you what I want because you ain't got no other way to go and no transportation to go and get it. So you want it, you need it, so I'll make you pay for it. You know you're gonna buy it."

These were poor Negroes speaking, all of them either welfare recipients or women working at very low-paid jobs, and I have heard such discussions fairly often during the past year. In the area of Los Angeles where they live, no adequate transportation system exists, so there is no place for them to do their shopping except at the fringes of the housing project. And before August, 1965 when the burning and rioting took place, most of the furniture and clothing, and a good many of the liquor and grocery stores in the area were Jewish-owned, and many of the owners did act in the way described by the women. Specifically, in addition to charging high prices for often inferior merchandise or standard brands, some shopkeepers also made the women purchase an item like a broom or a mop before they would cash their welfare checks. The liquor store owners, too, often insist that a bottle of expensive liquor be purchased before they will cash the checks. [. . .]

When I talk with poor Negroes, it never occurs to them that I am Jewish, and when I tell them that I am, they refuse to believe it. Since they have little or no connection with the civil rights movement, they know nothing of the Jewish role in it, and the names of Mickey Schwerner or Andrew Goodman are only vaguely familiar to them. When I identify them and explain that they were two Jewish boys killed by white men in the south, they find it hard to accept. [. . .]

It is very difficult to assess how much hostility is directed towards the Jew, as being separate from the whites: my own estimate, based on only the evidence I have seen, is that the Jews are *not* the primary target of the Negroes' frustration. Instead the order of hate runs, I think, roughly about as follows: white people, police, merchants, and the Jews, as a separate group, last. [. . .]

At the same time, a kind of bitter admiration exists, directed toward the way in which the Jews allegedly stick together, take care of their own and wield effective political power. No significant forces exist within the ghettoes combating that view of the Jew, and I see little possibility of any developing. None of the Jewish organizations concerned with anti-Semitism have any impact in the ghettoes. [. . .]

I get a terrible feeling of depression of *déjà vu* as I listen and argue. [. . .] I remember in the 'thirties hearing a North Dakota farmer, the militant head of a farmers' organization fighting mortgage foreclosures, inveigh against the "Jew bankers who were screwing the farmers." When I was a union organizer, I heard workers shout at people going through a picket line, "Don't go to work in a Jewshop! Don't go to work in a Jewshop!" And I have heard union officials, too, talk about the "Jewshop owners" and their smart "Jewboy lawyers."

I have heard the answer given by the Jewish store owners and employers before, too. "The *schwartzers* steal me blind so I'm gonna charge them more." "The colored people don't make their payments, so we have to have a high rate of interest in order to make up for our losses." "In a way, I'm doing the niggers a favor selling them. No one else will go down there and if I didn't they wouldn't have anything." And the final answer: "Business is business."

If I seem depressed in what I write, and offer little hope for change, this reflects accurately how I feel. As long as some Jewish businessmen exploit poor Negroes, they will help reinforce some Negroes' distorted and generalized view of the Jew, which is just as inaccurate as the distorted and generalized view of the Negro held by some Jews. But why should a Jewish businessman behave differently than a Christian one or one who worships Buddha? We Jews keep insisting we're no different from anyone else, don't we?

In This Moment of Grief

IRVING HOWE

For all of three days there was hope. Lyndon Johnson announced he would not run again; a bombing pause, of sorts, had been declared for North Vietnam; Hanoi's response indicated that negotiations might at last begin to end the war. We felt this to be a vindication of democracy. We saw it as evidence that with enough popular pressure and involvement, detestable policies could be changed and the men who spoke for them dislodged from office. For three days it seemed as if finally this country might take a turn toward reason and reconstruction.

And then came the news of the murder of Martin Luther King.

Let there be no rhetoric. By the time this will be read, you will have had enough of that. All of us know what a loss we have suffered. All of us know what the disastrous consequences are likely to be. What we cannot yet know fully is the amount of damage certain to be sustained within the Negro community itself.

In the murder of Martin Luther King we saw the other side of America. Yes, the events leading to President Johnson's withdrawal did—they still do—represent a triumph for democracy. But the murder of Martin Luther King shows the ugliness of American racism. It is a society, our America, that is shot through with racism from top to bottom and in which democracy is violated each day. The people who killed Martin Luther King may have been fanatics or lunatics, but they do not exist in isolation. They cannot be understood apart from the encasing atmosphere of violence and hatred which has always been a significant part of American life. Whoever pulled the trigger, the blood of Martin Luther King also lies on the head of George Wallace, and on the heads of many others, North and South, high and low, who have enacted or tolerated the humiliation of the American Negro.

No one can fail to understand why American Negroes should now respond with rage—or even violence. There comes a moment when a man cannot take any more, a moment at which he no longer cares to reason or think. His only recourse is to strike a blow. His only assertion of self-hood is to smash his fist, at a white policeman or through a store window. And he has to do this even if he knows that his own destruction will result—perhaps especially when he knows.

Yet if we still wish to save this country, we must say with absolute firmness: whoever counsels or acquiesces in violence is totally irresponsible. If we wish to keep American Negroes from being butchered in the streets this summer, we must say with absolute firmness: whoever counsels or acquiesces in violence is helping pave the way for an American fascism.

Here is the two-sidedness, the terrible ambivalence of America: the power of democracy and the power of racism, the way of community and the way of blood, the value of fraternity and the value of hatred.

These words, together with the happier ones that follow on the next few pages, reflect that doubleness. As for ourselves, there can be no doubt which course we choose. In a day or two we shall join the thousands of trade unionists and other people who will march in Memphis, under the leadership of Bayard Rustin, to show their solidarity with the striking garbage workers for whom only a few hours ago Martin Luther King spoke.

And yet, remembering that voice, who can contain his grief?

The Negro and the (Orthodox) Jew

RABBI BERNARD WEINBERGER

Many Jews will argue that it is intellectual chauvinism for the Orthodox Jew to react to the riots and bloodshed in urban streets on the basis of such presumably picayune considerations as how such turmoil may affect his going to and from the synagogue in the evening. Many will argue that it is such a viewpoint which is sending Orthodox youth away from their tradition, a youth which criticizes Orthodox Jewish leadership for not reacting to the burning issues of the day and for thinking in such narrow terms.

These youthful critics point to Reform and Conservative leaders who daily release statements to the press on the injustices perpetrated by the American society on the disadvantaged and the poor. Orthodox Jews do not sponsor conferences on urban problems or "dialogues," and have no social action committees, thus presumably lacking the universalism which is the essence of "prophetic Judaism." In such specific issues as the proposal to decentralize the New York City school system, which affects many Orthodox Jewish teachers, nothing is heard from Orthodox leadership.

The required answer to such criticisms must begin with the perhaps shocking counter-charge that those Jews who are thus involved in the social clashes of the day may well threaten the survival of the Jewish community in America. The survival of Jews in a hostile world is a miracle due in substantial degree to Jewish awareness that Jews simply cannot afford to tell their neighbors how to govern their lives. The reality is that Jews simply cannot speak their mind, openly and honestly, without jeopardizing Jewish lives. Every statement by the northern liberal Jew for the civil rights of the Negro causes some Jew to suffer at the hands of white racists in the south. It may not be obvious to the rabbi who joins the vigil in Washington protesting United States involvement in Vietnam that his participation may affect a million and a half of his brethren in Israel or other remote places in the world because his action may affect United States policy in the Middle East.

The irony and agony is that the Jews who are thus involved and purportedly speaking for the Jewish community are rarely affected personally by their public stands. Very few Reform and Conservative leaders live in the ghetto areas where the riots occur. Insulated in the "silk stocking" areas of the city or in split level suburban homes, they offer advice on integration. It is the Orthodox Jews in New York City, Los Angeles, Detroit, Baltimore, Chicago and other urban centers, who live in the slum neighborhoods, who account for whatever integration actually exists in such areas, and it is only after ethnic friction becomes intolerable that the Orthodox Jew finally leaves the community, thus ending whatever degree of integration it has achieved. The affluent Jewish leaders far removed from direct confrontation with slum living are quick to offer advice on coping with tensions in those ghettoes, but Orthodox Jews who live with those tensions remain silent. The image of appearing "relevant" cannot supplant both the determination to survive as a Jewish community and Orthodox Jewish reluctance to hurt any Jew.

The position that public silence is both prudent and just for Jews must not bar consideration within Jewish circles on development of a common strategy on how to exist in high-tension areas. It is the Jewish merchant whose stores are looted during riots. It is the homes of Orthodox Jewish residents which are vandalized and burglarized. The fact is that Jews can live with some measure of security only where law and order does exist because Jews are the easiest victims for all combatants when there is a breakdown of civil order. It is possible that America will survive even if the Kerner Commission prediction of a two-fold society of whites and blacks becomes true, but Jews will not be able to function in such a divided society. [. . .]

It is the responsibility of all Americans to overcome prejudice in the housing, education and employment that the Negro must have to extricate himself from his crippling poverty, but with that help must go an injection of self-esteem and self-reverence. Black power must be understood as the Negro's way of telling the white community that Negroes do not want to be treated like a small helpless child who needs mothering by the benevolent white man. [. . .]

A new Jewish strategy should begin with Jews getting out of the way of the black community. This could mean Jews giving up exploitative businesses in the ghettoes and public non-interference in Negro efforts to decentralize school systems. It certainly means desisting from overtly paternalistic efforts to help Negroes. Orthodox Jews must also learn to live with blacks and not to fear them. Orthodox Jews have too many resources invested in ghetto areas to afford the luxury of constant running. They must learn to adjust to the reality of integration from which a dialogue between the leadership of Jews and Negroes emerges naturally and a determination to co-exist becomes a reality.

The greatest contribution which Jews living in such areas can make to the black community is to encourage a stable family life. The example provided by the Orthodox Jewish community affords the Negro the inspiration which is worth infinitely more than all anti-poverty programs. Orthodox Jews should support changes in the social structure which tend to work against disadvantaged Negroes, as well as against impoverished Jews. [. . .] Jews have not had any share in the development of the white racism which engulfs America but they cannot remain indifferent to an injustice that corrodes our society.

5

The Struggle for Soviet Jewry

Antisemitism was hardly a new phenomenon in the Soviet Union of the 1960s. Since at least the late 1930s, the Stalinist regime had engaged in a series of punitive and deadly assaults against Jews and Jewish culture. It conducted show trials (in which many defendants were Jewish); it purged Jews from all top governmental positions; it sought to eliminate all Yiddish-language publications; and it imprisoned and executed leading Jewish writers and intellectuals deemed hostile to the regime. But after Stalin's death in 1953, there was a perception internationally that Soviet antisemitism might decrease.

However, in the first years of the 1960s, there was renewed concern that the Soviet Union planned to escalate its repressive efforts against its Jewish population. There were three major reasons for this concern. First, there was a Soviet ban on the baking of matzoh bread for Passover. Second, there was a controversy over whether or not to construct a monument at Babi Yar, a ravine outside of Kiev where a Nazi *Einsatzgruppe* slaughtered tens of thousands of that city's Jews in 1941. Already in 1961, the poet Yevgeni Yevtushenko had achieved international acclaim for his poem about the massacre; now, two years later, the Kiev City Council sought to sidestep the proposal for a memorial by erecting a sports arena instead. And finally, as the Soviet Union confronted an extended period of economic downturn, there was a concern that Soviet authorities intended to scapegoat Jews as a means to divert attention from their own failures. Most distressingly, there were reports in the early 1960s of "economic executions" of individuals (a remarkable percentage of whom were Jewish) convicted of embezzlement.

And yet there was also one additional area of major concern that, at least for some American Jewish observers, seriously outweighed everything else. This concern revolved around a perception that Jews in the United States were exhibiting a tremendous indifference toward the suffering of Jews in the Soviet Union. If this apathetic attitude did not change—and change quickly—many were fearful that Soviet Jewish lives and culture might eventually be eradicated.

The selections in this chapter each address this final concern. Each represents a dramatic appeal to American Jews to recognize the cost of their indifference to the plight of Jews in the Soviet Union. Poet and journalist Judd L. Teller openly expresses his frustration with American Jews who (he indicates) are more concerned with whether or not a local country club will admit them than they are with the plight of millions of their brethren in the Soviet Union. Writer Elie Wiesel's firsthand account of his visit to the Soviet Union in 1966 was widely circulated and discussed. In this brief excerpt, he expresses the fear that time is running out and not enough is being done. Comparable sentiments—as well as a possible solution to the dilemma—are also voiced by Erich Goldhagen, at that time director of the institute of East European Jewish Affairs at Brandeis University.

The final brief selections are taken from *S.O.S. Soviet Jewry,* a mimeographed newsletter distributed by the Student Struggle for Soviet Jewry (SSSJ). Organized in 1964, the SSSJ was the brainchild of Jacob Birnbaum and Glenn Richter, and it was altogether committed to less talk and more direct action and public protest when it came to saving Soviet Jewish lives. As such, the organization's tactics were reflective of a wider culture of student protest during the sixties. SSSJ's many mass demonstrations, vigils, marches, and rallies over the course of the decade were great successes. And the group's slogan, "I am my brother's keeper!" succinctly summarized the attitudes of all who lent their support to the movement to save Soviet Jewry.

American Jews and Soviet Anti-Semitism

JUDD L. TELLER

It is time to reflect on the nature and effectiveness of American-Jewish protest against Soviet anti-Semitism. It is time also to consider why it was not until April, 1964, that a conference was convened to express the indignation of a unanimous American Jewry over Soviet anti-Semitism, although the Soviet campaign against the Jews has been underway at least since 1948. Furthermore, there has been some dragging of feet since the Washington conference. The committee of major Jewish organizations which orchestrates the protests hesitated about the discharge of its commitment to the Washington conference until a blaze of local initiative in communities across the country late last year woke the national committee from its lethargy. In Cleveland, a group of Jewish academicians assumed such initiative some three years before the national bodies convened the Washington conference.

It is worth considering the reasons for the long hiatus between 1948 and April, 1964, and the shorter hiatus between the spring of 1964, when the Washington conference was held and the late fall of that year when the high command named by that conference finally convened a mass rally in Hunter College (capacity 2,500 in a city of two and a half million Jews) and led a candlelight parade to the Soviet U.N. Mission. By pinpointing the causes, it may perhaps be possible to strike down the inhibitions that have impeded action.

The first cause is classical. Respectable Jewish quarters counseled so-called "diplomatic actions" instead of public protest. There were once times of rebellious gallery voices in the councils of American Jewry, the Zionists chief among them. They have become respectable since 1948 when the State of Israel was established. Some Zionists have been sagacious counselors of paralyzing caution on the issue of Soviet anti-Semitism. They have urged subordination of public protest to "diplomacy" lest the Kremlin be provoked into retributive action. Although protests are now sweeping the country, paralleling unpublicized intervention, the advocates of no public action are only in temporary strategic retreat.

There were other inhibitive causes, peculiar to the Soviet situation. Jews cannot help but remember that the Soviet regime, on seizing power, opened opportunities to the Jew that he dared not hope for under Czarist rule. They remember, too, that under Communist rule anti-Semitism became a punishable crime in a country that had been the land of pogroms. Communist effectiveness, in the 1930's, in presenting Moscow as the ostensible steward of the global struggle against Nazism strengthened the impression of Soviet immunity to anti-Semitism. The support of the Kremlin for the Mufti-led attack on Jewish settlements in Palestine in 1929 and in 1936 was interpreted as an ideological war against Zionism and not as anti-Semitism. Moscow support of the Mufti corresponded to the Communist pattern everywhere of supporting arch-reactionaries against democratic forces if this momentarily served the Kremlin purpose. The Stalin-Hitler pact which placed Polish Jewry under Nazi rule and resulted in the expulsion of Jews from high diplomatic and military posts in the Soviet Union, was a traumatic experience which exploded the myth of Soviet immunity to anti-Semitism. But the valiant Soviet resistance to the Nazi invader, and the horrible suffering of the Soviet peoples in that war, restored grandeur to the old myth.

When Stalin, for the first time in Soviet history, launched an outright anti-Semitic drive in 1948, shutting down the Jewish Anti-Fascist Committee and liquidating thousands of Jewish intellectuals, including the most assimilated, this old myth served to camouflage his deeds. Another reason why so many Jews abroad did not believe what was taking place in the U.S.S.R. at the time was that Soviet support of Israel in 1948 seemed inconsistent with reports of anti-Semitism.

These several factors—the caution, the myth, Soviet support of Israel in the U.N.—were evidently still operative and potent in 1953 when an international Jewish conference to protest anti-Semitism was convened in Zurich in reaction to the Kremlin announcement of an alleged "Jewish doctor's plot" to assassinate Stalin and his adjutants through medical mistreatment. At least one major Jewish organization which had reluctantly consented to participate, withdrew from the conference and forced its cancellation just two days before it was to open. The reason was the newsflash from Moscow that the Soviet dictator was dying. The contention was that it would be in bad taste to protest the actions of a dying man, as if Soviet anti-Semitism were a consequence of Stalin's private paranoia and not the outgrowth of domestic and foreign considerations. It was argued that Jewish protests, when his successors were in "mourning," could only provoke them into more violent action against Soviet Jewry. It was also argued that with the eyes of the world focused on the dying man in the Kremlin no one would pay attention to the conference whose purpose was to stir world opinion through maximum publicity. That was an opportunity missed. For it is not at all unlikely that, under the pressure of protest, Stalin's successors, including the anti-Semitic Khrushchev, might have permitted the general thaw also to affect Soviet policy towards Jews.

* * *

There was no unified American Jewish protest on this issue until April, 1964, and there was only arrested impetus thereafter. Fortunately, the protest has now been accelerated, but some of the emphasis by the protestors should be corrected. Priority has been accorded to the religious issue. This priority is mistaken on several counts. The issue should be stressed, of course, because there is a great difference between the persecution of Judaism and that of Christian denominations. Furthermore, religious discrimination affects a relatively small segment of Soviet Jewry. The majority are not religious. The Soviet authorities might find it expedient to concede on this one point: they might, for example, provide more matzohs than are required for next Passover. They might even cease harassing the half-dozen students at the Moscow Yeshiva and continue to fawn upon Chassidic pilgrims from America to the tombs of *tzadikim*. Overemphasis of the religious issue as the primary discrimination practiced against Soviet Jewry does more to create a favorable image of the Jews in American Christian opinion than to relieve the plight of Soviet Jewry. The leaders of American Jewry have enthusiastically endorsed the concept of American society as a Protestant-Catholic-Jewish tripod. They insist that American Jewry is primarily a religious denomination. Their protests present a similar image of Soviet Jewry. It is a false image. East-European Jews, with the exception of the assimilationist segment, always regarded themselves as an ethnic nationality. In municipal and national elections, the Jews offered separate slates of candidates. This was the pattern of all East-European ethnic groups. This was the reason that Soviet Jews were granted Yiddish cultural autonomy. On the other hand, since Communism has branded all religions an "opiate," the Soviet authorities could find ample ideological justification in their scriptures for discriminating against the Jews as a purely religious denomination.

It has also become the habit of some Jewish leaders to deny the existence of Soviet anti-Semitism by distinguishing between the denial of cultural autonomy to the Jews as a group and discrimination against the Jew as an individual. Although they protest against the first, it is still a specious differentiation. That which is now taking place in the U.S.S.R. *is* ordinary anti-Semitism. On his passport, to be used within Soviet Russia, the Jew is compelled to identify himself as a member of the Jewish nationality. Yet he is denied the privileges of nationality. The result is that he can neither be a Jew nor cease being a Jew. Wherever the Jew applies for a job, for school admission or housing he is, because of the ethnic designation in his passport, given secondary consideration. Priority is accorded the "native" ethnic nationals—Ukrainians in the Ukraine, Uzbeks in Uzbekistan, and Russians everywhere in the U.S.S.R. This type of anti-Jewish discrimination is widespread and practiced by the Soviet bureaucracy on all levels.

The majority of U.S. Jewish leadership fortunately calls anti-Semitism by its true name. Yet its emphasis remains confused and confusing. It protests the exclusion of Jews from the Soviet diplomatic corps and the few Jews among the top-defense brass. Yet it has overlooked the multitude of Jews who live in slums and who must wait years before they are allotted an apartment in a new housing project, for example in Kiev, while Galician peasants, unfamiliar with the use of plumbing, are sometimes moved into new apartments within six months after their arrival. It has overlooked discrimination against Jews in the menial occupations. The reason is the socio-economic composition of American-Jewish leadership. It is an upper-bracket leadership. In America, it is concerned with breaking down the bars against Jews in the exclusive country clubs and the resistance to employing Jews in top executive positions by the utilities. It pays no attention to the failure of utilities and banks to hire Jewish clerks and tellers. The same pattern is applied in protesting economic discrimination against Soviet Jews.

If we use the charge of anti-Semitism sparingly, we spare the Soviet authorities serious ideological embarrassment. There is nothing in Communist doctrine to legitimize discrimination against Jews individually because of their ethnic origin. Lenin denounced anti-Semitism. In the early 1930's, even Stalin branded anti-Semitism as a weapon of the foes of the Soviet system. Recent charges of Soviet anti-Semitism have compelled Soviet denials. They have also compelled intervention with the Soviet authorities by Communist parties abroad, but the charge of cultural discrimination has elicited little more than bland excuses.

Considerable ideological basis, however, may be found in the Communist scriptures for denying the Jews the privilege of an ethnic nationality. Marx, Lenin and Stalin have all defined the Jews as a medieval phenomenon that has endured into our own time because of capitalism. Lenin and Stalin contended that only capitalist discrimination has preserved Jewish group identity. All three have argued that Jewry would dissolve under socialism. But Lenin countervened his own Written Law by his Oral Law. Confronted with multitudes of Jews in the Soviet realm who spoke no language but Yiddish, he authorized government-subsidized Yiddish schools, theaters, newspapers and book publishing, and in some areas of White Russia, in the early 1920's, the use of Yiddish in court and municipal proceedings. We shall not discuss here the perverse purposes to which these Yiddish language instrumentalities were bent. Yet their very existence and the designation of Jew on Soviet internal passports confirmed that the Jews were a distinct nationality.

The Crimean and Birobidjan projects, whatever their purpose, were similar confirmations. Thus, from the start, there has been a conflict between Leninist ideology and Leninist practice. It is on the latter that demands for Jewish cultural autonomy are based. It would serve no serious purpose, however, if these demands centered primarily on the restoration of Yiddish publishing. Included also should be Hebrew and Russian-language publications of Jewish interest. Many Soviet Jews neither read nor speak Yiddish yet they seek information on their Jewish identity and ways of expressing that identity. Books, periodicals, theaters and seminars of Jewish content in the Russian language would satisfy their needs. There is a precedent for Hebrew in early Soviet practice. In the early days following the Revolution, Hebrew was taught in Soviet Yiddish secondary schools. Israel's famous Habimah theater, the first Hebrew theater in the world, began its distinguished career on Soviet territory. It is curious that American Jewish organizations stress Yiddish and make only peripheral mention of Hebrew in their resolution protesting Soviet anti-Semitism.

If American Jewish leadership had the courage it would make yet another demand. It would request the Soviet authorities to explain the failure to include a sufficient number of Jews who contributed to Soviet society in war and peace among those for whom Soviet streets and cities are named. Such recognition would prove the simple factor that the Jews in the U.S.S.R. serve Soviet society no less loyally than American Jews serve American society. The purpose of the economic trials and anti-Semitic press agitation is to impale Soviet Jewry on disloyalty charges. However, this would of course impair the carefully nurtured American-Jewish image of Jews everywhere as opposed to Communism.

The demand for the reunion of Soviet Jews with their families in Israel has likewise been accorded relatively low priority on the list of American Jewish demands. This has been defended on the ground that it is one demand the Soviet authorities are least likely to grant. If they will feel compelled by pressure of protests to consider some concessions to the Jews, the Soviet masters will no doubt assess the list of Jewish demands. It is unlikely that they would make the least desirable choice from their viewpoint, if they would find that the Jews have placed matzohs first and exodus, or reunion of families, near the bottom of their list.

Those who claim the mandate of Jewish leadership are under obligation, whatever their ultimate decision, to at least consider a change of emphasis and tactics.

Fear and Heroism

A Visit with Russian Jews

ELIE WIESEL

Since my return from Russia, I am frequently asked whether the position of Soviet Jews is as grave as I visualized. The answer is: "Much worse and yet infinitely better!"

The fear is worse than I expected; so is the sense of isolation, the conviction that the world does not know—and does not want to know of—the overwhelming danger threatening the future of Judaism in Russia. Terrible is the mutual suspicion between people, the endless fear of the informer, the secret agent, the unutterable oppression which people's eyes betray.

My astonishment was therefore the greater that under such conditions masses of Russian Jews everywhere refuse to give up and make mighty efforts to survive as Jews. Everywhere I witnessed their sense of closeness to one another and to all Israel in the synagogues of Moscow, Leningrad, Kiev, Tbilsi and smaller places on the Festivals in particular. Most wonderful of all is the awakening among many young Jews. I shall never forget the experience of being among 30,000 of them outside the Moscow Synagogue on Simchas Torah.

I heard of many acts of heroism. There was the case of the synagogue of Kutasi, Georgia, where a very active Jewish life persists. The authorities attempted to close down one of the three remaining synagogues. When demolition vehicles closed in, large numbers of Jews—men, women and children—lay down in front of the synagogue. No demolition took place.

At this year's Warsaw Ghetto Memorial meeting in the Moscow Synagogue, an old engineer arose and, amidst a most eloquent silence, openly defended the state of Israel and called for a monument at Babi Yar. Gedalye Pecharsky, the leader of the Leningrad synagogue, was imprisoned for his open efforts for Yiddishkeit. He had the nerve to collect signatures asking for a Jewish school—his right under the Soviet constitution. [. . .]

The story is told of a clandestine Mohel who was awakened in the middle of the night by a high army officer, taken from his weeping wife, put in a car blindfolded, ordered to circumcise the officer's recently-born son, presented with 25 rubles and two bottles of vodka and brought home again blindfolded by the officer in a military car.

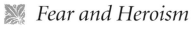

It is barely credible that such people, taking such risks, exist in Russia today. But they do and so I would say that there is far more hope for Russian Jewry than might rationally be expected. [. . .]

On my return flight to Paris, I found myself next to a French Jew who managed to chat with me about every subject imaginable except that of Soviet Jewry. I suddenly asked him where he'd been on Yom Kippur. "In the Leningrad shul," he replied. His pleasant smile froze on his face and then he burst out crying. [. . .]

By reason of our neglect and indifference we are sinning grievously. Would that we could learn from them but a small portion of the self-sacrifice and overwhelming love of Klal Yisroel which I found among them. But *we* do not really want to know. *We* have other worries. Surely, we will one day bitterly regret our apathy, our lack of burning concern—but by then it may be too late.

Soviet Jewry
Range of Repression

ERICH GOLDHAGEN

The Jews of the Soviet Union form the second largest Jewish community in the world. This community, once full of vitality, the source of most modern cultural and religious movements in Jewry, has been reduced by Soviet rule to a state of cultural and religious dessication without parallel among the religious and ethnic minorities of the Soviet Union. Before the Bolshevik Revolution, the Jews of Russia had seven thousand Jewish schools, thousands of rabbis and synagogues, and numerous publications in Hebrew, Yiddish and Russian. Today, the second largest Jewish community in the world is denied even a single Jewish school; the teaching of Hebrew and Yiddish to the young is prohibited by the authorities; the Yiddish theater, abolished in 1948 by Stalin in the course of his destruction of Yiddish arts and letters, has not been revived; and the production of ritual objects, such as prayer shawls and Bibles, is proscribed. The world of Jewish culture and religion in the Soviet Union consists of one literary journal and 62 synagogues. Groups much smaller than the Jews have been afforded richer cultural and religious facilities.

EXTINCTION OF RELIGIOUS LIFE

One may ask wherein is the plight of the Jewish religion graver than that of the Russian Orthodox, the Muslim or the Baptist. Is it not true that the Communist dictatorship constricts all religions under its sway, seeking to hasten the day of their disappearance? But the day of the disappearance of the Russian Orthodox, Baptist and Muslim religious establishments is remote. These are still well established churches, each possessing its own theological seminaries (or access to seminaries abroad), its central organizations, and its publications. They are much less vulnerable than organized Jewish religion, whose extinction in the Soviet Union can be predicted with certainty if the present policies of the Soviet Government continue. There are only forty or fifty rabbis in the Soviet Union whose average age is 65. Their ranks are rapidly diminishing; for unlike the other religions, the Jews have no theological school where young rabbis are trained.

Synagogues, made leaderless, will be closed, and the whole fabric of the Judaic tradition, robbed of its custodians and fosterers, will fall into oblivion. In ten or fifteen years it will be difficult to find within the Soviet Union a man capable of performing a Jewish religious burial ceremony, a Jewish wedding ceremony, or a Bar Mitzvah. For the first time in the history of the Jewish people, the orderly perpetuation of the Judaic heritage will have been broken. Many decades and perhaps generations will elapse before the other religions in the Soviet Union will have reached a state of such gravity. [. . .]

TOKEN CONCESSIONS

The charge of anti-Semitism frequently leveled at the Soviet Union strikes at a sensitive point. It casts a shadow on the pedestal of virtue from which the Soviet leaders denounce ethnic and racial repressions throughout the world. It provides grist for the mills of her enemies; it provokes protests from influential Jewish communities; and it disturbs and perplexes foreign Communists, especially in the Western world, whose unquestioning faith has been so rudely shaken by the revelations of Stalin's crimes. Thus, the restrictions and the denial of cultural facilities tarnish the image of the Soviet Union abroad at a time when it seeks friendship and admiration everywhere in the world. In order to counter the frequent reproaches the regime has made token concessions.

The apprehensions that protests and demands from abroad would worsen the plight of Soviet Jews are unfounded. The restrictive policies spring from Communistic outlook; they are not reprisals for the solicitude shown by foreigners for Soviet Jews. The meager cultural outlets granted by the regime are a tribute to the effectiveness of the influences from the West. Without them the cultural life of Soviet Jewry would be utterly desolate. The voice of Russian Jews has been muted. They can speak only through their brethren abroad.

But are we indeed justified in pinning the label of anti-Semitism on the Soviet Union? To my mind it would not be very profitable to pursue the question of whether the Soviet Government could be properly called "anti-Semitic." The confusion generated by discussions of that question could be dispelled by a precise definition of the word "anti-Semitism." But what is in a name? In imposing upon the treatment of the Jews in the Soviet Union a common label, one obscures its uniqueness—as unique as the Soviet system itself.

Jewish history has known a few regimes that have imposed a total ban on Jewish cultural life; but none has succeeded as thoroughly as the Soviet Government in paralyzing the cultivation and transmission of the cultural heritage of the Jewish community under its sway. The atomization of Soviet Jews is without precedent in the experiences of the Jewish people. Except for an occasional Jewish concert and several scores of synagogues, there is hardly a public place in the Soviet Union where Jews can meet for the purpose of common self-expression. The heavy and ubiquitous hand of the dictatorship isolates the Soviet Jews from one another, thwarting their natural urge to coalesce into a coherent ethnic body. There are 2,500,000 Jews in the Soviet Union, but no Jewish "community."

The picture of the condition of Soviet Jews would, however, be distorted if these dark features were not complemented by some brighter aspects. In many aspects of their physical life the Jews are accorded equality of treatment with non-Jews. The Jewish aged received the pensions due to them as Soviet citizens; medical treatment is dispensed to all without regard for ethnic origin. Elementary and secondary education, though not university education, is provided for Jews and non-Jews alike. It is not so much the Jewish body but the Jewish spirit that is in distress.

POPULAR ANTI-SEMITISM

So far we have discussed the official policies of the regime. Let us now say a word about the popular hostility to Jews and its interaction with the attitude of the leaders. Popular anti-Semitism in the Soviet Union is widespread but not uniform in intensity. It is pervasive, deep-seated and venomous in the Ukraine and the Baltic lands; it is less pronounced in White Russia and still milder in Russia proper. The source on which it feeds is a manifold compound: the anti-Jewish legacy of the Czars; discontent with conditions under the Communist regime which by well-known processes of psychological alchemy is transmitted into hatred of Jews; and the effects of Nazi propaganda in the areas occupied by the Germans during World War II.

In the 1920s the Soviet Government tried to combat anti-Semitism by means of a program of enlightenment. After the ascendancy of Stalin, however, all such enlightenment ceased; condemnations of anti-Semitism by Soviet leaders became rare; and when they were made, they were hurried and almost furtive. The Soviet leaders have even sometimes not shrunk from exploiting anti-Semitism for purposes of state. And it is this exploitation, combined with the lurid campaign against the Jewish religion, that, perhaps inadvertently, fosters the anti-Semitism of the people at large.

Is there a solution to the Jewish problem in the Soviet Union, at once a source of embarrassment to the Soviet leaders and a source of distress to the Soviet Jews? The distress of Soviet Jewry could be relieved by a stroke of the pen of the Soviet authorities, if only the Soviet leaders would shed the idea that Jewishness was an archaic relic to be dissolved rather than a culture to be tolerated within the framework of the Soviet system, if only the Soviet leaders would cease looking upon the Jews through the distorting lenses of ideological preconceptions, if only they would accept what they have hitherto stubbornly resisted on the Jewish question—a portion of reason.

"I Am My Brother's Keeper"

STUDENT STRUGGLE FOR SOVIET JEWRY

Just a few short days ago on the eve of Simchas Torah, tens of thousands of young Russian Jews defied the aura of official anti-semitism which hangs over the USSR to dance and sing, all night long, in front of the Great Moscow Synagogue.

In Riga, at a performance given by the noted Israeli singer Geulah Gil, police tried to prevent Jews from speaking to Miss Gil—and the Jews showed a remarkable resistance.

This resistance is the vanguard of a new hope which has found its way into the hearts and minds of many Russian Jews. To them, there may be a hope for tomorrow.

But what about our own commitment? Do we go, perhaps, to one rally or write one letter, and then think our "duty" is done? Do we say that it is not worth the effort to protest because even though positive change is seen, it is too slow?

Yes, change is slow and it is painful—*but for the first time we have been able to change the official policy of the Soviet Government*. It is not an easy task, but as brethren of those who languish in spiritual and cultural isolation, or even just as human beings, our commitment must never waver.

This coming *SUNDAY, OCTOBER 30th, at 1:30 p.m.*, there will be a massive GRAND CONCOURSE MARCH and RALLY. The MARCH and RALLY, sponsored by the new Bronx Council to Aid Soviet Jewry, will begin at East 167th Street and Grand Concourse, near the YMHA. The East 167th Street stop of the "D" train is very near. The MARCH will end at the Bronx County Courthouse on East 161st Street & Grand Concourse.

The Zamir Choir will lead the march, and among the many noted speakers will be Senator Jacob Javits, Attorney-General Louis Lefkowitz, and a number of congressmen. [. . .]

The MARCH and RALLY is important in another sense. It marks the near-completion of formation of New York regional Councils for Soviet Jewry. The Student Struggle for Soviet Jewry is proud of its crucial role in creating the Bronx Council to Aid Soviet Jewry, under the chairmanship of the noted Rabbi Heschel.

We would like to see all our members and supporters in the New York area at this important event. Bring picket signs; use the usual slogans; use string, no wood. Read the enclosed poster, remember the essential information, and pass it on or post it up in a conspicuous place. Tell everybody you know. For those not in the New York area, use the poster to remind yourself to call up the local radio and T.V. stations and the newspapers to ask them to carry the story.

Enclosed is your sheet of fifty Soviet Jewry seals, the latest effort by the Student Struggle for Soviet Jewry to maintain a continued awareness on the part of an international public of the still-critical situation of the Jew in the Soviet Union. Use these seals on envelopes and books, especially during this Passover season, the Festival of Freedom, so meaningful to Russian Jews.

In the past three years of SSSJ's existence, we have seen a problem that seemed almost forgotten due to lack of information and apathy—only one generation away from the silence of the Thirties—burst into the public recognition as a result of direct action and education by this now-vibrant international student movement. [. . .]

But as SSSJ continues to expand and to arouse others to action, its financial needs daily grow greater than ever. As an example, two of our latest SSSJ affiliate groups have just been established in Chicago, U.S.A. and Jerusalem, Israel.

Your obligation to support a movement that has vowed never to commit the sin of silence is crystal clear.

We urge you to give generously—at the least, a dollar, more if you possibly can—so we may move the world to cry out: "I *am* my brother's keeper!"

Very sincerely yours,

Jacob Birnbaum	Glenn Richter
National Coordinator	N.Y. Coordinator

6

The Jewish Stake in Vietnam

In November 1963, when he took the oath of president of the United States after the assassination of John F. Kennedy, Lyndon B. Johnson inherited a foreign policy that was already on track to further American military involvement in Southeast Asia. But Vietnam did not yet dominate discussion of American foreign policy; when Johnson took office, there were fewer than twenty thousand American troops in Vietnam. Over the course of the next several years, however, Johnson insisted that the United States dramatically intensify its involvement in Vietnam; by the time he left office early in 1969, there were more than half a million American troops in Southeast Asia.

In many respects, the year 1965 represents a critical turning point. It was then that the White House first ordered the massive and systematic bombing campaign against North Vietnam. It was also then that Johnson authorized the first substantial buildup of U.S. ground troops. Before 1965, there was little broad public discussion of (or dissent from) U.S. military policy in Vietnam. After 1965, when Johnson decided to increase exponentially the number of American combatants in Vietnam, there developed also a furious and deeply divided national debate over U.S. involvement in the war.

The essays in this chapter reflect this post-1965 debate as it played out within the American Jewish community. American Jews found themselves at odds with neighbors and friends over this controversy. Hawks and doves alike argued why Jews *in particular* had a special stake in Vietnam. Doves argued that the full-scale air war against North Vietnam was resulting in many innocent civilian deaths and that American soldiers were committing atrocities in a combat zone where it was often impossible to distinguish ally from bystander from enemy. Doves called on Jews to uphold the prophetic tradition of Judaism and demand an immediate cessation of all American military operations and a call for a diplomatic resolution to the conflict.

Hawks argued it was foolish and potentially dangerous to challenge the foreign policy of the president of the United States. Such opposition might jeopardize the administration's support for Israel in the future. Additionally, hawks cited reports that both the Soviet Union and the Palestine Liberation Organization (PLO) were offering (or were planning to offer) military aid to North Vietnam. Thus, to oppose U.S. military involvement in Vietnam was to offer support—even if indirectly—to the sworn opponents of the State of Israel. So far as Jewish hawks were concerned, this was not a risk worth taking.

There was also the specter of the Holocaust. As the selections in this chapter indicate, the Holocaust found its way into the arguments of *both* Jewish hawks and doves. One history came to the service of multiple rhetorical positions.

Writing in 1966, Albert Vorspan, director of the Commission on Social Action for the Union of American Hebrew Congregations (Reform), suggests how difficult it was for some Jewish doves to balance the pros and cons of this conflict. On the one hand, Vorspan raises the analogy between appeasement at Munich and in Vietnam only to dismiss it as absurd. Communism is not comparable to Nazism, Vorspan writes. But he also voices condescension for the student peace movement and suggests that a diplomatic settlement in Vietnam should not mean an immediate withdrawal of U.S. troops.

Also in 1966, Arthur J. Lelyveld and Michael Wyschogrod exchanged opinions on whether Judaism dictated a call for peace in Vietnam. Lelyveld, a prominent Reform rabbi who had been active in the civil rights movement, argues in the affirmative; the struggle for peace in Vietnam follows from the teachings of Jewish tradition. Wyschogrod, a philosophy professor, answers in the negative. In the contribution included here, Wyschogrod argues that Judaism does not automatically translate into a call for peace—or war. (Nonetheless, Wyschogrod would in 1967 write the first defense of the war for *Tradition,* a journal of Orthodox Jewish thought.)

Writing for the *Jewish Press,* an Orthodox newspaper in Brooklyn, Meir Kahane states his case that Vietnam and Israel are inseparable issues. Drumming up a cold war fear that communism seeks the eradication of all Jewish people, Kahane also makes effective use of the Holocaust. While these opinions represent the most right-wing and hawkish elements of the Jewish community, Kahane was no minor figure. He would soon emerge as the national leader of a Jewish vigilante organization: the Jewish Defense League.

In the autumn of 1969, an antiwar demonstration brought more than a half million protesters to Washington, D.C. Organized by the Vietnam Moratorium Committee and the more left-leaning New Mobilization Committee to End the War in Vietnam (New Mobe), the demonstration also saw a significant Jewish student presence. Mike Masch, a reporter for Philadelphia's *Jewish Exponent,* outlines in his newspaper article the many activities during the moratorium organized specifically for Jewish demonstrators. And in the months and years after the moratorium, Jewish antiwar activists began also to distribute widely a "Jewish People's Peace Treaty," a version of which is reprinted here.

Finally, Balfour Brickner's essay from 1970 mourns how successful the Jewish hawks within the Jewish community have been. Brickner strives here to argue once more the importance of an antiwar position for American Jews. He also returns—as did so many—to the subject of the Holocaust.

Vietnam and the Jewish Conscience

ALBERT VORSPAN

At its Biennial Assembly in San Francisco in November, 1965, the Union of American Hebrew Congregations adopted a resolution calling for a cease fire and a political settlement of the war in Vietnam. The following article is an expression of personal opinion with respect to the course of events in Vietnam and we recognize our obligation to publish diverse views on so troubling and controversial an issue. Reactions from readers will appear in forthcoming issues of American Judaism.

Should the American Jewish community, as such, be concerned with the moral issues raised by the growing crisis in Vietnam? The Union of American Hebrew Congregations and the Central Conference of American Rabbis have vigorously answered this question in the affirmative, and Reform Judaism has taken the lead in mobilizing the entire Jewish community to this challenge. For if such issues of war and peace are not within our province, then we reside in the province of Chelm or Never Never Land. There are many grounds for Jewish concern, not the least of which is our stake in maintaining a healthy and vigorous climate of civil liberties in America itself.

If the war in Vietnam continues its spiral of escalation, we may enter a dark and dangerous era in American life in which a spirit of repression and hysteria and hatred will make the McCarthyism of the 50's look, in retrospect, like a mild national aberration. The tension over the Korean conflict spawned the madness of McCarthyism. As I write, we have resumed bombing in North Vietnam and the Security Council of the United Nations is preparing to debate the question. What lies ahead no man can see, but it could well be a storm which would unleash the passions and furies of repression here in the United States. [. . .]

There is another rationale for our concern. It is the Great Society. Despite President Johnson's assurances to the contrary, I fear that an escalated war in Vietnam will also spell the epitaph to the Great Society. Not only are we not rich enough to wipe out poverty, racial ghettos, illiteracy and misery here at the same time that we conduct a protracted major war there, but I believe that an intensification of this war will so brutalize and blunt our moral sensitivity as to drain most of the idealism out of the vision of a Great Society.

I believe that our deepest rationale is the imperative of Judaism itself. Our unique history has made us specialists in the survival of human crisis; indeed, I think this accounts in part for the growing fascination on the part of non-Jews with literature about the mystery of Jews, Judaism and Jewish history. We tend, correctly, to attribute our drive for social justice to Jewish religious values. We explain our position on racial justice in terms of the Judaic concept of the sanctity of the human personality and the equality of all the children of God. Yet the commandment to seek peace, to pursue it, to be messengers of peace unto the nations—that commandment is infinitely more emphatic and unambiguous. It was our prophets who gave the world the vision of universal peace; and our rabbinic literature is an unceasing demand that Jews stand, as co-partners with God, in shaping the messianic vision of a time when nations shall beat their swords into plowshares. But never before in human history have Jews had the freedom and the security and the access to the ears of the world to give universal meaning to this mandate. The insights of Jewish tradition, the lessons of Jewish history, the ethical values of Judaism are acutely relevant, I believe, to an America sick and hungry for values to live by. [...]

One can criticize religion and its place in the social order, but one cannot discount the significance of the Vatican Council schema on war and peace, of Pope John's Pacem in Terris, and especially the moral leadership on this issue which the current Pope of Rome is bringing to bear. The same is true of the statement by the National Council of Churches of Christ, which similarly related a great religious tradition to the issues of our day. Nobody would care what a Jewish bowling club has to say about Vietnam, but I think they do care where Judaism stands, what we at the UAHC said in San Francisco and what the leaders of the three faiths will say when they meet in a conference on religion and peace in Washington. [...]

The Communist monolith is dissolving and dividing before our very eyes, but we cannot seem to lay down the clichés and the slogans which have befogged us for twenty years. And so we proceed on a course which drives Hanoi into the arms of Peking, which impairs the possibility of the Soviet-American détente which could lead to broad areas of settlement, which cannot possibly be resolved by military victory, which earns the fearful trembling but not the support of our allies throughout the world, which wastes American blood and wealth while China has a propaganda field day at our expense while she loses not a single Chinese soldier, and which raises the frightful possibility of a nuclear holocaust. On top of that is the folly of turning revolution over to the Communists who, of course, seek to debase and capture the revolution for their own purposes, while we embrace the hated generals and the keepers of the status quo.

But, we are told, we Jews especially must realize that this is Munich all over again and we must not permit appeasement. In my judgment this is demagoguery and nonsense. Communism and Nazism are both noxious but they are not identical. Rumania, Poland, Yugoslavia are Communist nations as well; they are not our enemies. In 1938, the main force operating against the Czech status quo was an outside force, Hitler's Germany; the major force operating against the status quo in South Vietnam has been an inside force, formed in 1960 into the NLF. The largest outside force in Vietnam is American troops, although North Vietnam pours more regiments into South Vietnam as the war escalates. The Czech government was a stable, strong, democratic government; the South Vietnamese is a dictatorship which we buy, sell and manipulate like puppets on a string. Ho Chi Minh is a ruthless and bloody tyrant, but he is not Hitler. Standing firm in 1938 might have ended the danger of Hitler's Germany. Fighting in Vietnam today, even if we gained total victory which would mean the decimation of all Vietnam, does not even engage our central foes—the Chinese Communists and perhaps the Soviets. To engage what we regard as our real foes would require nuclear bombs, and except for a few Pentagon madmen, we do not seem ready for that. The analogy between Vietnam and Munich is a spurious one; when used to frighten Jews it is a transparent and indefensible piece of demagoguery.

Should we withdraw from Vietnam? No, that is manifestly impossible. We should renew the cessation of bombings in North Vietnam and maintain unceasing quiet diplomatic efforts to get negotiations started among all parties to the conflict, including the Viet Cong, which will lead to a cease fire and an honorable settlement. As a Jewish community, we should speak and act in behalf of peaceful settlement of conflicts, in behalf of all movements in the direction of a world at law, in behalf of all efforts to deal with the poverty and hunger and disease which lie at the root of the revolutionary fever of this age, in behalf of conciliation, negotiation and peace. And, in my opinion, any Jewish agency which speaks out of a Jewish value stance will speak out for precisely these kinds of things. Isn't that a tender-hearted position? Yes. That's what the Jewish position has always been. *Rachmanim, b'nai rachmanim*—merciful sons of the Merciful! Neither America nor the world needs us to join the mob howling for more blood, more bombs, more military power or to develop position papers or strategy and realpolitik. We do not need a Jewish desk of the Rand Corporation. The Communist world is already dehumanized and we are rushing to catch up. No, America and the world need Jews, who are really Jews, to keep man human, to remind us again that man is a precious thing, that there is only one family of man, that the spilling of blood is something more serious than cracking a nut, that he who saves a life saves the world, and that man has a higher destiny than that revealed in the cesspool of Vietnam.

Long after this war disappears into history, the world will still remember the words of the Hebrew prophets of 2000 years ago, pointing the pathways of morality out of the jungle of inhumanity to that day when men will not hurt nor destroy in all this holy mountain. That was our mission in ancient days and it is still our mission today.

Peace
Jewish Imperatives

ARTHUR J. LELYVELD

[. . .] No committed Jew would hesitate to say that absence of compassion, exultation in violence are "un-Jewish." [Yet] we do have our ambivalences. The post-Emancipation Jew has known the influence of modern nationalisms, and our posture of *rachmanut*—compassion—has been warped. We seek a warless world but succumb to the belief that armaments will insure it.

The value-stance of the folk is, therefore, an unreliable guide. Unless it has the anchorage of conviction it is subject to the possibilities of eventual loss. This is why we are searching for imperatives. The search becomes crucial in a world where all violence is attended by ultimate threat—the threat of total extinction—which can be met only by Ultimate Demand—the demand for *kiddush ha-chaim,* the sanctification of life.

This, and not peace, is the supreme value in Judaism. More important than any other abiding determinative of our choices is the recognition that the Divine Presence—*kedusha,* holiness—abides in life itself. Man bears the mark of divinity and whatever depreciates men depreciates the divine image.

Life may be taken only to preserve life or to protect that human dignity which the Divine Presence in life makes supremely precious. Anything else is *chamas*—cruel violence. Modern mass warfare is in the category of *chamas* because it inevitably depreciates life. It inflicts degradation and death on innocent civilians. It results in the enthronement of expedience and the brutalization of human beings who must burn villages and use cruel weapons to exact the casualties of modern war. Those who wage it must put the best face on their actions. Thus, we talk about "our commitment to the government of South Vietnam," when we mean our own puppets of Saigon, while the majority of the South support the National Liberation Front. [. . .]

ULTIMATE EVIL

When we read the history of our involvement in Vietnam the word that comes to mind is *yosher*—the folk-insistence on equity or simple fairness. When we read what is happening to the peasants of South Vietnam, however, we confront that depreciation of life which in the light of our conviction as to its supreme value is intolerable. In the Talmud, the principle of respect for human beings (*k'vod ha'b'riyot*) outweighs every negative command of the Torah.

If this can be said of non-nuclear warfare, then surely the use of nuclear weapons is the ultimate sacrilege. Indeed, obliteration bombing, whether "nuclear" or "tactical," manifests in quantitative terms final disesteem for life.

Here we come face to face with the fact that international conflict has today a totally new qualitative content—what Karl Jaspers calls a "new dimension." The old terminology grows steadily more archaic. A nuclear exchange which would annihilate more than 200 million passive human beings cannot with any continuity of meaning be called "war." A situation of perpetual nuclear threat cannot be called "peace."

This is an example of our use of outmoded terminology to hide from ourselves "the discontinuities created by the atom" (David Riesman). We engage in limited warfare and convince ourselves that we are not marching mindlessly toward the final cataclysm. Yet every day we accommodate ourselves more easily to the thought of indiscriminate civilian extermination. This accommodation has taken place with horrifying rapidity and foretells the possibility of tomorrow's callousness, inconceivable today. The first obliteration bombing of a civilian population took place in 1937 when the Germans bombed Guernica. The entire civilized world responded with horror at this action. Picasso immortalized the nightmare with a great mural. It was an action, we thought, of which only Fascist brutes would be capable. The Second World War gave us the opportunity to grow accustomed to the obliteration bombing of defenseless civilians culminating in Hiroshima and Nagasaki. The psychological mechanisms of denial, distortion and displacement protect us against a realization of nuclear danger—the danger to ourselves and the greater danger that we may stain ourselves with the wholesale murder of others.

There is a new dimension for us as Jews as well. Ultimate Demand speaks differently to us than it did to our great-great-grandfather. Cut off from the larger world, he retained the ideal of mankind's ultimate perfection in his liturgy and in his aspirations and in his obligation under the covenant *l'takaym olam*—"to perfect the world." But the only task that was within his capacity as a Jew was to be faithful, to observe the commandments and to practice *kiddush hashem* in his relationship to the world. He prayed for the time when the just would exult and wickedness would vanish, when God would be King over the earth; but he didn't have to *do* anything about it. The quarrels among kings and princes, the violence and the cruelty, the servitude of the peasants, were all part of the world of the Gentiles—he had no access to it. Even when he recognized that the most stringent troubles were the troubles that affected *both* Israel and the world, he could not but feel that the only action required of him was personal witness and prayer.

We, in contrast, are part of the larger world. We cannot say, "What's Vietnam to me or I to Vietnam?" We are participant, in destiny and in responsibility, with all men. We cannot avoid making judgments—not technical judgments as to the most effective means of achieving certain ends—but judgments of value as to ends and means.

It may be inevitable that institutions such as governments are at times forced to choose the lesser evil. But relevant religion may not make a virtue of such choices lest it be in the class of those who "call evil good and good evil" and begin to prophesy deceits and say smooth things to the state. Rather, the response of religion should be: "Judgment will I lay to the line and righteousness to the plummet."

The judgments that we must lay to the line are those which proceed from the imperatives of the Jewish heritage. They must include, in relation to Vietnam:

1) *Fairness.* Our involvement in Vietnam must be placed in the context of the painfully long struggle of the Vietnamese people for self-government and freedom.
2) *Truth.* We must avoid half-truths and selection of facts and see the situation whole.
3) *Freedom to dissent.* This is a self-evident demand of our heritage. The Congressional hearings are in accord with this imperative.
4) *The continuing search for peace.* Negotiation is the ideal, violence is a defeat. We are told, in the Talmud, to seek peace and pursue it—"Seek it where you are (*bim'kom'cha*) and pursue it everywhere else (*b'makom acher*)." The Administration deserves applause for its effort to bring North Vietnam to the conference table just as it provoked censure by its harsh and incompatible words spoken at Honolulu to those who question our posture in Vietnam.

With all this, it is easier to know what *not* to do than it is to know what to do. The intelligent response of a man who is walking more and more deeply into a fatal maze is to stand still until he finds his direction. Let us, in General Gavin's phrase, "desist" in Vietnam. For this too is an insight from our tradition—"Cease to do evil. Learn to do good." We must cease to do evil before we can learn to do good.

Peace: The Real Imperatives

A Letter to Arthur J. Lelyveld

MICHAEL WYSCHOGROD

Dear Rabbi Lelyveld:

I cannot tell you how difficult it is for me to write this letter.

How can one take exception to a call for peace? And what is more, to a Jewish call for peace? ["Peace: Jewish Imperatives," CONGRESS BI-WEEKLY, March 21] It is not easy for a believing Jew to be reminded of the Mishnah that "he who destroys one human soul is regarded as though he had destroyed a whole world" at a time when our soldiers are engaged in a war that destroys hundreds of human lives every day. Is there a human being on this earth who fails to appreciate the cry raised by the Pope at the United Nations: "No more war"? Please believe, Rabbi Lelyveld, that I share your anguish and anxiety, that my days are as troubled as yours.

But can we leave it at that? You say: "It is easier to know what *not* to do than it is to know what to do." You add: "We must cease to do evil before we can learn to do good." How true! But, also, how vague! Can you blame me for expecting something more specific, something that deals with the realities of the situation, above all, with some specific recommendation?

GENERALITIES AND EVASIONS

Now I know that there are those who would say that this is not the task of a religious leader. Religious leaders lay down moral policy, they remind us of the great moral imperatives and then we leave it to the technicians at the State Department to work out the details. I know that you don't agree with this. Together with the most sensitive and most concerned religious figures of our day you are sick of a religion that dispenses pious platitudes and refuses to come to grips with the real, hard, ambiguous and tragic problems of our day. Religion must grapple with reality or it is not worth preserving. And, of course, I agree with you completely. But if this is so, can we go halfway? Can we escape the responsibility of having to be specific and concrete, well informed and precise, of criticizing a policy only when we have a thought-out alternative that we can offer in its place? If we don't do this, aren't we back at the generalities and the evasions?

But if vagueness were the only problem, I would be only half disturbed. Instead, where you become specific, I regret that you are not more vague. You complain that "we talk about 'our commitment to the government of South Vietnam,' when we mean our own puppets in Saigon, while the majority of the South support the National Liberation Front." Can you state that as plain fact, without qualification or explanation (it is you who speaks of fairness and truth as imperatives of the Jewish heritage)? But let us assume for argument's sake what I wholly deny, that the majority in the South does support the National Liberation Front, does that settle the issue? Didn't the majority of the German people in 1933 support Hitler and the Nazi Party? And if some decent country in those bitter years had shaken off its lethargy and put an end to Nazism in Germany in spite of the German people's support, would not all of mankind be eternally in the debt of that country?

CONFRONTING EVIL

Isn't the basic issue then the nature of Communism? You know as well as I do that when we bombed the cities of Germany we inflicted "degradation and death on innocent civilians" (to use your description of modern mass warfare). All good men weep for every innocent human child killed in the fire raid on Dresden and the assault on Berlin. But the Hitler Moloch had to be destroyed and good men therefore fought, knowing that to do otherwise would have meant becoming an ally of evil, even if from the best of motives. Perhaps you will reply that Communism is not Nazism. If this is your claim, then at least we are discussing *the* issue. Let's face it.

It is true: Communism is not Nazism. Nothing that I know of is. But Nazism was an evil of such magnitude that in its shadow almost all other evils appear puny. Yet they can still be very great evils indeed. Perhaps Soviet Communism no longer is what it was, though for Jews this would become significantly more obvious if Soviet Jews were granted the same rights enjoyed by other ethnic and religious minorities. But Chinese Communism is worse than it was; the one point agreed on by all the Far Eastern experts who recently testified before the Fulbright committee was that the withdrawal of American power from Southeast Asia would create a dangerously unstable situation. It must be remembered that China is the only nation in the world, as far as I know, that contemplates the possibility of nuclear war with some degree of equanimity. It has said so for the record.

I must finally say a word about the Jewish tradition which you find inconsistent in its attitude toward war and peace but in which we must distinguish "between that which is normative . . . and that which is atypical." If your conclusion is—though you are not really clear on this point—that normative

Judaism stands for pacifism and the rest is atypical, you are simply not right. Judaism abhors war but it also considers it necessary to wage war against evil when there is no other way to contain it. I find nothing inconsistent in this attitude.

The way of Israel is the way of peace. In this atomic age it must be the way of all men if the human race is to survive. We must therefore never cease our search for peace, patiently waiting for the day when Asian Communism will have learned the lesson that Soviet Communism seems, we pray, already to have learned: that its power cannot be extended by force of arms. But until that day comes, we must continue, with fear and trembling, to shoulder the responsibilities history has thrust upon us. If by our deeds and words we give Peking and Hanoi the impression that in a showdown we will back down, much of the responsibility for the ensuing inevitable catastrophe will be ours. And that must not happen.

As Jews, we cannot be hawks. But neither can we be doves—we must be men.

The Jewish Stake in Vietnam

MEIR KAHANE

United States forces are today fighting in Vietnam to check Communist aggression. All Americans have a stake in this grim war but Jews have a very special interest in the successful outcome of this struggle. For, wherever the Communist machine achieves power, not only are political, social and economic rights swept away, but spiritual persecution is inevitable and mercilessly practiced. Because of this, it is vital that the Jew realize the danger to his very survival as a free human being should Communism ever achieve victory. He should know that Judaism will be mercilessly attacked and his children torn from their faith. He should know that the State of Israel is a bitter target of the Communists in general and the Chinese and Vietcong in particular. The JEWISH PRESS, in line with its policy of alerting America to the dangers of totalitarianism from Right and Left, is writing a comprehensive series on The Struggle For Freedom In Vietnam. The writer of the series aside from being a regular contributor to the JEWISH PRESS, is also chairman of the American Jewish Friends of Vietnam and an expert on Communist threats to democracy and religious freedom.

It has not been a good two weeks for the opponents of United States efforts to defend the integrity of a small country in Southeast Asia and live up to its commitments. It was just a few weeks ago, on May 24, that a letter appeared in the New York Post from someone named Ben Marcus. It read, in part:

> **"We peacenicks . . . are really the ones who support the boys in Vietnam. We would like them to come home to a normal life, not to be killed IN SOME HALF-COUNTRY IN EASTERN ASIA." (boldface ours).**

The contemptuous phrase "some half-country"; so reminiscent of the isolationist slogan opposing war with Hitler, "who wants to die for Danzig?" apparently makes the point that small nations—"half-countries" are not worth dying for. Indeed this point is one that is raised over and over again by opponents of the war:

> **"Why should we die for some small country halfway around the world that we never heard of and with whom we have no ties?"**

Of course, once upon a time very few people heard of places as Guadalcanal or Iwo Jima or El Alamein or Bastogne. They, too, might have been excused for asking what these places had to do with people in New York or San Francisco or Kansas City. With hindsight we can now look back and realize that, in those places, in the battles that were fought there and where thousands of Americans died, freedom and civilization were preserved from the hands of the Nazi and fascist hordes. It was these places—less than half-countries these miserable islands and deserts, which helped guarantee that the spirit of Auschwitz would not be able to claim more than the six million Jews it did.

A little later, very few Americans had heard of places as Seoul and Inchon or Yalu. Today, they go down in the history of our time as landmarks in the struggle for Korean freedom. Is there anyone—aside from the know-nothing Marxist—who disputes the fact that the courage of an American President, Harry S. Truman, in going against the outraged protests of the pacifists of 1950 and sending American troops to stop the North Korean hordes, prevented Communism from swallowing up another "half country" and stopped Communist domination of the Far East?

The point, quite obviously, is that for people who pretend to don the mantle of morality and who were indignant at President Lyndon Johnson for daring to use force in Vietnam, the argument that "half-countries" are not worth dying for is as morally reprehensible as it is politically naive.

The history of aggression demonstrates quite graphically that the tyrant's meal begins with tiny or "half" countries. Adolph Hitler did not begin his aggression with "whole" or great countries. It was the Rhineland and the Saar and a small Austria and a tiny Danzig that first felt the hot breath of his aggressive appetite. They were testing grounds for the madman of Berlin, to see how far he could count on fearful people who sought to buy peace and security for themselves at the expense of the "half-country." He learned, to his delight, that there were a great many such people who were prepared to sell out a great many other people and he correctly foresaw that Munich was an integral part of the spiritual baggage of the pacifist and the fearful.

In the end, of course, not only have such people been guilty of moral bankruptcy but they did not even have the satisfaction of enjoying the peace they thought they had bought for themselves. For they learned to their sorrow that the more one appeases the aggressor the more his appetite is whetted. In the end, they had to go to war anyhow; in the end their sons and daughters died anyhow; the difference was, that, having waited and allowed the aggressor to gain time and strength and resources, the war was infinitely more bitter, eternally more desperate.

No country is a half-country morally; no country is unworthy of being protected from an international aggression which looks upon every "war of national liberation" as part of a world-scheme which would make a universal hell of the earth.

Certainly, we Jews stand in sorrowful and fearful realization of all this today. As the Arab hordes, urged on by their Communist patrons so eager to destroy yet another democratic world outpost, threaten the existence of the State of Israel, we urge and we demand that the force of the free world be brought to bear in defense of the Jewish State. We demand this despite the fact that Israel might very well be called a "half-country," both because of its size and the fact that, like South Vietnam it is a product of partition. We demand this despite the fact that it might be argued that millions of Americans have never heard of such places as Bnei Brak of Netanya or Mishmar Ha Emek. The point is an irrelevant one. A small nation, a small people is at the mercy of saboteurs and terrorists—it deserves to be saved this fate. A small nation is threatened with extinction by its neighbor and by guerrilla bands who claim that the land is theirs. It should be saved. Morally this is the only stand a person of integrity can take. Practically, it is the only foreign policy that great nations who wish to remain free themselves, can follow.

The principle of great power intervention on behalf of the small state is one that all men of justice must fight for—IN ISRAEL AND IN VIETNAM.

Those of us—the great majority of American Jews—who have backed President Johnson throughout in his Vietnam policy—stand sincerely and unashamedly and staunchly in our demands that he do no less for the State of Israel. [. . .] For the Ben Marcuses and other misguided ones there is only one course. To confess their moral and political sins so that they, too, can join the Jewish people AND ALL OTHER AMERICANS who desire justice, in demanding that their chief executive continue the struggle for world freedom through the defense of the "half-state" of Israel.

Anti-War Marchers Turn Out En Masse in Washington

MIKE MASCH

Washington, D.C.—One of the many remarkable aspects of the anti-war activity which took place here this past weekend was the unprecedented amount of support and participation it enjoyed from the Jewish community. Certainly there have been many Jews, especially college students, taking part in such demonstrations previously as individuals, but never before was such an organized Jewish presence felt.

Types of support and activity varied, of course. Some groups, such as the Washington Board of Rabbis and the American Jewish Congress, contented themselves with a verbal endorsement of the Nov. 15 march. Most synagogues in the area held special services Friday night and Saturday morning relating to the theme of peace. [. . .]

Without a doubt the most impressive program of the weekend was the Jewish Movement Center established and staffed by the National Jewish Organizing Project. The NJOP is a confederation of Jewish activist groups from several cities, including Jews for Urban Justice in Washington, the New York Jewish Organizing Project, and Na'aseh in Philadelphia.

The NJOP tried without success to obtain a Jewish site for the Movement Center, but received a chilly response from the leaders of the Washington Jewish community, who were apparently willing to house kids who were coming to the march anyway but were more reluctant to allow their own facilities to be used for anti-war activities. As a result the NJOP was forced to take advantage of an offer of assistance from the more progressive elements in the Christian community and the Jewish Movement Center was set up in the Christ Methodist Church.

The Jewish Movement Center was an integral part of the Mobilization (New Mobe) plan for handling the fantastic number of marchers who flooded the city Thursday and Friday. There were 25 such centers in all, run by such diverse groups as the Resistance, Federal Employees against the War, SDS, Clergy and Laymen Concerned, the Conspiracy 8, Vets for Peace and the Southern Christian Leadership Conference.

These centers provided information and special programs on just about every aspect of the war and the protest movement. As thousands of anti-war demonstrators swept into the city, they were directed to the New Mobe's four delegate reception centers where they could obtain maps, hot coffee, housing, medical aid, and just about anything else they needed.

BUSES TO ARLINGTON

The reception centers were also the staging areas for the March against Death, a 38-hour procession of more than 40,000 demonstrators, each one of them carrying the name of an American soldier who died in Vietnam or the name of a destroyed Vietnamese village. Shuttle buses took marchers from the reception centers to Arlington Cemetery. There the long winding solemn line began to bend its way to the Capitol, where the placards with their tragic contents were deposited into a dozen coffins.

Activities began at the Jewish Movement Center early Friday evening, while the March against Death was still going on. An Orthodox minyan started off the evening, followed by a communal dinner in which everyone shared what food they had brought. A creative Sabbath service, whose emphasis was on peace, led off the evening program. It was conducted by Danny Siegel, leader of Na'aseh and a student at Philadelphia's Reconstructionist Rabbinical College.

The Oneg Shabbat at the center was to have featured a panel discussion on "Jewish Tradition, the War and the Draft" conducted by Arthur Waskow, from Jews for Urban Justice; Burton Weiss, from the Jewish Peace Fellowship; Bob Greenblatt, from the New York Havurah; and Rabbi Everett Gendler, from Brandeis University. However, just as this was getting underway word was received that there had been violence up at DuPont Circle. Consternation and dismay broke out among the several hundred people that had come to the center by that time. [. . .]

As it turned out, the incident was not as serious as it first appeared. What actually had happened was that the Contingent in Solidarity with the Vietnamese People, a ragtag assortment of radicals including some members of the various factions of SDS, the Black Panthers and other militant groups, had attempted to march on the Saigon Embassy and, for the most part, were dispersed by the police with relatively little violence.

Despite reassurances that this was the case the people at the center still felt it in order to do something to reaffirm their commitment to having a nonviolent march Saturday and to express their disapproval of incidents of violence on the part of either police or demonstrators.

A number of suggestions were made, and finally it was agreed that the NJOP group would take part in the March against Death as a symbolic protest and as an expression of support of the New Mobe's non-violent policy. [. . .]

The mood was more cheerful Saturday morning as hundreds of thousands of people assembled in the mall for the major activity of the weekend. The crowd was enormous, stretching far beyond the line of vision. Besides the National Jewish Organizing Project, groups that marched included the Jewish Liberation Project, the Labor Zionist youth group Habonim, radical Jewish student groups from Columbia, Brandeis and the University of Wisconsin, and students from all the seminaries, including the two new experimental ones, the New York Havurah and Havurat Shalom in Boston.

The Saturday evening program at the Movement Center included workshops on the Middle East; the Jewish community and racism; Havurah, community and counter-institutions; Jewish education; organizing in the Jewish community; and creative resistance. The workshops were followed by a M'alava Malka and Tikun Hatzot.

TO WHITE HOUSE

The main event of the NJOP program took place Sunday morning. Due to the fact that it applied for it early, the NJOP was the only group in Washington that had been able to obtain a permit to march in front of the White House, and march they did, about 150 Jewish radicals, some in *talit,* others blowing *shoferot* and singing songs like *Lo Yisah Goy el Goy Herev* ("Nation shall not lift up sword against nation; neither shall they learn war anymore"—from Isaiah).

Once at the White House they held a brief *Yizkor* service. Then Weiss introduced the first of three symbolic blowings of the shofar.

"Although we are here for the purposes of peace," he explained, "we should remember that the blowing of the shofar was also a call to war. It was a way of waking people up and calling them to war against idolators and false gods. In America today the false gods are the images of material powers—the god of money, the god of war and the god of technology—a rampant technology that has nothing to do with human needs. Our children and our young men and women are sacrificed to these."

With that the shofar was blown as the demonstrators proceeded to destroy a dollar-sign strewn "golden calf" specially constructed for the occasion and to smash a number of war toys.

"Besides being blown to issue the call to war," continued Danny Siegel, "the shofar is blown in Jewish tradition to initiate a call to fast." He then went on to issue, in the name of the Jewish Organizing Project, a call for a one-day fast for all Jews on the first day of the December Moratorium.

Waskow, who was the author of the controversial "Freedom Seder" printed in *Ramparts* last spring, introduced the third shofar blast: "It is said that the shofar will also be blown to usher in the redemption of mankind, the days of the Messiah, an age of peace and justice. Yesterday we celebrated the Sabbath, the day which is supposed to be the prefiguration of the days of the Messiah. Yet we had that day only among ourselves—in Vietnam the bombs kept falling, the people of the ghettoes of Washington were still being eaten by rats, the air was still being poisoned. So we are not yet ready to welcome the Messiah. But let us instead welcome the struggle which will *bring* the Messiah."

With that, the group began marching around in front of the White House. There was some speculation on the seventh time around "the walls would come tumbling down." Alas, such an event failed to occur and the group had to content itself with a few rousing choruses of "Joshua Fought the Battle of Jericho."

What they, and the hundreds of thousands of other people who came to Washington, had accomplished in terms of influencing the President's Vietnam policy is, of course, moot. But if their presence did not have an immediate effect on the U.S. Government, it had a very great one on the many Jewish college students who participated. It showed them that there is a very real alternative to the kind of Judaism they had known from their parents. It is certain that this first appearance of the Jewish radical movement will not be its last.

Jewish People's Peace Treaty

We, the undersigned organizations and individuals who are members of the Jewish People in the United States, are committed as Jews and Americans to live in peace with the peoples of Indo-China. We now live subject to the laws of the U.S. government that compel our support for a war against the peoples of Indo-China, but our beliefs and traditions as Jews impel us to separate ourselves from that war. Moreover, we believe that by creating a vigorous, meaningful, and unalienated Jewish community in America, we will not only be freeing ourselves to live out our deepest needs, but making less likely in the future the use of the power of the United States government in unjust and murderous ways. For these reasons we support the adoption by Jews in the United States of this Joint Treaty of Peace, as well as its adoption by all other Americans.

We ourselves shall beat our swords into plowshares, our spears into pruning hooks, and we ourselves shall undo the thongs of the yoke and let the oppressed go free.

1. The Americans agree to immediate and total withdrawal from Vietnam and publicly to set the date by which all American forces will be removed. The Vietnamese pledge that as soon as the U.S. Government publicly sets a date for total withdrawal:
2. They will enter discussions to secure the release of all American prisoners, including pilots captured while bombing North Vietnam.
3. There will be an immediate cease-fire between U.S. forces and those led by the Provisional Revolutionary Government of South Vietnam.
4. They will enter discussions of the procedures to guarantee the safety of all withdrawing troops.
5. The Americans pledge to end the imposition of Thieu, Ky, and Khiem on the people of South Vietnam in order to insure their right to self-determination and so that all political prisoners can be released.
6. The Vietnamese pledge to form a provisional coalition government to organize democratic elections. All parties agree to respect the results of elections in which all South Vietnamese can participate freely without the presence of any foreign troops.
7. The South Vietnamese pledge to enter discussion of procedures to guarantee the safety and political freedom of those South Vietnamese who have collaborated with the U.S. or with the U.S. supported regime.

8. The Americans and Vietnamese agree to respect the independence, peace and neutrality of Laos and Cambodia in accord with the 1954 and 1962 Geneva conventions and not to interfere in the internal affairs of these two countries.
9. Upon these points of agreement, we pledge to end the war and resolve all other questions in the spirit of self-determination and mutual respect for the independence and political freedom of the people of Vietnam and the United States.

By ratifying the agreement, we pledge to take whatever actions are appropriate to implement the terms of this joint Treaty and to insure its acceptance by the government of the United States.

Q. Well, I'm against the war, of course, but why is it *Jewish* to be against the war?

A. The most important fact about being Jewish is that Jews ought not to separate religious and ethical commitments, on the one hand, from politics or everyday life, on the other. Jewishness at its best is a whole life process, and the war is part of our daily lives. (For example, all of us pay for it through taxes even if we speak out against it.) So if we're committed to being Jewish, then dealing with the war is part of being Jewish—we can't just feel we're Jewish on Yom Kippur.

Admittedly, this is Jewishness *at its best*—not the way we have often practiced it in America. But we think the separation between being "Jewish"—that's for Yom Kippur—and being "people"—that's for all the rest of the time—is one of the reasons our lives are so empty. It's also one of the reasons we haven't stopped the war yet—because we act as if being "Jewish"—that is, having religious and moral commitments about the war—is just something for Moratorium Day, while being "Americans" or "people"—that is, paying for the war and not making trouble—is what we should do all the rest of the time. It's clear now we're never going to stop the war *that* way. So we think that because the Treaty pledges us to be at peace with the Vietnamese people in our daily lives, the Treaty is both a step in reconnecting our whole lives to a sense of being Jewish, and a step toward ending the war. We don't think those two goals are contradictory: we think the war will end a lot quicker if Jews get themselves together, along with other peoples, to end it; and we think Jews will get themselves together as a community with a whole life process that is Jewish, if we try to incorporate peace with the Vietnamese, instead of war against the Vietnamese, into our daily lives.

A2. Jews have good reason to support the whole "Nuremberg idea" which came out of World War II, of preventing war crimes like the ones the Nazis perpetrated on us. Yet here our own government is not only letting things like My Lai happen but is making a *policy* out of burning whole countrysides from the air, forcibly moving whole towns into concentration camps, etc.

What's worse, that policy makes all of us morally responsible, and some of us maybe even legally responsible, for those war crimes.

Q. But won't signing this as Jews make Mr. Nixon less willing to give Israel the support she needs?

A. Mr. Nixon makes up his mind on the Middle East on the basis of what he thinks will most benefit the political and financial interests of the U.S. government and some major private companies. He doesn't support Israel for the reasons most Jews do, and he doesn't support her just to be nice to the Jews. If he changes his mind it will be a result of his thinking the situation in the Middle East has changed—not us.

Let's remember that living here in the Diaspora, we have our own obligations to Judaism—just as Jews in Israel have theirs. Those obligations are timeless—they don't stop because of a particular political situation, and they don't just apply to Jews. We have an obligation to struggle for justice and freedom for Israelis, but also for the Vietnamese. Is not their blood as red as ours? Or as Hillel said, "If we are not for ourselves, who will be? But if we are for ourselves only, what are we?"

Q. Isn't the war winding down? Why go ahead with this now?

A. The war is spreading out. It is already the longest war in U.S. history. To quote Hillel again: "If not now, when?"

Vietnam and the Jewish Community

BALFOUR BRICKNER

American Jewry seems to be caught in a conflict of interests. As a result, many American Jewish "peaceniks" who only a few months ago were conspicuously vocal in opposition to their government's conduct of the war in Vietnam now seem to have lost their tongues, silenced by a fear—whether imagined or real—that such criticisms might jeopardize American political or military support for Israel. By subtly suggesting that this support might erode if American Jews continue vigorously to oppose the war in Vietnam, the Nixon administration has as cleverly neutralized the Jewish community as it has effectively outmaneuvered the peace movement.

Strategically, President Nixon seems to be winning on both fronts. The loss of momentum within the peace movement is obvious. And the silence of Jewish spokesmen is deafening. Only two national Jewish organizations, the Union of American Hebrew Congregations and the American Jewish Congress, have refused to succumb to the threats and pressures. Their statements have not endeared them to the rank and file of American Jewry; indeed they have been almost totally ignored. Instead of realizing that the right to protest is the one option remaining by which to protect Israel, unfortunately the majority of American Jews and the preponderance of American Jewish organizations have seen the situation in just the opposite way, accepting the logic that a moratorium on American Jewish criticism of our government's conduct of the Vietnam war is good for Israel.

One wonders how to put things right side up. Should we again recite the sad, sordid story of how the United States first got involved in Vietnam, should we describe the contortions that administrations past and present have gone through in an effort to obtain the American people's sanction of that involvement? It all seems like ancient history—or worse, a nightmare of sophomoric logic and twisted rationalizations designed to capture the passions of uninformed citizens too many of whom reduce arguments concerning national policy to such neat simplicities as "America: love it or leave it."

The plain fact is that there is no legitimatizing our involvement in Vietnam. Neither legal nor moral nor practical considerations justify what we have done or what we are now doing there. Slowly the American people are coming to see all this, but it has taken a painfully long time. What intellectuals, students and some members of the religious community saw three or four years ago, the "average American" is now beginning to see—or is now being allowed to see (depending on how one evaluates how the news is brought to the people). A growing number of Americans now agree that the war in Vietnam was and is a terrible mistake.

Tragically, the war has cost us far more than money. Our nativistic penchant for simplistic patriotism, our adolescent propensity to "put our faith in our leaders" who "know much more than we do," has cost the nation the lives of more than 45,000 of its precious youth. Most of these men came from black and "Middle American" families—sons of people who because of or in spite of their limited intellectual capacities, their lack of social sophistication, have traditionally been the most avid supporters of the "my country right or wrong" ideology. What a cruel hoax has been played on them and on their children.

But the war has cost more than money and life. It may well be costing us a considerable part of our souls. The disclosure of what may have occurred at My Lai; the recurring "revelations" regarding our soldiers' capacity for indiscriminate murder, rape and even torture; the contempt that so many of our "boys" overseas exhibit for "gooks," "geeks" and "yellow bellies," as if Asians were not human beings (or at least not humans equal to Americans); the way we back home seem overly ready to discredit the reports of how our sons comport themselves—all this seems to suggest that the iron fist may have replaced idealism in our view of things, that brutality may have pre-empted our traditional commitment to giving bread to the hungry, shelter to the homeless, clothing to the naked. For "prestige of the spirit" we are substituting an acceptance if not a glorification of adolescent pugnacity, of violent confrontation at home as well as abroad, and we are beginning to tell ourselves that such violence is "as American as apple pie." What we rejected from the mouth of Rap Brown as he sought to justify black militancy, we accept as a fact of life when we seek to explain and justify white militarism. The costs are too high—in terms of the lives of our youth, the health of our economy, our credibility abroad and the trauma being suffered by our national psyche. Such heavy costs indicate that we are committing spiritual suicide by remaining in Vietnam. [. . .]

How would we as a nation fare were we to be judged by the Nuremberg principles we imposed on the Germans in 1945? What has happened to our national conscience when we apparently can endorse the "acting under orders" rationale we utterly condemned in 1945? What has happened to our ability to discriminate between right and wrong when an action is viewed as wrong if engaged in by our enemies, while a similar action involving our side is viewed as tolerable or as something to be dismissed with the cliché "war is hell"? What is happening to us when, as a consequence of the war, dissent becomes treason, criticism is equated with disloyalty, patriotism is measured by whether or not one sent a supporting letter to the President after his November 3 speech, and the President boasts of watching a football game in the White House the day half a million Americans peacefully protested for peace outside his door? [. . .]

By our silence we implicitly accede to those who suggest that a valid analogy obtains between the situation in Israel and that in Vietnam. Nothing could be further from the truth. The war in Vietnam is a civil war in which an unstable, unpopular government is being supported by the U.S. government; unbidden by the populace, we have interceded in behalf of one of the contestants in that civil war. The imbroglio between Israel and her Arab neighbors can hardly be so described. In the latter instance Israel, a stable democratic government, having the full support of the populace, is fighting for her life against a coalition of nations which, in violation of every international agreement, is intent on wiping her off the face of the map. Israel seeks only to repel an external aggression directed against her very existence.

Moreover, unlike the government of South Vietnam, Israel has not asked for the intervention of foreign troops on her soil. To the contrary, she has explicitly rejected any such proposal. All Israel asks of the United States and the other world powers is that they stand by their historic pledges to defend a nation's right to exist as a sovereign state under provisions of the United Nations Charter. [. . .]

There is, then, no analogy between Israel and Vietnam. Rabbi Solomon Sharfman, president of the Synagogue Council of America, was courageous enough to make that point when on December 8, 1969, he criticized "public statements [contending] that Jews who are critical of the administration's policy in Vietnam are doing a disservice to Israel." Vietnam and the Middle East are different problems requiring separate and different solutions. The Vietnam war must not be used as a club with which to beat into silence those in the American Jewish community who, seeing the absence of any analogy, are critically impatient with their government for continuing its presence in Vietnam, while at the same time they are equally critical and impatient whenever their government exhibits any tendency to reverse its historic commitment to Israel's survival. [. . .]

Admittedly the American Jewish community is in a difficult situation, but it is not yet in a bind. It will end up in a bind, however, if it gives up its right to be independent—to be critical, if need be, of its own government, of Israel, of itself. It will find itself discredited by the other American communities with which it must work and unheeded by its government, which will look on it as merely a group of special pleaders whose loyalties if not allegiances are subject to question. Just as we must not permit ourselves to be the puppet of any foreign group or government that seeks to manipulate us, so we must never give up our right to dissent from our government's policies when we feel dissent is warranted. Such independence requires that we become sophisticated, critical political acrobats; but that is precisely what is needed now. Balance is the most difficult facet of courage—and these are days that call us to be courageous.

7

After the Six-Day War

After three weeks of heightening tensions, Israel was attacked by Arab nations on the morning of June 5, 1967. More than four hundred thousand Egyptian, Syrian, and Jordanian troops amassed against Israeli positions. And yet, principally as a result of a remarkably efficient air campaign, the Israel Defense Forces quickly gained a decisive strategic advantage. Within three days, Israeli troops captured the Gaza Strip and the West Bank. On June 8, Israel took the Sinai, and Egypt surrendered. On June 10, Syria agreed to a cease-fire but continued shelling until Israel took the whole of the Golan Heights. On the evening of June 10, the war officially ended.

Despite Israel's swift victory over its opponents, most American Jews were deeply shaken by the experience of the Six-Day War. It reawakened terrible memories of the Holocaust; at that time, few nations had responded to the plight of Europe's Jews. Now American Jews responded fervently—and generously—to help save Israel from aggressors.

In the wake of the war, many American Jews unabashedly celebrated the tough military might of the Israel Defense Forces. Moshe Dayan, who had led the IDF to victory, became a folk hero for Jews around the world. In this way, the brilliant success of the Israeli army was—also—a magnificent (if vicarious) means finally to crush the old stereotype of the scrawny and neurotic Jewish man unable to defend himself against a bully (an image soon ironically popularized in the early comedic films by Woody Allen). The victory was as well read by some as a sort of divine expression that Israel would both survive and triumph over all who sought to destroy it. Feelings of anxiety and adulation, chauvinism and pride, commingled for many American Jews after June 1967.

The war was brief, but its consequences on American Jewry have been long-lasting. It was with this war that the Israeli government assumed control of huge swaths of Palestinian land—land it occupies to this day. It was also here that increasingly deep fissures emerged in the traditional American Jewish liberal consensus. To be sure, such a consensus was largely chimerical before 1967;

however, in the wake of the Six-Day War it was no longer possible to ignore the fact that more and more influential Jewish leaders were abandoning their liberalism only to embrace values that would soon earn the new label "neo-conservative."

The four selections in this chapter are all responses—in ways both direct and indirect—to the events of June 1967 in the Middle East. M. Jay Rosenberg's eloquent—and harrowing—account of his experiences as a college student affiliated with the New Left both before and after the Six-Day War captures well the sense of dilemma many young Jewish radicals felt. Alienated from their Jewishness before 1967, many young Jews rediscovered their heritage (albeit revised) after the June war. The difficulty was how to reconcile a left-wing outlook with a Zionist perspective, especially since so many on the American Left rejected Zionism as a form of imperialism. Steven S. Schwarzschild's contribution, by contrast, is more concerned to warn about the dangers of triumphalism in the aftermath of war. Invoking the lessons and legacies of the six million Jewish lives lost in the Holocaust, Schwarzschild outlines in painstaking detail the moral bankruptcy of any position that exults in militarism or concludes that the Israeli victory represents a sort of payback for the Shoah.

Sharon Rose's essay, meanwhile, articulates a dilemma that resembles Rosenberg's. Yet she arrives at an utterly dissimilar analysis. Her call for a binational, democratic, and secular state in Israel remains unanswered more than a generation later.

The final selection is by Balfour Brickner, a member of an older generation of Zionists. Attempting to balance a love for Israel with his frustration at its actions, Brickner also speaks plainly about his sense of alienation from an American Jewish community increasingly hesitant to take any stand that might contradict official Israeli policy. Brickner cites examples of instances when American Jewish groups worked actively to stifle the right to dissent when the topic turned to Israeli affairs.

My Evolution as a Jew

M. JAY ROSENBERG

Born in Brooklyn, raised in upstate New York, I had very little Jewish consciousness prior to June 1967. My family is not religious and I had only the most superficial Jewish education. Even that ended when I was thirteen. My parents, born in Midwest America, were not involved in Jewish causes. They supported Israel but not actively. They were certainly not Zionists. They came out of the various internationalist socialist movements of the nineteen thirties, and, until the very late sixties were true to their origins. The patron saints of our household were Norman Thomas, Henry Wallace, Adlai Stevenson and, of course, Mrs. Roosevelt. My parents were left-liberals in the nineteen forties and they are liberals now. I was brought up on "New York Post" liberalism. *That* is my heritage.

Intensely political, I came of age in the non-Jewish world that exists ninety miles north of Times Square. My causes paralleled those of my parents. At thirteen, I was bitter at Adlai Stevenson's Los Angeles defeat by John F. Kennedy. But I rang doorbells for the Massachusetts Senator and rejoiced in his election. In high school I was outraged by my classmates' indifference to the civil rights struggle. Birmingham, the Alabama "freedom rides," and the August nineteen sixty-three "March on Washington" made me realize that there would have to be some drastic changes in this country. In November of that year, I was crushed by the murder of President Kennedy, the instrument of all my hopes for the future. By the time I began college in nineteen sixty-five, I was actively opposing the war in Viet Nam.

Those were quiet and disheartening days at the State University of New York at Albany. I was one of, at the most, two dozen kids who composed the anti-war movement at State. The one pervasive feeling was that of isolation. Nobody really cared about the war despite the two thousand American dead. Viet Nam was just not an issue. I wrote articles, marched, and fasted with the Quakers. Our group was spat upon, heckled and denounced by everyone. The rest of the campus went to fraternity beer parties.

It was not until April nineteen sixty-seven that a substantial minority at the State University swung into the anti-war cause. Though not as fashionable as we were later to become, our group was able to send five buses to the Spring Mobilization in New York. And nationally, Martin Luther King was now on our side. We radicals were to be vindicated.

The campus was quiet in late May nineteen sixty-seven. Exams were approaching and we all were desperately trying to make up for the fact that we hadn't studied all semester. Our anti-war booth was closed for the year. Our last demonstration was against General Maxwell Taylor who was speaking in Albany. Afterwards we turned to our books and our thoughts were on summer jobs.

However, my attention was focused on another front, the Middle East. The *Times* was reporting ominous news about the Straits of Tiran, about nooses tightening around Israel's neck, about imminent war. One evening during the exam period I took a half hour break to watch the seven o'clock news. One filmed report from Baghdad showed Arabs demonstrating in the streets of the city. "Haifa, Jaffa, Tel Aviv," they chanted. It was chilling. Logistical charts showed that Israel could be in serious trouble. One gentile boy turned to his Jewish companion and remarked, "You Jews are really going to be creamed this time." They laughed. I was scared.

At that time I would have denied that I was reacting as a Jew. I was a radical, a democrat, of course an American and "everyone" supported Israel, didn't they. As for myself, I didn't know much about the political situation in the Middle East. In fact, I did not even know that Jerusalem was a divided city. But despite my ignorance of the political realities, I felt for Israel. It was not until later that I understood why.

School ended and I went home. In a week I was to start work at Old Westbury, Long Island as a student assistant to Harris Wofford of the Peace Corps who was planning a new university. The Middle East seemed to quiet down. On Monday June fifth, I awoke to the news that Israel was at war. I ran upstairs and found my family anxiously sitting around the heretofore neglected table radio. We turned from station to station. The reports were agonizingly slow in coming.

As we listened, I knew that for years I had lived with the fear that this would happen, that Israel would be destroyed. And as we waited for more bulletins from Tel Aviv, I knew that my concern was not as a leftist or even, at that moment, as an American. I did not fear for Israel because she was "the only democracy in the Middle East" or because she was a "socialist enclave" surrounded by "feudal sheikdoms." I cared because Israel was the Jewish State and I was a Jew. Her anguish was mine, the anguish of my people. I would not forget that.

In those hours of fear and then relief and exultation that Israel had survived, I was certain that all the good people were on her side. All the anti-war kids, all my radical friends, everyone supported Israel. Or so I thought. In fact, the reason I was so sure that all my college allies felt as I did was that they, besides being socially concerned, humanitarian radicals, were also all Jewish.

During the war, but after it had been decided, there was an article in the *Times* that should have alerted me to trouble looming ahead. The *Times* reported that the American left was split on the subject of Israel. In fact, certain spokesmen for SNCC, SDS and the Young Socialists Alliance were openly anti-Israel. They called Israel "imperialist" and a tool of the Central Intelligence Agency. I didn't take the charges of those radicals very seriously though. They were too absurd.

During the summer I read all I could about Israel, about Zionism, and about the Jews. I desperately wanted to know. Maybe in a book, I would find a passage that would grant me the key to my feelings about Israel.

I returned to school in September. The campus newspaper offered me a weekly column. I wrote about Viet Nam, about Johnson, about Bobby Kennedy. I wrote a column on the Middle East that called for direct negotiations and the recognition by all nations of Israel's permanence. The response was massive. For weeks the paper printed letter after letter from outraged Arab students and their sympathizers. Their letters referred to "Zionist gangsters," "racist Zionists," and "Jewish imperialists." They were not subtle. Suddenly everyone was discussing that newspaper column, those letters to the editor, and Israel.

It was not long after this that I was first called a "fascist" by one of my erstwhile friends and allies. He was not joking.

I continued my personal campaign. I debated, wrote and eventually made speeches. My only visible support was from two very sharp, radical Jewish girls and from two Zionist professors.

I rapidly became aware of the games pro-Arab professors play, both in and out of the classroom. All this talk about "Palestine." Courses on the modern Middle East that didn't mention Israel. Mid-East nationalism courses that ignored Zionism. One professor, in discussing the geography of the Middle East, used a map that ignored national boundaries but showed every Arab refugee camp. He didn't have to add any comment. And then there were the professors who signed a newspaper ad saying that they were tired of the world's "bleeding" for the Jews. I was unsophisticated enough to name, in my column, the professors who had signed such ads. I called them anti-Semites. A sympathetic lawyer had to rescue me. The issue grew and grew.

I soon realized that I was embarrassing many of the Jewish students. Everyone was choosing sides on the issue, and I was accused of fomenting anti-Semitism. My former allies of the left ignored me. When we did speak, they asked me why I had become so "religious." I asked them how they could support and claim to understand black nationalism when they were so hostile and blind to Jewish nationalism. It was simple, they told me. Black nationalism was progressive. Jewish nationalism was reactionary. Just like that.

I had planned to go to Chicago in the summer of nineteen sixty-eight. My candidate needed all the help he could get. His assassination in Los Angeles on the fifth of June affected me deeply. I had to get out of America. I spent three months in Israel. My hopes and expectations for that country were confirmed. In a Jerusalem hotel room, I learned that Prague had fallen and that, in Chicago, my brothers were being tear gassed and beaten.

By my senior year in college, I had lost all my political illusions. Regarding the Middle East, the New Left was at best "objective" and at worst openly pro-Fatah. I. F. Stone, Noam Chomsky and Tom Hayden were openly against Israel. Senator Fulbright was not a friend. Arthur Schlesinger felt that it was inconsistent to oppose American involvement in Viet Nam and yet support Israel. The conservative head of a major American Zionist organization agreed, he went out of his way to endorse Israel and the war in Viet Nam. The choice seemed to be one between the anti-Zionist left and the reactionary Zionists.

I had a problem. How could I reconcile my leftist proclivities with my new, admittedly Zionist ones? Did I have to choose between the Fatah-supporting SDS and the ultra–middle class, lox and bagel breakfast club, "Hillel Society?" There could be no doubt but that the most interesting Jewish kids were on the left. The Jews of the anti-war movement were infinitely more intellectually exciting than the business majors of State's Hillel. The choice was an impossible one. I felt that there had to be a third route.

That third route was Zionist radicalism. I took out a full page ad in the campus paper denouncing anti-Zionist professors, pro-Arab leftists, the war in Viet Nam and all reactionaries. Borrowing from the black nationalists, I announced the formation of a militant, radical campus Zionist organization called the "Hebrew Students Alliance." Our first meeting was to be later in the week. The local news media picked it up. I was interviewed on television and radio and in the press. The free publicity was what we needed. Although Hillel is grateful to have twenty-five kids at a meeting, we had over three hundred. The television cameras and the cluster of radio microphones gave it all a dramatic air. A few of us spoke, including a radical professor. We called for support for Israel and endorsed the Student Mobilization against the war in Viet Nam. The students in attendance were radical, well-informed, and anything but parochial in interest. They called for planks condemning Arab terror, the Nigerian government, Northern Ireland's Reverend Ian Paisley, the Sudanese government, the Soviet invasion of Czechoslovakia, and all manifestations of anti-Semitism. It was an exciting meeting. I knew, at last, that I was not alone. There were hundreds of college kids at Albany who were progressive, activist and assertively pro-Israel. To illustrate just where they stood, they changed the name of our organization from the "Hebrew Students alliance" to "Am Yisrael," the people of Israel.

What happened to me in Albany happened to thousands of young Jews throughout America at about the same time. And out of all this evolved a political philosophy. It is the philosophy of all those Jewish young people across the country who will not surrender their identity just so they can be accepted by their "revolutionary" peers. Nor will they give up their radicalism to accommodate the Jewish establishment.

What we say is this: We are radicals. We actively oppose the war in Viet Nam. We support the black liberation movement as we endorse all genuine movements of liberation. And thus, first and foremost, we support our own. We will march with our brothers of the left. We will support them.

But when they call for the death of Israel, when they acquiesce in plans for the liquidation of the Jewish state, we then have no choice but to fight them. We shall denounce anti-Semitism whether it emanates from the right or the left. There is no such thing as "progressive" anti-Semitism. And we shall not allow the "revolutionaries" to escape our indictment of racism by claiming that they are "anti-Zionist but not anti-Semitic." If they can reconcile themselves to the existence of every nation on the planet but Israel, if they call for revolution in every country but only death for Israel, then they are clearly against the Jewish people. One may call that what he will.

Radical Zionism is a growing movement. Organizations far more successful than Albany's "Am Yisrael" have been established on campuses throughout the country. These groups publish newspapers with a circulation of one hundred and fifty thousand. The movement will continue to grow because our philosophy involves no compromise. We can be accused of anything but inconsistency. Our position in support of black, Vietnamese, African and other national movements is a natural outgrowth of our identification with Israel. So is our recognition of the evolution of a new Palestinian Arab nationalism which exists and must be considered.

Our position as Jews, as Americans and as radicals was more than adequately epitomized over a century ago by the great Italian patriot, Mazzini. He said:

> I love my country because I love the idea of country. What I covet for myself, I covet for all other men. Because I demand and insist upon a spot on this earth where my race and my people, my culture and my nation, recognize and are recognized as sovereign and at home, I demand and insist upon the rights of all others to do the same.

I have come a long way in the twenty-three months since the Six Day War. I feel that my Zionist *Weltanschauung* is not a result of some atavistic impulse but rather a natural product of the American liberalism that is my birthright. Self-determination for all peoples is the basic tenet of the Declaration of Independence and the Atlantic Charter. But, most important, I am a Jew. In a very real sense, I am a child of the Holocaust. The Six Million dead is an incubus that hangs over all my post-war generation. That may just be the key to my awakening of the fifth of June nineteen hundred and sixty-seven. I think it is.

On the Theology of Jewish Survival

STEVEN S. SCHWARZSCHILD

When people think in 1968 about Jewish survival it can be assumed that the occasion for their consideration is the Six Day War of 1967 and its continuing consequences. We, too, will want to revert to that episode, but I wish to begin our exploration at another and more decisive point in contemporary Jewish history: the early summer of 1945—i.e., the hour when the Jewish people stood on both sides of the open doors of Bergen-Belsen, of Auschwitz, of Maidanek and Theresienstadt and the other camps of extermination, and when the full weight of what had happened to us there and throughout the Holocaust came bearing down on us.

The reality of the situation at that point was twofold: on the one hand, it was brutally clear that death and destruction, infinite pain and incurable physical and spiritual dislocations had reaped an abundant harvest in our midst. We were on the very verge of expiration; indeed, in some ways we had died, beyond revival. At the same time, we must remember, this condition prevailed, in varying ways and degrees, in all the countries and among all the peoples of the Old World, from the British Isles through the entire heartland of Eurasia to the islands of Japan and beyond. Slaughter and fire, the lie and the eraser had cut a wide swath not only through the peoples but also through the institutions and cultures of these continents. So we looked around us—we saw the scene—and, though with cracked voices and with bitter hearts, we first hummed softly and then sang in a swelling chorus the refrain of the Partisan song: "*Mir zennen do*"—"Never say we have walked our last road"; when all the roads will have been trod, and when all others will have fallen by the wayside, we—or at least a small remnant of Israel, the true "remaining remnant"—will yet present ourselves to proclaim: "We are still here—*mir zennen do.*" The greatest, the world-shaking and heaven-rending, the inexpungeably traumatic tragedy of Israel was accompanied, contrapuntally, as it were, by the increasing consciousness of the ineluctable, unextirpatable survival of the Jewish people throughout history—and if through that history then surely throughout eternity. [. . .]

The crucial question which—consciously or unconsciously—has arisen for all who have lived since is this: how did this survival, broken yet triumphant, tortured yet exultant, decimated yet fortified, come about? What can we learn about how we are to survive from how did we survive?

At the Eichmann trial the Israeli attorney-general Hausner asked most European-Jewish survivors of the Holocaust who gave testimony: Why did you not resist? Ben-Gurion, among others said that one of the major purposes of the trial was to purge Jewish consciousness of a haunting guilt-feeling for not having fought back against the Nazis but—as the Biblical phrase, frighteningly transvalued, which is usually cited at this point, goes—having "gone like sheep to the slaughter." Clearly, the premise of the question is, in the first place, that it is better to "fight back" than to die, without physical retaliation or defense, as martyrs, and, in the second place, that the survival of the "remaining remnant" was due to those who, as heroes on the walls of the Warsaw Ghetto, soldiers in the Jewish Brigade, members of the roaming Partisan groups, or after the war as soldiers in the *Haganah* or other military or quasi-military outfits, fought against the Nazis and for the establishment of the State of Israel. There can be little doubt that it is on the basis of essentially such premises that organized Jewry concentrates its memorializations of the victims of the Holocaust on anniversaries of the Warsaw Ghetto Revolt. Hence issues forth also a new worldwide Jewish admiration for heroes of brawn—Israeli, healthy, clear-eyed, wiry boys and girls with machine guns under their arms, Colonels Marcus, tanks and planes on Sunday-school bulletin boards, etc.

This view of how Israel survived its most horrible threat has undergone a rapid escalation. It began, shortly after the war, with the glorification of the Jewish military and paramilitary fighters while the "passive" martyrs were lamented but, for the rest, relatively neglected. From this followed shortly two different but supplementary theses: the Hausner thesis we have mentioned, that there was something, perhaps something crucial, that was demeaning, immoral, possibly even traitorous about not having physically fought back, and the Hannah Arendt thesis that significant elements of the Jewish leadership and communities in Europe had actually collaborated with their people's exterminators. Mind you, even most of those who vehemently argued against the Arendt thesis accepted the premise that to die unresistingly is somehow shameful, and they, therefore, concentrated their attention on revolts in ghettos and concentration camps and on Jewish leaders who were active in the war against the Nazis in order to try to refute Arendt's thesis. The next step in the escalation was, of course, the resolution, in Israel and abroad, not to let ourselves be decoyed into such a situation again but rather, from the outset, to be ready to take arms and other counteraggressive measures against any actual or potential (and thus preemptive) enemy. This was certainly the underlying and usually proclaimed psychological posture immediately before and during the Six Day War; it was part of the *déja-vu,* the *déja-senti* atmosphere of those weeks when the beleaguered spirit of the Second World War was rife in the Jewish community—and it is the source of the predominant "hawkishness" in

Jewish circles since then. The last and grotesquely Satanic degree of escalation which this interpretation of the Jewish history of our time has hitherto undergone is the doctrine enunciated in the current wave of Polish, neo-Stalinist Communist anti-semitism—that, by and large, it was the Poles—*mirabile dictu!*—who fought against the Nazis while the ranks of Jewry were shot through with traitors, collaborators, and cowards.

The subject is too painful, and I, therefore, want to try to summarize what is historically and morally wrong with this attitude as briefly as possible. In Israel and in this country a Jewish triumphalism has spread which is not lovely to behold. In the "Movement for the Greater Land of Israel" phrases are slung around which sound most ominous to anyone who has lived through the 'thirties of our century: "liberated territories," "the Greater Israel," "the call of the historic soil," "the metaphysical unity of the people and the land," "the irresistible destiny of the millennia," etc. Policy discussions are held about how to keep the numbers and the fertility of the Arabs (and sometimes even also of the Sephardim) in manageable proportion to those of the rest of Israel—satellite states are proposed as a more liberal way of dealing with the Near Eastern problem than wholesale removal of populations—the Israeli army is further enhanced as the chief tool of integration, education, and decision-making, where the Kibbutz had, surely, been originally cast in that role—generals become cabinet members and ambassadors, together with previously proscribed terrorist leaders and right-wing chauvinists—let these examples stand for others as well.

In a more technically theological sense the Israeli victory in the Six Day War has produced an immensely aggravated danger of pseudo-faith and pseudo-Messianism. It is by now a cliché how Israeli as well as *galut* Jews without religious faith suddenly came to believe in miracles (performed by a nonexistent God) and thought they were witnessing the *"Atchalta d'Geulah"*—the beginning of redemption. To which my teacher Prof. Akiba Ernst Simon replied epigrammatically: "I, too, would believe that it was a miracle—if I didn't believe in God so much."

In March 1968 the "Newsletter on Religious and Cultural Affairs" put out by the Consulate General of Israel in New York carried a rather stunning and worrisome summary of this pseudo-Messianic mood in certain circles. [. . .] Rabbi M. Fogelman of Kiryat Motzkin is quoted: "Is the miracle of our day less than that of Hanukkah?" Rabbi Techorsh, member of the Chief Rabbinate Council, advocated the recital of *"She-hecheyanu"* and *"Al ha-Nissim."* Rabbi Y. Abuhatzirah, also a member of the Council and spiritual head of Israel's North African community, maintained (and perhaps, such views can be indulged depending on the history of those who hold them) that last year's "recovery of the Land of Israel constituted the final step before the advent of the Messiah," warranting special readings from Torah and Prophets.

This is extremely dangerous talk. Theologically I would adduce at least three arguments against it, the first two cited from—if you please—the Satmerer Rebbe's recent *Kunteros al ha-Geulah viha-Temurah:* 1) "Miracles" are miracles only when they are in accord with the Torah and the *Halachah;* otherwise, like the miracles of the Egyptian magicians, they are deceptions of Satan; 2) Victories in wars, even those of the few over the many, are always natural events, not miracles. Thus Hanukkah celebrates the miracle of the oil, not the victory of the Hasmoneans. Indeed, military victories are special opportunities for the seductions of Satan. I should like to add a third reason for not regarding a victory in war a divine act, and I regret that this kind of thinking is hard to come by nowadays in Orthodox, Reform, or any other Jewish circles: R. Yochanan, the central teacher in the eschatological discussion of *Perek Chelek,* interpreting Jer. 30:6, asks why, in the Messianic fulfillment, "all faces will turn pale." He answers that the angels and Israel will turn pale because the salvation of Israel carries along with it a comparative demotion of other peoples: "At that time the Holy One, praised be He, will say: 'Those (Israel) are the works of My hands, and the others (Gentiles) are the works of My hands. How can I cause the ones to perish in favor of the others!'" And Rav Pappa (and Rashi *ad locum*) expatiate further on this consideration. It might be argued that, despite their misgivings, all the parties concerned nonetheless pray for the Messianic fulfillment and therefore the corollary derogation of the Gentiles—but it must be remembered that R. Yochanan makes the statement which we have quoted in order to explain why he, like a number of others, exclaims: "*Yatei vilo Itmeneh*"—i.e., R. Yochanan prefers not to experience the Messianic advent rather than be an accessory to the plight of the non-Jews. Much further genuine Jewish morality—or any other—cannot go! Can we say less in the presence of Moslems and Arabs?

Turning to American Jewry, the triumphalism which we have illustrated manifests itself here perhaps more flagrantly than in Israel, perhaps precisely because it is at one remove. Hundreds of rabbis sign full-page newspaper ads insisting that all of the conquered land must be retained by Israel because—if you please—otherwise the Soviet Union will have succeeded in pushing the United States out of its strategic strongholds in the Near East. Liberal Jewish professors, who had been in the vanguard of the movement against the Vietnam War, demand full American political and military commitment on the side of Israel, and, though their dissenting voices are heard on every other subject, a strange silence prevails toward the Israeli government on the delicate but crucial question of Arab-Jewish relations; the center of Jewish attention in this country has now become "Negro anti-Semitism" and campus anarchism where previously it had been equality and peace, etc. I confess with great sadness, that I see a dominant note of rampant self-assertiveness and self-righteousness in world Jewry, which may be compared with the ideology of those against whom Jeremiah prophesied, who thought that their strength lay in their own arms and in alliances with foreign, pagan powers.

One is sorely tempted, at this point, to want to assert one's Jewish "patriotism" against the inevitable accusations which will be leveled. But let us, instead, go back to the original thesis about the nature of Jewish survival as we witnessed it in 1945, and let us see what happens to the real interests of the Jewish people when that fragmented survival is looked at in another light.

Certainly the Jews of the Warsaw Ghetto had every human right to defend themselves and to fight back. The same is true of all the other military or paramilitary expressions of resistance and counterattack. Rightly do we honor their memories. But let us remember: in the first place, we lament to say that they, too, died—if survival is to be the yardstick of tactical or ethical worth, then we have to mourn to conclude that neither military resistance nor martyrdom availed. In the second place, it has been and is a terrible defamation of the third of the Jewish people who went to their deaths to claim or to imply that because they did not fight back they either did not resist or—God forbid!—collaborated. To be *menschen* in the midst of inhumanity, to sanctify the name of God while surrounded by a flood of heathenism, to study, teach, and pray in a world in which only murder, rape, and brutality reigned, to squeeze a precious drop of life through the sieve of all-consuming death, and finally to go to one's death in ranks of thousands because the world had turned into hell and no longer had a place for decent human beings—who will rise and have the forwardness to claim that this was not, in its way, the greatest, the most admirable, the most heroic form of resistance—that the more than five million who did not, as it happens, resort to guns, knives, stones, and fire did not plant the banner of Israel, God, and humanity fluttering high on the battlefield of history?

Two thousand years of Jewish exilic history had taught the Jewish people that the tree planted by the waters could bend its branches to the storm and afterwards rise up again and grow its fruit for the coming season. One has to be an assimilated, Westernized secularist to see something dishonorable—as Bialik did in "The City of Death" and as so many Jews do today—in crouching in cellars until, it is hoped, the beasts have passed by, in order to save one's own and one's family's lives. To be sure, the gentlemanly thing to do is to stand up straight, meet the badman in the open street and get the first draw on him, but then, as Maurice Samuel has put it, we choose to be Jews, not gentlemen. And, when all is said and done, in 1945 a small but viable remnant from the Holocaust had in fact survived. They stumbled out of the camps, they raised their heads from the floor, they walked blinkingly into the light, they came out of hiding and disguise, and whispered: "*Mir zennen do.*" And this was not a very small minority of our surviving people—it was the overwhelming majority of those who had, by God's unfathomable and cruel grace, somehow or other come through. They *were*, indeed, the Jewish people. They own our unqualified piety and love—as do all those who, to the end and into horrible deaths, exemplified what it is to be Jews, human beings, citizens of "the lands of the living."

It is almost universally said that the Holocaust is an irrefutable blemish on—if not denial of—God. This is true. It is equally true that the survival of the Jewish people—at all times and especially through the Holocaust—is an inexplicable handiwork of His. (It is, incidentally, little less cruel than the slaughter, as Elie Wiesel and others make clear.) We are entitled to put it blasphemously: God was so vicious as to kill us, and He was so vicious as to preserve us; to Him go all blame and all glory. The Jew came out of this furnace—dead or alive—pure as the driven snow. Under the Law those put to death by an [oppressive] government are, regardless of their personal merits or previous conditions, martyrs "for the sanctification of God's name." Again we conclude: we survive by God's harsh decree, and those who survive testify, willingly or no, knowingly or no, gladly or sadly, to His majesty and sovereignty. [. . .]

The transvaluation of all Jewish values which has already seriously set in in Israeli and world Jewry could soon completely overwhelm us. The problem of our Jewish generation and of our children is whether we can live with the ethics and politics of the persecuted, having, in some ways, ceased to be the persecuted. I implore you and me and all of us not to prove Nietzsche to have been right—that morality is the rationalization of the weak.

At this point, finally, I can articulate my own form of Jewish superchauvinism. What we have been saying is simply that the survival of the Jewish people is guaranteed by God—that we need not really concern ourselves with it—that to preoccupy oneself with it is a form of sickness, as health-faddists are invariably sick people—that to attribute our survival to human instrumentalities including and primarily our own, inevitably leads to the acts of *hybris, ga'avah,* which victimize other human beings and result in unending conflict and eventual defeat—and that, on the contrary, the God Who has brought us this far will also redeem His other promises to Israel. Like the Movement for the Greater Land of Israel I, too, am unable to surrender—*le-atid la-vo*—one inch of sacred soil of the Land of Israel. We may implicitly believe that in the Redemption not only will the historic land revert to its divinely designated occupants but that, as Rabbinic literature amply proclaims, it will be vastly expanded—yes, Hebron and Jericho, the cedars of Lebanon and the great river: "And He said to me: 'These waters go out into the eastern Galilee, descend into the Arabah, and end in the sea'" (Ez. 47:8). The late Chayim Weizman was asked about this Messianic claim by a member of the Peel Commission when, back in 1936, he was ready to accept the first partition plan for Palestine, and he answered, not facetiously: God made the promise—God, not we, will redeem it. Our task is to be menschen and thus—and thus only—to hasten the Messiah's coming, not by force or by magic or by superarrogation. [. . .]

Zionism in the Middle East

SHARON ROSE

Once, in another life (nice Jewish girl from New York, just graduated from college, about to launch brilliant career as mathematician-computer expert) I traveled to Israel. I stayed on a Kibbutz and picked grapes and peaches and dug the whole scene: the communal dining hall and children's houses; the pioneer-farmers, rifles at their sides, who had unearthed enough prehistoric artifacts to fill their own small museum. Using the Bible as a guide book, I reached out to touch the walls on either side of a narrow street in Nazareth—a street that hasn't changed much—except for the Coca Cola stand—since Jesus walked down it. Riding a bus in Haifa on the Sabbath I learned how the Labor Movement is powerful enough in that city to defeat the ultra-Orthodox who keep public facilities in the rest of the country shut down on that day. Wandering in the Mea Shearim quarter of Jerusalem, I tried to comprehend in what sense the strange people there, in their long black costumes, are kin to me. I disdained the American tourists who complained of the service at the posh Tel Aviv (read Miami Beach) hotels, and joined them, weeping, at the Anne Frank memorial to the six million.

I did see things that troubled my liberal head. I stood on the shore at Elath, looked across the Gulf to its twin city, Jordanian Acaba, and bemoaned the wasted duplication, the millions spent on armaments to keep two economies separated: two economies where there should be one. And I asked embarrassing questions: Why are all the dock workers and other laborers dark skinned Moroccan Jews and Arabs? Why are all the ditch diggers and workers on the roads dark skinned Yemenite Jews and Arabs? Why do the "socialist" Kibbutzim join in the exploitation of this labor? Why do the Arab villages live under military rule? Why are crucial civil rights denied Palestinian Arabs who remained in Israel? My Mapamnik (Left wing, Socialist Zionist) friends had high-minded answers: "It's just that the oriental Jews have not yet acquired the skills of our technological (read Western) economy. As soon as they do they will be integrated, or their children will be. After all, we cannot allow our country to be Levantine." "It's just that peace has not come yet. As soon as it does the Israeli Arabs will become full citizens."

And I answered: "But you are Levantine, or you should be. It is you who should be integrated: into the Middle East."

So I saw that I am not a Zionist, and I came home to my brilliant career. The day I arrived was the day Martin Luther King led his march on Washington. And I said, "Right—the struggle for civil rights is the same wherever it is fought!"

Now, in this life, I know that liberation is not achieved by finding optimal solutions to neat equations. If a system requires a pool of cheap labor to exploit, it will not be changed by asking the exploiters for part of the pie. If I was not a Zionist then, I am certainly not one now. For me, my own liberation, and liberation for all the Jewish people is inexorably tied to liberation for all peoples. My life is dedicated to organizing for that liberation through revolutionary change. Fully recognizing the dialectic that exists between Marxism and my cultural nationalism, I choose to organize in the community I think I can still talk to best: the Jewish community.

I say I believe that we can talk best to the Jewish community, but I admit it is becoming more difficult to do so all the time. One reason is that the Jewish community is becoming harder and harder to find. If a "community" is a set of people with common cultural experiences, supportive of common needs and interests, perhaps we should not so designate American Jewry, perhaps we should call it instead, the "Jewish rung" on the economic ladder that is the Amerikan system. And where is the Jewish rung? In suburbia, of course (or at least, on the suburban fringes of large cities) where all "good" white people who consent to be melted down in the Amerikan melting pot are eventually sent to reap the dubious "rewards" of having undertaken the climb up the ladder in the first place.

So off we go to suburbia, to the Jewish communal places, such as they are, to talk about how, as long as the ladder exists, those who oppress the people on the rungs below them will be equally oppressed by those on the rungs above them; about how it is that the Jews of Amerika remain a marginal people, as do all ethnic minorities; about how it is the responsibility of the Jewish community to help Jewish merchants get out of Black ghettoes, and to see to it that there are no Jewish slumlords and segregationists; about why so many Jewish young people are rejecting a brand of religion that is irrelevant to the real struggles of our time, and what the community might do about it. And a dialogue of sorts, strained and tenuous as it may be, is established, until the inevitable moment when someone in the room asks: "And what is your position on Israel?"

Now that question is a trap, because the person who asks it recognizes only two possible positions: the position he or she attributes (equally) to El Fatah and all the Arab states (namely, that "All the Jews of Israel will be pushed into the sea"), and the position he or she views as the only "Jewish" position (namely, the rigid, militaristic, morally and tactically indefensible stance of the present Israeli regime).

We must not fall into that trap, for the very inevitability of that question and the fact that it admits of only two responses lies at the heart of what is wrong with our system. A rich cultural heritage based on a prophetic religious tradition has been largely forfeited to the Amerikan melting pot, to be replaced by an uneasy, guilt-ridden quasi-loyalty to a foreign state. It is a blind loyalty—one which forces Amerikan "Zionists" into the absurd position of favoring disestablishmentarian religious liberty here, while defending the existence of a theocracy in the Middle East, of attesting to the survival of the Jewish people through two millennia of "dispersion" from their homeland, while denying the existence of a Palestinian people after their twenty-five years or less as refugees.

From what does that uncritical loyalty of "Zionists" in Amerika stem? I put the word in quotes to indicate that the people to whom I refer actually have no serious desire or intention to emigrate to Israel. When pushed, most of the same people admit that their "Zionism" is based on a real fear that Amerika could produce another wave of anti-Semitism from which they could take refuge in the Jewish state. That this fear is real, however, is no reason to allow it to go unchallenged. For the "refuge" theory is a dangerous self-delusion. The Amerikan system does show every sign of becoming expert at genocide. Unless we stop it now, there will be no piece of real estate far enough away, no cave deep enough in the earth to protect any of us. My organizing to help stop that genocide requires that I ally myself with brothers and sisters in the black community who are organizing to prevent a race war here, and against whom the repression has already begun to be unleashed. I think they are dead wrong whenever they attempt to use anti-Semitism to increase the class consciousness of their own people, but I will not allow even that to put me in the position of defending unequivocally the foreign policy of any government.

The revolution will come to Israel. There are indications that some left wing Israelis have learned that they must help build it. The Palestinian Arabs will gain self determination, despite the best efforts of the present regimes of the Arab states and their Amerikan oil company supporters. I believe that a binational, democratic, secular state, encompassing the entire area of the original mandate, will provide the best environment to carry out such revolutions, to create a truly just economic system for all the peoples of the area. If I were a Zionist, I would be there, working for that.

That is my "position" on the Middle East. But we are here, and we have a country to turn around, before it destroys the entire world, the Middle East included. Sometime soon, I hope, we will begin seriously to discuss our own oppression and liberation—liberation from a system which has forced us to relinquish our heritage. Where should that liberation begin? Why, with the very ground we stand on. It will be necessary to liberate the synagogues (and, by the way, the churches, which, I think, have become equally irrelevant to the Christianity they were built to serve) from the power-worshipping Amerikan anti-religion they foster. We will breathe new life and meaning into our traditions. For we understand that it is better to be Jewish, Catholic, Irish, Buddhist, Italian, Black, Spanish, Puerto Rican . . . anything but melted down, homogenized, assimilated, and dead, Amerikan. Then "all peoples will walk every one in the name of his god, and we will walk in the name of the Lord our God for ever and ever." (Micah, 4:4)

My Zionist Dilemmas

BALFOUR BRICKNER

Years ago things were simpler. I could love God, serve the United States, and be a Zionist all at the same time. Today nothing integrates easily. Herewith two recent experiences in loyalty leading to intense personal conflict.

The first agony came just after the Jordanian-guerrilla war began. A radical Jewish friend phoned from Washington. He had heard the U.S. was about to intervene and thought it disastrous. He was rounding up goyish names for a protest. Would I take the lead in collecting Jewish names.

Once again I could see myself at odds with the American Jewish community. And the Israelis would also descend upon me. Why rock the boat now? Hadn't Golda and Nixon just concluded one of the most celebrated love fests in the annals of Israeli-U.S. relations? Undoubtedly, what was good for America had to be good for Israel. And, if the United States decided to intervene to protect its citizens, what right did anyone have to object? Besides, this was a case of Arabs killing Arabs. How could that be anything but "good for the Jews"?

The issue might have been simple for the ordinary American Jew who, at the instruction of most national Jewish agencies over the past couple of years, had often been taught to swallow his anger at the administration. But not for those who, despite their love of Israel, had long and loudly protested their country's intervention into the Vietnamese civil war. Was the Jordanian situation any different? And what if the U.S. either dragged or pushed Israel into Jordan with her? Neither was it beyond imagining Hussein silently welcoming a few Israeli Phantoms over northern Jordan to blast Syrian tanks, an action which would later be explained to the world as a self-defensive response to Syrian aggression. Imagine the weapon such an action would place in the hands of those who at every available opportunity chant about Israeli imperialism.

THE SUFFERING BEGINS

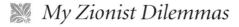

My dilemma was real. An American army of 12,000 was being alerted in Germany and South Carolina and the 6th fleet in the Mediterranean was being deployed to do more than save a few hundred Americans. After all, the International Red Cross was already working on that job. As for what the hucksters might shout—well, they're always shouting anyway so to hell with them. How could I ever again publicly protest against our immorality in Vietnam if I didn't protest a similar immorality in Jordan?

But was the immorality similar? I am not a pacifist. Pacifists see intervention in dimensions of moral absolutism. I do not. U.S. intervention in Vietnam is wrong, not because it is always wrong but because in Vietnam we are an aggressive intervenor on the side of one party in a civil war. Our intervention in Jordan could have been wrong for the same reason only the Syrian intervention had changed the situation from a Jordanian civil war to a war of national defense. The violation of a recognized international border legitimatized U.S. involvement on the side of Hussein. The 17th parallel dividing South from North Vietnam is not such a border, so that is a different case. Clearly, those who would take a negative view of U.S. intervention into the Jordanian situation must base it on other grounds than analogy to Vietnam: that it is unwise and has too many risks, viz. a Soviet response. That swayed me. But my response was now practical, not moral. I wondered whether I was fooling myself. I didn't know. I did know I had learned from situation ethics that the situation cannot be left out of an ethical decision.

I began to wonder what American Jews who support Israel but are absolutists against intervention would say about U.S. intervention to protect Israel from a united Arab-Russian attack. I was glad I wasn't that rigid. Not knowing when intervention might be right isn't comfortable. I hurt plenty after that phone call.

Practically speaking, what happened was that I adopted a non-interventionist posture based on a pragmatic evaluation. It would not be good *at this time.* When I called my friend back he seemed to understand but, in talking, he threw me into turmoil a second time, asking how I would feel if Hussein overwhelmed the guerrillas. Ouch.

THE ALTERNATIVES ARE TRAUMATIC

Establishment-type Zionists and Israelis have been supporting the Hashemite monarchy. They constantly say that a sovereign nation can negotiate only with another sovereign nation. Since the Palestinian groups are certainly not an established government, Israel cannot negotiate with them. It was Golda Meir who repudiated the notion of a separate Palestinian entity when she so glibly remarked: "A Palestinian—what's a Palestinian? I, too, was once Palestinian!"

The logic of this position loses cogency with each passing day. Witness the surprising student support for Nahum Goldmann when, last spring, he wanted to accept Nasser's invitation to talk. Witness the growing, though admittedly still small, support for Israeli doves like Shlomo Avineri, Yaakov Talmon, Ernst Simon, Arieh Eliav, and others. But the cruelest paradox is that though Israelis, despite their emergency, freely debate what attitude to take to the Palestinians, in America merely to raise the issue is to risk being branded a heretic or an enemy of the Jews.

Someone more concerned with ethics than organizational discipline, has shown me a confidential memo that one national organization sent to its regional offices. It warned its constituents against becoming involved with an Israeli, a member of the Knesset, no less, who was coming on a tour to this country. Why? Because, in the words of the memo: "He advocates the abolition of Zionist ideology in Israel, its institutions and traditional Jewish aspirations." Which means, as the memo continues, "He is against any incorporation or annexation of the administered territory and is against the establishment of Jewish settlements in administered areas until peace is achieved . . . he advocates that all Arab refugees be given the choice between repatriation or compensation." Should not the settlement question, such as the recent move by a group of Orthodox Jews to Hebron, be debated? Is the compensation alternative so heretical? In 1954 Michael Comay, then Israel's ambassador to the U.N., offered a measure of compensation. In 1958, Abba Eban did the same and reiterated it in his Nine Point Peace proposal of October, 1968.

The memo admits that this Israeli dove has repeatedly stated (a) his commitment to the continued existence of the State of Israel (b) his opposition to Al Fatah, and (c) his opposition to any Israeli withdrawal from territories until peace is established. Nonetheless, it urges no contact with him.

CIVIL LIBERTIES FOR WHOM?

This is a particularly disgusting example of the kind of "adhere-to-the-party-line" approach which has become standard in the American Jewish community and which has caused many thinking Jews to turn away from its organizations. How can we take seriously their call for free speech in every other facet of American life when they themselves deny it? The day for this kind of blindness is over. The Middle East cannot afford to go again to the brink to which the Palestinians in their extreme frustration brought it during two fateful weeks in September. The Palestinians may have lost the military shoot-out but just as the NLF won their right to sit at the Paris peace talk table, so the Palestinians have probably made good their demand to be a part of whatever negotiations finally take place between Israel and the Arab world. It was their frustration which drove them to the barbaric extremes of plane hijacking and the murderous military escapade from which they emerged so mauled. Unless they are accorded some recognition now, the world can anticipate that they will re-group and have another go at it. Uri Avnery is right when he writes: "We Israelis have been the activating force in the Middle East for the last three generations. We have been the victors, militarily at least, of three wars. Now, I believe, it is up to us to take the initiative and the first step toward peace—a view which makes me sound heretical in Israel. If no solution is found soon, the guerrilla war of organizations like Al Fatah will start a vicious circle of its own, a steep spiral of terror and counter terror, killing and retaliation, sabotage and mass deportations, which will bring undreamed of miseries to the Palestinian people. It will poison the atmosphere and generate a nightmare that will make peace impossible in our lifetime, turning Israel into an armed and beleaguered camp forever, bringing the Arab march toward progress to a complete standstill."

One who agrees with this position is no less a lover of Israel for so agreeing than one who does not. Indeed, to fail to see the truth of these words may do a greater disservice to Israel than can be imagined. [. . .]

I agree with those radical Jewish youths who talk about the necessity of Israel's recognizing the Palestinians. But they are wrong when they identify the militant Palestinians as true revolutionaries and thus much to be admired. This September's events should have made the falsity of such an equation painfully clear. The actions of the National Front for the Liberation of Palestine have revealed them to be gangsters. That they may end up having helped their people win recognition does not make them less criminal or their crimes less reprehensible. To say less is to badly confuse means and ends. To try to defend them is to try to legitimatize every defiance of international law and to make an unquestioned virtue out of bloody civil strife. Many of these same Jewish radicals are always trying to tar Israel with the brush of imperialism. Is not that charge now more properly evoked against Syria or, for that matter, even against the Palestinians themselves?

I have learned from these experiences that I live in a special sort of exile. I love the State of Israel, but I cannot stand some of the tactics of its supporters. I think moral imperatives can and must govern more of our political life, but I am repelled by the self-hate and self-delusion of some of the people who try to take civic morality most seriously. I am sure there are many other American Jews wandering in this no-man's-land, but mostly I feel very lonely.

8

How Jewish Is It?

What makes an American writer a *Jewish* writer? Is it a simple question of family origins, that is, all writers born of Jewish parents simply are Jewish writers? Or are writers obligated to, in effect, *earn* this distinction through a consistent affirmation of—or at least engagement with—Jewish culture and tradition in their work? Thus, would it be possible for Jewish-born artists really to relinquish their own Jewishness if their art did not reflect "appropriate" Jewish values? What are "appropriate" Jewish values? And should those writers deemed "inappropriate" be labeled "self-hating" Jews? Or does this label amount to a most peculiar and unfortunate expression of censorship?

While such questions may strike many as arcane or rhetorical today, they were taken quite seriously—perhaps too seriously—in the 1960s. As Jewish writers moved swiftly from the periphery to the center of American culture in the years after the Second World War, they also no longer felt (if they ever did) an obligation to write strictly and solely as insiders to an ethnic enclave. For one thing, their experiences had broadened tremendously as the quotas on professional advancement ended and the full-scale assimilation of Jews and other white ethnics into white Protestant mainstream American life proceeded apace. While Saul Bellow, Bernard Malamud, Grace Paley, Herman Wouk, Norman Mailer, Arthur Miller, and a host of other writers certainly continued to address Jewish themes and subjects in their writing, there was no necessary assumption that this was all they could—or should—address.

However, there was frequently a concern, made especially acute after Philip Roth won the National Book Award in 1960 for his collection of short stories, *Goodbye Columbus,* that Jewish writers should be held accountable for their portraits of American Jewish life. Some, like Roth himself and literary critic Leslie Fiedler, chose to address that concern head-on. Roth and Fiedler appeared together in June 1963 at a conference sponsored by the American Jewish Congress and held in Jerusalem and Tel Aviv. At that time, both encountered some sharp criticism from other conference attendees, who contended that American Jewish writers no longer identified adequately with a Jewish point of view but rather chose (as one commentator put it) to go "shopping" for other identities they felt better suited them. Fiedler's address to the conference is reprinted here, as is an essay Roth published several months later that takes up the complex issue of what it meant to him to be a Jewish writer in America.

On the other hand, not all Jewish writers cared to address these concerns or expressed any special anxiety that their writing might—or might not—win a seal of approval from professional Jewish groups or spokespersons. On the contrary, writer and raconteur Norman Mailer often seemed eager to provoke his readers rather than assuage their fears that he was a bad person, let alone a bad Jew. His 1960 essay included here, as he tells us, was prompted by a questionnaire—and written in the middle of the night, while partially drunk. Nonetheless, it offers no small insight into the views and opinions of a man whose very name would become synonymous with a combative, acerbic, funny, and often brilliant style of nonfiction prose for the remainder of the decade. How Jewish is it? That's for the reader to decide.

Like Mailer's piece, cultural critic Susan Sontag's 1967 essay was initially intended as an answer to a questionnaire. In this case, though, Sontag did formally—if also iconoclastically—respond. And so, for the record, these were the questions she had been asked to answer:

1. Does it matter who is in the White House? Or is there something in our system which would force any President to act as [President Lyndon B.] Johnson is acting?
2. How serious is the problem of inflation? The problem of poverty?
3. What is the meaning of the split between the Administration and the American intellectuals?
4. Is white America committed to granting equality to the American Negro?
5. Where do you think our foreign policies are likely to lead us?
6. What, in general, do you think is likely to happen in America?
7. Do you think any promise is to be found in the activities of young people today?

And as you shall see, although the questions are far from fascinating, Sontag produced a reply that really is. Note especially not only the opening discussion of American power but also Sontag's blistering retort to Leslie Fiedler and his condescension to the youth counterculture.

Finally, there is the case of poet Allen Ginsberg, who was a witness for the defense at the Chicago conspiracy trial in late 1969. It is almost impossible to recapture for a contemporary audience the theatrical (and often surreal) quality of these legal proceedings. Ginsberg's testimony certainly contributed its part to this remarkable event. For the record, the defense attorneys are William Kunstler and Leonard Weinglass; the prosecuting attorney is Thomas Foran. The part of the judge (or Court) is performed by Julius J. Hoffman. With the exception of Foran, everyone is Jewish.

A Program for the Nation

NORMAN MAILER

Last August I received a letter from Esquire *magazine. Its first two paragraphs read:*

Looking ahead to the 1960 presidential election, this magazine feels that it would be an interesting and useful undertaking to present the opinions of outstanding men of ideas regarding the candidates proposed and the issues involved. For the political parties and the electorate, there is the decision of which candidate, among the several already prominent, is to be given presidential authority and responsibility. Yet during the campaign there may be such concentration on the personalities of the candidates that issues to be debated and decided become neglected. We believe that the publication of the opinions of leaders in fields other than politics will be a contribution to intelligent public discussion.

Accordingly, we should be grateful if you will consider, and answer, these two questions:

1. Among those mentioned as possible presidential candidates, whom do you prefer for president in 1960?

2. What, to your mind, should be the most important issues in the election?

Attached is a list of those who, like yourself, are being asked to participate. There has been a fair attempt to select persons whose individual opinions are valued within their fields, and whose collective opinions will present a wide spectrum of response.

I went no further with the letter, but took a look at who had been invited. There were 150 names. About ten of us in the literary garden, and a wide range of other minds, frauds, generals, stuffed shirts, bureaucrats, after-dinner speakers, and figures in the news: Bernard Baruch, Dr. Ralph Bunche, Gen. Lucius Clay, Henry Ford II, Gen. James M. Gavin, William Randolph Hearst, Jr., Ernest Hemingway, Dr. Sidney Hook, Rev. Martin Luther King, Jr., Henry R. Luce, Gen. Douglas MacArthur, George Meany, Edward R. Murrow, Dr. Reinhold Niebuhr, Walter Reuther, Rear Adm. Hyman G. Rickover, Dr. Jonas Salk, Gen. David Sarnoff, Francis Cardinal Spellman, Dr. Frank Stanton, Bishop Fulton J. Sheen, Dr. Wernher von Braun, DeWitt Wallace, Hon. John Hay Whitney.

Over breakfast, I decided the hell with it, I was not going to answer, and went through the rest of the day without thinking any more about the letter. Late that night, after a party, I tried to go to sleep half-drunk, and instead found myself awake with that particular intense and false clarity alcohol can give in the last thirty minutes before it starts to wear away. I was thinking about the letter from Esquire, *and at three in the morning it seemed right to answer it. So I went downstairs, and worked at fever speed for an hour or less, not altogether innocent of manic glee at the thought of how this long answer to question 2 would look in the pages of a mass-media magazine. The draft written, I went to bed and enjoyed a self-satisfied sleep.*

In the morning I thought to take another look at the letter from Esquire. *In its third paragraph was the following sentence:*

> Answers to Question 2 will be collated, with a discussion of the issues cited by the author of the article, William Friedenberg, a scholar-journalist and Fellow of the Institute of Current World Affairs.

As an afterthought, the letter remarked:

> *Esquire* holds no political position and will advance none.

So I did not mail in my suggestions; it occurred to me they might roil the processes of collation.

What follows is the first draft as I wrote it, touched here and cut there to make it a little less unreadable.

I think I would be in favor of legislation whose inner tendency would be to weaken the bonds of legislation. As examples:

1. I would like to see a law passed which would abolish capital punishment, except for those states which insisted on keeping it. Such states would then be allowed to kill criminals provided that the killing is not impersonal but personal and a public spectacle: to wit that the executioner be more or less the same size and weight as the criminal (the law could here specify the limits) and that they fight to death using no weapons, or weapons not capable of killing at a distance. Thus, knives or broken bottles would be acceptable. Guns would not.

   The benefit of this law is that it might return us to moral responsibility. The killer would carry the other man's death in his psyche. The audience, in turn, would experience a sense of tragedy, since the executioners, highly trained for this, would almost always win. In the flabby American spirit there is a buried sadist who finds the bullfight contemptible—what he really desires are gladiators. Since nothing is worse for a country than repressed sadism, this method of execution would offer ventilation for the more cancerous emotions of the American public.

2. Cancer is going to become the first political problem of America in twenty years. The man who finds a cure could run successfully for President. But I doubt if a cure will be found until all serious cancer researchers, and most especially the heads of department are put under sentence of mortal combat (with a professional executioner) if they have failed to make progress in their part of the program after two years. This would keep committeemen out of the project—it would also help in the search for a cure, since one may suspect that only a brave man living in the illumination of approaching death could brood sufficiently over the nature of disease to come up with a cure which was not worse than the illness. (Cancer may well have proliferated because the medical minds pound out cures for other diseases which so violate the inner rhythms of the body that one's potential for cancer is increased—as for example the hoggish therapy of illness by antibiotics whose after-effects and psychic effects are still unknown.)
3. Pass a bill making legal the sale of drugs. I happen to think that people who take drugs burn up the best part of their minds and gut their sex, but the same is true for those who drink too much, and alcohol is in a favored legal position because the liquor industries are so rich. While it would not necessarily be attractive to see a larger proportion of people destroy themselves with drugs, it must be recognized that the right to destroy oneself is also one of the inalienable rights, because others cannot know the reason for the self-destruction. It is possible that many people take heroin because they sense unconsciously that if they did not they would be likely to commit murder, get cancer, or turn homosexual.
4. Since the Russians seem to have more vigor than we do at the moment, I would make every effort to pass them our diseases. I would encourage the long-term loan to them of countless committees of the best minds we have on Madison Ave. If our hucksters have been able in fifteen years to leech from us the best blood of the American spirit, they should be able to debilitate the Russians equally in an equivalent period; if not, my admiration for the soporific power of Madison Ave. is misplaced.
5. I would pass a bill abolishing all forms of censorship. Censorship is an insult to democracy because it makes men unequal—it assumes that some have more sexual wisdom than others, and it imprisons everyone in excessive guilt. Besides, pornography is debilitating to sex—the majority of people would stay away from it once they discovered how wan it left them. Given the force of the hangover, most people do not get drunk

every night, and the same, I believe, would apply here. It is possible I am indulging a shallow liberal optimism, and America would become a cesspool of all-night pornographic drive-in movies, the majority of the population becoming night people who meet for cocktails at one in the morning. But this could also serve as the salvation of the Republic, for America would then become so wicked a land that Russia would never dare to occupy us, nor even to exterminate us by the atom bomb, their scientists having by then discovered that people who are atomized disseminate their spirit into the conqueror.

Writing about Jews

PHILIP ROTH

Ever since some of my first stories were published in 1959 in a volume called *Goodbye, Columbus,* my work has been attacked from certain pulpits and in certain periodicals as dangerous, dishonest, and irresponsible. I have read editorials and articles in Jewish community newspapers condemning these stories for ignoring the accomplishments of Jewish life, or, as Rabbi Emanuel Rackman recently told a convention of the Rabbinical Council of America, for creating a "distorted image of the basic values of Orthodox Judaism," and even, he went on, for denying the non-Jewish world the opportunity of appreciating "the overwhelming contributions which Orthodox Jews are making in every avenue of modern endeavor. . . ." Among the letters I receive from readers, there have been a number written by Jews accusing me of being anti-Semitic and "self-hating," or, at the least, tasteless; they argue or imply that the sufferings of the Jews throughout history, culminating in the murder of six million by the Nazis, have made certain criticisms of Jewish life insulting and trivial. Furthermore, it is charged that such criticism as I make of Jews—or apparent criticism—is taken by anti-Semites as justification for their attitudes, as "fuel" for their fires, particularly as it is a Jew himself who seemingly admits to habits and behavior that are not exemplary, or even normal and acceptable. When I speak before Jewish audiences, invariably there have been people who have come up to me afterward to ask, "Why don't you leave us alone? Why don't you write about the Gentiles?"—"Why must you be so critical?"—"Why do you disapprove of us so?"—this last question asked as often with incredulity as with anger; and often when asked by people a good deal older than myself, asked as of an erring child by a loving but misunderstood parent.

It is difficult, if not impossible, to explain to some of the people claiming to have felt my teeth sinking in, that in many instances they haven't been bitten at all. Not always, but frequently, what readers have taken to be my disapproval of the lives lived by Jews seems to have to do more with their own moral perspective than with the one they would ascribe to me: at times they see wickedness where I myself had seen energy or courage or spontaneity; they are ashamed of what I see no reason to be ashamed of, and defensive where there is no cause for defense.

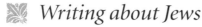

Not only do they seem to me often to have cramped and untenable notions of right and wrong, but looking at fiction as they do—in terms of "approval"

and "disapproval" of Jews, "positive" and "negative" attitudes toward Jewish life—they are likely not to see what it is that the story is really about.

To give an example. A story I wrote called "Epstein" tells of a sixty-year-old man who has an adulterous affair with the lady across the street. In the end, Epstein, who is the hero, is caught—caught by his family and caught and struck down by exhaustion, decay, and disappointment, against all of which he had set out to make a final struggle. There are Jewish readers, I know, who cannot figure out why I found it necessary to tell this story about a Jewish man: don't other people commit adultery, too? Why is it the Jew who must be shown cheating?

But there is more to adultery than cheating: for one thing, there is the adulterer himself. For all that some people may experience him as a cheat and nothing else, he usually experiences himself as something more. And generally speaking, what draws most readers and writers to literature is this "something more"—all that is beyond simple moral categorizing. It is not my purpose in writing a story of an adulterous man to make it clear how right we all are if we disapprove of the act and are disappointed in the man. Fiction is not written to affirm the principles and beliefs that everybody seems to hold, nor does it seek to guarantee us of the appropriateness of our feelings. The world of fiction, in fact, frees us from the circumscriptions that the society places upon feeling; one of the greatnesses of the art is that it allows both the writer and the reader to respond to experience in ways not always available in day-to-day conduct; or if they are available, they are not possible, or manageable, or legal, or advisable, or even necessary to the business of living. We may not even know that we have such a range of feelings and responses *until* we have come into contact with the work of fiction. This does not mean that either reader or writer no longer brings any moral judgment to bear upon human action. Rather, we judge at a different level of our being, for not only are we judging with the aid of new feelings, but without the necessity of having to act upon judgment, or even to be judged for our judgment. Ceasing for a while to be upright citizens, we drop into another layer of consciousness. And this dropping, this expansion of moral consciousness, this exploration of moral fantasy, is of considerable value to a man and to society.

I do not care to go at length here into what a good many readers take for granted are the purposes and possibilities of fiction. I do want to make clear, however, to those whose interests may not lead them to speculate much on the subject, a few of the assumptions a writer may hold—assumptions such as lead me to say that I do not write a story to make evident whatever disapproval I may feel for adulterous men. I write a story of a man who is adulterous to reveal the condition of such a man. If the adulterous man is a Jew, then I am revealing the condition of an adulterous man who is a Jew. Why tell that story?

Because I seem to be interested in how—and why and when—a man acts counter to what he considers to be his "best self," or what others assume it to be, or would like for it to be. The subject is hardly "mine"; it interested readers and writers for a long time before it became my turn to be engaged by it, too.

One of my readers, a man in Detroit, was himself not too engaged and suggested in a letter to me that he could not figure out why I was. He posed several questions which I believe, in their very brevity, were intended to disarm me. I quote from his letter without his permission.

The first question. "Is it conceivable for a middle-aged man to neglect business and spend all day with a middle-aged woman?" The answer is yes.

Next he asks, "Is it a Jewish trait?" I take it he is referring to adultery and not facetiously to the neglecting of business. The answer is, "Who said it was?" Anna Karenina commits adultery with Vronsky, with consequences more disastrous than those that Epstein brings about. Who thinks to ask, "Is it a Russian trait?" It is a decidedly human possibility. Even though the most famous injunction against it is reported as being issued, for God's own reasons, to the Jews, adultery has been one of the ways by which people of *all* faiths have sought pleasure, or freedom, or vengeance, or power, or love, or humiliation. . . .

The next in the gentleman's series of questions to me is, "Why so much *shmutz?*" Is he asking, why is there dirt in the world? Why is there disappointment? Why is there hardship, ugliness, evil, death? It would be nice to think these were the questions the gentleman had in mind, when he asks "Why so much *shmutz?*" But all he is really asking is, "Why so much *shmutz* in that story?" This, apparently, is what the story adds up to for him. An old man discovers the fires of lust are still burning in him? *Shmutz!* Disgusting! Who wants to hear that kind of stuff! Struck as he is by nothing but the dirty aspects of Epstein's troubles, the gentleman from Detroit concludes that I am narrow-minded.

So do others. Narrow-mindedness, in fact, was the charge that a New York rabbi, David Seligson, was reported in the New York *Times* recently as having brought against myself and other Jewish writers who, he told his congregation, dedicated themselves "to the exclusive creation of a melancholy parade of caricatures." Rabbi Seligson also disapproved of *Goodbye, Columbus* because I described in it "a Jewish adulterer . . . and a host of other lopsided schizophrenic personalities." Of course, adultery is not a characteristic symptom of schizophrenia, but that the rabbi should see it this way, as a sign of a diseased personality, indicates to me that we have different notions as to what health is. After all, it may be that *life* produces a melancholy middle-aged businessman like Lou Epstein who in Dr. Seligson's eyes looks like another in a parade of caricatures. I myself find Epstein's adultery an unlikely solution to his problems, a pathetic, even a doomed response, and a comic one, too, since it does not even square with the man's own conception of himself and what he wants; but none of this *unlikeliness* leads me to despair of his sanity, or humanity. I suppose it is tantamount to a confession from me of lopsided schizophrenia to admit that the character of Epstein happened to have been conceived with considerable affection and sympathy. As I see it, one of the rabbi's limitations is that he cannot recognize a bear hug when one is being administered right in front of his eyes.

The *Times* report continues: "The rabbi said he could only 'wonder about' gifted writers, 'Jewish by birth, who can see so little in the tremendous saga of Jewish history.'" But I don't imagine the rabbi "wonders" anymore about me than I wonder about him: that wondering business is only the voice of wisdom that is supposed to be making itself heard, always willing to be shown the light, if, of course, there is light to be pointed out; but I can't buy it. Pulpit fair-mindedness only hides the issue—as it does here in the rabbi's conclusion, quoted by the *Times:* "'That they [the Jewish writers in question] must be free to write, we would affirm most vehemently; but that they would know their own people and tradition, we would fervently wish.'"

However, the issue is not knowledge of one's "people." At least, it is not a question of who has more historical data at his fingertips, or is more familiar with Jewish tradition, or which of us observes more customs and rituals. It is even possible, needless to say, to "know" a good deal about tradition, and to misunderstand what it is that tradition signifies. The story of Lou Epstein stands or falls not on how much I "know" about tradition, but on how much I know and understand about Lou Epstein. Where the history of the Jewish people comes down in time and place to become the man whom I called Epstein, that is where my knowledge must be sound. But I get the feeling that Rabbi Seligson wants to rule Lou Epstein *out* of Jewish history. I find him too valuable to forget or dismiss, even if he is something of a *grubber yung* and probably more ignorant of history and tradition than the rabbi believes me to be.

Epstein is pictured not as a learned rabbi, after all, but the owner of a small paper-bag company; his wife is not learned either, and neither is his mistress; consequently, a reader should not expect to find in this story knowledge on my part, or the part of the characters, of the *Sayings of the Fathers;* he has every right to expect that I be close to the truth as to what might conceivably be the attitudes of a Jewish man of Epstein's style and history, toward marriage, family life, divorce, and fornication. The story is called "Epstein" because Epstein, not the Jews, is the subject; where the story is weak I think I know by this time;

but the rabbi will never find out until he comes at the thing in terms of what *it* wants to be about rather than what he would like it to be about.

Obviously, though, his interest is not in the portrayal of character; what he wants in my fiction is, in his words, "a balanced portrayal of Jews as we know them." I even suspect that something called "balance" is what the rabbi would advertise as the most significant characteristic of Jewish life; what Jewish history comes down to is that at long last we have in our ranks one of everything. But his assumptions about the art of fiction are what I should like to draw particular attention to. In his sermon Rabbi Seligson says of Myron Kaufmann's *Remember Me to God,* that it can "hardly be said to be recognizable as a Jewish sociological study." But Mr. Kaufmann, as a novelist, probably had no intention of writing a sociological study, or—for this seems more like what the rabbi really yearns for in the way of reading—a nice positive sampling. *Madame Bovary* is hardly recognizable as a sociological study, either, having at its center only a single, dreamy, provincial Frenchwoman, and not one of every other kind of provincial Frenchwoman too; this does not, however, diminish its brilliance as a novel, as an exploration of Madame Bovary herself. Literary works do not take as their subjects characters and events which have impressed a writer primarily by the *frequency* of their appearance. For example, how many Jewish men, as we know them, have come nearly to the brink of plunging a knife into their only son because they believed God had commanded them to? The story of Abraham and Isaac derives its meaning from something other than its being a familiar, recognizable, everyday occurrence. The test of any literary work is not how broad is its range of representation—for all that breadth may be characteristic of a kind of narrative—but the depth with which the writer reveals whatever it may be that he has chosen to represent.

To confuse a "balanced portrayal" with a novel is finally to be led into absurdities. "Dear Fyodor Dostoevsky—All the students in our school, and most of the teachers feel that you have been unfair to us. Do you call Raskolnikov a balanced portrayal of students as we know them? Of Russian students? Of poor students? What about those of us who have never murdered anyone, who do our school work every night?" "Dear Mark Twain—None of the slaves on our plantation has ever run away. We have a perfect record. But what will our owner think when he reads of Nigger Jim?" "Dear Vladimir Nabokov—The girls in our class," and so on. What fiction does, and what the rabbi would like for it to do are two entirely different things. The concerns of fiction, let it be said, are not those of a statistician—or of a public-relations firm. The novelist asks himself, "What do people think?"; the PR man asks, "What *will* people think?" But I believe this is what is actually troubling the rabbi, when he calls for his "balanced portrayal of Jews." What will people think?

Or to be exact: what will the *goyim* think?

II

This was the question raised—and urgently—when another story of mine, "Defender of the Faith," appeared in the *New Yorker* in April 1959. The story is told by Nathan Marx, an Army sergeant just rotated back to Missouri from combat duty in Germany, where the war has ended. As soon as he arrives, he is made First Sergeant in a training company, and immediately is latched on to by a young recruit who tries to use his attachment to the sergeant to receive kindnesses and favors. His attachment, as he sees it, is that they are both Jews. As the story progresses, what the recruit, Sheldon Grossbart, comes to demand are not mere considerations, but privileges to which Marx does not think he is entitled. The story is about one man who uses his own religion, and another's uncertain conscience, for selfish ends; but mostly it is about this other man, the narrator, who because of the ambiguities of being a member of his particular religion, is involved in a taxing, if mistaken, conflict of loyalties.

I don't now, however, and didn't while writing, see Marx's problem as nothing more than "Jewish": confronting the limitations of charity and forgiveness in one's nature—having to draw a line between what is merciful and what is just—trying to distinguish between apparent evil and the real thing, in one's self and others—these are problems for most people, regardless of the level at which they are perceived or dealt with. Yet, though the moral complexities are not exclusively characteristic of the experience of being a Jew, I never for a moment considered that the characters in the story should be anything other than Jews. Someone else might have written a story embodying the same themes, and similar events perhaps, and had at its center Negroes or Irishmen; for me there was no choice. Nor was it a matter of making Grossbart a Jew and Marx a Gentile, or vice versa; telling half the truth would have been much the same here as telling a lie. Most of those jokes beginning, "Two Jews were walking down the street," lose a little of their punch if one of the Jews, or both, are disguised as Englishmen or Republicans. Similarly, to have made any serious alteration in the Jewish factuality of "Defender of the Faith" as it began to fill itself out in my imagination, would have so unsprung the tensions I felt in the story that I would no longer have had left a story that I wanted to tell, or one I believed myself able to.

Some of my critics must wish that this had happened, for in going ahead and writing this story about Jews, what else did I do but confirm an anti-Semitic stereotype? But to me the story confirms something different, if no less painful to its readers. To me Grossbart is not something we can dismiss solely as an anti-Semitic stereotype; he is a Jewish fact. If people of bad intention or weak judgment have converted certain facts of Jewish life into a stereotype of The Jew, that does not mean that such facts are no longer important in our lives, or that they are taboo for the writer of fiction. Literary investigation may even be a way to redeem the facts, to give them the weight and value that they should have in the world, rather than the disproportionate significance they probably have for some misguided or vicious people.

Sheldon Grossbart, the character I imagined as Marx's antagonist, has his seed in fact. He is not meant to represent The Jew, or Jewry, nor does the story indicate that it is the writer's intention that he be so understood by the reader. Grossbart is depicted as a single blundering human being, one with force, self-righteousness, cunning, and on occasion, even a little disarming charm; he is depicted as a man whose lapses of integrity seem to him so necessary to his survival as to convince him that such lapses are actually committed in the name of integrity. He has been able to work out a system whereby his own sense of responsibility can suspend operation, what with the collective guilt of the others having become so immense as to have seriously altered the conditions of trust in the world. He is presented not as the stereotype of The Jew, but as a Jew who acts like the stereotype, offering back to his enemies their vision of him, answering the punishment with the crime. Given the particular kinds of denials, humiliations, and persecutions that the nations have practiced on their Jews, it argues for far too much nobility to deny not only that Jews like Grossbart exist, but to deny that the temptations to Grossbartism exist in many who perhaps have more grace, or will, or are perhaps only more cowed, than the simple frightened soul that I imagined weeping with fear and disappointment at the end of the story. Grossbart is not The Jew; but he is a fact of Jewish experience and well within the range of its moral possibilities.

And so is his adversary, Marx, who is, after all, the story's central character, its consciousness and its voice. He is a man who calls himself a Jew more tentatively than does Grossbart; he is not sure what it means, means for him, for he is not unintelligent or without conscience; he is dutiful, almost to a point of obsession, and confronted by what are represented to him as the needs of another Jew, he does not for a while know what to do. He moves back and forth from feelings of righteousness to feelings of betrayal, and only at the end, when he truly does betray the trust that Grossbart tries to place in him, does he commit what he has hoped to all along: an act he can believe to be honorable.

Marx does not strike me, nor any of the readers I heard from, as unlikely, incredible, "made-up"; the verisimilitude of the characters and their situation was not what was called into question. In fact, an air of convincingness that the story was believed to have, caused a number of people to write to me, and the *New Yorker,* and the Anti-Defamation League, protesting its publication.

Here is one of the letters I received after the story was published:

Mr. Roth:

With your one story, "Defender of the Faith," you have done as much harm as all the organized anti-Semitic organizations have done to make people believe that all Jews are cheats, liars, connivers. Your one story makes people—the general public—forget all the great Jews who have lived, all the Jewish boys who served well in the armed services, all the Jews who live honest hard lives the world over. . . .

Here is one received by the *New Yorker:*

Dear Sir:

. . . We have discussed this story from every possible angle and we cannot escape the conclusion that it will do irreparable damage to the Jewish people. We feel that this story presented a distorted picture of the average Jewish soldier and are at a loss to understand why a magazine of your fine reputation should publish such a work which lends fuel to anti-Semitism.

Clichés like "this being Art" will not be acceptable. A reply will be appreciated.

Here is a letter received by the Anti-Defamation League, who out of the pressure of the public response, telephoned to ask if I wanted to talk to them. The strange emphasis of the invitation, I thought, indicated the discomfort they felt at having to pass on—or believing they had to pass on—messages such as this:

Dear——,

What is being done to silence this man? Medieval Jews would have known what to do with him. . . .

The first two letters I quoted were written by Jewish laymen, the last by a rabbi and educator in New York City, a man of prominence in the world of Jewish affairs.

The rabbi was later to communicate directly with me. He did not mention that he had already written the Anti-Defamation League to express regret over the decline of medieval justice, though he was careful to point out at the conclusion of his first letter his reticence in another quarter. I believe I was supposed to take it as an act of mercy: "I have not written to the editorial board of the *New Yorker,*" he told me. "I do not want to compound the sin of informing. . . ."

Informing. There was the charge so many of the correspondents had made, even when they did not want to make it openly to me, or to themselves. I had informed on the Jews. I had told the Gentiles what apparently it would otherwise have been possible to keep secret from them: that the perils of human nature afflict the members of our minority. That I had also informed them it was possible for there to be such a Jew as Nathan Marx did not seem to bother anybody; if I said earlier that Marx did not strike my correspondents as unlikely, it is because he didn't strike them at all. He might as well not have been there. Of the letters that I read, only one even mentioned Marx and only to point out that I was no less blameworthy for portraying the Sergeant as "a white Jew" as he was described by my correspondent, a kind of Jewish Uncle Tom.

But even if Marx were that and only that, a white Jew, and Grossbart only a black one, did it in any way follow that because I had examined the relationship between them—another concern central to the story which drew barely a comment from my correspondents—that I had then advocated that Jews be denationalized, deported, persecuted, murdered? Well, no. Whatever the rabbi may believe privately, he did not indicate to me that he thought I was an anti-Semite. There was a suggestion, however, and a grave one, that I had acted like a fool. "You have earned the gratitude," he wrote, "of all who sustain their anti-Semitism on such conceptions of Jews as ultimately led to the murder of six million in our time."

Despite the sweep there at the end of the sentence, the charge made is actually up at the front: I "earned the gratitude. . . ." But of whom? I would put it less dramatically, but maybe more exactly: of those who are predisposed to misread the story—out of bigotry, ignorance, malice, or even innocence. If I did earn their gratitude, it was because they failed to see, even to look for, what I was talking about. . . . Such conceptions of Jews as anti-Semites hold, then, and as they were able to confirm by misunderstanding my story, are the same, the rabbi goes on to say, as those which "ultimately led to the murder of six million in our time."

"Ultimately"? Is that not a gross simplification of the history of the Jews and the history of Hitler's Germany? People hold serious grudges against one another, vilify one another, deliberately misunderstand one another, and tell lies about one another, but they do not always, as a consequence, *murder* one another, as the Germans murdered the Jews, and as other Europeans allowed the Jews to be murdered, or even helped the slaughter along. Between prejudice and persecution there is usually, in civilized life, a barrier constructed by the individual's convictions and fears, and the community's laws, ideals, and values. What "ultimately" caused this barrier to disappear in Germany cannot be explained only in terms of anti-Semitic misconceptions; surely what must also be understood here is the intolerability of Jewry, on the one hand, and its usefulness, on the other, to the Nazi ideology and dream.

By simplifying the Nazi-Jewish relationship, by making *prejudice* appear to be the primary cause of annihilation, the rabbi is able to make the consequences of publishing "Defender of the Faith" in the *New Yorker* seem very grave indeed. He doesn't appear to be made at all anxious, however, by the consequences of his own position. For what he is suggesting is that some subjects must not be written about, or brought to public attention, because it is possible for them to be misunderstood by people with weak minds or malicious instincts. Thus he consents to put the malicious and weak-minded in a position of determining the level at which open communication on these subjects will take place. This is not fighting anti-Semitism, but submitting to it: that is, submitting to a restriction of consciousness as well as communication because being conscious and being candid is too risky.

In his letter the rabbi calls my attention to that famous madman who shouts "Fire!" in "a crowded theater." He leaves me to complete the analogy myself: by publishing "Defender of the Faith" in the *New Yorker:* (1) I am shouting; (2) I am shouting "Fire!"; (3) there is no fire; (4) all this is happening in the equivalent of "a crowded theater." The crowded theater: there is the risk. I should agree to sacrifice the freedom that is essential to my vocation, and even to the general well-being of the culture, because—because of what? "The crowded theater" has absolutely no relevance to the situation of the Jew in America today. It is a grandiose delusion. It is not a metaphor describing a cultural condition, but a revelation of the nightmarish visions that must plague people as demoralized as the rabbi appears to be: rows endless, seats packed, lights out, doors too few and too small, panic and hysteria just under the skin. . . . No wonder he says to me finally, "Your story—in Hebrew—in an Israeli magazine or newspaper—would have been judged exclusively from a literary point of view." That is, ship it off to Israel. But please don't tell it here, now.

Why? So that "they" will not commence persecuting Jews again? If the barrier between prejudice and persecution collapsed in Germany, this is hardly reason to contend that no such barrier exists in our country. And if it should ever begin to appear to be crumbling, then we must do what is necessary to strengthen it. But not by putting on a good face; not by refusing to admit to the intricacies and impossibilities of Jewish lives; not by pretending that Jews have existences less in need of, less deserving of, honest attention than the lives of their neighbors; not by making Jews invisible. The solution is not to convince people to like Jews so as not to want to kill them; it is to let them know that they cannot kill them even if they despise them. And how to let them know? Surely repeating over and over to oneself, "It can happen here," does little to prevent "it" from happening. Moreover, ending persecution involves more than stamping out persecutors. It is necessary, too, to unlearn certain responses to them. All the tolerance of persecution that has seeped into the Jewish character—the adaptability, the patience, the resignation, the silence, the self-denial—must be squeezed out, until the only response there is to *any* restriction of liberties is "No, I refuse."

The chances are that there will always be some people who will despise Jews, just so long as they continue to call themselves Jews; and, of course, we must keep an eye on them. But if some Jews are dreaming of a time when they will be accepted by Christians as Christians accept one another—if *this* is why certain Jewish writers should be silent—it may be that they are dreaming of a time that cannot be, and of a condition that does not exist, this side of one's dreams. Perhaps even the Christians don't accept one another as they are imagined to in that world from which Jews may believe themselves excluded solely because they are Jews. Nor are the Christians going to feel toward Jews what one Jew may feel toward another. The upbringing of the alien does not always alert him to the whole range of human connections which exists between the liaisons that arise out of clannishness, and those that arise—or fail to—out of deliberate exclusion. Like those of most men, the lives of Jews no longer take place in a world that is just *landsmen* and enemies. The cry "Watch out for the *goyim!*" at times seems more the expression of an unconscious wish than of a warning: Oh that they were out there, so that we could be together in here! A rumor of persecution, a taste of exile, might even bring with it that old world of feelings and habits—something to replace the new world of social accessibility and moral indifference, the world which tempts all our promiscuous instincts, and where one cannot always figure out what a Jew is that a Christian is not.

Jews are people who are not what anti-Semites say they are. That was once a statement out of which a man might begin to construct an identity for himself; now it does not work so well, for it is difficult to act counter to the ways people expect you to act when fewer and fewer people define you by such expectations. The success of the struggle against the defamation of Jewish character in this country has itself made more pressing the need for a Jewish self-consciousness that is relevant to this time and place, where neither defamation nor persecution are what they were elsewhere in the past. Surely, for those Jews who choose to continue to call themselves Jews, and find reason to do so, there are courses to follow to prevent it from ever being 1933 again that are more direct, reasonable, and dignified than beginning to act as though it already is 1933—*or as though it always is.* But the death of all those Jews seems to have taught my correspondent, a rabbi and a teacher, little more than to be discreet, to be foxy, to say this but not that. It has taught him nothing other than how to remain a victim in a country where he does not have to live like one if he chooses. How pathetic. And what an insult to the dead. Imagine: sitting in New York in the 1960's and piously summoning up "the six million" to justify one's own timidity.

Timidity—and paranoia. It does not occur to the rabbi that there are Gentiles who will read the story intelligently. The only Gentiles the rabbi can imagine looking into the *New Yorker* are those who hate Jews and those who don't know how to read very well. If there are others, they can get along without reading about Jews. For to suggest that one translate one's stories into Hebrew and publish them in Israel, is to say, in effect: "There is nothing in our lives we need to tell the Gentiles about, unless it has to do with how well we manage. Beyond that, it's none of their business. We are important to no one but ourselves, which is as it should be (or better be) anyway." But to indicate that moral crisis is something to be hushed up, is not of course, to take the prophetic line; nor is it a rabbinical point of view that Jewish life is of no significance to the rest of mankind.

Even given his own kinds of goals, however, the rabbi is not very far-sighted or imaginative. What he fails to see is that the stereotype as often arises from ignorance as from malice; deliberately keeping Jews out of the imagination of Gentiles, for fear of the bigots and their stereotyping minds, is really to invite the invention of stereotypical ideas. A book like Ralph Ellison's *Invisible Man,* for instance, seems to me to have helped many whites who are not anti-Negro, but who do hold Negro stereotypes, to surrender simple-minded notions about Negro life. I doubt, however, that Ellison, reporting as he does not just the squalid circumstances Negroes must put up with but certain bestial aspects of his Negro characters as well, has converted one Alabama redneck or one United States Senator over to the cause of desegregation; nor could the novels of James Baldwin cause Governor Wallace to conclude anything more than that Negroes were just as hopeless a lot as he'd always known them to be. As novelists, neither Baldwin nor Ellison are (to quote Mr. Ellison on himself) "cogs in the machinery of civil rights legislation." Just as there are Jews who feel that my books do nothing for the Jewish cause, so there are Negroes, I am led to understand, who feel that Mr. Ellison's work has done little for the Negro cause and probably has harmed it. But that seems to place the Negro cause somewhat outside the cause of truth and justice. That many blind people are still blind, does not mean that Mr. Ellison's book gives off no light. Certainly those of us who are willing to be taught, and who needed to be, have been made by *Invisible Man* less stupid than we were about Negro lives, including those lives that a bigot would point to as affirming his own half-baked, inviolable ideas.

III

But it is the treachery of the bigot that the rabbi appears to be worried about and that he presents to me, to himself, and probably to his congregation, as the major cause for concern. Frankly, I think those are just the old words coming out, when the right buttons are pushed. Can he actually believe that on the basis of my story anyone is going to start a pogrom, or keep a Jew out of medical school, or even call some Jewish schoolchild a kike? The rabbi is entombed in his nightmares and fears; but that is not the whole of it. He is also hiding something. Much of this disapproval of "Defender of the Faith" because of its effect upon Gentiles, seems to me a cover-up for what is really objected to, what is immediately painful—and that is its direct effect upon certain Jews. "You have hurt a lot of people's feelings because you have revealed something they are ashamed of." That is the letter the rabbi did not write, but should have. I would have argued then that there are things of more importance—even to these Jews—than those feelings that have been hurt, but at any rate he would have confronted me with a genuine fact, with something I was actually responsible for, and which my conscience would have had to deal with, as it does.

For the record, all the letters that came in about "Defender of the Faith," and that I saw, were from Jews. Not one of those people whose gratitude the rabbi believes I earned, wrote to say, "Thank you," nor was I invited to address any anti-Semitic organizations. When I did begin to receive speaking invitations, they were from Jewish ladies' groups, Jewish community centers, and from all sorts of Jewish organizations, large and small.

And I think this bothers the rabbi, too. On the one hand, some Jews are hurt by my work; but on the other, some are interested. At the rabbinical convention I mentioned earlier, Rabbi Emanuel Rackman, a professor of political science at Yeshiva University, reported to his colleagues that certain Jewish writers were "assuming the mantle of self-appointed spokesmen and leaders for Judaism." To support this remark he referred to a symposium held in Israel this last June, at which I was present; as far as I know, Rabbi Rackman was not. If he had been there, he would have heard me make it quite clear that I did not want to, did not intend to, and was not able to, speak *for* American Jews; I surely did not deny, and no one questioned the fact, that I spoke *to* them, and hopefully to others as well. The competition that Rabbi Rackman imagines himself to be engaged in hasn't to do with who will presume to lead the Jews; it is really a matter of who, in addressing them, is going to take them more seriously—strange as that may sound—with who is going to see them as something more than part of the mob in a crowded theater, more than helpless and threatened and in need of reassurance that they are as "balanced" as anyone else. The question really is, who is going to address men and women like men and women, and who like children. If there are Jews who have begun to find the stories the novelists tell more provocative and pertinent than the sermons of some of the rabbis, perhaps it is because there are regions of feeling and consciousness in them which cannot be reached by the oratory of self-congratulation and self-pity.

The Jewish Intellectual and Jewish Identity

LESLIE FIEDLER

I don't propose to speak to you tonight about the situation of the writer who is a Jew as well as an Israeli, since I know little or nothing about this subject—as my opposite number surmised. What you will hear from me is only the testimony of one writer who is a Jew, as well as an American, about what seems to me one of the strangest events in the history of Jewish culture anywhere, at any time.

I shall not be judging, or blaming, or praising anybody or anything. I shall merely attempt to describe to you the facts, as I see them—though I can't forbear saying that some of the writers whom I name tonight—and I think you will have no difficulty in distinguishing the ones I mean—have written some of the most brilliant and some of the truest books of our time.

I am in some doubt about what use any of this that I propose to say will be to the Israelis, except that I have a deep belief that it is good, on both sides, to know everything concerned with the continuing existence of our people—and I am sure that it's good, on both sides, for us to know as much about each other as possible. As far as the Americans in this audience are concerned, I hope that some of them will find it instructive and useful to hear about a situation of which they may not be deeply or entirely aware.

Everybody who is concerned with matters of culture at all must be aware of the fact that in the arts in the United States, especially in literature, American Jews have, in the last decade or two, for the first time become central figures on the American scene, and that their success is a little dazzling and rather embarrassing. The novelists who most move Americans—and I mean not only Jewish Americans, but all Americans—are writers ranging from such sentimental and trivial falsifiers of experience as Herman Wouk and Leon Uris to such serious artists as Saul Bellow and Bernard Malamud and Philip Roth. Novelists of this latter kind have not merely written works which seem to us important but which seem to us to be at the center of American concern. And I am sure you scarcely have to be reminded that the figure who stands at the center of the single, major poetic movement of the last decade or so is Allen Ginsberg.

You know, it becomes clearer and clearer to me that we're not having a Dialogue between Israel and the United States but between Judea and Philistia—in the higher sense of the word. Despite the fact that people are aware of the things which I have just mentioned, it has seemed to me that few have taken the time to think these matters through to their ultimate implications; and I propose to follow them through to what seem, at least to me, some of those ultimate implications.

The first deep implication which comes to my mind is that at the present moment certain Jewish American characters, in books by certain Jewish American authors, characters who speak a language whose intonations are dictated by the intonations of Jewish American speech and the traditions of Yiddish which lie behind it—these characters have come to stand, in the events which happen to them as described in these books, for the deepest aspirations of the American public on all levels. The traditional Jew, the Jew of the *Galut,* in his rootlessness, in his commitment to urban life, in his desperate sense of humor, in his awareness of suffering as the essence of human history, in his way of connecting together the most violent kind of vulgarity and the most absolute spirituality, in his ability to stand (as somebody once said of the Arabs) up to his eyes in dung and to have his brows touch the heavens, that the sons and grandsons and the great-grandsons of Eastern European Jews, the last inheritors of *Yiddishkeit*—these have come to seem to Gentile Americans mythic Americans, Americans who stand for the mythical or archetypical essence of being an American.

It seems to me worthy of remark that the Ulysses and Achilles of the recent American epic which is being commonly written are Jews and that this has happened in a Gentile country. The questions arise: who could have foreseen it, and how did it happen, and what are we going to do about it?

Yet I must introduce you to a further twist of irony before I can talk about the situation—and I think it's already implicit in what I said—and that is simply this: that at the very moment in which Jewish American writers have been enjoying such a triumph, at the moment when philo-Semitism is rampant in certain cultural and literary circles in America, the Jewish American writer's awareness of himself as a Jew is reaching the vanishing point, and the gesture of passionate rejection seems to him his last possible connection with the historical past.

Now perhaps we're ready to ask the question of how and why? Some general sociological answers are very easy to give, though not, finally, very satisfying. The Jewish American writer is the beneficiary of a general *détente* in relations with non-ethnic groups, as we Americans like to say in the United States. There has spread through our country wave after wave of what we call intergroup understanding; and with the decay of religious belief a kind of *ersatz* toleration comes into existence, since people who don't really believe anything anyhow find it easy to endure other people who don't really believe anything in different churches.

Part of the general *détente* depends upon this; part of it, of course, depends upon certain historical facts. There is the whole history of the Nazi régime and a feeling of guilt in the American Gentile community over Hitler and the destruction of the Jews. There is also a general feeling in America of satisfaction at the emergence of Israel as an independent state—a satisfaction which sometimes is a genuine satisfaction that the Jews have found a place of refuge and a homeland, but which sometimes seems to me to be the satisfaction which Americans always have when anyone licks the English anywhere, from the American Revolution to the Irish, and so on.

Now, as a result of what I have described there has occurred a Judaization of American culture which is beyond belief. And it occurs to me to note that at the point where American culture is being Judaized, world culture is being Americanized—and what does this mean when one gets down to the second, third, fourth level.

I live in a remote provincial town, in a state which most people who have seen the other states in the United States may not have ever got to. I live in Missoula, Montana. As I walk into the local taverns I see the bums who come off of the freight-trains walking up to the bar and ordering Mogen David wine. As I walk down the streets of my home town, past a little junk shop which sells gifts to tourists, I see looking out at me from the windows, on ashtrays, stationery and greeting-cards, the character of the *Nebbish* who has passed into general American culture.

I turn on radio or television and I hear Jewish comics—Jewish American comics, let's say—bringing to the great multitudes the kind of humor which was built by the Jews at the point of ultimate desperation. I move through a country where the secular sanctification of Anne Frank has been utterly astonishing and where the glorification of Harry Golden is utterly appalling. I live in a country which has witnessed the strange conversions to Judaism of the mythical, erotic figures we see on the screen, Marilyn Monroe and Elizabeth Taylor.

The best American writers, I think, are troubled and embarrassed to find themselves part of this general development. Yet I think when the American writer, whoever he may be, searches his deepest conscience he discovers that it is true that what has happened to him and to his country is what he has all along desired, though he may have concealed from himself the full meaning of his wishes. We now come to the first crux of what I am trying to say to you. The success of American writers represents the success of an assimilationist dream which is not accidental but essential to the act of becoming a Jewish American writer. It is an assimilationist dream—a cultural, assimilationist dream I would say—a not ignoble or cowardly dream, not the kind of assimilationist dream of escaping from something but of entering into something. [...]

* * *

When Walt Whitman—a man who says: "I contain multitudes," who wanted to encompass everything and spew it back again; a man whose proudest boast was "I am a man, I suffered, I was there"; a man who was called by the first critics of his own time "the dirtiest beast of the age"—when Walt Whitman comes back to life, he's a Jewish boy from Paterson, New Jersey, and his name is Allen Ginsberg. He writes a book which destroys the world of his father, chops it up into little pieces; and then he writes a second book and calls it: *Kaddish.*

When we move down on to a lower level, when the pale Anglo-Saxon virgin—the great favorite of female popular literature in the United States, who weeps and pleads seduction for page after page—is reinvented, it turns out she's not really the Gentile Anglo-Saxon girl we thought she was all along; she's just changed her name to Marjorie Morningstar.

Generation after generation now, in the recent years, there have come out of American homes originally founded by refugee Jews from Eastern Europe, writer after writer who make books that seem to a whole class of readers—many of them Gentiles—to discover the actual shape of the lives those readers live: Saul Bellow, Bernard Malamud, J. D. Salinger, Norman Mailer, Philip Roth, Grace Paley, Norman Fruchter. The list goes on and on.

Finally, there are even protests which come up from certain quarters, at least humorous ones, so that I was amused recently to read by Gore Vidal a little note which says: "Every year there is a short list of OK writers. Today's list consists of two Jews, two Negroes and a safe, floating *goy* of the American Establishment." Rattling description of the way the critics judge the scene.

But it's not only true in the United States. I enjoy travelling about the world, talking to anybody who'll listen to me. And when I talk to the sixth-formers of Manchester Grammar School, they say: "What about Norman Mailer?" When I go to a school in Milan, they say: "What about *Giovanne Holden*?"—"Young Holden," which is the title they've given to the book *The Catcher in the Rye.*

And yet—I come back to the sad part of my talk—all this occurs at the point when the Jewish American writer, the kind I have been talking about, is painfully aware that his own Jewishness is certainly vestigial, if it is not at absolute zero. Now, what such writers choose to do about this fact, as American citizens and children of Jews, is up to them. They can applaud the fact that their Jewishness is about to disappear, or they can deplore that fact. The writer can want to become *more* Jewish rather than *less* Jewish, if he chooses, or he can let his Jewishness disappear. That's as a human being. *As a writer,* though, the Jewish American writer of the kind I've been describing, who is alive and registering in the present world, *has no choice!* The only thing there is for him to describe is what he is and what he knows—Jews who are sometimes terminal Jews and, more often, penultimate Jews. [. . .]

What's Happening to America

SUSAN SONTAG

Everything that one feels about this country is, or ought to be, conditioned by the awareness of American *power:* of America as the arch-imperium of the planet, holding man's biological as well as his historical future in its King Kong paws. Today's America, with Ronald Reagan the new daddy of California and John Wayne chawing spareribs in the White House, is pretty much the same Yahooland that Mencken was describing. The main difference is that what's happening in America matters so much more in the late sixties than in the twenties. Then, if one had tough innards, one might jeer, sometimes affectionately, at American barbarism and find American innocence somewhat endearing. Both the barbarism and the innocence are lethal, outsized today.

First of all, then, American power is indecent in its scale. But also, the quality of American life is an insult to the possibilities of human growth; and the pollution of American space, with gadgetry and cars and TV and box architecture, brutalizes the senses, making grey neurotics of most of us, and perverse spiritual athletes and strident self-transcenders of the best of us.

Gertrude Stein said that America is the oldest country in the world. Certainly, it's the most conservative. It has the most to lose by change (60 per cent of the world's wealth owned by a country containing 7 per cent of the world's population). Americans know their backs are against the wall, that "they" want to take it away from "us." And I must say America deserves to have it taken away.

Three facts about this country.

America was founded on a genocide, on the unquestioned assumption of the right of white Europeans to exterminate a resident, technologically backward, colored population in order to take over the continent.

America had not only the most brutal system of slavery in modern times, but a juridically unique system (compared with other slaveries, say in Latin America and the British colonies) which did not, in a single respect, recognize slaves as persons.

As a country (as distinct from a colony), America was created mainly by the surplus poor of Europe, reinforced by a small group who were just *Europamüde,* tired of Europe (a literary catchword of the eighteen forties). Yet even the poorest knew both a "culture," largely invented by his social betters and administered from above, and a "nature" that had been pacified for centuries. These people arrived in a country where the indigenous culture was simply the enemy and was in process of being ruthlessly annihilated, and where nature, too, was the enemy, a pristine force, unmodified by civilization, that is, by human wants, which had to be defeated. After America was "won," it was filled up by new generations of the poor, and built up according to the tawdry fantasy of the good life that culturally deprived, uprooted people might have at the beginning of the industrial era. And the country looks it.

Foreigners extol the American "energy," attributing to it both our unparalleled economic prosperity and the splendid vivacity of our arts and entertainments. But surely this is energy bad at its source and for which we pay too high a price, a hypernatural and humanly disproportionate dynamism that flays everyone's nerves raw. Basically it is the energy of violence, of free-floating resentment and anxiety unleashed by chronic cultural dislocations which must be, for the most part, ferociously sublimated. This energy has mainly been sublimated into crude materialism and acquisitiveness. Into hectic philanthropy. Into benighted moral crusades, the most spectacular of which was Prohibition. Into an awesome talent for uglifying countryside and cities. Into the loquacity and torment of a minority of gadflies: artists, prophets, muckrakers, cranks and nuts. And into self-punishing neuroses. But the naked violence keeps breaking through, throwing everything into question.

Needless to say, America is not the only violent, ugly and unhappy country on this earth. Again, it is a matter of scale. Only three million Indians lived here when the white man arrived, rifle in hand, for his fresh start. Today, American hegemony menaces the lives not of three but of countless millions who, like the Indians, have never even *heard* of "The United States of America," much less of its mythical empire, "the free world." American policy is still powered by the fantasy of Manifest Destiny, though the limits were once set by the borders of the continent, while today America's destiny embraces the entire world. There are still more hordes of redskins to be mowed down before virtue triumphs; as the classic western movies explain, the only good Red is a dead Red. This may sound like an exaggeration to those who live in the special and more finely modulated atmosphere of New York and its environs. Cross the Hudson. You find out that not just *some* Americans, but virtually all Americans feel that way.

Of course, these people don't know what they're saying, literally. But that's no excuse. That, in fact, is what makes it all possible. The unquenchable American moralism and the American faith in violence are not just twin symptoms of some character neurosis taking the form of a protracted adolescence, which presages an eventual maturity. They constitute a full grown, firmly-installed national psychosis, founded, as are all psychoses, on the efficacious denial of reality. So far it's worked. Except for portions of the South a hundred years ago, America has never known war. A taxi driver said to me on the day that could have been Armageddon, when America and Russia were on collision course off the shores of Cuba: "Me, I'm not worried. I served in the last one, and now I'm over draft age. They can't get me again. But I'm all for letting 'em have it right now. What are we waiting for? Let's get it over with." Since wars always happen Over There, and we always win, why not drop the bomb? If all it takes is pushing a button, even better. For America is that curious hybrid—an apocalyptic country and a valetudinarian country. The average citizen may harbor the fantasies of John Wayne, but he as often has the temperament of Jane Austen's Mr. Woodhouse.

To answer, briefly, some of *PR*'s questions:

1. I do *not* think that Johnson is forced by "our system" to act as he is acting. For instance, in Vietnam, where each evening he personally chooses the bombing targets for the next day's missions. But I think there is something awfully wrong with a *de facto* system which allows the President virtually unlimited discretion in pursuing an immoral and imprudent foreign policy, so that the strenuous opposition of, say, the Chairman of the Senate Foreign Relations Committee counts for—exactly nothing. The *de jure* system vests the power to make war in the Congress—with the exception, apparently, of imperialist ventures and genocidal expeditions. These are best left undeclared.

   However, I don't mean to suggest that Johnson's foreign policy is the whim of a clique which has seized control, escalated the power of the Chief Executive, castrated the Congress and manipulated public opinion. Johnson is, alas, all too representative. As Kennedy was not. If there is a conspiracy, it is (or was) that of the more enlightened national leaders hitherto largely selected by the eastern seaboard plutocracy. They engineered the precarious acquiescence to liberal goals that has prevailed in this country for over a generation—a superficial consensus made possible by the strongly apolitical character of a decentralized electorate mainly preoccupied with local issues. If the Bill of Rights were put to a national referendum as a new piece of legislation, it would meet the same fate as New York City's Civilian Review Board. Most of the people in this country believe what Goldwater believes, and always have. But most of them don't know it. Let's hope they don't find out.

4. I do not think white America is committed to granting equality to the American Negro. So committed are only a minority of generous and mostly educated, affluent white Americans, few of whom have had any

prolonged social contact with Negroes. This is a passionately racist country; it will continue to be so in the foreseeable future.

5. I think that this administration's foreign policies are likely to lead to more wars and to wider wars. Our main hope, and the chief restraint on American bellicosity and paranoia, lies in the fatigue and depoliticization of Western Europe, the lively fear of America and of another world war in Russia and the Eastern European countries, and the corruption and unreliability of our client states in the third world. It's hard to lead a holy war without allies. But America is just crazy enough to try to do it.
6. The meaning of the split between the Administration and the intellectuals? Simply that our leaders are genuine Yahoos, with all the exhibitionist traits of their kind, and that liberal intellectuals (whose deepest loyalties are to an international fraternity of the reasonable) are not *that* blind. At this point, moreover, they have nothing to lose by proclaiming their discontent and frustration. But it's well to remember that liberal intellectuals, like Jews, tend to have a classical theory of politics, in which the state has a monopoly of power; hoping that those in positions of authority may prove to be enlightened men, wielding power justly, they are natural, if cautious, allies of the "establishment." As the Russian Jews knew they had at least a chance with the Czar's officials but none at all with marauding Cossacks and drunken peasants (Milton Himmelfarb has pointed this out), liberal intellectuals more naturally expect to influence the "decisions" of administrators than they do the volatile "feelings" of masses. Only when it becomes clear that, in fact, the government itself is being staffed by Cossacks and peasants, can a rupture like the present one take place. When (and if) the man in the White House who paws people and scratches his balls in public is replaced by the man who dislikes being touched and finds Yevtushenko "an interesting fellow," American intellectuals won't be so disheartened. The vast majority of them are not revolutionaries, wouldn't know how to be if they tried. Mostly a salaried professoriat, they're as much at home in the system when it functions a little better than it does right now as anyone else.

A somewhat longer comment on the last question.

Yes, I do find much promise in the activities of young people. About the only promise one can find anywhere in this country today is in the way some young people are carrying on, making a fuss. I include both their renewed interest in politics (as protest and as community action, rather than as theory) and the way they dance, dress, wear their hair, riot, make love. I also include the homage they pay to Oriental thought and rituals. And I include, not least of all, their interest in taking drugs—despite the unspeakable vulgarization of this project by Leary and others.

A year ago Leslie Fiedler, in a remarkably wrongheaded and interesting essay (published in *PR* and titled "The New Mutants") called attention to the fact that the new style of young people indicated a deliberate blurring of sexual differences, signaling the creation of a new breed of youthful androgens. The longhaired pop groups with their mass teen-age following and the tiny elite of turned-on kids from Berkeley to the East Village were both lumped together as representatives of the "post-humanist" era now upon us, in which we witness a "radical metamorphosis of the western male," a "revolt against masculinity," even "a rejection of conventional male potency." For Fiedler, this new turn in personal mores, diagnosed as illustrating a "programmatic espousal of an anti-puritanical mode of existence," is something to deplore. (Though sometimes, in his characteristic have-it-both-ways manner, Fiedler seemed to be vicariously relishing this development, *mainly* he appeared to be lamenting it.) But why, he never made explicit. I think it is because he is sure such a mode of existence undercuts radical politics, and its moral visions, altogether. Being radical in the older sense (some version of Marxism or socialism or anarchism) meant to be attached still to traditional "puritan" values of work, sobriety, achievement and family-founding. Fiedler suggests, as have Philip Rahv and Irving Howe and Malcolm Muggeridge among others, that the new style of youth must be, at bottom, apolitical, and their revolutionary spirit a species of infantilism. The fact that the same kid joins SNCC or boards a Polaris submarine or agrees with Conor Cruise O'Brien *and* smokes pot and is bisexual and adores the Supremes, is seen as a contradiction, a kind of ethical fraud or intellectual weak-mindedness.

I don't believe this to be so. The depolarizing of the sexes, to mention the element that Fiedler observes with such fascination, is the natural, and desirable, next stage of the sexual revolution (its dissolution, perhaps) which has moved beyond the idea of sex as a damaged but discrete zone of human activity, beyond the discovery that "society" represses the free expression of sexuality (by fomenting guilt), to the discovery that the way we live and the ordinarily available options of character repress almost entirely the deep experience of pleasure, and the possibility of self-knowledge. "Sexual freedom" is a shallow, outmoded slogan. What, who is being liberated? For older people, the sexual revolution is an idea that remains meaningful. One can be for it or against it; if for it, the idea remains confined within the norms of Freudianism and its derivatives. But Freud *was* a Puritan, or "a fink," as one of Fiedler's students distressingly blurted out. So was Marx. It is right that young people see beyond Freud and Marx. Let the professors be the caretakers of this indeed precious legacy, and discharge all the obligations of piety. No need for dismay if the kids don't continue to pay the old dissenter-gods obeisance.

It seems to me obtuse, though understandable, to patronize the new kind of radicalism, which is post-Freudian and post-Marxian. For this radicalism is as much an experience as an idea. Without the personal experience, if one is looking in from the outside, it does look messy and almost pointless. It's easy to be put off by the youngsters throwing themselves around with their eyes closed to the near-deafening music of the discothèques (unless you're dancing, too), by the longhaired marchers carrying flowers and temple bells as often as "Get Out of Vietnam" placards, by the inarticulateness of a Mario Savio. One is also aware of the high casualty rate among the gifted, visionary minority among the young, the tremendous cost in personal suffering and in mental strain. The fakers, the slobs and the merely flipped-out are plentiful among them. But the complex desires of the best of them: to engage and to "drop out"; to be beautiful to look at and touch as well as to be good; to be loving and quiet as well as militant and effective—these desires make sense in our present situation. To sympathize, of course, you have to be convinced that things in America really are as desperately bad as I have indicated. This is hard to see; the desperateness of things is obscured by the comforts and liberties that America does offer. Most people, understandably, don't really believe things are that bad. That's why, for them, the antics of this youth can be no more than a startling item in the passing parade of cultural fashions, to be appraised with a friendly, but essentially weary and knowing look. The sorrowful look that says: I was radical, too, when I was young. When are these kids going to grow up and realize what we had to realize, that things never are going to be really different, except maybe worse?

From my own experience and observation, I can testify that there is a profound concordance between the sexual revolution, redefined, and the political revolution, redefined. That being a socialist and taking certain drugs (in a fully serious spirit: as a technique for exploring one's consciousness, not as an anodyne or a crutch), are not incompatible, that there is no incompatibility between the exploration of inner space and the rectification of social space. What some of the kids understand is that it's the whole character-structure of modern American man, and his imitators, that needs rehauling. (Old folks like Paul Goodman and Edgar Z. Friedenberg have, of course, been suggesting this for a long time.) That rehauling includes Western "masculinity," too. They believe that some socialist remodeling of institutions and the ascendance, through electoral means or otherwise, of better leaders won't really change anything. And they are right.

Neither do I dare deride the turn toward the East (or more generally, to the wisdoms of the nonwhite world) on the part of a tiny group of young people—however uninformed and jejune the adherence usually is. (But then, nothing could be more ignorant than Fiedler's insinuation that Oriental modes of thought are "feminine" and "passive," which is the reason the demasculinized kids are drawn to them.) Why shouldn't they look for wisdom elsewhere? If America *is* the culmination of Western white civilization, as everyone from the Left to the Right declares, then there must be something terribly wrong with Western white civilization. This is a painful truth; few of us want to go that far. It's easier, much easier, to accuse the kids, to reproach them for being "non-participants in the past" and "drop-outs from history." But it isn't real history Fiedler is referring to with such solicitude. It's just *our* history, which he claims is identical with "the tradition of the human," the tradition of "reason" itself. Of course, it's hard to assess life on this planet from a genuinely world-historical perspective; the effort induces vertigo and seems like an invitation to suicide. But from a world-historical perspective, that local history which some people are repudiating (with their fondness for dirty words, their peyote, their macrobiotic rice, their Dadaist art, etc.) looks a good deal less pleasing and less self-evidently worthy of perpetuation. The truth is that Mozart, Pascal, Boolean algebra, Shakespeare, parliamentary government, baroque churches, Newton, the emancipation of women, Kant, Marx, Balanchine ballets, *et al.*, don't redeem what this particular civilization has wrought upon the world. The white race *is* the cancer of human history; it is the white race and it alone—its ideologies and inventions—which eradicates autonomous civilizations wherever it spreads, which has upset the ecological balance of the planet, which now threatens the very existence of life itself. What the Mongol hordes threaten is far less frightening than the damage that Western "Faustian" man, with his idealism, his magnificent art, his sense of intellectual adventure, his world-devouring energies for conquest, has already done, and further threatens to do.

This is what some of the kids sense, though few of them could put it in words. Again, I believe them to be right. I'm not arguing that they're going to prevail, or even that they're likely to change much of anything in this country. But a few of them may save their own souls. America is a fine country for inflaming people, from Emerson and Thoreau to Mailer and Burroughs and Leo Szilard and John Cage and Judith and Julian Beck, with the project of trying to save their own souls. Salvation becomes almost a mundane, inevitable goal when things are so bad, really intolerable.

One last comparison, which I hope won't seem farfetched. The Jews left the ghetto in the early nineteenth century, thus becoming a people doomed to disappear. But one of the by-products of their fateful absorption into the modern world was an incredible burst of creativity in the arts, science and secular scholarship—the relocation of a powerful but frustrated spiritual energy. These innovating artists and intellectuals were not alienated Jews, as is said so often, but people who were alienated *as* Jews.

I'm scarcely more hopeful for America than I am for the Jews. This is a doomed country, it seems to me; I only pray that, when America founders, it doesn't drag the rest of the planet down, too. But one should notice that, during its long elephantine agony, America is also producing its subtlest minority generation of the decent and sensitive, young people who are alienated *as* Americans. They are not drawn to the stale truths of their sad elders (though these are truths). More of their elders should be listening to them.

Witness for the Defense at the Chicago Conspiracy Trial

ALLEN GINSBERG

Mr. Weinglass: Will you please state your full name?
The witness: Allen Ginsberg.
Mr. Weinglass: What is your occupation?
The witness: Poet.
Mr. Weinglass: Have you authored any books in the field of poetry?
The witness: In 1956, *Howl and Other Poems;* in 1960, *Kaddish and Other Poems;* in 1963, *Empty Mirror;* in 1963, *Reality Sandwiches,* and in 1968, *Planet News.*
Mr. Weinglass: Now, in addition to your writing, Mr. Ginsberg, are you presently engaged in any other activity?
The witness: I teach, lecture, and recite poetry at universities.
Mr. Weinglass: Now, did you ever study abroad?
The witness: Yes. In India and Japan.
Mr. Weinglass: Could you indicate for the Court and jury what the area of your studies consisted of?
The witness: Mantra Yoga, meditation exercises and sitting quietly, breathing exercises to calm the body and calm the mind, but mainly a branch called Mantra Yoga, which is yoga which involved prayer and chanting.
Mr. Weinglass: How long did you study?
The witness: I was in India for a year and a third, and then in Japan studying with Gary Snyder, a zen poet, at Dai Tokuji Monastery, D-A-I T-O-K-U-J-I. I sat there for the zazen exercises for centering the body and quieting the mind.
Mr. Weinglass: Are you still studying under any of your former teachers?
The witness: Yes, Swami Bahkti Vedanta, faith, philosophy; Bahkti Vedanta, B-A-H-K-T-I V-E-D-A-N-T-A. I have seen him and chanted with him the last few years in different cities, and he has asked me to continue chanting, especially on public occasions. This involves chanting and praying, praying out loud and in community.
Mr. Weinglass: In the course of a Mantra chant, is there any particular position that the person doing that assumes?

The witness: Any position which will let the stomach relax and be easy, fall out, so that aspiration can be deep into the body, to relax the body completely and calm the mind, based as cross-legged.

Mr. Weinglass: And is it—chanting—to be done privately, or is it in public?

Mr. Foran: Oh, your Honor, I object. I think we have gone far enough now—

The Court: I think I have a vague idea now of the witness' profession. It is vague.

Mr. Foran: I think I might also indicate that he is an excellent speller.

The witness: Sir—

The Court: Yes, sir.

The witness: In India, the profession of poetry and the profession of chanting are linked together as one practice.

The Court: That's right. I give you credit for that.

Mr. Weinglass: Mr. Ginsberg, do you know the defendant Jerry Rubin?

The witness: Yes, I do.

Mr. Weinglass: Do you recall where it was that you first met him?

The witness: In Berkeley and San Francisco in 1965 during the time of the anti-Vietnam war marches in Berkeley. I saw him again at the human be-in in San Francisco. We shared the stage with many other people.

Mr. Weinglass: Would you describe for the Court and jury what the be-in in San Francisco was?

The witness: A large assembly of younger people who came together to—

Mr. Foran: Objection, your Honor.

The Court: Just a minute. I am not sure how you spell the be-in.

Mr. Weinglass: B-E I-N, I believe, be-in.

The witness: Human be-in.

The Court: I really can't pass on the validity of the objection because I don't understand the question.

Mr. Weinglass: I asked him to explain what a be-in was.

Mr. Foran: I would love to know also but I don't think it has anything to do with this lawsuit.

The Court: I will let him, over the objection of the Government, tell what a be-in is.

The witness: A gathering-together of younger people aware of the planetary fate that we are all sitting in the middle of, imbued with a new consciousness, a new kind of society involving prayer, music, and spiritual life together rather than competition, acquisition and war.

Mr. Weinglass: And was that the activity that was engaged in in San Francisco at this be-in?

The witness: There was what was called a "Gathering of the Tribes" of all the different affinity groups, spiritual groups, political groups, yoga groups, music groups and poetry groups that all felt the same crisis of identity and crisis of the planet and political crisis in America, who all came together in the largest assemblage of such younger people that had taken place since the war in the presence of the Zen master Sazuki and in the presence of the rock bands and the presence of Timothy Leary and Mr. Rubin.

Mr. Weinglass: Now, later on in the year of 1967 did you have occasion to meet again with the defendant Jerry Rubin?

The witness: Yes. We met in a cafe in Berkeley and discussed his mayoral race for the city of Berkeley. He had run for mayor.

Mr. Weinglass: Did you have any participation in that campaign?

The witness: I encouraged it, blessed it.

Mr. Weinglass: Now, do you know the defendant Abbie Hoffman?

The witness: Yes.

Mr. Weinglass: Now, calling your attention to the month of February 1968, did you have any occasion in that month to meet with Abbie Hoffman?

The witness: Yeah.

Mr. Weinglass: Do you recall what Mr. Hoffman said in the course of the conversation.

The witness: Yippee—among other things. He said that politics had become theater and magic; that it was the manipulation of imagery through mass media that was confusing and hypnotizing the people in the United States and making them accept a war which they did not really believe in; that people were involved in a life style that was intolerable to young folks, which involved brutality and police violence as well as a larger violence in Vietnam; and that ourselves might be able to get together in Chicago and invite teachers to present different ideas of what is wrong with the planet, what we can do to solve the pollution crisis, what we can do to solve the Vietnam war, to present different ideas for making the society more sacred and less commercial, less materialistic; what we could do to uplevel or improve the whole tone of the trap that we all felt ourselves in as the population grew and as politics became more and more violent and chaotic.

Mr. Weinglass: Now, did he ascribe any particular name to that project?

The witness: Festival of Life.

Mr. Weinglass: After he spoke to you, what, if anything, was your response to his suggestion?

The witness: I was worried whether or not the whole scene would get violent. I was worried whether we would be allowed to put on such a situation. I was worried, you know, whether the government would let us do something that was funnier or prettier or more charming than what was going to be going on in the Convention hall.

Mr. Foran: I object and ask that it be stricken. It was not responsive.

The Court: Yes. I sustain the objection.

The witness: Sir, that was our conversation.

Mr. Weinglass: Now, during that same month, February of 1968, did you have occasion to meet with Jerry Rubin?

The witness: I spoke with Jerry Rubin on the phone, I believe.

Mr. Weinglass: Will you relate to the Court and jury what Jerry Rubin said to you?

The witness: Jerry told me that he and others were going to Chicago to apply for permission from the city government for a permit to hold a Festival of Life and that he was talking with John Sinclair about getting rock and roll bands together and other musicians and that he would report back to me.

Mr. Weinglass: Mr. Ginsberg, do you recall anything else that Mr. Rubin said to you in the course of that telephone conversation?

The witness: Yes, he said that he thought it would be interesting if we could get up little schools like ecology schools, music schools, political schools, schools about the Vietnam war, schools with yogis.

He asked if I could contact Burroughs and ask Burroughs to come to teach nonverbal, nonconceptual feeling states.

Mr. Weinglass: Now you indicated a school of ecology. Could you explain to the Court and jury what that is?

The witness: Ecology is the interrelation of all the living forms on the surface of the planet involving the food chain—that is to say, whales eat plankton; larger fishes eat smaller fish, octopus or squid eat shellfish which eat plankton; human beings eat the shellfish or squid or smaller fish which eat the smaller tiny microorganisms—

Mr. Foran: That is enough, your Honor.

The Court: Yes. We all have a clear idea of what ecology is.

The witness: Well, the destruction of ecology is what would have been taught. That is, how it is being destroyed by human intervention and messing it up with pollution.

Mr. Weinglass: Now you also indicated that Mr. Rubin mentioned nonverbal education. Will you explain what that is to the Court and jury?

The witness: Most of our consciousness, since we are continually looking at images on television and listening to words, reading newspapers, talking in courts such as this, most of our consciousness is filled with language, with a kind of matter babble behind the ear, a continuous yakety-yak that actually prevents us from breathing deeply in our bodies and sensing more subtly and sweetly the feelings that we actually do have as persons to each other rather than as talking machines.

Mr. Weinglass: Now, Mr. Ginsberg, on March 17, where were you?

The witness: I took part in a press conference at the Hotel Americana in New York City.

Mr. Weinglass: Who else was present at this press conference?

The witness: Abbie Hoffman and Jerry Rubin were there as well as Phil Ochs, the folk singer, Arlo Guthrie, some members of the USA band, some members of the Diggers groups.

Mr. Weinglass: Could you indicate to the Court and jury what Jerry Rubin said?

The witness: He said that a lot of younger people in America would come to Chicago during the Convention and hold a Festival of Life in the parks, and he announced that they were negotiating with the City Hall to get a permit to have a life festival in the parks.

Mr. Weinglass: Do you recall what Abbie Hoffman said?

The witness: He said that they were going to go to Chicago in groups to negotiate with representatives of Mayor Daley to get a permit for a large-scale Gathering of the Tribes and he mentioned the human be-in in San Francisco.

Mr. Weinglass: Did you yourself participate in that press conference?

The witness: Yes. I stepped to the microphone also. My statement was that the planet Earth at the present moment was endangered by violence, overpopulation, pollution, ecological destruction brought about by our own greed; that our younger children in America and other countries of the world might not survive the next thirty years; that it was a planetary crisis that had not been recognized by any government of the world and had not been recognized by our own government, not the politicians who were preparing for the elections; that the younger people of America were aware of that and that precisely was what was called psychedelic consciousness; that we were going to gather together as we had before in the San Francisco human be-in to manifest our presence over and above the presence of the more selfish elder politicians who were not thinking in terms of what their children would need in future generations, or even in the generation immediately coming, or even for themselves in their own lifetime and were continuing to threaten the planet with violence, with war, with mass murder, with germ warfare. And since the younger people knew that in the United States, we are going to invite them there, and that the central motive would be a presentation of a desire for the preservation of the planet. The desire for preservation of the planet and the planet's form was manifested to my mind by the great Mantra from India to the preserver god Vishnu whose Mantra is the Hare Krishna. And then I chanted the Hare Krishna for ten minutes to the television cameras, and it goes:

Hare krishna/hare krishna/krishna krishna/hare hare/hare rama/hare rama/rama rama/hare hare.

Mr. Weinglass: Now in chanting that did you have an accompaniment of any particular instrument? Your Honor, I object to the laughter of the Court on this. I think this is a serious presentation of a religious concept.

The Court: I don't understand. I don't understand it because it was—the language of the United States District Court is English.

Mr. Kunstler: I know, but you don't laugh at all languages.

The Court: I didn't laugh. I didn't laugh.

The witness: I would be happy to explain it.

The Court: I didn't laugh at all. I wish I could tell you how I feel. Laugh—I didn't even smile.

Mr. Kunstler: Well, I thought—

The Court: All I could tell you is that I didn't understand it because whatever language the witness is using—

The witness: Sanskrit, sir.

The Court: Well, that is one I don't know. That is the reason I didn't understand it.

The witness: Might we go on to an explanation?

The Court: Will you keep quiet, Mr. Witness, while I am talking to the lawyers?

The witness: I will be glad to give an explanation.

The Court: I never laugh at a witness, sir. I protect witnesses who come to this court. But I do tell you that the language of the American court is English unless you have an interpreter. You may use an interpreter for the remainder of the witness' testimony.

Mr. Kunstler: No. I have heard, your Honor, priests explain the mass in Latin in American courts and I think Mr. Ginsberg is doing exactly the same thing in Sanskrit for another type of religious experience.

The Court: I don't understand Sanskrit. I venture to say the jury members don't. Perhaps we have some people on the jury who do understand Sanskrit, I don't know, but I wouldn't even have known it was Sanskrit until he told me. I can't see that that is material to the issues here, that is all.

Mr. Weinglass: Let me ask this: Mr. Ginsberg, I show you an object marked 150 for identification, and I ask you to examine that object.

The witness: Yes.

Mr. Foran: All right. Your Honor, that is enough. I object to it, your Honor. I think it is outrageous for counsel to—

The Court: You asked him to examine it and instead of that he played a tune on it. I sustain the objection.

The witness: It adds spirituality to the case, sir.
The Court: Will you remain quiet, sir.
The witness: I am sorry.
Mr. Weinglass: Having examined that, could you identify it for the Court and jury?
The witness: It is an instrument known as the harmonium, which I used at the press conference at the Americana Hotel. It is commonly used in India.
Mr. Foran: I object to that.
The Court: I sustain the objection.
Mr. Weinglass: Will you explain to the Court and to the jury what chant you were chanting at the press conference?
The witness: I was chanting a mantra called the "Maha Mantra," the great mantra of preservation of that aspect of the Indian religion called Vishnu the Preserver. Every time human evil rises so high that the planet itself is threatened, and all of its inhabitants and their children are threatened, Vishnu will preserve a return.

9

On Jewish Radicals and Radical Jews

During a several-year period after the Six-Day War in June 1967, a radical Jewish movement emerged whose core constituency was university students and other young people from across the United States and Canada. This radical Jewish youth movement articulated a number of important shared views. It considered mainstream American Jewishness to be superficial and inauthentic. It likewise criticized professional American Jewish organizations for lacking a commitment to genuine or meaningful Jewish values. It denounced as "Uncle Jakes" those Jews who "collaborated" with conservative (gentile) elements in U.S. society. It often saw the central conflict in American Jewish (*and* American) life in intergenerational terms—as in "Don't trust anyone over thirty." It was melodramatic, insolent, shocking, and theatrical. It seldom hesitated to bash and belittle Jewish elders for all sorts of crimes.

However, there was also very little consensus within the Jewish youth movement. Many involved in this insurgent confederacy of radical Jews first experienced the politics of direct action in the African American civil rights struggle and/or in the context of activities for the Student Nonviolent Coordinating Committee (SNCC) and Students for a Democratic Society (SDS). Yet this shared sense of an activist past did not translate into a shared vision for a radical Jewish future.

Unquestionably, these internal disagreements were largely a result of the major shake-up in the New Left after the Six-Day War. In June 1967, Jewish radicals heard their New Left friends harshly criticize the actions of an "imperialist" Israel. At the same time, the Palestinian cause grew immensely popular with the New Left, causing Jewish New Leftists angrily to denounce it. Some young Jews—calling themselves radical Zionists—reconfigured their allegiances so that Israeli survival was now the priority of their left-wing political outlook.

At the same time, there were also radical Jews who did not endorse Zionism but rather sought to bring together New Left ideology *and* Jewish pride. These radical Jews often invoked the prophetic tradition of Judaism, and they rejected the view that they had to choose between "Jewish" and "non-Jewish" causes. Thus, efforts to rescue Soviet Jews and efforts to end the war in Vietnam were seen as equally important causes. These Jewish radicals were also more willing than radical Zionists to attack the right-wing Zionism of the Jewish Defense League.

The topic of Jewish radicalism remains underacknowledged. This is surprising not least because there were dozens of radical Jewish student newspapers that spanned the spectrum of political debate and religious affiliation. But it is most surprising in view of the fact that many former radicals would later run many of the very same professional Jewish organizations they had criticized in their youth. This chapter offers a brief sampling from the radical Jewish movement.

M. Jay Rosenberg and Aviva Cantor Zuckoff were early leaders of the radical Zionist movement. Rosenberg, a student at the State University of New York at Albany, rose to national prominence after he published the essay included here: "To Jewish Uncle Toms." It was frequently reprinted and sparked great controversy. Rosenberg's attack on the acculturated suburban Jewish middle class was especially incendiary; his impact on subsequent debate was considerable. In 1969, Zuckoff cofounded the *Jewish Liberation Journal*. Published in Manhattan, *JLJ* became one of the most influential of the radical Jewish journals at the turn of the decade. And its articles mainly lived up to the ideals stated in this first editorial, also included here.

Meanwhile, some radical Jews opted for political humor as their weapon of choice. The short article by David Weissman foregrounds the playfulness that typified many of the actions conducted by radical Jewish groups. Likewise, although on a national stage, the testimony of Yippie leader Abbie Hoffman during the Chicago conspiracy trial suggests that nothing is more deadly for political action than humorlessness. Hoffman injected an often distinctly Jewish kind of humor and irreverence into virtually every public declaration he made.

Indeed, as mentioned in the introduction to the prior chapter, the Chicago Eight conspiracy trial was an unusually Jewish event. Judge Julius J. Hoffman was Jewish, as were both defense attorneys (although prosecutor Richard G. Schultz was not). And several of the best-known defendants (including Abbie Hoffman and Jerry Rubin) were also Jewish. Facing charges that they had crossed state lines with the intent to incite a riot at the Democratic National Convention in 1968, the defendants—and Abbie Hoffman in particular—missed few opportunities to mock the prosecution and the court. The selections from the trial transcript reprinted in this chapter indicate once again how bizarre an encounter with authority this trial often was. Included is a brief exchange toward the end of the proceedings that suggests how the odd subtext of Jewishness functioned in this courtroom drama.

The next three selections outline the goals of the radical Zionist movement. There is a news report from the Boston-based *Genesis 2* that announces the formation at Camp Ramah in western Massachusetts of the Radical Zionist Alliance and cites from its manifesto. This is followed by Aviva Cantor Zuckoff's elaborate—but quite provocative—essay, "Oppression of Amerika's Jews." Zuckoff takes on a host of Jewish stereotypes and argues that American Jews have internalized these myths. (Her decision to use the German spelling of "Amerika" also emphasizes the disturbing parallels she sees between contemporary U.S. and Nazi German society.) While problematic in the way she revives the cliché of Jewish passivity under Nazism, Zuckoff's essay nonetheless encapsulates key elements of radical Zionist philosophy at the end of the 1960s.

The dialogue between a young radical Zionist, Jonathan Goldin, and a leading member of the Jewish Old Left, *Jewish Currents* editor Morris U. Schappes, illuminates radical Jewish intergenerational tensions. Schappes had been closely aligned with the Communist Party in the early 1950s and had broken with the party only after the revelations surrounding Stalin's purges of Jewish intellectuals had proven indisputable. Schappes then refashioned *Jewish Currents* into a progressive (but noncommunist) voice of American Jewry, although—as this dialogue suggests—still a voice hesitant to endorse Zionist ideology.

Brooklyn Bridge was a non-Zionist New Left underground journal. The inaugural editorial included here combines Jewish pride with a continued Jewish commitment to the struggles of other oppressed minorities in the United States. On the other hand, the interview with Jewish Defense League leader Meir Kahane by two radical Zionist students suggests how cleverly Kahane courted radical Zionist young people's support. Finally, Steve Cohen severely critiques Kahane's appropriation of the Holocaust to advance the right-wing causes sponsored by the JDL.

To Jewish Uncle Toms

M. JAY ROSENBERG

It has become fashionable in certain liberal (and predominantly Jewish) circles to scoff at anything that smacks of Jewishness. The Jew, the classic bumbling liberal, is today subject to scorn by virtually every left-wing spokesman. And the young American Jew is falling into line. He sees nothing inconsistent in his support of black "leaders" who warn of "Zionist conspiracies," and he can fit, albeit uncomfortably, into political organizations that advocate the liquidation of Israel. At one time such a Jew would be ridiculed and perhaps referred to a competent psychotherapist. Today he is respected and is, at the very least, considered legitimate. His more rational Jewish peers avoid the subject of the "Jewish question" with him while his Gentile allies rejoice at the sight of this "liberated" Jew.

It is about time that this intellectual misfit be challenged. One must make clear that not all Jewish leftists subscribe to the militantly pro-Arab and anti-Jewish line of such organizations, popular on campus, as the Al-Fatah supporting "Socialist Workers Party." But it must also be said that any Jew, regardless of how pro-Israel he might personally be, who remains in one of these organizations, supports it financially or merely helps distribute its literature under the pretense that there are more important issues than the Middle East, is guilty of the greatest crime. And he will be dealt with.

It is most ironic. The self-hating Jew should have died with the creation of Israel. If the drama enacted in Cyprus, Europe and Palestine between 1945 and 1948 did not convince him of the blood and guts of his own people then I am not sure that anything would. But in this time of exploding nationalism we should be less than tolerant of any Jew who chooses the route of self-denial and submission. One can sympathize with an individual who feels such self-hatred and yet we are also entitled to condemn him.

In the context of America, 1968, it is all the more amazing. The black American is the first to openly abjure the idea of assimilation, to recognize the inherent lie in the concept of the melting-pot. Through black nationalism he has developed a new black pride and hence the ticket to liberalism.

The young American Jew is a good deal slower. He desperately craves assimilation; the very idea of "Jewishness" embarrasses him. If you tell him that he doesn't "look Jewish," he will invariably take it as a compliment. The concept of Jewish nationalism, Israel notwithstanding, he finds laughable. The leftist

Jewish student—and this also applies to such apolitical college-age Jews as the fraternity boys, although to a far lesser degree—is today's "Uncle Tom." He scrapes along ashamed of his identity and yet obsessed with it. He goes so far as to join black nationalist organizations, not as a Jew, but as a white. He does not and will not understand that his relevance is as a Jew, a fellow victim, and that his only effectiveness is as such. His destiny is that of the Jews but he denies what is apparent to the rest of us; he wants to be an "American," a leftist American talking liberation and an aspiring WASP. In relating to blacks, he will not come on as a Jew but as a white; he is hardly ready to relegate his precious whiteness to a secondary position. This potential Jewish WASP is a ludicrous figure. If certain black spokesmen have been sounding anti-Semitic, we can attribute part of this feeling to the inherently racist attitude of the leftist Jew. The black militant comes into contact only with these self-hating Jews; it is not hard for him to realize that any man who cannot accept his own national identity is hardly likely to honestly accept any other man's. He can only see the self-abnegating Jewish leftist as the hypocrite that he is.

If he accepts the most basic tenets of the black nationalist movement, he should get himself out of it. Blacks don't want his "leadership" and they certainly don't need it. They realize the need for auto-emancipation even if he doesn't. The sad fact is that the Jewish "Tom," so desirous of flagellation, is an inevitable product of American civilization. But it is time that he realizes that he is truly the invisible man. He, not today's black, is wandering in a no-man's land.

The Jew can be an ally of the black liberation movement and he should be. But first he must find himself. He must realize that his own struggle for liberation is a continuing one, that he also has much to fear and also much to take pride in. The miracle of Israel, a national liberation deferred for two thousand years, should be his inspiration. As the late Robert F. Kennedy said, "Israel's creation . . . has written a new chapter in the annals of freedom and courage—a story that my children and yours will tell their descendants to the end of time." This is recognized by free men everywhere. In Biafra, the struggling Ibo looks to Israel as a symbol of man's never ending fight for survival and freedom. It would be doubly tragic if the young American Jew does not see clearly what is so apparent to a Biafran, a Czech, a free Irishman or a West Berliner. The miracle of 1948 was that the Jew did it alone, with the guns he could smuggle and the iron will that is the legacy of Auschwitz. The Jew prevailed and he did it without a single ally. This makes it so imperative that we ensure that what was won by Jewish heroes on the fields of Palestine will not be lost with the aid and connivance of Jewish moral cowards here at home.

Therefore it is as a Jew that I must accept black nationalism. The black nationalists may or may not be the equivalents of the militants of the early

Zionist organizations, and Malcolm X may or may not be a black Vladimir Jabotinsky, but surely the parallel is there. The Jewish War of Liberation differs from that of the black American or of the Viet Cong only in that the Jewish struggle has seen its greatest aim realized, however tenuously. So will the black revolution succeed. And yet I know that when the black man wins his freedom, he will lose all his white "friends." He will be called "anti-progressive." He will be labeled an "aggressor." If he wins again and again, he will be called an "oppressor." The black in America will then realize that he stands completely alone; as he, in fact, does now.

He can learn this much from the Jewish experience. When they slaughtered six million Jews, the good people muttered sympathetic noises. But the gates of America and Britain remained closed. And when the war ended, these good people wanted to help the few remaining Jews. They told them that they would help them return "home"—to Germany, to Poland and to Rumania. But the Jews wanted more. It was only when the fighting Jew arose from the blood and ashes of Europe, when the pitiful skeletons of Dachau resolved that they would now fight for their own land, that the Jews lost their newly-found friends. The world reluctantly came to accept our national existence but was prepared to mourn our imminent demise. For as it was said from the British Foreign Office to the halls of the American Department of State: "My God, man, you know Jews can't fight."

But fight and win they did. And for twenty years it appeared as though the world really did care about the fledgling Jewish state. Who can forget those days before the Six-Day War when every free world capital saw massive rallies in support of Israel. From London to Warsaw the common man supported Israel in its fight to live. Even the leftists backed Israel, although one can only feel that the Left would have rather avoided the subject entirely. But Israel's victory lost her any left-wing support she had. Israel suddenly became a "force of reaction," and a bastion of "anti-revolutionary activity." If Israel had lost the war, she could truly have ingratiated herself with the leftists. They would have held their sympathy rallies and would wear the "Star of David" as the symbol of national liberation. She could have come to represent the fight for freedom; the universal struggle to exist. Her people, unfortunately "driven into the sea," would have been martyrs to the cause. It could have been beautiful; but Israel lost her one golden chance to be loved by the left. She survived. And for that she shall be punished. Many Jewish nationalists have remarked that our recent history has conclusively proved that the Jews are "damned if they do and damned if they don't." For hundreds of years they said we were too passive, couldn't fight and finally that we allowed ourselves to be led "like sheep" to the slaughter. Today they say that we are a militaristic people with a fiercely bellicose streak.

So we have been condemned both for a lack of action and for strong deterrent action. In the final analysis we must prefer the latter condemnation. It is better by far to be damned for action than for the lack of it. As the black nationalists have said, when the issue is survival, we must prevail "by any means necessary."

But Israel is not the central issue at this point. The issue is one of Jewish pride. The Jewish professor who makes a point of teaching on Yom Kippur with subtle mockery of those students who stay home, the Jewish kids who lower their heads when a Philip Roth story is up for discussion in their literature course, the Jewish radicals who are prepared to fight for the Czechs, the Greeks and the Biafrans and yet reject Israel; these are our Uncle Toms and our shame. The Jew must accept his identity; and, like it or not, his Jewishness is his destiny. Hermann Goering was not far from the point when he said that, "I determine who is a Jew." Our only answer, as Jean-Paul Sartre has advised us, is to accept our Jewishness with pride. No anti-Semite, National Socialist or Socialist Worker, will define my existence. The sad lesson of the past thirty years is that, in the final analysis, we shall stand or fall together. To speak figuratively, in the shower-rooms it will little matter that one fellow was once Albert Shanker and the other was once Mark Rudd. Their destinies and fates are intertwined, for better or for worse. If we haven't learned that, we have learned nothing.

Black nationalism and Jewish nationalism will exist concurrently. To accept one, you must accept the other. The black is America's Jew and a common fight can be waged. But not at the expense of our own pride. Thus, when some black nationalist calls us "racist Zionists" or tells us that we are poisoning his children's minds; then we must see him for what he is; just another *goy,* using the Jew, the available and acceptable scapegoat. We must then fight him with all we have. That's the way it has to be; we must scrape for no one.

And thus from this point on, I will support no movement that does not accept my people's struggle. If I must choose between the Jewish cause and a "progressive" anti-Israel SDS, I shall always choose the Jewish cause. Not blindly, not arbitrarily, but always with full knowledge of who I am and where I must be. If the barricades are erected, I will fight as a Jew. It has been written that after "Auschwitz we retain but one supreme value—to exist." Masada will not fall again.

There is still time but the burden of proof is not on the Jewish nationalist; it is on you—you who reject your identity and attempt to evade the inescapable fact that it follows you wherever you go. You who mockingly reject every lesson of your people's history. You who are so trapped by your Long Island split-level childhood that you can't see straight. You who fight against everything you are—and against the one element that gave you your goddam social consciousness: your Jewish social idealism.

In the aftermath of the crematoriums, you are flippant. In the wake of Auschwitz, you are embarrassed. Thirty years after the Holocaust you have learned nothing and forgotten everything. Ghetto Jew, you'd better do some fast thinking.

Editorial

JEWISH LIBERATION PROJECT

This is the first issue of a publication which we of the Jewish Liberation Project hope will become a forum for the exchange of ideas and information among young Jews who feel that new and positive alternatives to the present Jewish way of life, both in the United States and other diasporas and in Israel, must be worked out.

The need for such alternatives has become more than obvious to anyone who is committed, as is the JLP, to the survival and flourishing of the Jewish people and its culture, and of Israel. With such a commitment, we cannot help being concerned about the sorry way things are going for and in Israel, and the American Jewish community.

Israel provides a unique historical opportunity for social experimentation leading to the working-out of new Jewish life-styles. However, under the pressures of security, a growing materialism and a moral-political crisis derived from the bankruptcy of the world Left, it has to a large extent moved away from its original pioneering ideals.

The American Jewish community is neither Jewish in essence or content nor a community in structure. It has rejected the basic Jewish ethical and communal traditions as they have evolved from the Prophets on down in exchange for the mess (and it is a mess) of pottage which is the American middle class way of life. Neither is it a community, because community means a group of people which *knows itself* and knows the realities it is facing and responds to them in a manner relevant to the concerns of its people and the situation it finds itself in. Those rich Jews and their hired bureaucratic hacks who have, with incredible chutzpah, appointed themselves the "leaders" of American Jewry are no more representative of the Jews and their interests than the American establishments of the American people.

The real pay-off is the attitude of the Jewish establishment toward American Jewish young people. They weep crocodile tears about the assimilation and alienation of Jewish youth and intellectuals while they themselves engage in a mad rush to throw off the last vestiges of Jewishness because that is their ticket to acceptance in American society. They talk about Jewish education but spend their money on fancy synagogues and even fancier homes, neither of which have much Jewish content. They talk about the Jewish ideal of social justice and then show the greatest surprise when young Jews get turned off because the Jewish establishment has no more intention of carrying out these ideals than did the "fat cows of Samaria" that the prophet Amos thundered against thousands of years ago

The American Jewish community must undergo radical change. Many young Jewish radicals have come to realize that their job should be to work within the Jewish community to bring about such a revolution and to create new alternatives, new approaches and new organizations.

Such alternatives never spring full-blown from the brains of some genius but, alas, must evolve, slowly and painfully, from individual and collective analyses of the situation, from experimentation based on these analyses and from the free exchange of ideas, however contrary, contradictory or controversial.

The purpose of this publication is to provide the opportunity for such an exchange of ideas.

It should be obvious from all this that, although this Journal is published by the JLP, it is not our "house organ" or the vehicle for pushing the JLP "line." *There is no JLP line.* We will print articles by our own members who, being Jews, disagree violently among themselves; by people who agree with us on some things and dissent on others; and by those violently opposed to our ideas. We will also publish news of interest to young American Jews dealing with what is going on in the rapidly developing Jewish radical movement, the American Jewish establishment, the "New Left" beginning in Israel—as well as material on Israeli and American society, the Israel-Arab problem, the Left, Black-Jewish relations and world Jewry.

We welcome articles, letters, think-pieces, news reportage and so on from anyone this periodical finds its way to. We welcome controversy and opinion, however way-out. We look forward to having a real dialogue (despite the way this word has been abused it is the only word for the gut-level kind of discussion we mean) in these pages, and hope you do, too.

Radicals Invade Federation, Glue 200 Mezuzahs to Doors

DAVID WEISSMAN

Los Angeles—A group of radicals invaded the premises of the Jewish Federation-Council here, but no one seems to be complaining except the janitor.

The Jewish radicals affixed some 200 mezuzahs to the doors in the building at 590 No. Vermont Ave. after "invading" the premises on a Sunday morning. Before the invasion only the front and rear doors of the building sported mezuzahs.

When the janitor became aware of the "desecration," he protested bitterly, and threatened to remove the mezuzahs. He was balked when the young people started a "sit-in."

The young people are members of Ohr Chadash–New Light—and are students at Calstate. When they decided to act in the case of the mezuzahs they raised $200 for their purchase only to find the mezuzahs were examined by the Lubavitcher rebbe and that they were not religiously fit—they were not "kosher" to use the correct terminology. They then borrowed $400 to buy correct mezuzahs.

Six members of Ohr Chadash, two of them girls, took on the task. As they were gluing the mezuzahs to the doors, they were confronted by the janitor who ordered them to take down the religious objects. They then began their sit-down, at which point the janitor relented and put off any action until the officials of the JF-C could make the decision on Monday.

At the Chicago Conspiracy Trial

ABBIE HOFFMAN ET AL.

Mr. Schultz: It was in December of 1967 that you and Rubin and Krassner created the Yippie myth, is that right?

The witness [Abbie Hoffman]: And Nancy Kurshan and Anita Hoffman—that's the woman I live with. It's not just men that participate in myths.

Mr. Schultz: And the myth was created in order to get people to come to Chicago, isn't that right, Mr. Hoffman?

The witness: That's right, Mr. Schultz—that was one reason, to create—the other was to put forth a certain concept, a certain life style.

Mr. Schultz: And one of the reasons for coming to Chicago was to create a liberated area as part of your revolutionary movement, is it not?

The witness: It's a concept, yes. Free space and liberated zones are concepts in this revolutionary movement, as you call it—

Mr. Schultz: No, you call it a revolutionary movement.

The witness: We use the word differently, Mr. Schultz.

Mr. Weinglass: Your Honor, if I could interrupt Mr. Schultz a minute. The Government is now going to cross-examine the witness on a book they wouldn't allow me to ask direct questions on.

Mr. Schultz: Your Honor, Mr. Weinglass is desperately trying to explain away this man's writings. I use the book because it obviously shows what this man's intent is.

Mr. Weinglass: We are not ashamed of a word in this book. In fact I will have fourteen copies of the book for the jury in the morning and then they can all read the entire book.

The Court: No. You will not. You may have fourteen copies, but they will not go to the jury.

Mr. Weinglass: Then you should admonish the U.S. attorney not to say that we are afraid of this book.

The Court: I will admonish the jury—the United States Attorney, if it is required that he be admonished.

The witness: Wait until you see the movie.

The Court: And you be quiet.

The witness: Well—the movie's going to be better.

Could I have a copy of the book? I've never read it. Could I have a copy—

The Court: The remarks of the witness may go out, and the jury is directed to disregard them.

Mr. Schultz: This is a copy of what is called *Revolution for the Hell of It,* and I'm showing the witness page 69, the bottom.

The witness: Yes. I think you have taken the term "liberated area" out of context, though.

Mr. Schultz: Put it in context, please.

The witness: It says:

"When we put on a large celebration the aim is to create a liberated area. People can do whatever they want. They can begin to live the revolution, even if only within a confined area. We will learn how to govern ourselves."

Mr. Schultz: Your idea of your revolution is first start with limited, confined areas, subject to your own laws and disregard the laws of the community, that's the beginning, is it not, sir?

The witness: The beginning of what?

Mr. Schultz: Of your revolution.

The witness: I would say that it's not done in the sinister tone you imply, no, there's an element of joy. That's what "revolution for the hell of it" means. That's what "celebration" means. That's what liberation means.

Mr. Schultz: May I have that answer stricken, your Honor, and have the witness respond.

The Court: Yes, that answer may go out. Miss Reporter, please read the question to the witness.

(question read)

The witness: It's the beginning of world conquest, yes, that's right.

Mr. Schultz: And in these liberated areas—

The witness: One has to begin somewhere.

Mr. Schultz: Are you done, Mr. Hoffman, so I can—

The witness: Yes.

Mr. Schultz:—ask another question? Or do you want to entertain your friends?

Now, you were at demonstrations at the Pentagon which you have testified to, isn't that right?

The witness: I don't call them demonstrations, but if you want to call it that, no, I was at the exorcism of the Pentagon.

Mr. Schultz: And there were entertainers there, were there not?

The witness: Yes. Mr. Jerry Rubin was one. Phil Ochs was there, and, I assume, Peter, Paul and Mary.

Mr. Schultz: You use entertainers—

The witness: Dr. Spock.

Mr. Schultz: You use entertainers to attract young people to come to your—

The witness: The CIA.

Mr. Schultz: Are you done, Mr. Hoffman?

The witness: People in the Pentagon are entertainers, generals.

Mr. Schultz: You use entertainers to bring young people from all around the United States to various demonstrations, isn't that right?

The witness: Entertainers, as you would call the rock personalities, are in a sense the real leaders of the cultural revolution, yes. The idea that we have control over them is quite the reverse.

Mr. Schultz: Did you see numerous instances of people attacking the Guardsmen at the Pentagon, Mr. Hoffman?

The witness: I do not believe that I saw any instances of people attacking National Guardsmen. In fact, the attitude was one of comradeship. They would talk to the National Guardsmen continuously and tell them they were not the people that they had come to confront, that they were their brothers and you don't get people to oppose [their ways] by attacking them.

Mr. Schultz: Mr. Hoffman, the Guards and the troops were trying to keep the people from entering into the Pentagon for two days, isn't that right?

The witness: I assume that they were there to guard the Pentagon from rising in the air possibly. I mean, who knows what they are there for? Were you there?

You probably watched it on television and got a different impression of what was happening. That is one aspect of myth-making—you can envisualize hordes and hordes of people when in reality that was not what happened.

Mr. Schultz: Did you see some people urinate on the Pentagon?

The witness: On the Pentagon itself?

Mr. Schultz: Or at the Pentagon?

The witness: There were over 100,000 people. People have that biological habit, you know.

Mr. Schultz: Did you symbolically urinate on the Pentagon, Mr. Hoffman?

The witness: I symbolically urinate on the Pentagon?

Mr. Schultz: Yes.

The witness: I didn't get that close. Pee on the walls of the Pentagon?

You are getting to be out of sight, actually. You think there is a law against it?

Mr. Schultz: Are you done, Mr. Hoffman?

The witness: I am done when you are.

Mr. Schultz: Did you ever state that a sense of integration possesses you and comes from pissing on the Pentagon?

The witness: I said from combining political attitudes with biological necessity, there is a sense of integration, yes.
Mr. Schultz: You had a good time at the Pentagon, didn't you, Mr. Hoffman?
The witness: Yes I did. I'm having a good time now too. I feel that biological necessity now. Could I be excused for a slight recess?
The Court: Ladies and gentlemen of the jury, we will take a brief recess.

(brief recess)

Mr. Schultz: On the seventh of August, you told David Stahl that at your liberated area you—
The witness: What meeting was this, August 7?
Mt. Schultz: That's when you just flew in from New York.
The witness: Crossing state lines—
Mr. Schultz: At this meeting on the evening of August 7, you told Mr. Stahl that you were going to have nude-ins in your liberated zone, didn't you?
The witness: A nude-in? I don't believe I would use that phrase, no. I don't think it's very poetic, frankly.

I might have told him that ten thousand people were going to walk naked on the waters of Lake Michigan, something like that.
Mr. Schultz: You told him, did you not, Mr. Hoffman, that in your liberated zone, you would have—
The witness: I'm not even sure what it is, a nude-in.
Mr. Schultz:—public fornication.
The witness: If it means ten thousand people, naked people, walking on Lake Michigan, yes.
Mr. Kunstler: I object to this because Mr. Schultz is acting like a dirty old man.
Mr. Schultz: We are not going into dirty old men. If they are going to have nude-ins and public fornication, the City officials react to that, and I am establishing through this witness that that's what he did.
The Court: Do you object?
Mr. Kunstler: I am just remarking, your Honor, that a young man can be a dirty old man.
The witness: I don't mind talking about it.
The Court: I could make an observation. I have seen some exhibits here that are not exactly exemplary documents.
Mr. Kunstler: But they are, your Honor, only from your point of view—making a dirty word of something that can be beautiful and lovely, and—
Mr. Schultz: We are not litigating here, your Honor, whether sexual intercourse is beautiful or not. We are litigating whether or not the City could permit tens of thousands of people to come in and do in their parks what this man said they were going to do. [. . .]

[. . .]

The Court: I have beseeched you and Mr. Kunstler throughout this trial, beginning with the Seale episode, to please try to get your clients to behave in this courtroom. [. . .]I have been very patient for nearly five and a half months.

Mr. Rubin: You haven't been patient at all. You interrupted my attorney right in the middle of his argument. He was right in the middle of his argument and you interrupted him.

You are not being very patient at all. That is not patience.

The Court: Ask that man to sit down.

Note who he is. That is Mr. Rubin.

Mr. Rubin: Jerry Rubin.

Can he finish his argument?

Can he finish his argument?

The Court: I will ask you to remain quiet, sir.

Mr. Rubin: I will ask you to remain quiet when our attorney represents us in making his arguments. [. . .]

The Court: I have the authority to maintain order in this courtroom.

Mr. Weinglass: But—

The Court: It was very difficult when profanity is being uttered by defendants and the judge is called various kinds of names. A defendant has to be tried and so I must let him be here, but in the circumstances of this case he could have been denied bail right from the beginning without his conduct here.

Mr. Weinglass: Well, if your Honor please, I would like to just answer the Court's remarks without interruption, if I may. If I may—

The Court: I will interrupt you whenever I choose. Any judge has a right to—

Mr. Rubin: That is called justice? That is called justice?

The Court: Will you ask your—is he your client? Is Mr. Rubin one of your clients?

Mr. Weinglass: Your Honor, I am—

The Court: Will you ask him to remain silent?

Mr. Weinglass: I am an officer of this court, but I am not a United States Marshal.

The Court: At times you have not acted as one.

Mr. Weinglass: I represent Mr. Rubin's interests here and Mr. Rubin, I feel, has a right when he feels—

The Court: If you feel that way, sir, that I have no right to interrogate a lawyer or say something to a lawyer when he is making an argument before me, I deny your motion.

That will be all.

Mr. Weinglass: Your Honor is not going to permit me to continue—

The Court: That will be all, sir.

Mr. Weinglass:—my argument—

The Court: I deny the motion. I shall not hear Mr. Kunstler on it. I rely on the record.

Mr. Kunstler: That is disgraceful.

The Court: And note that he said that was disgraceful. [. . .]

The Court: Mr. Marshal, please have that lawyer sit down—both of them.

Mr. Davis: May we defend ourselves if our lawyers can't?

Mr. Kunstler: I think the marshal is going to have to put me in my seat this time. I am not going to sit down unless I am forced to sit down.

The Court: I direct you to.

Mr. Kunstler: I think we ought to argue the motion.

The Court: I ask you to sit down and there will be no further argument.

Mr. Hoffman: Your idea of justice is the only obscenity in the room. You schtunk. *Schande vor de goyim,* huh? [. . .]

The Court: Mr. Marshal, will you ask the defendant Hoffman to—

Mr. Hoffman: This ain't the Standard Club.

The marshal: Mr. Hoffman—

Mr. Hoffman: Oh, tell him to stick it up his bowling ball.

How is your war stock doing, Julie? You don't have any power. They didn't have any power in the Third Reich either.

The Court: Will you ask him to sit down, Mr. Marshal?

The marshal: Mr. Hoffman, I am asking you to shut up.

Mr. Rubin: Gestapo.

Mr. Hoffman: Show him your .45. He ain't never seen a gun.

The Court: Bring in the jury, Mr. Marshal.

Mr. Rubin: You are the laughing stock of the world, Julius Hoffman; the laughing stock of the world. Every kid in the world hates you, knows what you represent.

Marshal Dobkowski: Be quiet, Mr. Rubin.

Mr. Rubin: You are synonymous with the name Adolf Hitler. Julius Hoffman equals Adolf Hitler today.

The Court: You may bring the jury in.

(jury enters)

Ladies and gentlemen of the jury, good morning. [. . .]

Radical Zionist Manifesto

Members of the radical Jewish student movement met recently in Palmer, Massachusetts, in the first nation-wide attempt to clarify their ideological position.

The conference, held on the weekend of February 13–15, brought together American, Canadian, and Israeli students from campuses throughout North America to discuss "Jewish Radicalism: A Search for a Renewed Zionist Ideology." The participants attempted to formulate a synthesis of radicalism and Zionism.

Acrimonious and heated debate marked the conference sessions. A major source of disagreement was where to place the focus of radical Jewish student action. Some stressed the centrality of the individual's confrontation with Jewish religion and culture. Others focused on a social, political and economic analysis of the Jews in American society: they emphasized the need for cooperation between the Jewish student movement and the general radical movement, with special reference to the Black nationalists. Still others saw in Israel the culmination of Jewish radicalism.

Despite these differences, there was common ground in the deep commitment to the Jewish people, the State of Israel, and the revitalization of Jewish life in America. The conference reached its emotional peak during the final sessions; speaker after speaker voiced total rejection of the assimilationist position and strong affirmation of the need for a liberation movement for the Jewish people.

One concept that dominated conference discussions was that of "radical Zionism." Various expressions of this idea were presented. The position of one Israeli participant, Yaron Ezrahi, is printed in this issue of *Genesis 2.*

A group of conference members came together in caucus to try to formulate a concise statement of their position on radical Zionism. They agreed to form an alliance of the organizations they represented, to advance and develop a movement based on these ideas.

The founding statement of the Radical Zionist Alliance, drafted at the Palmer conference, is reprinted below. It represents only a minimal set of principles, and not a full platform or program for action.

"Recognizing the vital need for united action and contact among the various sectors of the Jewish left, representatives of the following organizations, pending ratification, hereby form the Radical Zionist Alliance; ACIID of St.

Louis, Boston Area New Zionists, Ichud Habonim, the Jewish Liberation Coalition of Providence, the Jewish Liberation Project of New York, JLP of Saskatoon, JLP of Washington, D.C., the Jewish Socialist Union, Jewish Student Movement, Oberlin Radical Jewish Movement, the Seattle Jewish Student Union, the Student Zionist Organization (of Montreal) and the University of Michigan Coalition of Jewish Students.

"North American Jews are a marginal people in a society of economic, political, and cultural oppression. The Jewish community has adopted a tradition of ignoring its own needs, and has structured itself in an undemocratic manner geared toward assimilation and disappearance as a functioning nation.

"We call for the liberation of the Jewish people and the restructuring of our people's existence in such a way as to facilitate self-determination and development of our own institutions so as to control our destiny as a nation.

"To this end, we see Israel as central to the liberation of the Jewish people. The Jewish state, Israel, is the modern expression of people's right to national life in its own land. As such, settlement in Israel is the primary option facing each Jew in the diaspora. We see the only other viable option as being the struggle for Jewish self determination in the countries where Jews live.

"We are committed to the creation of a socialist society in Israel. We look toward mutual recognition of the national rights of the Jews and Palestinian Arabs, and the cooperation of all people in the area toward the realization of socialism and human justice.

"All those, individuals and organizations, adhering to the general policies stated above are invited to join the struggle for Jewish liberation." The Radical Zionist Alliance can be contacted through:

Ira Gelnick
2308 40th Avenue N.W.
Washington, D.C. 20007
(202 965-0302)

Jonathan Brandow
Box 239
Brown University
Providence, R.I. 02912

Oppression of Amerika's Jews

AVIVA CANTOR ZUCKOFF

Are the Jews in the United States oppressed?

As the term is used in this essay, oppression in its various forms means the denial of the most basic human right: to be yourself. It means being forced into a situation where your own destiny is not in your own hands but in those of others, usually of your enemy. It is a condition of being powerless to act to gain control of your destiny, of being reacted upon by events without the capacity to affect, change or prevent them. It means being exploited and used in the interests of the oppressor and against your own, and of being programmed for and forced into certain roles for his benefit. It is being forced to adapt to these conditions in such a way as to prevent retaliation on the part of the oppressor. The threat of retaliation may be blatantly physical or covertly subtle, but it is always there and it paralyzes action by the oppressed against the oppressor.

Thus, we should not be side-tracked by the fact that the Amerikan Jews happen to be, by and large, economically well-off and not subject at the moment to physical oppression.

For centuries Jews have been programmed into certain roles in the society which they still play: the middle-man, the "oppressor surrogate" and the scapegoat. Historically, Jews have been kept from owning land, and until today they have not been involved in the production process but are predominant in the distribution end of the economy.

Jews have always been allowed and even encouraged, however, to enter new areas of the economy that were too risky for anyone else. Jews were essential in the incipient stages of capitalism; the rising goyish bourgeoisie took it over when it became too profitable.

Nowhere is the Jew allowed to be in a position where he is so essential, so central to the functioning and survival of the economy that it could rise and fall with him. This is, in essence, the meaning of the Jews' "marginality": if all the Jews went to the moon tomorrow the economy would still function.

Jews are also programmed to be the surrogate of the ruling elite in doing its dirty work of helping keep down other oppressed groups; today they are welfare caseworkers, teachers, slumlords, and pawnbrokers in the black ghettoes of Amerika's cities. Thus the Jews are constantly forced into the dangerous position of being trapped between the peasants and the nobles, the ruling elite and other oppressed groups. In this role of oppressor surrogate, and otherwise, the Jew functions as society's "lightning rod" for absorbing and deflecting the rage of oppressed groups that might otherwise be turned on the ruling elite.

DIVIDE-AND-RULE

An oppressed group always poses a potential threat to the oppressing elite. Throughout the history of the Jews in Galut (Exile), the ruling elite feared the Jews might become the focal or rallying point for a revolt of other oppressed groups in the society. The Jews, by their act of refusal to give up their religion and culture, denied the ruling elite complete domination; this rebellion was obvious to other oppressed groups. Also, because the Jews were perceived as being different in values and life-style, the ruling elite feared it would be harder to keep them under control as successfully as other oppressed groups who did accept society's values and could be kept down by early and continuous brain-washing. The ruling elite, therefore, found it expedient to take certain definite means to make sure the Jews would not initiate a revolt that might be joined by other oppressed groups.

The most successful method was the classic divide-and-rule. The Jews had to be kept apart from other oppressed groups. The invention and wide circulation of ugly stereotypes and myths such as the Christkiller, host desecration and blood libels served to "inoculate" oppressed goyim against getting together with Jews. When the ruling elites became truly panicky about their loss of power, they resorted to expelling or ghettoizing the Jews.

PASSIVITY CONDITIONING

Another method of keeping the Jews down was to make the threat of retaliation so frightening that it served as an effective deterrent. Periodic pogroms served not only to keep the mind of other oppressed groups off the real source of their troubles, but to keep the Jews paralyzed by fear for their survival and unable to think beyond it.

The best way of keeping the Jews down has involved conditioning from childhood to certain patterns of behavior which the ruling elite rewarded by letting the Jews survive. One obvious pattern is passivity and non-assertiveness in relation to individual goyim and society in general. Jews are taught not to "antagonize the goyim": do not provoke them by asserting your rights. Never give cause for criticism. "Nice" is a favorite word in the Jewish lexicon.

As part of passivity conditioning, Jewish anti-social behavior is always judged more harshly than similar behavior by goyim—a double standard

Jews accept. Too many Jews believe that if all Jews behaved "properly" antisemitism would disappear. Whenever a Jew deviates from the prescribed non-assertiveness, i.e., asserts himself as much as a goy would, he is put down as "pushy."

Then there's the "sha-shtil" pattern. On the theory that if you are not conspicuous, they won't go after you with an axe, Jews try to fade into the woodwork and emerge in the pale, lifeless reincarnation of "good Amerikans."

DANGEROUS DEFENSELESSNESS

Jews are taught to feel guilty about seeking or using political power or taking political actions solely in their own interests. For years the so-called Jewish "defense" organizations "combatted" antisemitism under the cloak of fighting for civil rights for all; apparently it is not considered kosher for a Jewish organization to fight only for Jews. [. . .]

Jews are constantly looking to the goyim for approval. This is reflected in the Jews' striving to prove how well they fit into whatever they view society, or a particular "ally" demanding they be or do. This may be part of the reason they are pushed to achieve, achieve, achieve. Jews bend over backwards to show the goyim that they can be harsher in judging their own people than would a goy in the particular circles from which they crave acceptance. A non-Jewish judge would probably not have sentenced the Rosenbergs to death. Many young radical Jews go beyond their goyish comrades in denouncing Israel or parroting a particular group's line (even if it's antisemitic). Worst of all is our eternal nauseating gratitude to those goyim who behave with the most elemental kind of decency expected by one human being of another.

In the past two centuries ruling elites have invented a second method of keeping Jews down: the assimilationism game.

THE ASSIMILATION GAME

It should be obvious that the complete assimilation of the Jews (or any other oppressed group) is not in the interests of the ruling elite. Oppression and power is too advantageous for the oppressor to give up or share; moreover, if the Jews would assimilate, who would fill the roles they are programmed for?

Assimilationism, however, achieves very desirable ends for the ruling elite. One: by getting Jews to accept its values, they become better and more pliable tools, more easily exploited and manipulated; and two: breaking down Jewish cohesiveness so that the ruling elite has to deal with Jewish individuals instead of with a Jewish people, ensures Jewish powerlessness. Peoplehood is powerful; keeping Jews apart means keeping Jews down.

The Jew who gives up his distinctiveness is indeed "rewarded": he is allowed to rise on the socio-economic ladder. He is not, of course, allowed to cross the boundary into the ruling elite, but is kept tantalized with this prospect. In this state of anticipation and frustration he is scared to do anything that will jeopardize his chances and is thus even more susceptible to exploitation and less willing to acknowledge the existence of hostility.

ETHNIC AMNESIA

In such a state, the Jewish assimilationist feels a great deal of rage against his oppressor (whom he does not define as such). Unable to turn this rage on them, he turns it on himself and on the Jews: if only he could eradicate the vestiges of his Jewishness made conspicuous by the all-too-visible existence of the Jewish group! It is these assimilationist Jews who rule the Jewish community. Denied the high status they crave in the goyish bourgeoisie, they accept substitute high status among the Jews. The Jews choose them as "ambassadors" or "court Jews."

Assimilationism is, in essence, the conditioning and programming of the Jews to ethnic amnesia. The ruling elite with its Jewish collaborators, in order to get the Jews to give up their distinctiveness in return for a promised end to antisemitism, has to lead Jews to believe that 1) their distinctiveness was worthless to preserve, and 2) giving it up was paying off, i.e., antisemitism had disappeared. Since it really has not disappeared, Jews had to be conditioned into not perceiving its existence.

The perception and expectance of antisemitism had always been an important Jewish defense. Jews developed exquisitely sensitive antennae to antisemitism and learned that it was real and to be expected. This defense was and is necessary. Jews do have enemies; it is a bare 25 years since the Holocaust. Should any Jew be surprised that antisemitism is alive and well?

The ruling elite and the assimilationist Jews, however, have led us to believe that it is "paranoid" to recognize antisemitism as such in the U.S. ("Amerika is different"), that the feeling of insecurity we experience is some sort of weird atavistic throwback (or perhaps a neurosis to enrich a shrink), in other words, an irrational response to a non-existent danger. Jews are taught to feel guilty about harboring these feelings instead of recognizing them as real; Jews absolutely refuse to confront the implications of the Holocaust. We were conditioned to feel guilty about distrusting goyim (regardless of the fact that antisemitism was engineered by the ruling elite, most goyim have participated to some degree, actively or passively in our 2000 years of oppression). We were taught to repress our rage when hostility was dumped on us, and even to feel guilty about using the word "goyim." Most important, Jews are vulnerable because they are not conscious of their enemies.

DIFFERENCE AND DEFENSES

It is, however, useful to the ruling elite to have Jews feeling guilty about distrusting or hating goyim. For thousands of years antisemitism has been a perfectly acceptable attitude; even today it will not get you fired from Personnel or censured by the Senate. But a Jew who recognizes goyim as his oppressors threatens them. So Jews are taught to repress this as "paranoia."

The Amerikan Jew who faces antisemitism today faces it alone and unprepared. What should we do when a goy makes an antisemitic remark? Smile and pretend he didn't hear or he's above all that? walk out of what may be a very important meeting? speak out and face the accusation that he's simply "too emotional" and that his "over-sensitivity" led him to "misunderstand"? Because Jews fail to expect antisemitism and discuss it, they experience it as a traumatic shock and have no way of coping with their rage. [. . .]

Jews are conditioned to feel guilty and act defensive and apologetic about being and wanting to remain different. They are taught that being Jewish is "petty" "narrow" and "confining," and somehow disqualifies one from being a human being.

POPULARITY CONTEST MENTALITY

The oppressor always advocates the concept that it is the difference of the oppressed that is causing the oppression. The oppressor knows that the difference was the excuse or rationalization for the oppression, but not the cause.

Amerikan Jews have fallen right into the trap. Most of the efforts of the organized Jewish community, outside of fund-raising, go into creating the image that the Jews are like the goyim.

Many Amerikan Jews have internalized the attitude that being different (Jewish) is bad (or retrogressive, reactionary, what you will) so that they actually regard it as a compliment when someone says, "you don't look Jewish." Jewish women have their noses shortened and bleach their hair to conform to the Anglo-Saxon ideal of beauty, or at least, minimize their Jewish differences. We spend years trying to eradicate what the high school and college speech mavens call a "Yiddish intonation" or a "Brooklyn accent." Some Jews go so far as to change their family names to something Anglo-Saxon sounding. [. . .]

Assimilationist Jews try to over-compensate for their differences by being more British than the British, more American than the Americans, and so on. They hope that by doing this they will not only "pass," but that the outer personality will become, by force of habit, the inner personality. It sometimes does.

To these Jews, a conspicuous committed Jew or Jewish group is a threat. The hassid's garb is the external symbol of his refusal to assimilate; he is a living, breathing, walking reminder of Jewishness. His conspicuousness makes us conspicuous.

Similarly with Israel. Assimilationist Jews, of the right and the left, who seek to escape their Jewish identity are put up-tight by Israel's highly conspicuous existence. Significantly, what they find objectionable about Israelis is always their "arrogance" i.e., their prideful Jewish identity and assertiveness, which contrast with the assimilationist's lack of these characteristics. Many left assimilationists reject Israel for this emotional reason, and other more complicated ones discussed below. Many right assimilationists, involved in Jewish communal affairs, use their power to try to make Israel become bourgeois Amerikan like them, i.e., less Jewish.

Too many of us have internalized Jewish stereotypes invented by goyim—the money-grubbing Jew, for instance. It is a tragedy—that Jewish emotionalism and expressiveness, one of the really healthy and positive characteristics of our tradition, has been so put down that we are intimidated into repressing them, particularly among goyim—and embarrassed when a Jew is emotional.

OTHERS DEFINE US

Jews are kept powerless by being taught to feel guilty about being together. Brain-washed into believing that the warm feeling of concern Jews feel for each other is "chauvinistic" and that the freeness Jews experience only in each others' company is "racist," Jews will always try to refute that most terrible of all terrible accusations: Jews are "clannish." The technique of keeping people powerless by keeping them apart is used with other oppressed people. [. . .]

Jews acquiesce in the definition of themselves by the ruling elite and the majority of goyim as a "religion." This is convenient because Amerikan society is tolerant about religious differences, because nobody really cares about them any more. But ethnic differences, the recognition and encouragement of which lead to ethnic solidarity and power to the peoples, are a threat to the ruling elite. The "melting pot" is designed to break down ethnic groups and render them powerless. So Jews masquerade as a religion and have even come to believe this definition and function as a religion and not a people—with far-reaching implications beyond this essay's scope.

Jews accept with alacrity the nauseating term "Judeo-Christian civilization." The term is a fraud because it misleads people into thinking that it really includes the Jewish tradition of the past 5,000 years, while in reality the only "Judeo" part is the "Old Testament." It successfully deceives Jews into believing that the two civilizations are really alike (when they are at opposite extremes), and again minimizes our distinctiveness and the uniqueness of our tradition and culture. [. . .]

This conditioning goes hand in hand with severe cultural deprivation—the absence of anything positively Jewish in the life experiences of young Jews. It is in the interests of the ruling elite to keep groups, including the Jews, culturally deprived, meaning, separated from the resources of their history and tradition. The Jewish tradition contains strong positive elements that develop pride and cohesiveness. A solid knowledge of Jewish history would give Jews the tools to analyze their oppression and rebel against it. Of course, this is against the interests of the ruling elite.

BREAKDOWN OF SOCIALIZATION

The almost total absence of quality Jewish education is no accident: assimilationist Jews do not want their children to be raised as Jews.

The creation of a Jew takes place mostly in the home. It consists of the absorption, imitation and internalization by the child of the parents' Jewish gut feelings, attitudes and values. What has occurred in Amerika is the partial or sometimes even total breakdown of the Jewish socialization process. [. . .]

Oppression is always destructive and dehumanizing for the oppressed. But oppression that is experienced as oppression at least frees the oppressed from his self-hatred and alienation. He stops internalizing the oppressors' hostility and begins to fight it with his sisters and brothers.

Oppression that is not experienced as oppression is, however, far more destructive to a human being. He internalizes the oppressors' hostility and mythology and turns it on himself, or more accurately in the case of the Jews, the Jewish parts of himself. He tries to cut these pieces out in order to fit into and be accepted by those of his oppressors that he identifies with.

ZIONISM VS. OPPRESSION

It is the Zionist thesis that all the various forms of the oppression of Jews discussed above derive from the inherently oppressive nature of Galut, where Jews are always a tiny and "different" minority.

It is the ruling elite, of course, which engineers the oppression of the Jews. But it is the Galut condition which places Jews at the mercy of the ruling elite.

The Galut condition forces Jews, if they want to survive, to adapt to the values and roles set by the ruling elite. Being forced again and again to adapt to totally different environments makes any kind of natural cultural and social development impossible. If Jews will ever again produce a work of the creative stature of the Torah, it will have to evolve out of their unimpeded cultural development, and that means outside of Galut, i.e., in Israel.

The process of liberation begins with the consciousness of oppression. What Jews in Amerika lack most is this consciousness; this keeps them paralyzed in a state of ethnic amnesia. It is to raising the Jewish consciousness of Amerikan Jewry, then, that our efforts should be directed.

Dialogue with a Radical Jewish Student

JONATHAN GOLDIN AND MORRIS U. SCHAPPES

I have enjoyed reading Jewish Currents for about two years and in some times of stress it has been the only thing saving me from despair about the American Jewish community. But recently there has been a Jewish reawakening and radical Jewish groups have formed in every large city almost spontaneously. Coupled with this has been the spreading of the Jewish Defense League, which has chapters in almost every large American city, and we find a substantial and growing mobilization of the Jewish community. It's about time! And I'm sure you feel the same way.

Yet in some ways you appear out of step with radical Jewish youth, but not too far out of step that it can't be rectified. One of the strongest issues and in fact the central theme of your magazine seems to be Black-Jewish cooperation (I can't understand why you persist in using the term "Negro"). While I can understand this noble sentiment I hope that you can understand how little weight such idealistic sentiments will carry at this time with young radical Jews, even let alone the rest of the Jewish community. In the black community I would expect to see almost no positive reaction from young people. The reason I feel young Jews are turned off from the coalition right now is that while in theory it might sound nice, in practice it has always been the Jews who have suppressed their Jewishness for the "sake of the black cause." Other types of Black-Jewish relationships, such as black boy with Jewish girl, have usually figured in the Jew being the one exploited. Blacks feel the exact opposite and regarded the Jew as trying to dominate his movement.

I know of course that people such as you have never been hung up like that; that your Black-Jewish relations are of mutual recognition, respect and equality. But in your desire for Black-Jewish relations being number one in your focus you have overlooked more important issues of Jews in the world today.

Your coverage of Russian Jewry has been marginal at best. There seems to be a fear to admit that the Soviet Union is practicing a policy of cultural genocide against the Jews of the Soviet Union and must therefore be looked upon as an enemy of the Jewish people. If you have failed to make this assessment because you still have ties to the ideals of the Bolshevik Revolution and can't see that Soviet Russia since Stalin has destroyed all those ideals, then you are acting in bad faith when you consider yourself progressive Jews. The *token* concessions by the Soviet government must be seen as only measures to divert world opinion from the oppression of Soviet Jewry. The Soviet Union is not only destroying anything resembling a Jewish community but is practicing a policy of distorting European history so as to exclude the Jews from history books. They want to make us invisible, just as Ralph Ellison pointed out white society was trying to do to black people. I haven't even mentioned Soviet policy in the Middle East, which ranks with America's war against Vietnam as outstanding verities of imperialism.

The other policy I must question you on is your rejection of Zionism. In the Feb. issue you reject such theses of Zionism as "that the Jews throughout the world constitute a single nation (instead of a people) . . ." Could I ask, what is the difference? And "that Israel should be *central* in the life of Jews in all countries . . ." Israel is central right now to the Jewish question and to Jewish survival and must be recognized as such. To give just one example: world attention is increasing constantly and conspicuously in regards to Israel and that means the Jew is in the limelight. We must brace ourselves for this tough position and not be apologists in any way. If you don't feel enthused about Zionism then I imagine you might not support the Jews of Russia, the young Jews who are rebelling as militant Zionists against an oppressive anti-Semitic state. While I don't favor mass *aliya* to Israel (definitely not from America yet), I can see that possibly being the only real alternative for Russian Jews.

I think that if you focused a little more attention on the Mid-East you might include some of the excellent articles on the subject such as the ones that appeared in the Nov. *Liberation* magazine.

Don't get me wrong. Keep up the good work (you haven't fallen for the trap about a "New Germany" as you never fail to mention about the travesty of justice in W. Germany and Austria for war criminals).

Jonathan Goldin
Radical Jewish Union
Boston University
Boston, Feb. 16

MORRIS U. SCHAPPES COMMENTS:

We welcome these expressions of opinion from a young Jewish radical. We are pleased that he has found our magazine helpful in relating him to the American Jewish community. There is room for only brief comments on the many questions he raises.

1) We regard the Jewish Defense League (see our article in our Jan. issue) as a *reactionary* organization, which takes advantage of the weakness of some major Jewish organizations in responding to some real needs of the

Jewish people and tries to parade as the defender of the Jews. Rabbi Meir Kahane, head of the JDL, fully supports the Nixon policy on the Vietnam war and has a chauvinist attitude to the black people's movement for equality. His militant tactics are harnessed to a reactionary social program. The right wing can use militant tactics too—and a Jewish radical should not be lured into a right-wing trap by demagogic phrases about fighting the "establishment" when the actions of the JDL are mainly a response to anti-Negro "white backlash."

2) On relations of Jews and blacks, Jonathan Goldin recognizes that our concept is based on "mutual recognition, respect and equality." We believe an alliance between Jews and blacks is necessary and possible because they have a *common interest* in ending the war in Vietnam, in resisting racism and anti-Semitism, in struggling for civil liberties, in combatting inflation and hunger, in fighting for social progress.

If, as Goldin says, "young Jews are turned off from the coalition right now," it may be because these young Jews are responding in their way to the "white backlash." This being turned off is not a sign of radicalism but of confusion. We are not asking Jews to "suppress their Jewishness for the 'sake of the black cause,'" as Jonathan Goldin puts it, but to express their Jewishness in struggling for a proper alliance with the black movement. Black youth has reason to resent some old habits and practices of some white liberals and Jews, who entered the struggle for equality with a patronizing attitude of helping the "poor blacks" and, intentionally or unintentionally, often affronted black dignity by providing a "leadership" that was seen by black people as a tendency to dominate them.

Conscious allies, on the other hand, have the right to differ with each other and to criticize each other in relation to the common interests and common struggle. Equality permits and requires such candor. To withhold necessary dissent and criticism may be a sign either of a) a sense of superiority that you do not wish to reveal as unfitting for a liberal or radical (so you keep quiet), or, b) a sense of inferiority, of self-deprecation, self-disesteem, that leads you to sacrifice your own and your people's interest and really become subservient to the other group. A Jewish liberal or radical needs to combat both this disguised sense of superiority and this shame-faced inferiority.

3) We cannot agree with Jonathan Goldin that "the Soviet Union . . . must be looked upon as an enemy of the Jewish people." We disagree with current Soviet policy on the Middle East as one-sided and harmful to the State of Israel. We disagree with the Soviet practice of forced assimilation, as Aaron Vergelis admitted it to be, with regard to the Soviet Jewish population. We believe both policies can be changed, and we do what we can to help bring about such changes.

We report and condemn manifestations of anti-Semitism in Soviet life and publications. We report and encourage whatever Jewish cultural activities are carried on in the Soviet Union. We regard the phrase, "cultural genocide," as confusing and misleading: to us, genocide taken literally signifies the extermination of a people. You cannot exterminate a people's culture without exterminating the people itself. As long as the people lives, it has the capacity to revive its culture. We therefore welcome all signs of activity, including protest against forced assimilation, that appear in Soviet Jewish life.

Because we still believe that world peace requires peaceful coexistence between socialist and capitalist states, we oppose the anti-Soviet Cold War (and the anti-communist hot war in Vietnam and now Laos and Cambodia). Therefore we try to prevent our criticism of what is wrong in Soviet policy on the Middle East and on the Jewish question from being snared into the Cold War context. In this respect, our approach differs enormously from that of those loud critics of Soviet policy who are anti-socialist primarily and enjoy belaboring the Soviet Union for its wrong policies on the Middle East and the Jewish question. We have no such joy. In the past 50 years, socialism has changed the course of world history—for the better. Despite all its blunders and crimes committed in the name of socialism, including some crimes against the Jews, socialism has unloosed tides of change that are undermining imperialism and paving the way for basic social progress. Personally, I believe a socialist humanism is necessary and viable. Criticism of errors of socialist states is an indispensable ingredient of this outlook.

4) On our rejection of Zionism, we should first like to record the fact that Richard Yaffe, editor of the socialist-Zionist *Israel Horizons,* commenting in his Jan. issue (in which he generously printed my comment on his views) wrote: "I am grateful to Mr. Schappes that he has put the Zionist position so succinctly and well. I am only sorry that he still resists it."

Jonathan Goldin asks two questions: what is the difference between a nation and a people, and why do I say Israel is not "central in the life of Jews in all countries"?

A nation is a form of social organization in which its members live on a certain territory, have an interdependent economic life, develop interrelated political, social, cultural and other institutions, and on the basis of these common experiences exhibit a common psychology.

A people is a much looser form of social relation, without a common territory, a common political life in a single state, or an interdependent economic life. What binds a people together includes common ethnic origin, certain common experiences (as with anti-Semitism in different countries and at different times), common traditions and cultural patterns, religious and/or secular, common sentiments, common fears, common dangers, a continuing interest of one segment in the status and welfare of other segments of that people everywhere.

Concretely, Israel is a nation; the Jews there are citizens of the State of Israel, and are part of the economic, political, cultural and communal life of that State. Israeli Jews are of course also a part of the Jewish people, most of whom live outside Israel. Jews outside Israel are not Israelis, do not have Israeli citizenship, do not depend upon Israeli economy, culture and so on.

To Jews outside Israel, Israel is something *special* but not *central.* Because Israel is the one Jewish State, we know that Jews in every country outside Israel have a *special* interest in its existence, security, survival and inner life. American Jews, for instance, are interested in Jewish life in other countries with Jewish communities or populations. Thus United States Jews are interested in Canadian Jews, Russian Jews, Polish Jews, Iraqi Jews, etc., some more, some less, depending often on family ties, place of birth, cultural awareness, and so on. Similarly Canadian Jews are interested in American Jews, Russian Jews, Mexican Jews, etc. Argentinian Jews are interested in United States Jews, Spanish Jews, French Jews, Lebanese Jews, etc.

Yet the interest of all Jews in all countries in each other has a special element in it, in that in all countries, Jews are interested in Israel as a Jewish State. But for American Jews, *American* life is *central,* not Israeli life. No matter how much an American Jew may "do for Israel," as an American the bulk of his life activities is in the American scene, the American economy, polity, culture and so on. As American Jews we seek to develop Jewish cultural and communal institutions *here.* We cannot live on a culture imported from Israel (just as radicals cannot live on a culture imported from socialist countries), although cultural exchange (import *and export*) is a necessary part of an international outlook like ours. Therefore no matter how we enjoy Israeli cultural or other imports, they can only supplement our American Jewish culture.

We have found that Zionists who regard Israel as *central* in their life tend to underestimate the need to build American Jewish cultural and communal institutions with a life of their own and not merely as a fund-raising adjunct to Israel. On the other hand, progressive Jews, concentrating on developing American Jewish life, reflect their *special* interest in Israel in many ways, including aid to the existence and support of Israel.

Now Jonathan Goldin does not favor mass emigration of American Jews to Israel "yet," but he thinks mass emigration to Israel is possibly "the only real alternative for Russian Jews."

First about the "yet." We assume he means that there may come a time, if the U.S.A. for example were to become a fascist state, when mass Jewish emigration to Israel would be desirable. Our view is that if ours becomes a fascist country and state, with a fascist foreign policy in the Middle East, Israel might be the *least* desirable "haven" for American Jews. A fascist U.S. policy in the Middle East would certainly provoke a confrontation with the USSR. In such a situation, Israel, no matter which side it were on, would be in the very vortex of the hurricane—and far from a haven for American Jewish refugees from fascism. That is why we believe it is the duty of American Jews to extend their energies manifold in the struggle against the drift to reaction and the Ultra-Right, that is, to fascism, in our country.

As for the Jews in the USSR, first, we believe in the democratic right of all persons to emigrate to any country if they so desire. Soviet Jews who wish to emigrate, to Israel or any other country, ought to have the right to do so. But to expect the emigration of 3,000,000 Soviet Jews is sheer fantasy. And to mount an international campaign for such total emigration takes on the coloration of a Cold War operation, which many Soviet Jews legitimately resent.

Even if tens of thousands, or a few hundreds of thousands, were to go, the vast majority of Jews would stay. And they would continue to have the need of, and the right to, Jewish national identity and its cultural expression. That is why the Jewish question has to be settled *in* the Soviet Union. Emigration to Israel, no matter how important for those who wish to go, is not the central issue. Changing Soviet practice from forced assimilation to a socialist encouragement of the development of Jewish cultural life is the need of Soviet Jews and the answer to Soviet distortions of the Jewish question.

Well, Jonathan Goldin, enough for now. Thanks for writing to us. We hope you are listening and still with us, or "with it." Let us hear from you again. And that goes for Jewish radical students all over the country too.

We Are Coming Home

BROOKLYN BRIDGE COLLECTIVE

We are coming home. To Brooklyn. Those of us who have moved away and forgotten our birthplace, and those of us who still live here and always dreamed of getting out. We have been running away too long, cutting ourselves off from our roots too long, and it has stunted us. We are coming home to Brooklyn to live, to love, to begin building a new world, and to be Jewish.

Brooklyn Bridge is the road we are taking back home. It is a Revolutionary Jewish newspaper. Jewish, because that is what we are; because our Jewishness plays an important part in shaping our total selves, and in the world we are trying to create we want to be full human beings, not assimilated nonentities; because we have learned—as have women, and blacks, and gay people—that unless we look out for ourselves, we are just as likely to be the victims of oppression in a revolutionary society as we are in this one. Revolutionary, because we realize that playing the roles America forces on us will destroy us as it destroyed our parents; because we see that for our people to be free, all people must be free and the deadly hands of America lifted off our backs.

Our struggle begins at home, with the oppression we face as Jewish people in America. We have been trapped in the buffer-zone between other oppressed peoples and the ruling class; shunted into the bureaucracies of the military-industrial-education complex. The commitment of our people to find meaningful and human work—to build a decent society, as teachers, doctors, scientists—is impossible in obscene America. It only alienates us and is used against us. The age-old oppression of Jew-hating and Jew-baiting is like any other racism, both irrational and calculated at the same time. False myths and stereotypes have been imposed on us for centuries. The idea that assimilation through the "melting pot" will end Jew-hating is a dehumanizing lie. Assimilation means believing those myths and stereotypes. It means being cut off from our own history, being cut off from each other. Attempts to assimilate have led us to self-hatred. But no matter how much we might have effaced our spirit, Jews as a nation remain a reality in America, as much of a reality as Blacks, Puerto Ricans, Chinese, Italians.

Brooklyn Bridge is a voice in the struggle to define ourselves. Organized Judaism and the "Jewish establishment" have failed us. The institutions and organizations created to serve the needs and goals of Jewish People have been coopted to serve other interests. They represent us as a religion, rather than as the nation we are. Jewish philanthropy no longer aids Jews who need it; Jewish education tones down our people's historic fight to survive and teaches us to be "nice Jewish boys and girls." Our culture has been made rigid in the name of tradition and continues sexist oppression both in religious practice and in day-to-day life. Our synagogues are no longer the nexus of our community, but often only temples of ill-founded self-congratulation.

Brooklyn Bridge speaks to the totality of our lives. Our Jewishness is only part of the wholeness toward which we are struggling. Our oppression as Jews is only one of the ways in which we are oppressed. The ruling class in America oppresses all people; it denies basic life needs, perverting those needs for profit—in the supermarket, in health, in housing. It destroys the environment and murders people in its wars for profit and power.

As Jewish People we demand our right to self-determination. We will defend ourselves against oppression in every way it manifests itself. We are not naive about the struggle involved in achieving our goals. We hope to ally ourselves with other people who are struggling against the same enemies. However, we remember both our own personal histories and the history of our people in revolutionary movements. We will not sacrifice our own aims or struggle to fight for someone else's freedom. No longer will we efface our Jewishness or deny our needs and interests to fit into any current ideological framework. Our brothers and sisters are those people who treat our struggle with the same respect and fraternity that we give to theirs. We are totally committed to the freedom of Jewish People, and all oppressed people. And knowing our oppression, we know that our struggle is against anyone, "revolutionary" or "reactionary," "Jewish" or non-Jewish who oppresses us, who denies us our right to self-determination.

As Jews we have fully experienced the horrors of genocide, racism, and exploitation. As Jews we carry a vision rising out of our tradition of a radical and inclusive social justice. As women and men struggling to survive in America we know we must destroy sexism, elitism, and all other systems of domination that threaten to debilitate our struggle. We will grow in our struggle and we will win.

Brooklyn Bridge is a collective endeavor. An endeavor to open up a dialogue among our people and to begin building a liberated Jewish community. Join us in our trip back home. Take the *Brooklyn Bridge*.

An Interview with Meir Kahane

ZVI LOWENTHAL AND JONATHAN BRAUN

Do you think that the activist program of the J.D.L. has been the decisive factor in attracting so many youth to the J.D.L.?

I think that's probably the key to everything that we have done. The bankruptcy of Jewish leadership is manifested most clearly in the results that we see with Jewish youth. I don't always like to use the term "Establishment" but the fact is that it does exist. Our Jewish leaders carry the sin and the crime of negligence when it comes to Jewish youth.

How do you think they've failed the Jewish youth community?

They have not given the young Jew any reason to feel Jewish. When I speak in synagogues and temples out in the suburbs, the adults come there expecting me to agree with them when someone gets up and attacks the Jewish New Left youth as lousy kids with long hair, and so on. They're usually very stunned when I say—and all our people say—that, on the contrary, our great hope is not so much the apathetic youth, but the radical leftist who at least marches for something and feels something. If someone feels something he's alive.

And now, of course, you have to change them to the right way. How do you resurrect the dead? Both the dead Jews, the apathetic young Jews, and those who have gone into foreign fields, into strange fields, and marched with all sorts of non-Jewish and anti-Jewish causes—they have all done so because they've never received any reason for being proud to be Jewish. Everyone knows the incredible kind of training the young Jews get. A kid of eleven or twelve is brought to Hebrew school, not to be Jewish but for a *bar mitzvah*. If I had my way, I'd bury this entire ritual because it has buried us. A *bar mitzvah,* my God! That's not the beginning. That's it; that's the end of everything.

Judaism in this country is hypocrisy. It's a fraud. And when we come, we say to young people, "We don't want to give you anything; we demand of you something. You've got to help. You've got to march. You may even get arrested; you may have to fight police—but for something Jewish."

So you would say that the activism of the J.D.L. presents a viable alternative to the so-called Portnoy Judaism or the bagels-and-lox Judaism of the Jewish Establishment?

No question about it. I believe that there are only two meaningful Jewish trends at this moment on campus., They are the J.D.L. and the radical Zionist trends. These are two groups which offer sacrifices, which offer substance, not form. I feel very close in many ways to the Radical Zionist Alliance and to the Jewish Liberation Project. I differ with them strongly on certain issues. But I know there is substance there, and meaning and sincerity which young Jews sense both in them and in us.

You have indicated that you feel a closeness to the Radical Zionist Alliance and to the Jewish Liberation Project. Do you also feel a possible closeness toward other militant ethnic groups, such as the Puerto Rican Young Lords and the Black Panthers?

There is no question that despite the effort to paint us as racists—which is incredible nothingness—we certainly do feel and understand a great many of the things that, for example, the Panthers say. We differ with them on a number of things—for example, branding all police as pigs. But there are pigs. No one has to teach me that. I've seen cops charging and shouting, "Lousy kikes!" I've seen and heard those things. I myself, in the 90th precinct in Queens, when I was arrested last June, saw one of our people handcuffed, both hands cuffed to a chair as he was beaten by a cop. I've seen the anti-Semitism. So there are pigs, and if they can do this to us you can imagine what they can do to some poor black guy.

So we don't differ with the Panthers on that. And we don't differ with the Panthers in the sense that if after asking for 300 years for things from the government—federal or local—it becomes necessary to use unorthodox or outrageous ways. There is no question. On this we don't differ. We don't differ on their wanting to instill in their young people ethnic pride. Not at all. Where we do differ with them is where we think that nationalism crosses the boundary line and becomes Nazism; instead of just love of our own people, hatred of others.

What I believe is clear evidence of anti-Semitism on the part of Panthers is not just anti-Zionism. This is a cop-out. This is nothing. I remember reading the April 25, 1970 issue of the Panther paper where they attack those three well-known Zionists—Abbie Hoffman, Jerry Rubin, and William Kunstler. They're not Zionists. They're Jews. This is a code name, the kind of thing the Poles used two years ago to expel their Zionists when they meant Jews. So we empathize with the Panthers and sympathize with them; but we get turned off when they suddenly deviate from what we feel to be a legitimate nationalism and go on to hatred of other people.

What about their revolutionary goals and their revolutionary analysis of American society? You differ with them there also?

Yes, I believe that this country has a great many faults, that's for sure. I believe that nevertheless, at this moment still—and maybe this will change in a year or two years or a month—nevertheless, this country still affords a chance for democratic change. It may be slower than most people want. It's slower than I want it. Sometimes you have to pay a certain price in speed. But the only right thing that any group has the right to ask is, "Is there change possible and is change taking place?" I mean, this country is not the Soviet Union. No matter what one may say about Agnew, Agnew is not Brezhnev. He's not a good guy. He's not one of my favorite people in this country. There could be a great many worse people in this country. And unfortunately, I'm afraid that you'll see them yet.

Does that mean that you feel that the American Jewish community may be endangered in the near future?

There is no hope for the Jews in this country. I'm going to say that quite clearly. I've said this over and over again to adults in the suburbs. I'd go for 40 minutes and they'd eat it up and love it, and then I'd say, "Remember, the only place for a Jew to live is in Israel." That's it. Goodbye. But again, I'm not out to score points with people. I'm out to deal with what I honestly believe to be a serious, physical crisis for Jews arising in this country.

I think that I love Jews enough to say things to them for what I think is their benefit, without having to make points. This is why we did take the stand that we took on Vietnam. We didn't have to say that. We could have gotten—I know we could have had at this moment—thousands and thousands of new members on campuses if we didn't take that stand. I believed then and I believe to this day that any time there is a conflict between what I think is good for Jews and for J.D.L. there is no conflict. Jews come first. [. . .]

Getting back to J.D.L.'s youth appeal. In your campaign to attract more students to the organization you've spoken on a number of campuses. What do you think if the value of these meetings?

I speak at an average of three or four campuses every single week, which in itself tells something about the change in attitude on campuses to J.D.L. [. . .]

I can only tell you that the response has been tremendous . . . I think that we have seen perhaps the turning point on campus for Jewish youth. I think there's a hunger, a thirst for Jewishness.

I don't blame young people for not wanting to go to the more traditional things. I don't blame them for being turned off by Hillel. I really don't. I was turned off by Hillel, and even in the 1950s when it took a great deal to turn off Jews. And I don't blame them for being turned off by Hillel or by the average synagogue or the average rabbi. And if the American Jewish Congress has no youth it deserves it. Maybe they're looking for that which once was. I've always stated that we're not out to form any new Jew. We're out to resurrect the old Jew that once was. And the new Jew is a product of the *galut*. He's insecure, full of complexes. We'd like to bury that new Jew and resurrect the old one.

The JDL Politics of Jewish Experience

STEVE COHEN

The Jewish Defense League is the one current Jewish grass-roots organization that has penetrated into the public media. Rash and militant, its members have captured public attention for themselves, their slogans, and even some of the issues with which they deal. This article is a first step in analyzing the JDL as a Jewish movement with an implicit ideology about the Jewish position in America. It does not deal with the work of JDL in the Black-Jewish neighborhoods but some of the analysis applies to this aspect of their work as well. The article takes as its main substance for focus the JDL actions on Soviet Jewry.

THE PSYCHOLOGY OF OPPRESSION

We Jews were once great experts on the psychology of oppression. We understood the subtle first principle of that psychology, that most often you do not know the depth of your oppression. We struggled, through ritual and great feats of passive aggression, against the second principle of that psychology: the hatred of the oppressor can but blind the oppressed from choosing the best way to defeat their oppression and the best way is seldom the most direct way.

Not many of us are still experts. Instead American Jews have become experts on the psychology of oppression-of-everybody-else. Here the two main emotions are guilt and shame: guilt for failing to end the oppression; shame for having been shown to have failed to act strongly enough against it.

The guilt we feel tends to prevent us from engaging in sharp criticism of many who would raise their voices against the oppression. The shame we feel tends to force us into self-righteous anger against those who act shamelessly against the oppression.

It is this complex of feelings that makes discussion of the JDL on Soviet Jewry so difficult. We need an analysis that tries to free itself from the guilt and shame and to think clearly about the subject. We need to re-learn the psychology of oppression so that we can choose the best way to struggle against the oppression of the Jews in the Soviet Union, which may not turn out to be the most direct way. In order to do this we may have to re-examine the nature of Jewish oppression in the United States.

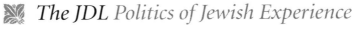

It would not be difficult to categorize the attacks on JDL, the defenses of it, and the silence about it, according to the relative predominance of these in various Jewish groups. For example, the Jewish leadership's great expression of anger stems from their having been shamed by the public demonstrations and declarations of their comparative silence and lack of action. They probably felt more keenly their anger at JDL than their anger at the Soviet Union.

What is common to the many attacks, and to many of the defenses, is the failure to engage the central justification of the JDL. The JDL claims to advance the Jewish interests. Any analysis of them must confront them in these terms. Attacks of the right about the propriety of tactics, or of the left about their rhetoric of anti-communism and alleged racism may be important to the critics but to the JDL are essentially beside the point.

For the JDL the actions are appropriate if they serve Jewish interests and red-baiting or the exploitation of Blacks would be justified if they would advance the Jewish interests. The question that confronts the JDL is whether in fact their political stance makes sense from the Jewish point of view.

THE PSYCHOLOGY OF JEWISH POLITICS

The Jewish interest in the problem of the Soviet Jew is simple. The interest is to mount pressure of the amount and kind that would bring influence on the Soviet Union to relax and then abolish its discrimination against Jews and to end its refusal of their emigration rights. To this end JDL has taken to personal harassment of Soviet officials and alleged bombing of selected Soviet agencies in the United States and recently Europe.

The model of political power that suggests these tactics to the JDL is twofold. On the one hand they identify themselves with the Irgun, the underground secret military organization of Mandate days in pre-state Israel. On the other hand they seem to more generally adopt the tactics of the petty terrorists in the United States in their caricature of guerilla warfare.

Will Jewish political power in America grow out of the barrel of a gun? This is the absurd question the JDL poses. While we can argue as to whether Jewish power in Palestine grew out of the barrel of a gun we must recognize that the analogy of the United States in 1971 to mandate Palestine is simply too far-fetched to make.

Even if we ignore the absurdity of this analogy we might ask if somehow American opinion and the American government would be impressed by this show of power. The answer is that this politics is that of despair. It only suggests that the Jews have no hope of influencing public opinion through persuasion or by bringing to bear whatever limited financial and political power they have.

The Jews of America can simply not be taken seriously as a people threatening massive violent destruction of America. They are both too vulnerable and too few in number. For most Jews to engage in such action would be to lose rather than gain influence. Jewish power must come from the use of the position of Jews in the society to persuade on their vital interests. The Jewish leadership of today is guilty of refusing to enlist and wield that power because its use for Jewish purposes might threaten the privileged position for other purposes. The JDL is guilty for positing a model of Jewish power which is romantically naive and leads down a dangerous path of self-delusion.

It is painful to recognize our powerlessness to make Soviet Jewry a moral issue for the world, a question of international diplomatic significance, as other questions of racism and oppression have become. It is true that we cannot use the flimsy excuse that "we do not know" reminiscent of another day. It is, however, imperative that we do not fool ourselves into equating romantic self-deluding politics with the hard work of creating an American Jewry willing to wage the battle for Jewish rights in the USSR with all its power and prestige without excusing itself for fear of the loss of this power and prestige. [...]

NEVER AGAIN?

The slogan of the JDL, "Never Again," has a mistaken political implication suggested above. It also cuts deeply into the uphill struggle for the Jewish people's consciousness. "Never again" has come to imply that the Jews shall never again be silent as they were in WW II, and this is deeply important but it implies as well that Jewish passivity in Europe shares the responsibility for the holocaust if not the guilt. This identification with the critics of European Jewry fails to appreciate the richness of the lives of European Jews while it deplores their failure to prevent the Nazis from taking their lives.

This is a common Jewish view of the holocaust: it may be the only perception of Jewish history shared by most Israelis, most JDL members, and most vehement anti-Zionist leftist Jews.

What can one say except to recognize this view as obscenity? For this analysis, the practical consequences of this point of view are of special concern. The JDL learned from their reading of history to concentrate on self-defense. Concentration on self-defense leads the JDL to become ADL, this time to the tenth power, searching out anti-Semites wherever they may be found. It exaggerates that of which there is already too much. It again sets the focus on what "they" are doing to us rather than on what we might do to transform ourselves. American Jewish life has its fill of defenders against limitations on Jewish freedoms. What it needs is an organization that focuses on the positive uses of Jewish freedom for the development of a true Jewish community. "Never

Again" is also a reminder that everything in Jewish experience is compared by the JDL to the holocaust. Not only does this make of the six million a political pawn in every controversy, but it makes it difficult to make the requisite distinctions between forms of oppression and anti-Semitism. It makes it impossible to see that others may disagree with one or oppose Jewish interests on the basis of their own interests without being anti-Semites. It allows other Jews off the hook because once they realize that the event in question is not as bad as the holocaust, they may come to feel no responsibility to act.

10

The Making of a Jewish Counterculture

The late 1960s were tough times for the liberal Jewish establishment. Assailed by Jewish radicals for its tepid attention to political change and social issues, this older Jewish generation soon also found itself on the defensive against charges from a new movement of Jewish youth that it was simply not Jewish enough. Especially after the Six-Day War in 1967, increasing numbers of Jewish youth argued that the alienation they too often felt from established Jewish institutions was due to the inadequate Judaism of their middle-class suburban upbringing. In search of a more meaningful Jewish identity, increasingly aware that there were Jewish traditions their parents and rabbis had hidden from them at Hebrew school, and frustrated that access to Jewish education remained largely unavailable on most college campuses (since the Hillel was often seen as part of the problem, and not the solution), these self-styled "New Jews" pursued their own experimentations, invented their own traditions, and followed their own agendas. In so doing, they self-consciously created an alternative Jewish cultural space, sustained by its own highly successful Jewish student press service, its own Jewish counterculture magazine (*Response,* first published in the summer of 1967), and a host of egalitarian communal houses dedicated to the pursuit of Jewish living and study (*havurot*).

Unsurprisingly, there were generational clashes. Many in the Jewish counterculture were outraged that national and regional Jewish philanthropic organizations were usually reluctant to subsidize autonomous student-led programs in Judaic study on university campuses, or hesitant to endorse or support alternative Jewish experiments in housing. The most memorable confrontation occurred in late 1969, when three hundred protesters, calling themselves Concerned Jewish Students, picketed the national convention of the Council of Jewish Federations and Welfare Funds. Calling for the CJF to reorder its priorities, the students threatened to crash the convention if they were not granted permission to present their demands. (The convention organizers relented.)

Other similar confrontations—some of them resolved far less amiably—between an older and a younger generation would follow.

The selections in this chapter offer just a few voices from or about the Jewish counterculture. In each case, the author is sympathetic to the cause of this new Jewish movement, even if he himself is not a member of it. Rabbi Balfour Brickner (or "Brick," as he was known to those in the Jewish youth movement) expresses his qualified admiration for the now legendary Freedom Seder held in April 1969, on the second day of Passover and the first anniversary of the assassination of Dr. Martin Luther King, Jr. Attended by several hundred participants, and held in an African American church (because no local synagogue was available), the Freedom Seder was broadcast live (on Pacifica radio in New York) and received international media coverage. As Brickner describes it, the radical Haggadah written by Arthur I. Waskow attempted to bring together a radical affirmation of faith and a commitment to political change. As such, it was often attacked by many in the organized Jewish community; yet, at the same time (and although this is far less acknowledged), Waskow's willingness to innovate led to countless further rewritings of the Haggadah—across the political spectrum—in the decades that followed.

Writer Bill Novak, editor at *Response* magazine, wrote as a full-fledged activist/participant in the new Jewish counterculture. Speaking in a New York radio address (and here reprinted from a Reform Jewish publication), Novak emphasizes how the Jewish counterculture is deeply invested in reinventing a useful Jewish tradition. Novak does not seek to minimize the political aspects of the movement, but he does work consciously to place those political engagements in the broader context of an abiding commitment to Judaism.

Stephen C. Lerner, a Conservative rabbi in New York City and a sympathetic chronicler of the Jewish counterculture, focuses his attention on controversies surrounding the Ramah camps. Not everyone within the Conservative movement accepted that the Ramah camps appeared to have evolved by the late 1960s into experimental incubators for the Jewish counterculture. Young people at Ramah were insisting on policy changes, and (depending on the specific camp) administrators had become increasingly permissive (if not outright supportive) of youth demands. Many who lived and worked at Ramah camps during these turbulent years (like Bill Novak) would afterward commit themselves to cooperative religious youth communities—like the *havurot.*

While the most influential *havurot* were based in Somerville, Massachusetts, New York City, and Washington, D.C., these informal Jewish communal living arrangements sprung up all over the place during the early 1970s. The article reprinted here from the *Cleveland Jewish News* describes one such experimental student community at Case Western Reserve University. Written by journalist Jerry Barach, it captures well how satisfying (if also disorganized) life in a *havurah* could be.

Finally, Mike Tabor discusses his belated rediscovery of the Jewish Labor Bund. Founded in Vilna in 1897, and soon thereafter an influential political force popular throughout Yiddish-speaking eastern Europe, the Bund was dedicated to democratic socialism and to secularism; it championed *Yiddishkeit* as a cultural alternative to Zionism. As such, Bundists challenged the notion that all Jews should ultimately make aliyah to Palestine, as they urged instead the transformation of societies in which they already lived. Tabor asks why such a tradition has been—and perhaps remains—largely forgotten by American Jews.

Notes on a Freedom Seder

BALFOUR BRICKNER

Lincoln Temple is a church in the heart of Washington's Black ghetto. By 8:30, Friday evening April 4th, the first anniversary of Martin Luther King's death, the basement of that church was "S.R.O.," with nearly 800 mostly White, mostly Jewish, mostly young people. They had come to participate in Arthur Waskow's much-publicized Freedom Seder.

I was there because I had been asked to be one of the leaders of that "seder." The experience proved to be as moving as it was unique. There were even moments that touched my calloused sense of spirituality.

The evening began with a fairly traditional religious service composed and conducted by Rabbi Harold White, Hillel Director at American University. If these young people are said to be contemptuous of Judaism (and some of them undoubtedly are) their participation in the service belied their contempt, and disarmed those whose opposition to the group and the seder was based on the charge that the evening was "blasphemous." To my amazement, those present refused to be "bored" spectators. They refused to content themselves with "watching the rabbi perform." They joined in, unbidden, line by line, chorus by chorus. In short, they were involved from the start, and that created a warm and positive atmosphere for what followed.

INNOVATIONS? PLENTY!

To be sure, Waskow's Haggadah took on its own "seder," its own order; but the traditional elements were all there: the four questions (deliberately asked by a young girl, rather than a boy, to satisfy those in the group who belong to the Woman's Liberation Movement), the blessing of the Pesah, the Matzah and the Maror, the welcoming of Elijah, the eating of the Karpas, the recitation of the story. Even the line, "let all who are hungry come and eat" was taken seriously, and, unlike so many congregational and communal sedarim, it was free!

Innovations? Plenty! Not just that among the participants were a Black Protestant minister (Rev. Channing Phillips, in whose church we met, and who was one of those nominated for the Presidency at the national Democratic convention last August); a Roman Catholic priest, Father George Malzone, one of the priests living at the D.C. Center for Christian Renewal

(Father Phil Berrigan couldn't make it); a Black nationalist, and sundry other lay persons. That is all common stuff nowadays. The seder broke new ground in other ways.

First, the fresh wording of the classic wish: "Next year may the entire household of Israel be free." Read again and ponder these lines from the Haggadah:

> For were we sitting tonight in Jerusalem we would still say: next year in Jerusalem. For this year, all men eat as aliens in a land not wholly theirs; next year we hope all men will celebrate in "the land of Israel"—that is in a world made one and a world made free.

Jerusalem thus ceases to be a place. It is here transposed into a state of mind and a condition. To live under oppression is to live "outside of Jerusalem," while total freedom is the "condition" of Israel. Thus, Jews can still meaningfully express the hope, "next year in Jerusalem," even though the physical city is now totally in Israeli hands.

PASSOVER POINTS TO REVOLUTION

The second innovative insight which these radical minds saw in and drew from the traditional words was that the entire Passover story pointed inexorably to revolution:

> Search further and inquire what our own fathers Moses and Joshua intended to do to our brothers the Canaanites, for as is said, "we took all his cities and the women, and the little ones, we left none of them remaining."

Ouch!

> But, let us remember the lesson of the plagues; the winning of freedom has not always been bloodless in the past.

> The theme they really wished to extract from the story begins to emerge:

> The heroes of our Biblical past whom we lionize have faced the issue of violence in the struggle for freedom.

Revolt requires violence! Revolution condones violence—for a holy cause: Freedom! This is the articulated mood of our generation's young radicals.

Waskow had done his homework. He mined out of the Jewish and American past those quotations which supported his point. The compilation was incredibly effective. The "shofet," Thomas Jefferson, speaking of the American revolution:

Can history produce an instance of rebellion so honorably conducted? God forbid we should ever be twenty years without such a rebellion. The tree of liberty must be refreshed from time to time, with the blood of patriots and tyrants.

THE LITANY OF HEROES

The Litany began to grow as the words of America's heroes were paraded before the Assembly:

> Thoreau wrote of the prophet John Brown: "It was his peculiar doctrine that a man has a perfect right to interfere by force with the slaveholder, in order to rescue the slave. I agree with him. Only they who are continually shocked by slavery have some right to be shocked by the violent death of the slaveholder."

The "judge" Lincoln said:

> If every drop of blood drawn by the lash must be paid by one drawn by the sword, still must it be said: the judgments of our Lord are true and righteous altogether.

Emanuel Ringelblum, writing from the Warsaw ghetto:

> Most of the populace is set on resistance. It seems to me that people will no longer go to the Slaughter like lambs. They want the enemy to pay dearly for their lives . . . Now we are ashamed of ourselves, disgraced in our own eyes, and in the eyes of the world, where our docility earned us nothing. This must not be repeated now. We must put up a resistance, defend ourselves against the enemy, man and child.

These words hurt. As "older liberals" we feel that we are being duped; the phrases are being torn out of context and used against us. It's not fair. But we know better. Like so many things the radicals say, they are just too right.

How far out of the legitimate stream is "shofet" Eldridge Cleaver who, we are reminded, "went into exile like Moses" (we wish Waskow would stop these painful analogies) when he said:

> This nation—bourgeois or not, imperialist or not, murderous or not, ugly or not—its people, somewhere in their butchered and hypocritical souls, still contained an epic potential which fires the imaginations of its youth . . .
>
> The young whites know that the colored people of the world, Afro-Americans included, do not seek revenge for their sufferings. They seek the

same things the White rebel wants; an end to war and exploitation. Black and White, the young rebels are free people, free in a way that Americans have never been before in the history of their country.

REVERSE "DAYENU"

Using the radical revolutionary behavior of Moses and God in Egypt, the Seder continued to focus the attention of its participants on the notion that radical revolution was and remains the undeniable necessity for a new social structure. I was impressed.

> For we must struggle for a freedom that enfolds stern justice, stern bravery and stern love. Blessed art thou, O Lord our God who hast confronted us with the necessity of choice and of creating our own book of Thy law. How many and how hard are the choices and the tasks the Almighty set before us.

The third *hiddush* (new thought) emerges. Waskow called it his "reverse dayenu":

> It would *not* be sufficient. . . . For if we were to end a single genocide but not to stop the other wars that kill men and women as we sit here, it would not be sufficient.
>
> If we were to end those bloody wars but not disarm the nations of the weapons that could destroy all mankind, it would not be sufficient . . . How much more then are we in duty bound to struggle, work, share, give, think, plan, feel, organize, sit-in, speak out, hope and be on behalf of Mankind. For we must end the genocide (in Vietnam), stop the bloody wars that are killing men and women as we sit here, disarm the nations of the deadly weapons that threaten to destroy us all, end the brutality with which the police beat minorities in many countries, make sure that no one starves, free the poets from their jails, educate us all to understand their poetry, allow us all to explore our inner ecstasies, and encourage and aid us to love one another and share in the human fraternity. All these!

Perhaps the most meaningful of all quotations was the one from Buber:

> Man, while created by God, was established by Him in an independence which has since remained undiminished. In this independence he stands over against God. So man takes part with full freedom and spontaneity in the dialogue between the two which forms the essence of our existence.

To which Waskow added:

> So let us remember that we celebrate both Mankind and God.

WHAT KIND OF REVOLUTION?

With this, I believe, the Seder reached its climax. The denouement followed easily, yet not without meaning. Laced throughout were the appropriate songs, sung at the right moments, led by two "Judy Collins" types, young girls with folk guitars and refreshing, folksy voices. Imagine singing "Solidarity Forever" at a seder in 1969. My grandfather must be smiling. I too smiled a little as I sang "The Times They Are Changing" immediately after reading:

> We speak to our children of the departure from Egypt because we know that in their generation too it will be necessary to seek liberation.

And I choked up when we sang "The Peat Bog Soldiers" immediately following the quote from the Ringelblum diary.

As for calling Cleaver, Nat Turner, Jefferson, Lincoln "shoftim"—judges, or Mustie, Robert Moses, Dr. Martin Luther King, Lloyd Garrison, John Brown, Ghandi, "prophets," it didn't bother me at all. The context and the purpose gave the poetic license a kind of fresh legitimacy.

So, there you have it—at least in capsule form. A group of Jews, most of whom consider themselves radicals, using history, Jewish and American, from which to mine a preachment of revolution. Maybe it's not legitimate. Granted it sees the Jewish past one-dimensionally, that's really not the issue. More important is to ask, "What do they mean?" There are revolutions and there are revolutions. What kind are they advocating? The kind their fathers and grandfathers shouted about when they came to these shores 40–50 years ago, or the kind that "Che" abortively led in Bolivia? Our young Jewish radicals know and use the language of both. Do they seriously advocate the physical overthrow of "the system" to attain their goals? I've talked and listened to some of them, and, honestly, I do not know. I don't think they know yet. But one thing is clear: they are fed up with the Jewish establishment and with the way the Jewish organizational structure functions. It goes without saying that they live outside of and indifferent to that structure.

WHERE THE ACTION WAS

Is their use of the Passover metier just a gimmick? I don't think it can be written off that easily. Listening to them, I cannot help feeling that some are taking a fresh look at their own Jewishness as, perhaps, the only way by which to establish their own identity. If that is the case, a number of factors have to be considered. Perhaps some of our radical Jewish youth are coming to see that the assimilation route, so unproductively trod by their parents' generation, is not the answer. Many young Jewish radicals are contemptuous of the older generation for having tried this approach, leaving their children with so little awareness of what Jewish authenticity really entails.

Moreover, the Black community has taught them that assimilation is too high a price to pay, even if it could be achieved. But the Black community may have done even more to and for our Jewish young. They may have forced our young people into the posture of self-identification by telling them (and us) there is no place for you, as a White person, in our world right now. "Do your own thing in your own community." If so, our young people are discovering that separatism means, for the present anyway, that there is little or no room for them in the Black world despite their own radicalism. Distressingly, some Jewish adults have been using that awareness as a pretext to justify their own desire further to disengage from the urban crisis and gleefully to retreat into their own Jewish atmospheres. Maybe out of this "evil" something positive is emerging—the realization on the part of some of our radical Jewish youth that they can't escape their Jewish selves and that what they have considered a liability might just as well be turned into an asset. I don't know.

Anyway, Friday night, April 4th, was a night when, for the first time in a long, long time, I felt that I was some place "where the action was." It felt good.

The Making of a Jewish Counter Culture

BILL NOVAK

[. . .] Jewish life in the 1950's was something less than glorious. Youth activities on an organized level made today's look good by comparison. If a Hillel foundation provided its quota of Jewish boys for Jewish girls, it was doing a fine job. And Jewish education—if you can imagine this—was in worse shape than it is now. It was certainly not a hopeful picture, and, given the mood of America at that time, there was little reason to expect a significant change.

But as the new decade began, things did change, and very rapidly, as new symbols arose to replace the old. The election of John Kennedy was at the heart of this symbol switch, as new qualities and ideas were paraded before the nation. Fashion and glamour. Minorities and politics. Youth and vigor. Involvement on all levels by all people. Charm and wit and chivalry. A sense of humor and a belief in the future of mankind. A new sense of cultural excellence. The country responded to all this as young people awoke one morning in 1961 to find themselves in a new age. Michael Harrington told them about poverty, John Galbraith about corporate capitalism, Paul Goodman and Martin Luther King about youth and dignity, while Bob Dylan (and later on, of course, the Beatles) filled in the gaps by drawing a more complete picture of the world and its visions. The system itself took on a new life, and Washington again became its focal point. The Peace Corps was born, and folk music swept the country. There was a great march on Washington, and the sit-in movement began in the south.

Jewish students were very much involved in the projects associated with the Kennedy administration. To be sure, they were involved as Jewish young people rather than as young Jewish people, but we should find nothing surprising about that. They became involved in the civil rights and peace movements. Liberal rabbis pointed at them with pride, while the more conservative elements in the Jewish community were frankly embarrassed by the Jewish identity of the activists. And, unfortunately, many of the young people themselves shared in that embarrassment.

The new spirit continued to grow, until the bullet that killed the youthful President brought that short-lived era to an abrupt and violent end. Another swift change in symbol sets, as ugliness moved into the White House. Power and Prestige took over. Quantity replaced quality, authority replaced style. And, finally, Vietnam.

Aside from the well-known and documented effects that the war has had on the youth culture, there were, I suggest, two key events during the Johnson administration that had a profound effect on Jewish young people and their situation. The first of these events was the gradual but obvious shift in what until that time had been called the civil-rights movement. In effect, black people told their white counterparts, and Jews in particular, that the struggle was more particular than universal. As a black movement there was really nothing that whites could do to help, except by withdrawing from the struggle. This was naturally a bitter pill to swallow for many Jewish liberals who had been honestly and significantly involved in the black struggle up to that point. When cries of anti-semitism were heard, and when some of the blacks allied themselves out of ignorance with the Arab cause, many Jews gave up on the whole thing. But some of the younger Jews responded differently and understood the message that had emerged. The lesson was, ironically, a Jewish lesson—identify with your own people. You are fortunate, said the black to the Jew, for you have a people: work with it. You are fortunate, said the black to the Jew, for your history is recorded: study it. You have your own culture, so dig it. That was the message in 1966. But it was a little too subtle, and had to be repeated, in a different form, a year later.

The massive response of the world Jewish community to the 1967 war in Israel was just that—the reformation of a world Jewish community. For the most part, the response did not extend to the American campus, except in a very personal way. While the war of 1967 had an effect on all Jews, it seemed in many cases to reach young people a little later than their parents. Perhaps their parents had other spectres haunting their collective memory. Whatever the reason, the Jew on campus reacted to Israel far more in 1968 and especially in 1969 than he did immediately after the six-day war.

In view, then, of the black revolution and the six-day war, what has become of the Jewish activist on campus? Many of them are still in the picture, as they have always been, ready to participate in any cause but their own. But a small minority has responded to recent events by attempting to merge their political views and their Jewish tradition. The New Left, at one point the only hope for a political morality in this country, sold him out by its pointless acceptance of the "good-guy-bad-guy" dualism in the Middle East. The logical response, one might think, would be for the young people to channel their energy into concerns that are at least in some way Jewish. But it is not as easy as it seems. Above all, many of my generation have been turned off long ago by an organized Jewish Community which is neither Jewish nor Community—only organized. Consequently, many young people have the impression that American Jewish life is really Judaism, and they want no part of it. So, to their minds, Judaism is another part of the system, because their elders have allowed it to happen.

We turn now to some of the results of this ferment. The new Jewish counter culture, it must be remembered, is in its initial stages. The entire movement is difficult to study because it is (intentionally) fragmented, decentralized, and particularistic. These anti-organizational tendencies are common to the new politics in general, as there is a built-in distrust of structured mass movements, often as the result of bitter and frustrating experience.

In an attempt to categorize the various features of the new Jewish counter culture, one turns first to the most obvious aspect—politics. The political counter culture in Jewish life is composed for the most part of people who have been involved in progressive or leftist causes of various kinds in the past few years. In many cases, they are just now realizing that there is some connection between their political radicalism and their Jewish backgrounds, however thinly they might have been exposed to Jewish values in earlier years, and however poorly they understand the link between the two. Examples of these political projects are the Jewish Liberation Project in New York, *Na-aseh* in Philadelphia, the New Jewish Committee in Minnesota, and Jews for Urban Justice in Washington. The Philadelphia group, for instance, has been active in calling for draft counselling in local synagogues. Groups in New York and Boston have been more concerned with how money is spent in the Jewish community. Just this past week a group of three hundred Jewish students picketed the national convention of Jewish philanthropic organizations, demanding that higher priorities be given to Jewish education, culture, and social action. In the recent peace march in Washington, hundreds of Jewish students met together under the banner of the National Jewish Organizing Project in an attempt to determine how they might best combine their politics and their heritage within the peace movement. And in Montreal, Madison and Toronto, new progressive Zionist groups have sprung up out of thin air at the local universities. In Long Island, the well-publicized Ruskay case attracted national attention when a Jewish student presented evidence to prove that it was impossible for him to be granted the status of C.O. by his local draft board, because his religion was not recognized as being traditionally pacifist.

But it would be a misreading of the situation to see the counter culture strictly in terms of politics. In Toronto, for instance, a group of young college people, faced with the dreary prospect of attending High Holy Day services at the local temple, as they had been doing for years, decided not to go, and instead formed their own underground congregation, and held their own services in the basement of one of the member's homes. In various other communities, young people are forming their own religious services, often radically different from the traditional Jewish liturgy. The *Havurat Shalom* in Cambridge and the House of Love and Prayer in San Francisco are but two of the more known communal places where a new form of experimental service is being developed, and where younger Jews can come to find appropriate modes of expression for their own religious quests.

Jewish culture and education have not remained unaffected by the increased activity in the youth community. In certain afternoon Hebrew schools, committed college students have taken over whole departments and are experimenting with new types of Jewish education. The 1960s have also seen the growth of more exciting projects within the establishment, such as the Ramah camps, and better youth programs. But these institutions are inadequate in themselves, and the impetus has finally come from the young people themselves. Performing groups in Hebrew music and dance have sprung up in the nineteen sixties, particularly in the New York area. In addition, Jewish kids are now reading Jewish books. Not only Philip Roth, who has been scapegoated by parts of the Jewish establishment for being, in a word, too good a writer, but also authors such as Agnon, Nellie Sachs, and Elie Wiesel, along with Americans such as Singer and Malamud are part of the new reading list. And, at long last, there is finally some agitation at various colleges for the establishment of departments of Judaica. At the State University in Albany, students have taken matters into their own hands by creating a free Jewish University.

One could go on listing projects, but there are two in which I have been involved which I would like to describe. Last year there were a number of conferences and meetings as it became clear that developments all over the country were leading in similar directions vis-à-vis radical Judaism. There were a number of individuals who felt that the movement in its totality was greater than the sum of its parts, i.e. that a merely political affiliation was in itself inadequate. What emerged was the Havurah in New York City. Havurah is the Hebrew word for fellowship or community, and it is within that framework that courses have been established to study Judaica on the graduate level. The Havurah is dedicated to a free and personal type of learning, and with a total membership of twenty-five and no administration at all, it is able to achieve this desired goal. Anyone interested in starting a course has an opportunity to do so, and the students decide whether they need a teacher, and, if so, they seek one out. Havurah members have a communal meal once a week, and spend shabbat together at least once a month. The group decided that the November retreat should take place at the March on Washington, and we participated in that event as a group. There is also a Havurah (group) in Boston, as well as New Brunswick. New groups will probably emerge in other cities as local people are ready to create them. The Havurah provides human contacts in a way that the university can not, and as a system of learning it may well become very popular in the near future among religious and even secular students. It should be added that most members of the Havurah continue their graduate programs at other colleges at the same time.

If the Havurah is sort of a culmination and summary of the recent developments, then RESPONSE is surely at the other end of the spectrum. When RESPONSE was started three years ago by a few dissatisfied undergraduates, there was no hint of a counter culture in Jewish life. The editors of the magazine wanted a forum to discuss the problems in American Jewish life, and suggest new models and ideas that might be useful, especially to other students. The first issue appeared in 1967, with five hundred copies. Two years later, RESPONSE is now a quarterly with over five thousand readers. The magazine has become somewhat of an unofficial intellectual organ for the new Jewish counter culture, for it is in the pages of RESPONSE that new theoretical models are discussed, while current structures and concepts are analyzed.

The counter culture I have spoken of is a new and growing organism. It is very small in actual numbers, but involved in it are some of the brightest and most creative young people in Jewish life today. The overall movement is intentionally vague, ad-hoc, and decentralized, for its members have learned to fear structures more than anything else. The Jewish establishment might do well to take note of the new counter culture, which seeks not so much to destroy what already exists as to bypass it. Rather than concentrating on attacking and destroying what is irrelevant, the movement has chosen instead to create new models and experiment with their uses.

As Jacob Neusner has pointed out, fellowship in Judaism is not exactly new. In fact, it is evident that most of the elements in the counter culture are very old ideas. Young people are going back to traditional models and ancient texts in their search for meaning, and it is in this sense that they are truly radical.

Ramah and Its Critics

STEPHEN C. LERNER

Ramah has been the Jewel of Conservative Judaism. When Professor Seymour Fox says, "Ramah makes Jews," that statement readily commands the assent of Jewish professionals and lay leaders. If Professor Louis Finkelstein declares more poetically, "Ramah saves lives," few take issue with the reality underlying his comment. For, since the first Ramah camp was founded in Wisconsin in 1947, Ramah has had incredible success in making committed Jews, in opening youth to the more meaningful aspects of American Jewish life.

While the effect of Ramah in producing a generation of rabbis, educators and dedicated laymen has not been measured scientifically, it is generally agreed that the camps have had a most powerful, even incalculable, role in producing a responsible American Jewish élite of professionals and laymen. Furthermore, the camp experience has stimulated hundreds of students to spend a year, and some of them a lifetime, in Israel.

Ramah's growth has been the result of the work of far-sighted laymen, dedicated rabbis, and key Seminary personnel, to which has been added the momentum of successful summers and growing acclaim. Rabbi Ralph Simon and the late Maxwell Abbell were instrumental in the establishment of the first camp in Wisconsin (1947). Under the leadership of Mr. Abe Birenbaum and Rabbis David Goldstein and Simon Greenberg, a Poconos camp was opened in 1950. Local groups in Chicago and Philadelphia, working closely with Seminary representatives, Rabbi Moshe Davis and Mrs. Sylvia Ettenberg, recognized the national implications of these camps and the need for constant professional supervision. The creation of a National Ramah Commission in 1951, under the guidance of the Teachers Institute, encouraged increasing coordination and centralization of educational camping programs.

Ramah grew. New camps were founded in Connecticut, California, Canada, Nyack (New York), the Berkshires, Glen Spey (New York), and Massachusetts (replacing the Connecticut camp). The Ramah Seminar and the Community Program in Israel were established. Ramah became "big time."

In the summer of 1970, close to 4,000 campers were at Ramah camps. The small initial staff of part-timers had expanded to a national Ramah director, seven full-time camp directors, a director of Ramah programs in Israel, and a number of professional administrators. The annual operating budget of Ramah was over two million dollars. The few thousand staff members included professors-in-residence, unit heads, teachers, and a contingent of Israeli "specialists" in particular fields. Ramah is clearly one of the most significant educational camping movements in America. [. . .]

In 1969, this reporter started to hear stories of strange doings in Massachusetts. I had sent one girl up to camp as a waitress, hoping that the intensely Jewish atmosphere of Ramah would help overcome seventeen years of comparative Jewish isolation and ignorance. Instead, her mother received dismaying letters which, in commenting on the staff, said among other things: "The dope in this camp is unbelievable—and the grass, so many kids smoke." What was going on?

The history of that 1969 summer ultimately begins and ends with Raphael Arzt, director of Ramah's New England installation for almost a decade. Arzt has been clearly one of the most gifted of the Ramah directors and far and away the most willing to experiment in programming. Ramah has never been a monolithic movement. Each camp director has been given wide latitude in running the individual camp. Thus, Arzt was able to embark on unique programs and to employ certain specialists who would not have been engaged at other Ramah camps. Over the years, Arzt's camp had developed a mystique about it. While every Ramah director had his own *hasidim,* those who opted to work specifically with Arzt felt that his camp was different from other Ramahs. Campers shared this feeling.

Arzt, ordained in 1961 and appointed a Ramah director that year, began to realize toward the end of his first summer as director that the youngsters he was encountering in Ramah and LTF (the élite conservative youth group) had a strong allegiance to the Jewish people, but no meaningful Jewish philosophy. At best they had "a survivalist, sociological formulation of Jewish life" but "no propelling system to transcend the orbit of Ramah." Arzt began a double search—to define his own underlying principles of Jewish life, and to develop an educational methodology to lead others to their own "personal, existential posture."

Under Arzt, Ramah became an extremely exciting place. The Winnipeg *hasid,* Professor Zalman Schachter, was at camp in 1963 and 1964 and had tremendous impact in sensitizing staff and youngsters to religious symbols and to deeply felt prayer. One method combined craftsmanship and religious sensitivity: campers began making their own *taliyot* in bright and varied hues, and later brought them home to add warmth and color to local synagogues. In the following years Rabbi Arthur Green and Alan Mintz, now of the Boston and New York *havurot,* respectively, continued along similar paths.

The demand for change grew. Arzt perceived that for many at Ramah, the tradition evoked little positive response, and that adherence to tradition often amounted to no more than a form of religious behaviorism. There was too much *keva* (routine) and insufficient *kavanah* (religious intensity). In time, Arzt came to feel that the Ramah policy of insisting on a fixed structure of prayer was not educationally justified, and that new approaches were needed to articulate the fundamental value concepts of the *Siddur* in a way comprehensible to youth.

One line of experimentation employed the "evocative word approach." An important idea found in the *siddur*—*ahavah* (love), for example—would become the center of a week's study. During this period the daily *Shaharit* service would be abbreviated. One day the campers would be asked to cite all the associations the word *ahavah* suggested to them; on another day they might relate the value concept to their own lives. Finally when the campers returned to pray the *ahavah rabbah* prayer, it hopefully would resonate with the extended intellectual and personal meaning which the week of intensive study had afforded them. Another technique involved examining the contents of a prayer, instead of *davening* it at a specific service. With such techniques, Arzt and his staff attempted to deal with the problems of prayer, of religious behaviorism, of *kavanah* versus *keva*. As Arzt noted, "The entire problem of *tefillah* was broken open, for better or worse." For educational purposes Arzt was willing to run the risks involved in this experimentation. [. . .]

Around 1968, the youth culture became a real factor in American life. Student activism and drugs were part of the scene wherever young people gathered. Ramah, drawing its staff and campers from among the most articulate and vital young people, did not escape the problems. Ramah did not create the youth culture; it inherited it.

The youth culture presented new challenges and demanded new responses. It was perhaps inevitable that Arzt, the most experimental of Ramah directors, would test them. It is also probably true that Arzt's camp, with its encouragement of diverse points of view, had a larger percentage of staff and campers sympathetic to many facets of the youth culture. Often they came to Palmer from other Ramah camps. One religiously radical student in the Seminary's Combined Program reported to a young faculty member that he was advised by people at *his* more staid Ramah camp to apply to Massachusetts the following summer, because that was where the radicals were. In addition, some of Arzt's previous associates did not return in 1969. The framework of commitment to Jewish tradition became somewhat more tenuous; the experiments became more radical.

In 1969, a new and enlarged LTF (the name was now applied to the oldest group of campers) was created, with 180 youngsters under three co-equal unit heads. The problems of structuring the program and of communicating decisions within so large a unit were enormous. The leaders working with Arzt had envisioned the creation of a camp community where pluralism was the norm, where exciting options were available—traditional *davening,* or creative services using outside materials. There was a real attempt to create meaningful experiences for smaller groups within LTF—separate *Shabbat* meals, "family" dinners, small *tefillah* groups, certain labs or workshops, such as one in sensitivity training.

In many ways, the plans went awry. With the extremely large size of the LTF unit and its subdivision into many groups, it was virtually impossible to supervise it adequately. A noticeable percentage of campers would manage to avoid their obligations at any given time. Given a choice of religious services, the majority of campers chose those which were minimally connected to the *siddur*. As Alan Mintz, one of that year's LTF leaders, noted: "We didn't realize the special advocacy and compensatory treatment the tradition must receive in a situation of educational pluralism." Jewish and Ramah traditions were often overturned. Furthermore, while there was no public policy of permissiveness, there was a *de facto* refusal to make demands on the campers. Mintz acknowledged that, as educators, his staff felt a tension between the claims of furthering the personal development of adolescents and the claims of Judaism. Again, *de facto,* personal development took precedence over Jewish claims.

Perhaps the crowning example of this process was the presentation by some members of LTF of the play "Hair" in English. Here, a decision was made to permit a small group of non-cooperative campers to do something constructive. That the content of "Hair" and its production in English were not expressive of Ramah's Jewish goals, were insufficient reasons to overrule this project and its supposedly positive effect on the personal growth of some campers.

Even more controversial was the 1969 *Mador* (counselor-training program). Arzt, who had been a critic of past programs, wanted to do more than merely train counselors to carry out tasks. The *Mador,* he believed, must begin to encourage future counselors to develop ideological commitments. He also hoped the *Mador* members would function as a community that would, through discussion, determine its own policies. Arzt and Rabbi Neal Kaunfer, a young educator increasingly outspoken in his criticism of establishment patterns of Jewish education, presented their conception of the *Mador* to the Ramah directorate, which accepted the plan and refined it in a series of meetings. Kaunfer was selected as *Mador* director.

It was Kaunfer's feeling that "conditioning people to Judaism is not necessarily the best way to firm commitment." He believed that the conditioning process was an extension of more authoritarian approaches to education. Adolescents on the threshold of maturity should have room to search out decisions on their own.

The *Mador,* in fact, was only minimally directive. Counselor-trainees spent half the season in bunks and took certain classes. During the remainder of the season, an experiment in community living was attempted, with much of the initiative left to the *madorniks.* What occurred most often were interminable meetings and discussions, little constructive programming, and a great deal of freedom to do nothing. *Tefillot* were "touch and go"; there was evidently not enough interest to maintain a *minyan* or provide Torah readers on weekdays.

The *Mador* did succeed, perhaps more than in previous years, in fostering self-discovery and personal maturation. Thus it proved valuable in helping high school graduates make the difficult transition to college. *Madorniks* of that summer remarked that the first thing the counselor-trainees did when granted all that freedom was to deal intensively with personal issues, something they had never done before. In terms of projects, one *madornik* noted, "nothing got off the ground." This was especially true in regard to Judaism. Little positive Jewish search seems to have been attempted. As James A. Sleeper, a member of the *Mador* staff, commented in a privately circulated paper, "Judaism—and by that we mean both willingness to live Jewishly, and enthusiasm for the study of Judaism—lost by a kind of default to more personal concerns. . . ."

According to Label Waldman, the 1970 *Mador* director, the previous summer's *Mador* incorrectly assumed that "kids are their own best physicians." He believed that the person on the threshold of college desperately needs structure even though he announces that he doesn't. Thus, in the 1970 *Mador,* the educators were the "senior partners" and the kids "junior partners" in the business of education.

Massachusetts Ramah in the summer of 1969 was a watershed. Daring experiments were tried; few were entirely successful. The religiously permissive atmosphere of the camp, the experimentation, the negative trappings of the youth culture which apparently were not adequately curbed, caused deep dismay among some staff members, Jewish leaders, and parents of campers. (Of all the Ramah camps, Massachusetts was the only one which did not meet its quota of campers in 1970.)

For many who were at Palmer, Massachusetts, the serious attempts to provide new educational approaches to major religious problems did not counterbalance the violence done Jewish tradition in the process. Rabbi Zvi Shapiro, who taught at Palmer in 1969, was so disturbed by what he saw there that he switched to the Berkshire camp the following summer. At Palmer, he "felt that there was no positive religious spirit." The staff was, by and large, not committed to any kind of religious tradition and thus made little attempt to enforce its observance. Gimmicks (girls putting on *tefillin*) and over-individualism became the order of the day. Thus, there was very little in the way of meaningful Jewish growth. Shapiro exempts from his charges the younger age group whose program was operated in a more traditional manner and was, therefore, more successful.

Nobody was completely contented with the 1969 *Mador* or with the Palmer summer in general. Arzt told me, "It was an important *Mador;* it was not a successful *Mador*." He lamented the fact that the *Mador* director became too much of a participant instead of remaining somewhat aloof as the group's advisor. Arzt also regretted that the size of the camp made it impossible for him to be on top of every project, so that some stupid experimentation went on. "At their best," he said openly, "the lines of communication [with the staff] didn't always turn out to be lines of communication."

Other members of the Ramah hierarchy were clearly unhappy with the ways things had turned out, but it was not easy for them to discuss the efforts of their friend and colleague critically. Mrs. Sylvia Ettenberg, to whom the national Ramah director is immediately responsible, admitted that the problems of New England had been building for several years. "We had a director in New England and a number of people who gathered around him, a man who wanted to experiment in certain ways with forging or forming a youth-centered society. He is a responsible person; he has integrity. He was given a chance to do his experiments. Most were responsible. . . . Some things got out of hand, were wrong religiously, wrong educationally. . . . We do not condone them; in fact, we condemn them." Seymour Fox spoke of the experiments in New England as "a remarkable failure. They undertook to solve very difficult problems with, I think, limited conceptions." He acknowledged that there was a legitimate tension between control and freedom. New England in 1969, he believed, "went 'gung-ho' for one extreme."

Perhaps the key to the problem is to be found in Alan Mintz's analysis. "We mistook the stage we were at, in terms of our own maturity, our own religious development, as being identical with the stage of development which the kids should have been brought into at that time." *Tesisah* (intellectual ferment) among the staff, Arzt proudly noted, helped give rise to two *havurot* and to *Response* magazine. On the camper-*Mador* level, this observer found that it apparently encouraged *hefkerut* (irresponsibility).

REDEFINING POLICY

After the problem of 1969, the Ramah hierarchy with its new national Ramah director, Rabbi David Mogilner, closely scrutinized its past program. Clearly, while the program of the camps had, as usual, been markedly successful, some things were radically wrong. Ramah decided to place some checks on experimentation and to make manifestly clear what the Ramah framework was. It was decided that the traditional prayers were to be part of every *Shaharit* service, that a curfew was necessary, that it was the role of the counselor to impose a value structure on young people, at least in certain areas. It was made absolutely clear, too, that drugs were not to be part of the Ramah community's experience. Before the 1970 season, directors stressed in interviews with staff and during orientation week that since "pot" was illegal, it would not be countenanced at Ramah.

Most important, the directors prepared a brochure, "An Experience Called Ramah," which was distributed to staff and to every camper above thirteen. The pamphlet delineated rather explicitly what Ramah's programs and expectations were in regard to *Shabbat, tefillah,* interpersonal relationships and safety regulations. One can almost read through the lines of the document and discern the directors' wrestling both with the peremptory demands of the youth culture and with the recognition that too much freedom is not necessarily a good thing: "Life at camp is in many ways more varied and fuller than one's normal routine at home. Therefore, each division, depending on the age of the campers, has a set curfew time." The significance of basic ritual was plainly reaffirmed: "Boys over Bar Mitzvah age pray each morning with a *talit* and *tefillin*. The *kipah* (*yarmulka*) is required at meals, at prayers and at class sessions."

While Ramah policies were being hammered out, Rabbi Arzt was in Israel on sabbatical. He returned to what he termed a new situation. The philosophic and programmatic retrenchment was in large measure due to "political" pressures, he suggested. He was not happy with some of the policy determinations that had been made, feeling that they were the result, not of educational needs, but rather of external conditions.

When Arzt speaks of political pressures, he means the protests of rabbis, scholars, and parents intent on maintaining the status quo of tradition irrespective of educational considerations. Arzt lamented, and this lament has been echoed by others, that many rabbis don't really understand what happens to youngsters of post–Bar Mitzvah age.

One frequently notes among Ramah people serious criticism of Seminary faculty and congregational rabbis who, lacking educational expertise, nevertheless carp at aspects of Ramah's programming and innovations. Ramah directors add that those who were all too willing to censure, were less than willing to cooperate in attempting to solve the host of problems that confront anyone who deals with today's generation of youth. Arzt scornfully recounted his periodic meetings with rabbis in the Northeast. When he would tell them of new projects at his camp, little of his presentation would exercise them positively or negatively, but when discussions finally turned to conflicts with the *shul* caterer, the rabbis would be roused to indignation. [. . .]

* * *

Everyone has criticisms of Ramah. At the same time, virtually everyone speaks highly of the camps. Steve Shaw may speak of the religious crisis at Ramah, but he returns to teach and be inspired in turn. David Weiss may recognize the immense difficulties of integrating Israelis into the camp framework, but he knows that American youth and Israeli adults return to their homes summer after summer very much influenced by the Jewish life which suffuses the camps. Even campers and, occasionally, staff members who are at odds with the Jewish religious outlook return because of the rare *hevrah* which is produced, a *hevrah* of sensitive souls who enjoy interacting with each other.

Ramah is alive, alive with study, with questioning, with exploration, with deeply felt prayer. A *Shabbat* at Ramah can well be a taste of *olam haba,* and can change the life of any youth fortunate enough to experience it. Rabbis and teachers return to camp because at Ramah Judaism works, and sloganizing gives way to education of the most rewarding kind. People learn and are changed—and that is what Judaism is all about.

A visit to Camp Ramah in Massachusetts in 1970 showed this reporter that Ramah has not lost its magic. The atmosphere was heady with Jewish life; the classes in *midrash,* in Bible, in Hebrew literature, on the Holocaust, were serious and rewarding. The spirit in the dining room on *Shabbat* was strong and unmanipulated; the *kabbalat Shabbat* service indicated just how wide of the mark our late Friday evening services are. At the *makhon* service on *Shabbat* morning, *hassidic niggunim,* colored *taliyot,* the open air, created a truly meaningful atmosphere. The bare feet may have been startling, but something was happening; youngsters were *davening*. They felt the prayers; I felt the prayers. It was a rare and moving service. [. . .]

On the Palmer campus, one young girl, a veteran of a few summers at the camp, related: "Last year, I got more of the feeling for Judaism through religious expression and experience. This year, I'm more into Torah, confronting questions about God, the Bible, Judaism. I'm here to learn; I have a lot to learn."

When Ramah works, its results last. Judi Feldman has spent eight years in the Ramah movement. Last summer she was a counselor at Camp Ramah in the Berkshires. This reporter had taught her four summers before at the same camp. Sitting at the edge of the baseball field, we talked about Ramah. "I love it; I love the people and the way they live here." She saw herself as an "advocate for Judaism" and hoped that she was managing to convey to her charges some of her feelings about Ramah, about Judaism, about the Jewish people.

Ramah tries to nourish sensitive Jewish souls. Very frequently, Ramah succeeds.

The Chavura Blend of Chaos, Tranquility

JERRY D. BARACH

What is life like in a chavura—a Jewish communal residence?

"Chaos," says one resident.

"Chaos," echoes another.

"Chaos," I agree to myself.

Having ventured forth to do a story about what life is like in a chavura—specifically Chavurat Aviv on the campus of Case Western Reserve University—I strived to look beyond the chaos that was an obvious fact of life among these 11 young Jewish men and women.

There is tranquility, too, I was assured. The tranquility that comes with a Shabbat that is spent in prayer (some of it original), festive dining, discussion and a good measure of resting.

I joined the chavura—all six women and five men—for an evening together recently to sample the life of the commune and to ask them what they feel they have gotten out of this share-all type of living.

I obviously chose an evening of more than normal chaos because the chavura members were all involved in helping to get ready for the recent Israel Independence Day celebration on the campus.

All over the place were balloons and those crazy plastic hammers that squeak when you hit someone over the head with them.

The telephone kept ringing, people kept arriving, and oh, yes, there was Grushie. Grushie is a dog but maybe thinks he is a person too. Anyway he eats well judging by the creature's size.

The chavura came into existence last January, when the students moved into a haunted-house looking old frame structure (a mansion at one time?) on E. 117th St., just off of Euclid Ave.

With donated furniture and a cash gift from a benefactor, the house was put into usable condition.

Why a chavura?

Basically to create the vehicle in which a living Judaism could operate. Where there would be kashrut, Shabbat, yom tov. Where discussions could take place among the participants together with others on what the real meaning of Judaism is.

For some, the chavura is the beginning—a sampling of what they hope to create in Israel as members of "irbutzim" (urban kibbutzim).

Generally speaking, the chavura has served to create a more intensive Jewish feeling among the members, one of the chaverim (or chavura members) told me.

Additionally, there is the heightened sense of responsibility and consideration for one another that comes in an atmosphere where each has his or her assigned duty to perform at a particular time and place.

There is no "sexism" in assignment of duties, and the fellows do cooking and cleaning on an equal footing with the girls.

Does the system work? Yes, all agreed, but naturally there are some frictions.

As one student put it, not entirely humorously, "I feel as though I've got ten mothers and fathers here."

Problems are discussed at a weekly meeting to deal with administrative and other matters, held each Sunday night.

The chavura has proved to be both a center of Jewish life where nonmembers also drop in, and a place which reaches out to the larger community.

An independent Sunday school for children which was begun before the chavura came into existence now meets there.

Also chavura members are active Jewishly in various roles such as teachers, youth leaders and in activities at Hillel.

What's to be the future of this commune, one of only a few such operations in the U.S.?

Well, next fall's continuation is apparently assured. Even though most of this year's members will be leaving Cleveland, more than enough have been signed up to replace them.

A more immediate concern faces the chavura, that of continued payment of expenses over the summer. Rent, at $450 per month, must be met even though the students will not be around.

To pay those expenses, even those chavura members not returning are seeking employment in various types of odd jobs in the week beginning May 21, with all proceeds to go to the chavura.

Young Jews Discover Their True Forebears

MIKE TABOR

My understanding of what's happened to Jews in America might seem a bit simplistic to some of you. But here it is.

A number of things happened. The most important was the natural urge, once one entered the "Golden Door," to be accepted. If you wanted to make it in America, you had to first of all stop behaving like a "greenhorn." To many that meant learning the business, language, ethics and cultural ways of the "promised land" and, in the process, forgetting the life of the old country—the shtetl, the rebbe, the shul, the poverty.

There's nothing unnatural or peculiar about this process. It happens to all sorts of ethnic groups. But the question is, did it have to happen? I think not. At least not as thoroughly and completely as it did here. But that's not important. What is is that the last two generations, their actions and direction, hold the key to Jewish survival, or its near complete demise in this part of the diaspora.

A number of us are groping for the pieces now strewn about. We know that what is labeled "Jewish" by the Jewish establishment, is not. Although many of our brothers and sisters accept that which they have been told is the authentic form of Judaism, we do not. We know it is aberration, distortion and desecration.

But enough of that.

How are we picking up the pieces you ask? Well, a couple of months ago, you'll be glad to know that we unearthed a truly delightful, moving, strange and relevant object. We discovered Yiddish! Washington's "Jews for Urban Justice," after its Friday night Shabbat celebration and communal dinner, invited Susan Roemer to sing a few Yiddish songs. Susan is a young woman who is active in the Women's Liberation movement in Washington. She was brought up in a Brooklyn home that stressed Yiddish. We, the products of various forms of typical American Jewish education, expected mostly lullabies.

Instead, what did we hear? Songs like "Vacht Oyf!"—Awake! And it rang with verses like "How long, oh how long will you suffer in bondage, in slavery still to remain? How long will you toil to create all the riches, for those who reward you with pain?" (The English of course hardly does it justice.)

What's this? We thought we had invented the revolution. Exactly who sang these songs? (Certainly not our parents.)

Our grandparents you say? No. Those half-literate old people? But, we checked it out and found that sure enough, something like three million of them in the Pale, for instance, were affiliated with the Socialist Labor BUND. Paul found out that his grandfather hid guns to be used by Bundist self-defense groups against the Czar and the Cossacks. Arthur discovered that his grandmother was in a Bundist support group. I found out that my grandfather wrote for a Yiddish anarchist paper called the "Freie Arbeiter Shtimme" (now in its 81st year).

Ah, all these skeletons came out of the closets. But they're such beautiful skeletons. So, we rediscover also, our grandparents, who, as it turns out, can't speak English as flawlessly as they can Russian, Polish, Yiddish and maybe a number of other languages.

But why were they hidden all this time? Why doesn't our understanding of Yiddish go beyond lullabies? Why are we so ashamed and alienated from life just two generations or so away (and stretching back many years—Poland, for instance, recently celebrated its thousandth year of Jewry).

Part of it is easily understood. All that poverty. All that oppression. Who needs it? Who wants to remember it? Well some of us do. Some of us, who can't identify with what you all have erected in the last couple of decades want to know, want to remember. Not just the holocaust. But the sorrow and anger and the warmth and the visions. The prophets, the poets, the mystics, the heretics, the radicals, the visionaries.

How many young Jews today know that poverty, oppression and resistance were just one or two generations away. How many know "religion" in anything but a synthetic, sterile, irrelevant package? How many know about contemporary Jewish resistance (beside the reactionary JDL)? Very, very few. Don't kid yourselves.

At a Ramah camp at which I spoke last summer, only eight out of 40 staff people (most in their 20's and 30's) had ever heard of the Bund. And out of 100 NFTY [North American Federation of Temple Youth] campers at Warwick, N.Y. only six (and half of those thought it was a neo-Nazi group).

It goes deeper than the Bund and leftist politics though. (That's something Jewish that I and many of my ilk can identify with and say "Look, we're not a bunch of freaks at all; our own people, when they were oppressed felt many of the same things.") This weekend I read "A Bintel Brief" (60 years of letters from the Lower East Side to the *Jewish Daily Forward*) just published by Doubleday & Company. Oy, oy, oy. All the letters are so moving. The most tragic I think was from grandparents whose daughter-in-law (and son) suggested that they visit their grandchildren only once every two weeks. Why? Because she didn't want them to hear English with a "Jewish accent." Oy, oy, oy.

As many of you know, that's not terribly untypical. If you want to take a look at how it works institutionally though take a look at Philip Roth's "Eli the Fanatic," hidden in the back of his paperback edition of "Goodbye, Columbus," and see what happens when a chassidic yeshiva tries to move into suburbia.

Am I wrong? Maybe so. But tell me different.

11

The Sexual Revolution

In effect, there was nothing "Jewish" about the sexual revolution of the late 1960s and early 1970s. Nearly every American—Jewish and gentile alike—found his or her own sexual mores and feelings about sexuality challenged by the seismic shift toward permissive sexual values. The signs were everywhere. Suddenly, there were reports that homosexuals no longer planned to remain secretive or ashamed about their desires. Just as suddenly, married women announced that they were fed up with playing the role of housewife and submissive spouse. Young people declared that they had no intention of getting married and that they considered monogamy an antiquated ideal. There was much titillating talk about "swinging singles," and many people felt both morally repulsed and personally curious about these developments.

For Jews, as for most non-Jews, there was tremendous ambivalence when it came to the sexual revolution. Many rabbinical authorities from all three major branches of Judaism assured their congregants that Jewish tradition was sex-friendly—and always had been. What got confusing was which kind of sex was Judaically preapproved. Most rabbis were quick to enunciate that they meant sex within heterosexual marriage—and nothing else. But this marital sex really should be excellent sex, also for the woman. Indeed, these authorities made abundantly clear that the sexual pleasure of the wife was a mitzvah—and even exceeded in importance the pleasure of the husband. In this respect, or so it was claimed, the American sexual revolution was a redundancy for American Jews, who had been enjoying sex (within marriage) since time immemorial.

Beyond this point, however, disagreements readily sprang up. For one thing, homosexuality was widely condemned except by the most liberal rabbis. Fledgling congregations for gay and lesbian Jews were broadly criticized by the mainstream Jewish community. Women's liberation (addressed in the next chapter) also met with profound mainstream Jewish resistance. The assertion of women's rights was interpreted (especially by Orthodox Jews) as destructive of patriarchal family values. Furthermore, the traditional authority of the

Jewish husband and father would be diminished if women and children were given equal rights within the nuclear family unit. This would yield an unhealthful state of affairs. And the sexual promiscuity of counter-cultural youth—many of whom were Jewish—was seen as additional evidence that things also within the Jewish community were running amuck.

The selections in this chapter offer a glimpse into the sexual revolution and its impact on American Jewish life. The opinions expressed range from the radical to the conventional. Although a pro-sex perspective might have appeared to be the one thing American Jews really could have agreed upon at the end of the 1960s, this was not the case at all.

The opening two selections document the rise of an open and proud gay and lesbian Jewish culture. The first article announces the first time a homosexual Jewish congregation conducted services, at the end of 1970. The second essay, by Jewish lesbian activist Martha Shelley, declares in no uncertain terms that the trouble with homosexuality in America is really a problem unhappy heterosexuals are having with themselves. While there may be nothing specifically "Jewish" about this analysis, Shelley's bitterness toward "liberal tolerance" might also be interpreted as a stab at many in the Jewish community.

The remaining articles in this section offer perspectives on how more mainstream American Jewish newspapers and spokespersons publicly discussed the sexual revolution. In the first, a Conservative New Jersey rabbi announces that he will no longer allow "hot pants" (that is, very short shorts) to be worn during services in his synagogue. In the second, Dr. Morris Mandel, a well-respected marriage and sex advice columnist for the *Jewish Press,* a Brooklyn-based Orthodox newspaper, responds to a letter from a husband whose wife now dominates their household—and him. The third article reports on the perspectives of rabbinic scholars David Feldman and Eugene Borowitz toward the sexual revolution as it pertains to Jewish tradition. And the final selection, by popular *Jewish Post and Opinion* columnist Helen Cohen, articulates her hostility toward the new so-called liberated sexual standards. It is quite conceivable that Cohen's opinions reflect attitudes that were held by many among her readership.

Rabbi Conducts Jewish Gay Service

GAY

New York, N.Y.—America's first homosexual Jewish congregation, The House of David and Jonathan, conducted its opening services on Friday evening, November 6, in an upper room at the Spencer Memorial Church, 152 Remsen Street, Brooklyn Heights. Rabbi Herbert Katz presided over a congregation of thirty-five persons.

The services took place primarily in English, with the congregation following responsive readings and chanting in the Union Prayer Book. The text for the sermon, on the evening of GAY's attendance, was Abraham's discussion with God about the saving of Sodom and Gomorrah. The Rabbi quoted Abraham's challenge to God: "Shall not the Judge of all the earth do justly?" and noted that in the Jewish religion, justice is tempered with Love and Mercy, and that our very human life could not exist without this tempering.

"Homosexuality in the Jew is perfectly acceptable," said the Rabbi. "There is nothing wrong when you love if you love dearly and cherish."

After the sermon there was a collection and the Cantor, Leigh Baldwin, of the Church of the Beloved Disciple, played the piano and sang for the Congregation.

The Rabbi spoke to GAY afterwards, explaining that he believed David and Jonathan had been physical lovers and that the Psalms of David were love poems to Jonathan.

Asked if there were any other examples of homosexual love in Jewish history, he said, "Ruth and Naomi were lovers too."

Asked if the question of the homosexual Jew had ever been discussed by any of the Jewish rabbinical groups, he said that in his personal experience the answer given whenever the subject was brought up was that there *are* no homosexual Jews.

Rabbi Katz was born in the Bronx in 1933 and now lives in Brooklyn at 20 Woodruff Avenue. He attended City College of New York for his secular education and the Jewish Theological Seminary for his religious instruction. He has a degree of BBA from City College and was ordained by Rabbi Hershey Goldstone of Brooklyn. Rabbi Goldstone died in Israel in 1969.

Rabbi Katz served in the U.S. Air Force as Chaplain for eight years in Texas, Korea and Vietnam. Following his release from the armed services, he served with the Beth Jacob congregation in Cumberland, Maryland, a Conservative congregation.

Rabbi Katz informed *GAY* that he belonged to the New York Board of Rabbis and would speak about homosexuality and the acceptance of gays into Jewish congregations at the Board's next meeting.

Gay is Good

MARTHA SHELLEY

Look out, straights! Here comes the Gay Liberation Front, springing up like warts all over the bland face of Amerika, causing shudders of indigestion in the delicately-balanced bowels of the Movement. Here come the Gays, marching with six-foot banners in Moratoriums and embarrassing the liberals, taking over Mayor Alioto's office, staining the good names of War Resister's League and Women's Liberation by refusing to pass for straight any more.

We've got chapters in New York/San Francisco/San Jose/Los Angeles/Wisconsin/New England and I hear maybe even in Dallas. We're gonna make our own revolution because we're sick of revolutionary posters which depict straight he-man types and earth mothers, with guns and babies. We're sick of so-called revolutionaries lumping us together with the capitalists in their term of universal contempt—"Faggot!"

And I am personally sick of liberals who say they don't care who sleeps with whom, it's what you do outside of bed that counts. This is what homosexuals have been trying to get straights to understand for years. Well, it's too late for liberalism. Because what I do outside of bed may have nothing to do with what I do inside—but my consciousness is branded, is permeated with homosexuality. For years I have been branded with your label for me. The result is that when I am among Gays or in bed with another woman, I am Martha Shelley, a person, not a homosexual. When I am observable to the straight world, I become homosexual. Like litmus paper. Dig it?

We want something more now, something more than the tolerance you never gave us. But to understand that, you must understand who we are.

We are the extrusions of your unconscious mind—your worst fears made flesh. From the beautiful boys at Cherry Grove to the aging queens in the uptown bars, the taxi driving dykes to the lesbian fashion models, the hookers (male and female) on 42nd Street, the leather lovers . . . and the very ordinary very unlurid gays . . . We are the sort of people everyone was taught to despise—and now we are shaking off the chains of self-hatred and marching on your citadels of repression.

Liberalism isn't good enough for us. And we are only just beginning to discover it. Your friendly smile of acceptance—from the safe position of heterosexuality—isn't enough. As long as you cherish that secret belief that you are a little bit better because you sleep with the opposite sex, you are still asleep in your cradle and we will be the nightmare that awakens you.

We are men and women who, from the time of our earliest memories, have been in revolt against the sex-role structure and the nuclear family structure. The roles that we have played amongst ourselves, the self-deceit, the compromises and subterfuges—these have never totally obscured the fact that we exist outside the traditional structure—and our existence threatens it.

Understand this—that the worst part of being a homosexual is having to keep it secret. Not the occasional murders by police or teen-age queer-beaters, not the loss of jobs or expulsion from schools or dishonorable discharges—but the daily knowledge that what you are is something so awful that it cannot be revealed. The violence against us is sporadic. Most of us are not affected. But the internal violence of being made to carry—or choosing to carry—the load of your straight society's unconscious guilt—this is what tears us apart, what makes us want to stand up in the offices, in the factories and schools and shout out our true identities.

(Do you think some of my school teachers will remember me, the quiet bespectacled painfully shy kid now metamorphosed into Super-dyke?)

We were rebels from our earliest days—somewhere, maybe just about the time we started to go to school, we rejected straight society. Unconsciously. Then, later, society rejected us, as we came into full bloom. The homosexuals who hide, who play it straight or pretend that the issue of homosexuality is unimportant are only hiding the truth from themselves. They are trying to become part of a society that they rejected instinctively when they were five years old, trying to deny that rejection, to pretend that it is the result of heredity, or a bad mother, or anything but a gut reaction of nausea against the roles forced on us.

(My mother was no prize—nor was she worse than most people's mothers of my acquaintance.)

If you are homosexual, and you get tired of waiting around for the liberals to repeal the sodomy laws, and begin to dig yourself—and get angry—you are on your way to being radical. Get in touch with the reasons that made you reject straight society when you were a kid (remembering now my own revulsion against the vacant women drifting in and out of supermarkets, vowing never to be like them, trivial endless gossip mah-jongging sicklysweet lipstick), and realize that you were right. Straight roles stink.

And you straights—look down the street, at the person whose sex is not really apparent. Are you uneasy? Or are you made more uneasy by the stereotype homosexual, the flaming faggot or diesel dyke? We want you to be uneasy, to be a little less comfortable in your straight roles. And to make you uneasy, we behave outrageously—even though we pay a heavy price for it sometimes—and our outrageous behavior comes out of our rage.

But what is strange to you is natural to us. Let me illustrate. Gay Liberation Front "liberates" a gay bar for the evening. We come in. The people already there are seated quietly at the bar. Two or three couples are dancing. It's a down place. And then GLF takes over. Men dance with men, women with women, men with women, everyone in circles! No roles. You ever see that at a Movement party? Not men with men—this is particularly verboten. No, and you're not likely to, while the Gays in the Movement are still passing for straight in order to keep up the good names of their organizations or to keep up the pretense that they are acceptable—and not have to get out of the organization they worked so hard for because they are queer.

True, some Gays play the same role-games among themselves that straights do. Isn't every minority group fucked over by the values of the majority culture? But the really important thing about being gay is that you are forced to notice how much sex-role differentiation is pure artifice, is nothing but a game.

Once I dressed up for an ACLU theatre benefit. I wore a black lace dress, heels, elaborate hairdo and makeup. And felt like a drag queen. Not like a woman—I am a woman every day of my life—but like the ultimate in artifice, a woman posing as a drag queen.

The roles are beginning to wear thin. The make-up is cracking. The roles—breadwinner, little wife, screaming fag, bull-dyke, Hemingway hero—are the cardboard characters we are always trying to fit into, as if being human and spontaneous were so horrible that we each have to pick on a character out of a third-rate novel and try to cut ourselves down to its size. And you cut off your homosexuality—and we cut off our heterosexuality.

But back to the main difference between us. We Gays are separate from you—we are alien. You have managed to drive your own homosexuality down under the conscious skin of your mind—and to drive us down and out into the gutter of self-contempt. We, ever since we became aware of being gay, have each day been forced to internalize the labels: "I am a pervert, a dyke, a fag, etc." And the days pass until we look at you out of our homosexual bodies, bodies that have become synonymous and consubstantial with homosexuality, bodies that are no longer bodies but labels; and sometimes we wish we were like you, sometimes we wonder how you can stand yourselves.

It's difficult for me to understand how you can dig each other as human beings—in a man-woman relationship—how you can relate to each other in spite of your sex-roles. It must be awfully difficult to talk to each other, when the woman is trained to repress what the man is trained to express and vice-versa. Do straight men and women talk to each other? Or does the man talk and the woman nod approvingly? Is love possible between heterosexuals; or is it all a case of women posing as nymphs, earthmothers, sex-objects, what-have-you; and men writing the poetry of romantic illusions to these walking stereotypes?

I tell you, the function of a homosexual is to make you uneasy.

And now I will tell you what we want, we radical homosexuals: not for you to tolerate us, or to accept us, but to understand us. And this you can only do by becoming one of us. We want to reach the homosexual entombed in you, to liberate our brothers and sisters, locked in the prisons of your skulls.

We want you to understand what it is to be our kind of outcast—but also to understand our kind of love, to hunger for your own sex. Because unless you understand this, you will continue to look at us with uncomprehending eyes, fake liberal smiles; you will be incapable of loving us.

We will never go straight until you go gay. As long as you divide yourselves, we will be divided from you—separated by a mirror trick of your mind. We will no longer allow you to drop us—or the homosexuals within yourselves—in the reject bin; labelled sick, childish, or perverted. And because we will not wait, your awakening may be a rude and bloody one. It's your choice. You will never be rid of us, because we reproduce ourselves out of your bodies—and out of your minds. We are one with you.

Several members of our collective felt that the author of this article was guilty of imposing her own definitions of sexuality on heterosexuals, and it is this imposition of values which she and all of us should be trying to avoid. Most members of the collective agreed with both her analysis and her semantics.

Rabbi Bans Hot Pants, See-Through Blouses

JEWISH POST AND OPINION

Haddon Heights, N.J.—A Conservative rabbi has laid down the law on hot pants and see-through blouses.

Rabbi Albert L. Lewis, of Temple Beth Sholom here, went so far as to advise parents of forthcoming bar mitzvahs to state in their invitations to relatives and friends "that the synagogue believes that good taste demands modest clothing."

"The very name hot pants," he wrote in his bulletin, "makes them trafe for synagogues. The thought of shorts in shul is bad enough. If you call them hot pants, they shift out of the realm of clothes and into a suggestive state of mind."

He said:

> I therefore apprise all females through the medium of this bulletin that to come to shul dressed in hot pants is unaesthetic, inappropriate and definitely not in good taste.

He said he could appreciate hot pants on a bathing beach or in an informal situation. "I cannot see them in a synagogue where one's clothes are to be muted in favor of the purpose of prayer which requires no distraction."

As for esthetics, he put it this way:

> I possess an aesthetic sense. It is this which is both violated and exalted when I see someone in "hot pants." When an older woman with thick thighs, or as we used to call them in our day, "pulkahs," wears "hot pants," my aesthetic sense is violated. On the other hand, if a younger person wears "hot pants," and wears them well, they are extremely aesthetic. My aesthetic sense is appreciative. But this appreciation in no way dovetails with the purpose for which we came to services, i.e. to pray.

Problems in Human Emotions

DR. MORRIS MANDEL

SHE RUNS THE WORKS!

Dear Dr. Mandel,

It takes great courage to write this letter to you because it means that I am admitting to myself things I have tried to hide. However, the time has come for me to save whatever pride I have left, and so I throw caution to the winds and write to you for advice.

I am married 10 years to a woman who has me bulldozed. It isn't that she orders me around, or belittles me, it is rather a situation where she talks me into submission. Believe me she talks such a mean streak, I just clam up. It has come to a point where I am actually afraid of crossing her in any area. My love for peace is more important to me than my burning desire to show her that I can stand up for my rights.

I am a warm, sensitive person and need someone with whom I can discuss my day's activities. At the start of our marriage I discussed all of my activities with my wife. But in the past 10 years she has become an authority on everything and makes authoritative judgments on any matter. This makes me so sick I feel I am burying my own personality in my quest for peace.

When we have a spat, discussion, debate, talk, disagreement (take your pick) I am left weak. If at this time company should come, I just don't know how to be civil or hospitable to them. The result is that we are fast losing friends and alienating family.

I must point out that she is a devoted mother, an excellent home-maker, a good cook, and a faithful wife—she had all these qualities, but she just talks much too much.

How do I handle this explosive situation? I am beginning to hate myself for being so weak. I'll be eagerly awaiting your reply in your wonderful column. Prudence and tact makes it impossible for me to give you my name.

Harried Husband

Answer:

Mutual respect is the principle which can help you live in harmony with others and with yourself. Mutual respect includes the acceptance of the idea that each person has a right to think and speak for himself. In a marriage, the feelings of both husband and wife must receive serious consideration. Hiding or denying any feeling you have is an act of disrespect toward yourself and automatically it causes a rift between the marital partners.

It is up to you to start asserting your own independence as an individual. No wife should bulldoze her husband. Better it should be said that no husband ought to permit himself to be bulldozed. There are areas in which she may know more and areas in which she should have control. On the other hand, there are areas where you as a husband should feel so secure that you will not tolerate any belittling. Realistic limits should be set on what might be termed unacceptable behavior on the part of your wife.

You indicate that your wife is an excellent mother as well as a good cook, a faithful wife, but that she talks too much. Well, what do you do when she talks? To whom does she talk? Is she conversing or lecturing to you? Do you discuss with her your own day's activities?

Could it be that all through your single life you listened too much to your mother? Did she have you bulldozed as well? Was she always making decisions for you? Think about these questions for a while.

In any event, it is time you acted like the head of the family and clearly demonstrate to your wife that you want no marathon lectures, that you don't feel she is an authority on everything, that though you recognize where her strengths lie, you know full well that she has weaknesses as well.

Don't hide! Don't cower! SPEAK UP! Who knows! If you will, she might sit up and take notice!

Fun in the Bedroom Is the Jewish View

JEWISH POST AND OPINION

Two Jewish scholars agreed that the Jewish attitude on sex was hardly puritanical, but there was some variation in their views when it came to "fun" in intercourse.

Rabbi David Feldman, who has done extensive research on the Talmudical attitude toward sex, said that "the traditional view is that anything goes in the privacy of the bedroom provided that what goes on meets with the approval of the wife."

Rabbi Eugene Borowitz said that one thing Jews can learn from today's liberated attitude toward sex is "the simple proposition that sex can be fun." The editor of *Sh'ma,* who is professor of Jewish Thought at Hebrew Union College–Jewish Institute of Religion in New York, said that "although there always has been a healthy attitude toward sex in Jewish life, exemplified by the tradition that between husband and wife almost everything is permitted, there has been a concomitant attitude that sex is a duty."

Rabbi Feldman, speaking at the Adult Institute of Temple Emanu-El in Providence, R.I., said that in Jewish tradition "it is recognized that the woman has the stronger sex need. It is the duty and responsibility, therefore, of the husband to satisfy his wife, and in no way is it the other way around as is usual in a puritanical tradition."

Continuing, he explained that the so-called "new morality" may be new to the Christian community, but is, in its major points, a restatement of Jewish tradition. Although an ascetic puritanical approach to sexuality at times did creep into rabbinic writings, such a view has never been in the mainstream of Jewish tradition.

Rabbi Borowitz' views were expressed in an address at B'nai Israel Congregation in Pittsburgh and were reported in the *Jewish Chronicle* by staff writer Vicki Rogal.

"The Jewish tradition has never been very concerned with having fun. Of course you should enjoy yourself, but you were told to take certain precautions," Borowitz said. "I don't know about you, but to relax and learn to enjoy ourselves more fits in with my Jewishness."

Pleasure cannot be an end in itself, he said. "Today there is so much pressure on people to perform, they often become impotent.

"To a Jew, pleasure is a secondary category, life comes first and joy comes from living," he said. Therefore he said, living with a person "eyeball to eyeball"—taking full responsibility for another person's life—must take priority over pleasure.

The Games Singles Play

HELEN COHEN

The term "sexual revolution" is bandied about these days as though we have taken a wonderful new step forward toward freedom and fulfillment. Off with our binding chains, our old out-moded rules reserving sex for marriage.

It's all going to be a blast for everyone, isn't it?

In the July 16 *Newsweek,* the cover story complete with cover picture of a shapely blonde in ultra-brief bikini with liquor glass in hand, is entitled "Games Singles Play."

After several descriptive pages of single life, singles bars, swinging single apartment complexes, singles clubs, all of which add up to uncommitted sex with first one bed partner and then another, the article gets down to evaluations.

Is it really a whole new ball game?

Suppose in the old days one was homely and lacking in confidence, especially a female? Is the revolution ushering in a new day for her? Let's see what *Newsweek* found:

"The dark side of the singles world: there are players who score and those who strike out, yet for both a sobering degree of loneliness and tristesse (sadness) seems to be built into the rules. It is no revelation that the physically unattractive and socially maladroit find the singles game a never-ending round of rejection.

"But what does surprise is the prevalence of unhappiness among the very singles who appear ostensibly to be living the Mary Tyler Moore life. Gail, a curvaceous, 25-year-old Manhattan stockbroker, confesses that no amount of dazzling the boys on the Fire Island beach can fill a gnawing emptiness in her existence. 'Sex has gotten so cheap,' she told the reporter with a sad smile. 'The biggest void in my life is children. I may have one even if I don't get married.'"

At Grossingers in the Catskills, *Newsweek* explains, singles come to meet and mingle. And now that girls are free with their favors, have things changed for them at Grossingers?

A game which aimed at getting couples together "seemed like a real fun idea, except that when the whistle blew, at least a dozen ignored girls were brushing tears from their mascara. 'I'm so depressed now,' blurted one Bronx secretary, 'I'm going to call Dial-a-Prayer.'"

So what's the improvement over the days when they held out for marriage?

One singles club in Boston throws a "new faces party" twice a year. "We call them meat markets," confides one male chauvinist (writes *Newsweek*), "because all the guys come to look over all that fresh meat." Bending over backward in an equalizing gesture to females, *Newsweek* adds that presumably the female guests arrive with somewhat similar goals. But *Newsweek,* cherie, didn't you observe what happened at Grossingers? Females took the beating, got looked over. They're the fresh meat.

Sounds like the same old tired game to me.

I can't resist quoting a few more sentences because it's what I've been saying for a long time now.

"The longer that 'swinging' singles play their roles, the harder it seems to unlearn the script, to break off the quest for new conquests and the conditioned adjustment to a paucity of communication and commitment. Some finally suffer from a kind of battle fatigue in this transient existence.

"One bright Chicago secretary, after two years at a singles complex, is turning in her key. 'The whole scene begins to seem so empty, so contrived. It's simply not the kind of place to be grown up in. I'm ready for the real world.'

"Inordinately indulged, prolonged singlehood tends to deaden the emotional and sexual palates, freezing its disciples in a state of suspended adolescence . . ."

An item about actor Omar Sharif has to fit in here somewhere. Reported by the press to be a ladies' man (one reporter counted 7 girls in 21 days) Sharif considers himself a romantic, to a point. And I suppose he's reached that point.

"I often wake up and look at the girl beside me," he is quoted as saying, "and I think: I just wish she wasn't here. I wish I could have my morning cup of tea alone . . ."

How depressing, when sex becomes such a bore and the long line of females become faces that pass in the night.

Ladies and gentlemen, I give you the sexual revolution, a lonely, dehumanizing ego-shattering treadmill going nowhere. That's the game singles play.

12

Jewish Women and Feminism

There can be little doubt that a major achievement of the 1960s and 1970s was the emergence of a Jewish women's movement. This movement, which grew out of and alongside a national women's liberation movement (and shared many key personnel with it), became necessary as Jewish women realized that the cause for equal rights for which they were fighting in society-at-large did not grant them those equal rights within their own families—or in their synagogues. Jewish women rejected the proposition that gender relations within the Jewish community should abide by a different standard, and so they fought their second-class status in all spheres of their lives. In this way, "coming out" as a feminist proceeded together with "coming out" as a Jewish woman. For many these self-assertions became inseparable.

At the same time, it is crucial to remember how difficult it was initially to make an argument for gender equality within the Jewish community. There was tremendous condescension and resistance from Jewish men (and also occasionally Jewish women) toward "women's lib." The Jewish community's reputation for sexual liberality actually served to minimize what possible good a Jewish women's movement might accomplish. (After all, had not Jewish tradition always respected the Jewish woman?) Thus, there was a concerted effort to belittle this movement; repeatedly, Jewish women were urged not to risk doing damage to communal life.

This last point might need some elaboration. How could a Jewish women's movement be said to damage the Jewish community? Arguments varied. Jewish feminism could damage Judaism because it might weaken the family unit and threaten the authority of already beleaguered Jewish fathers and husbands. Jewish feminism might lead to the further reduction of the fertility rate—already at a level well below replacement—and it might result in more intermarriage. Jewish feminism could encourage Jewish men to lessen their commitment to their religious life; if so, synagogues would become a "feminine" sphere that might further erode American Jewish religious affiliation. The hypothetical nature of these and other concerns made them especially difficult to counter. Certainly, though, one thing is clear, at least in retrospect. The widespread revitalization of Judaism that did take place after the 1960s was due in no small part to the *success* of—not the resistance to—a Jewish women's movement.

Before there was feminist success, however, there was feminist critique. And no critique of the subordinate role of the woman in the American family—both gentile and Jewish—had a greater impact than Betty Friedan's *The Feminine Mystique,* published in 1963. The book sold in the millions. And while Friedan would only acknowledge (and celebrate) her Jewishness many years later, there are passages in *The Feminine Mystique* that suggest how Jewishness was there for Friedan from the beginning. Friedan based her dramatic analogy between Nazi concentration camps and suburban American homes on the (itself deeply flawed) interpretation of concentration camp victims provided by psychologist Bruno Bettelheim. Friedan's outrageous claim communicates the intensity of desperation felt by countless women confined to the home at that time.

Also reprinted is an early manifesto of the Jewish women's movement produced by an underground group called the Brooklyn Bridge Collective. Here the society-wide sexism is translated expressly into Jewish terms. Note as well the troubling role ascribed to antisemitism in this analysis.

The contributions by Rachel Adler and Paula Hyman emphasize the religious dimensions of the Jewish women's movement. Adler's 1971 essay may be the first to address how Jewish law (Halacha) had historically been interpreted to deny equality to Jewish women. Adler calls for the end of the subordination of women defended in terms of Jewish law, declaring such a defense an injustice to all committed Jews. Hyman challenges those "apologists" in the community who would label a Jewish feminist a "self-hater." And like Adler, Hyman further argues that the community has historically denigrated the lives of Jewish women. Additionally, there is a short document from Erzat Nashim, or "Support for Women," a Jewish feminist group within the Conservative movement. Erzat Nashim distributed its "Jewish Women Call for a Change" at the 1972 annual meeting of the Rabbinical Assembly. It represents one of the earliest attempts to press for feminist demands at a national religious conference.

Finally, Shirley Frank looks back on a major communal debate that would dominate discussion in the 1970s. Frank's essay first appeared in 1977 in the Jewish feminist journal *Lilith,* and it outlines the ongoing sense of crisis about Jewish population statistics. As Frank perceptively notes, such debate quickly turns antifeminist. And Frank makes quite apparent that when Jewish men already in the 1960s raised concerns about the plummeting fertility rates of Jewish women, there was the clear implication that the proper place for those Jewish women was at home with the kids.

A Comfortable Concentration Camp?

BETTY FRIEDAN

It is not an exaggeration to call the stagnating state of millions of American housewives a sickness, a disease in the shape of a progressively weaker core of human self that is being handed down to their sons and daughters at a time when the dehumanizing aspects of modern mass culture make it necessary for men and women to have a strong core of self, strong enough to retain human individuality through the frightening, unpredictable pressures of our changing environment. The strength of women is not the cause, but the cure for this sickness. Only when women are permitted to use their full strength, to grow to their full capacities, can the feminine mystique be shattered and the progressive dehumanization of their children be stopped. And most women can no longer use their full strength, grow to their full human capacity, as housewives.

It is urgent to understand how the very condition of being a housewife can create a sense of emptiness, non-existence, nothingness, in women. There are aspects of the housewife role that make it almost impossible for a woman of adult intelligence to retain a sense of human identity, the firm core of self or "I" without which a human being, man or woman, is not truly alive. For women of ability, in America today, I am convinced there is something about the housewife state itself that is dangerous. In a sense that is not as far-fetched as it sounds, the women who "adjust" as housewives, who grow up wanting to be "just a housewife," are in as much danger as the millions who walked to their own death in the concentration camps—and the millions more who refused to believe that the concentration camps existed.

In fact, there is an uncanny, uncomfortable insight into why a woman can so easily lose her sense of self as a housewife in certain psychological observations made of the behavior of prisoners in Nazi concentration camps. In these settings, purposely contrived for the dehumanization of man, the prisoners literally became "walking corpses." Those who "adjusted" to the conditions of the camps surrendered their human identity and went almost indifferently to their deaths. Strangely enough, the conditions which destroyed the human identity of so many prisoners were not the torture and the brutality, but conditions similar to those which destroy the identity of the American housewife.

In the concentration camps the prisoners were forced to adopt childlike behavior, forced to give up their individuality and merge themselves into an amorphous mass. Their capacity for self-determination, their ability to predict the future and to prepare for it, was systematically destroyed. It was a gradual process which occurred in virtually imperceptible states—but at the end, with the destruction of adult self-respect, of an adult frame of reference, the dehumanizing process was complete. This was the process as observed by Bruno Bettelheim, psychoanalyst and educational psychologist, when he was a prisoner at Dachau and Buchenwald in 1939.

When they entered the concentration camp, prisoners were almost traumatically cut off from their past adult interests. This in itself was a major blow to their identity over and above their physical confinement. A few, though only a few, were able to work privately in some way that had interested them in the past. But to do this alone was difficult; even to talk about these larger adult interests, or to show some initiative in pursuing them, aroused the hostility of other prisoners. New prisoners tried to keep their old interests alive, but "old prisoners seemed mainly concerned with the problem of how to live as well as possible inside the camp."

To old prisoners, the world of the camp was the only reality. They were reduced to childlike preoccupation with food, elimination, the satisfaction of primitive bodily needs; they had no privacy, and no stimulation from the outside world. But, above all, they were forced to spend their days in work which produced great fatigue—not because it was physically killing, but because it was monotonous, endless, required no mental concentration, gave no hope of advancement or recognition, was sometimes senseless and was controlled by the needs of others or the tempo of machines. It was work that did not emanate from the prisoner's own personality; it permitted no real initiative, no expression of the self, not even a real demarcation of time.

And the more the prisoners gave up their adult human identity, the more they were preoccupied with the fear that they were losing their sexual potency, and the more preoccupied they became with the simplest animal needs. It brought them comfort, at first, to surrender their individuality, and lose themselves in the anonymity of the mass—to feel that "everyone was in the same boat." But strangely enough, under these conditions, real friendships did not grow. Even conversation, which was the prisoners' favorite pastime and did much to make life bearable, soon ceased to have any real meaning. So rage mounted in them. But the rage of the millions that could have knocked down the barbed wire fences and the SS guns was turned instead against themselves, and against the prisoners even weaker than they. Then they felt even more powerless than they were, and saw the SS and the fences as even more impregnable than they were.

It was said, finally, that not the SS but the prisoners themselves became their own worst enemy. Because they could not bear to see their situation as it really was—because they denied the very reality of their problem, and finally "adjusted" to the camp itself as if it were the only reality—they were caught in the prison of their own minds. The guns of the SS were not powerful enough to keep all those prisoners subdued. They were manipulated to trap themselves; they imprisoned themselves by making the concentration camp the whole world, by blinding themselves to the larger world of the past, their responsibility for the present, and their possibilities for the future. The ones who survived, who neither died nor were exterminated, were the ones who retained in some essential degree the adult values and interests which had been the essence of their past identity.

All this seems terribly remote from the easy life of the American suburban housewife. But is her house in reality a comfortable concentration camp? Have not women who live in the image of the feminine mystique trapped themselves within the narrow walls of their homes? They have learned to "adjust" to their biological role. They have become dependent, passive, childlike; they have given up their adult frame of reference to live at the lower human level of food and things. The work they do does not require adult capabilities; it is endless, monotonous, unrewarding. American women are not, of course, being readied for mass extermination, but they are suffering a slow death of mind and spirit. Just as with the prisoners in the concentration camps, there are American women who have resisted that death, who have managed to retain a core of self, who have not lost touch with the outside world, who use their abilities to some creative purpose. They are women of spirit and intelligence who have refused to "adjust" as housewives.

It has been said time and time again that education has kept American women from "adjusting" to their role as housewives. But if education, which serves human growth, which distills what the human mind has discovered and created in the past, and gives man the ability to create his own future—if education has made more and more American women feel trapped, frustrated, guilty as housewives, surely this should be seen as a clear signal that *women have outgrown the housewife role.*

It is not possible to preserve one's identity by adjusting for any length of time to a frame of reference that is in itself destructive to it. It is very hard indeed for a human being to sustain such an "inner" split—conforming outwardly to one reality, while trying to maintain inwardly the value it denies. The comfortable concentration camp that American women have walked into, or have been talked into by others, is just such a reality, a frame of reference that denies woman's adult human identity. By adjusting to it, a woman stunts her intelligence to become childlike, turns away from individual identity to become an anonymous biological robot in a docile mass. She becomes less than human, preyed upon by outside pressures, and herself preying upon her husband and children. And the longer she conforms, the less she feels as if she really exists. She looks for her security in things, she hides the fear of losing her human potency by testing her sexual potency, she lives a vicarious life through mass daydreams or through her husband and children. She does not want to be reminded of the outside world; she becomes convinced there is nothing she can do about her own life or the world that would make a difference. But no matter how often she tries to tell herself that this giving up of personal identity is a necessary sacrifice for her children and husband, it serves no real purpose. So the aggressive energy she should be using in the world becomes instead the terrible anger that she dare not turn against her husband, is ashamed of turning against her children, and finally turns against herself, until she feels as if she does not exist. And yet in the comfortable concentration camp as in the real one, something very strong in a woman resists the death of herself.

Describing an unforgettable experience in a real concentration camp, Bettelheim tells of a group of naked prisoners—no longer human, merely docile robots—who were lined up to enter the gas chamber. The SS commanding officer, learning that one of the women prisoners had been a dancer, ordered her to dance for him. She did, and as she danced, she approached him, seized his gun and shot him down. She was immediately shot to death, but Bettelheim is moved to ask:

> Isn't it probable that despite the grotesque setting in which she danced, dancing made her once again a person. Dancing, she was singled out as an individual, asked to perform in what had once been her chosen vocation. No longer was she a number, a nameless depersonalized prisoner, but the dancer she used to be. Transformed however momentarily, she responded like her old self, destroying the enemy bent on her destruction even if she had to die in the process.
>
> Despite the hundreds of thousands of living dead men who moved quietly to their graves, this one example shows that in an instant, the old personality can be regained, its destruction undone, once we decide on our own that we wish to cease being units in a system. Exercising the lost freedom that not even the concentration camp could take away—to decide how one wishes to think and feel about the conditions of one's life—this dancer threw off her real prison. This she could do because she was willing to risk her life to achieve autonomy once more.

The suburban house is not a German concentration camp, nor are American housewives on their way to the gas chamber. But they are in a trap, and to escape they must, like the dancer, finally exercise their human freedom, and recapture their sense of self. They must refuse to be nameless, depersonalized, manipulated, and live their own lives again according to a self-chosen purpose. They must begin to grow.

Jewish Women Life Force of a Culture?

BROOKLYN BRIDGE COLLECTIVE

> "In the days of horror of the later Roman Empire, it was not war alone that destroyed and annihilated all those peoples of which nothing remains but their name. It was rather the ensuing demoralization of home life. This is proved by the Jews; for they suffered more severely and more cruelly by wars than any other nation; but among them, the inmost living germ of morality—strict discipline and *family devotion*—was at all times preserved. This wonderful and mysterious preservation of the Jewish people is due to the *Jewish Woman*. This is her glory, not alone in the history of her own people, but in the history of the world." (M. Lazarus)
>
> "Be careful not to cause woman to weep, for God counts her tears. Israel was redeemed from Egypt on account of the *virtue of its women*. *He* who weds a good woman, it is as if *he* had fulfilled all the precepts of the Law." (Talmud)
>
> "Jewish custom bids the Jewish mother kindle the Sabbath lamp. That is symbolic of the Jewish woman's influence on her home, and through it upon larger circles. She is the inspirer of a pure, chaste, family life whose hallowing influences are incalculable; she is the center of all spiritual endeavors, the confidante and fosterer of every undertaking. To her the Talmudic sentence applies: 'It is woman alone through whom God's blessings are vouchsafed to a house.'" (Henrietta Szold)

The above quotations are seductive. They tell us that it is the strength of the Jewish family that has preserved the Jewish people. And they tell us that the responsibility for keeping that family strong fell to the Jewish Woman. There is no doubt this is true, but these quotations give a false sense of the real condition of Jewish Women.

The ideal pattern of family life in European Jewish communities was the "Talmudist" father and home-preserving mother: men who dealt with the "serious" issues of God, Torah, and Talmud, and Women who dealt with the "immediate" issues of emotion, human relations, and survival. Precisely like the sexual division of labor that occurs in all cultures, the men do what is considered important and significant, while the Women do everything that the men do not want to be bothered with. However, in Jewish culture, this division was even more destructive to Women because of the nature of the oppression of

Jewish people. Since Jewish men were forbidden to participate in the "manly" endeavors of the larger society in which they lived, they withdrew into the Yeshiva and the shul to study and argue about God's law. In order to preserve a shred of dignity for themselves, they were forced to deny the importance of activity directly related to daily survival. This they left to Women. Women embodied the softness of motherhood at the same time they developed the fortitude to deal with the repression of the outside world. It is no myth that Jewish Women were strong—we had to be. It is only surprising that we didn't collapse from exhaustion.

The flight to America and the ensuing pressure to assimilate further transformed the already oppressive Jewish family. Jewish men traded the status of Torah study for "Making it"—economically and intellectually. Jewish Women were not able to adapt the characteristic forms of behavior they had developed in the ghettoes of Europe to this new situation that Jewish men were defining for them in America. Their strength, their intelligence, their self-sufficiency, their demand for respect, were in complete contradiction with the image of the American Woman that Jewish men now needed in order to embellish and legitimate their new status.

Jewish daughters are thus caught in a double bind: we are expected to grow up assimilating the American image of "femininity"—soft, dependent, self-effacing, blonde, straight-haired, slim, long-legged—and at the same time be the "womanly" bulwark of our people against the destruction of our culture. Now we suffer the oppression of Women of both cultures and are torn by the contradictions between the two. These contradictions take some curious forms. Jewish men demand that their Women be intellectual sex-objects. So Jewish families push their daughters to get a good education. The real purpose is not to be forgotten however. While PhD's do make Jewish parents proud of their daughters, the universities are recognized as hunting-grounds for making a "good" marriage. Grandchildren assure the race.

We've been called "Jewish princess" and "castrating bitch" by the rest of the world and by our own men loud and clear. We've been defined as a "Jewess" and been the object of rape. As Jewish Women we were strong, but always the force *behind* our men. We were strong in order to survive, and kept things together for our families and our culture, and for this we are now attacked as being "Jewish mother," ridiculous and disgusting as that has come to be.

Any group of Women which has had their men and their culture crippled by the world, has had to be strong. What has gone down and continues to come down on Jewish men on the outside has affected us on the inside—in our homes, our bedrooms and kitchens. While our men are put down in their every contact with the "world," they come home and try to assert their manliness on us; any time we balk at this process and its dehumanizing effect, we are labeled bitches.

While the Jewish Woman is perceived as the life force and essence of Jewish culture, it is by living up to the role expected of her that her destruction is accomplished. For she is expected to be the essence and life force of a culture that has always been and continues to be completely centered around the Jewish man. How can a Jewish Woman *be* if she is nothing within her culture—a culture in which the Jewish male is god, to be worshipped and obeyed, a culture in which the Jewish female is property, where she can be only what he makes of her? And the more she carries out her cultural (and historic and religious) obligation of keeping that family and home together—the harder she works, cleans, cooks, and devotes herself to her children—the more complete is her destruction. The more she develops the posture "I am nothing."

What the world has *always* done physically to *all* Jews, Jewish men and Jewish Women, the Jewish man does psychically to the Jewish Woman. He oppresses her with the shitwork of living, he blames her for his difficulties, and the anti-semitism he suffers is taken out on her—he hates her Jewishness because it reflects his own. It is time now for Jewish Women to move out of the way and let Jewish men fall on their own asses. We will then be able to prove to Jewish men that we are not the proper target of their anger; that the roles forced upon both of us divide us, keep us fighting among ourselves, and make *their* manipulation that much easier.

Jewish Sisters, we *are* strong! Let us reap the benefits of that STRENGTH! It is time for us to get together and fight to determine for *ourselves* what is a Jewish Woman. We can then change life for all Jews, and fully join the struggle of all oppressed women.

The Jew Who Wasn't There
Halacha and the Jewish Woman

RACHEL ADLER

It is not unusual for committed Jewish women to be uneasy about their position as Jews. It was to cry down our doubts that rabbis developed their pre-packaged orations on the nobility of motherhood; the glory of childbirth; and modesty, the crown of Jewish womanhood. I have heard them all. I could not accept those answers for two reasons. First of all, the answers did not accept *me* as a person. They only set rigid stereotypes which defined me by limiting the directions in which I might grow. Second, the answers were not really honest ones. Traditional scholars agree that all philosophies of Judaism must begin with an examination of Jewish law, Halacha, since, in the Halacha are set down the ways in which we are expected to behave, and incontestably our most deeply engrained attitudes are those which we reinforce by habitual action.

Yet scholars do not discuss female status in terms of Halacha—at least not with females. Instead, they make lyrical exegeses on selected Midrashim and Agadot which, however complimentary they may be, do not really reflect the way in which men are expected to behave toward women by Jewish law. This latter is the subject no one wants to discuss. Nevertheless, I think we are going to have to discuss it, if we are to build for ourselves a faith which is not based on ignorance and self-deception. That is why I would like to offer some hypotheses on the history and nature of the "woman problem" in Halacha.

Ultimately our problem stems from the fact that we are viewed in Jewish law and practice as peripheral Jews. The category in which we are generally placed includes women, children, and Canaanite slaves. Members of this category are exempt from all positive commandments which occur within time limits.[1] These commandments would include hearing the shofar on Rosh Hashanah, eating in the Sukkah, praying with the lulav, praying the three daily services, wearing tallit and t'fillin, and saying Sh'ma.[2] In other words, members of this category have been "excused" from most of the positive symbols which, for the male Jew, hallow time, hallow his physical being, and inform both his myth and his philosophy.

Since most of the mitzvot not restricted by time are negative, and since women, children and slaves are responsible to fulfill all negative mitzvot, including the negative time-bound mitzvot, it follows that for members of this category, the characteristic posture of their Judaism is negation rather than affirmation.[3] They must not, for example, eat non-kosher food, violate the Shabbat, eat chametz on Pesach, fail to fast on fast days, steal, murder, or commit adultery. That women, children, and slaves have limited credibility in Jewish law is demonstrated by the fact that their testimony is inadmissible in a Jewish court.[4] The minyan—the basic unit of the Jewish community—excludes them, implying that the community is presumed to be the Jewish males to whom they are adjuncts. Torah study is incumbent upon them only insofar as it relates to "their" mitzvot. Whether women are even permitted to study further is debated.[5]

All of the individuals in this tri-partite category I have termed peripheral Jews. Children, if male, are full Jews *in potentio*. Male Canaanite slaves, if freed, become full Jews, responsible for all the mitzvot and able to count in a minyan.[6] Even as slaves, they have the b'rit mila, the covenant of circumcision, that central Jewish symbol, from which women are anatomically excluded. It is true that in Jewish law women are slightly more respected than slaves, but that advantage is outweighed by the fact that only women can never grow up, or be freed, or otherwise leave the category. The peripheral Jew is excused and sometimes barred from the acts and symbols which are the lifeblood of the believing community, but this compliance with the negative mitzvot is essential, since, while he cannot be permitted to participate fully in the life of the Jewish people, he cannot be permitted to undermine it either.

To be a peripheral Jew is to be educated and socialized toward a peripheral commitment. This, I think, is what happened to the Jewish woman. Her major mitzvot aid and reinforce the life-style of the community and the family, but they do not cultivate the relationship between the individual and God. A woman keeps kosher because both she and her family must have kosher food. She lights the Shabbat candles so that there will be light, and hence, peace, in the household. She goes to the mikva so that her husband can have intercourse with her and she bears children so that, through her, he can fulfill the exclusively male mitzvah of increasing and multiplying.[7]

Within these narrow confines, there have been great and virtuous women, but in several respects the tzidkaniot (saintly women) have been unlike the tzaddikim. Beruria, the scholarly wife of Rabbi Meir, the Talmudic sage, and a few exceptional women like her stepped outside the limits of the feminine role, but legend relates how Beruria came to a bad end, implying that her sin was the direct result of her "abnormal" scholarship.[8] There is no continuous tradition of learned women in Jewish history. Instead there are many tzidkaniot, some named, some unnamed, all of whom were pious and chaste, outstandingly charitable, and, in many cases, who supported their husbands. In contrast, there are innumerable accounts of tzaddikim, some rationalists, some mystics, some joyous, some ascetic, singers, dancers, poets, halachists, all bringing to God the service of a singular, inimitable self.

How is it that the tzaddikim seem so individualized and the tzidkaniot so generalized? I would advance two reasons. First of all, the mitzvot of the tzadeket are mainly directed toward serving others. She is a tzadeket to the extent that she sacrifices herself in order that others may actualize themselves spiritually. One has no sense of an attempt to cultivate a religious self built out of the raw materials of a unique personality. The model for the tzadeket is Rachel, the wife of Rabbi Akiva, who sold her hair and sent her husband away to study for twenty-four years, leaving herself beggared and without means of support, or the wife of Rabbi Menachem Mendal of Rymanov (her name incidentally, goes unremembered) who sold her share in the next world to buy her husband bread.

Frequently there is a kind of masochism manifest in the accounts of the acts of tzidkaniot. I recall the stories held up to me as models to emulate, of women who chopped holes in icy streams to perform their monthly immersions. A lady in the community I came from, who went into labor on Shabbat and walked to the hospital rather than ride in a taxi, was acting in accordance with this model. Implicit is the assumption that virtue is to be achieved by rejecting and punishing the hated body which men every morning thank God is not theirs.[9]

Second, as Hillel says, "an ignoramus cannot be a saint."[10] He may have the best of intentions, but he lacks the disciplined creativity, the sense of continuity with his people's history and thought, and the forms in which to give Jewish expression to his religious impulses. Since it was traditional to give women cursory religious educations, they were severely limited in their ways of expressing religious commitment. Teaching, the fundamental method of the Jewish people for transmitting religious insights, was closed to women—those who do not learn, do not teach.[11] [. . .]

The Talmudic sages viewed the female mind as frivolous and the female sexual appetite as insatiable.[12] Unless strictly guarded and given plenty of busywork, all women were potential adulteresses.[13] In the Jewish view, all physical objects and experiences are capable of being infused with spiritual purpose; yet it is equally true that the physical, unredeemed by spiritual use, is a threat. It is therefore easy to see how woman came to be regarded as semi-demonic in both Talmud and Kabbalah. Her sexuality presented a temptation, or perhaps a threat which came to be hedged ever more thickly by law and custom.[14] Conversing with women was likely to result in gossip or lewdness.[15] Women are classed as inadmissible witnesses in the same category with gamblers, pigeon-racers and other individuals of unsavory repute.[16]

Make no mistake; for centuries, the lot of the Jewish woman was infinitely better than that of her non-Jewish counterpart. She had rights which other women lacked until a century ago. A Jewish woman could not be married without her consent. Her ketubah (marriage document) was a legally binding contract which assured that her husband was responsible for her support (a necessity in a world in which it was difficult for a woman to support herself), and that if divorced, she was entitled to a monetary settlement. Her husband was not permitted to abstain from sex for long periods of time without regard to her needs and her feelings.[17] In its time, the Talmud's was a very progressive view. The last truly revolutionary ruling for women, however, was the Edict of Rabbenu Gershom forbidding polygamy to the Jews of the Western world. That was in 1000 C.E. The problem is that very little has been done since then to ameliorate the position of Jewish women in observant Jewish society.

All of this can quickly be rectified if one steps outside of Jewish tradition and Halacha. The problem is how to attain some justice and some growing room for the Jewish woman if one is committed to remaining *within* Halacha. Some of these problems are more easily solved than others. For example, there is ample precedent for decisions permitting women to study Talmud, and it should become the policy of Jewish day schools to teach their girls Talmud. It would not be difficult to find a basis for giving women aliyot to the Torah. Moreover, it is both feasible and desirable for the community to begin educating women to take on the positive time-bound mitzvot from which they are now excused; in which case, those mitzvot would eventually become incumbent upon women. The more difficult questions are those involving minyan and mechitza (segregation at prayers). There are problems concerning the right of women to be rabbis, witnesses in Jewish courts, judges and leaders of religious services. We need decisions on these problems which will permit Jewish women to develop roles and role models in which righteousness springs from self-actualization, in contrast to the masochistic, self-annihilating model of the post-Biblical tzadeket. The halachic scholars must examine our problem anew, right now, with open minds and with empathy. They must make it possible for women to claim their share in the Torah and begin to do the things a Jew was created to do. If necessary we must agitate until the scholars are willing to see us as Jewish souls in distress rather than as tools with which men do mitzvot. If they continue to turn a deaf ear to us, the most learned and halachically committed among us must make halachic decisions for the rest. That is a move to be saved for desperate straits, for even the most learned of us have been barred from acquiring the systematic halachic knowledge which a rabbi has. But, to paraphrase Hillel, in a place where there are no menschen, we may have to generate our own menschlichkeit. There is no time to waste. For too many centuries, the Jewish woman has been a golem, created by Jewish society.

She cooked and bore and did her master's will, and when her tasks were done, the Divine Name was removed from her mouth. It is time for the golem to demand a soul.[18]

NOTES

1. Kiddushin 29a.

2. ibid, but see also Mishna Sukkah 2:9 and Mishna Brachot 3:3.

3. Kiddushin 29a.

4. Shevuot 30a. See also Rosh Hashanah 22a.

5. Sotah 20a.

6. It must be admitted that Canaanite slaves were only to be freed if some overriding mitzvah would be accomplished thereby. The classic case in which Rabbi Eliezer frees his slave in order to complete a minyan is given in Gittin 38b.

7. Mikva is not in itself a mitzvah. It is a prerequisite to a permitted activity, just as shechita is prerequisite to the permitted activity of eating meat. See Sefer HaChinuch, Mitzvah 175.

8. Avoda Zara 18b. See Rashi.

9. In the Traditional Prayerbook see the morning blessing, "Blessed are You, Lord our God, King of the universe, who has not created me a woman."

10. Avot 2:6.

11. Exactly this expression is used in Kiddushin 29b, where it is asserted that the mitzvah of teaching ones own offspring the Torah applies to men and not to women.

12. Kiddushin 80b contains the famous statement, "The rational faculty of women weighs lightly upon them." Interestingly enough, the Tosafot illustrate this with an ancient misogynistic fabliau whose written source is the Satyricon of Petronius Arbiter. See also Sotah 20a.

13. Mishna Ketubot 5:5.

14. This is the context in which one may understand the statement of the Kitzur Shulchan Aruch, "A man should be careful not to walk between two women, two dogs, or two swine." Ganzfried, Rabbi Solomon, Code of Jewish Law I, trans. Hyman E. Goldin, 2nd ed. (New York: 1961), p. 7.

15. Avot 1:5. See also the commentaries of Rashi, Rambam, and Rabbenu Yonah.

16. Rosh Hashanah 22a.

17. Mishna Ketubot 5:6.

18. There is a famous folk tale that the scholar Rabbi Loewe of Prague created a golem or robot, using the Kabbalah. The robot, formed from earth, came to life and worked as a servant when a tablet engraved with the Divine Name was placed in its mouth. When the tablet was removed, the golem reverted to mindless clay.

The Other Half
Women in the Jewish Tradition

PAULA E. HYMAN

It has become fashionable in certain circles to label the more outspoken, and most often young, critics of Jewish life as self-haters. When those critics are also women, and their critique a feminist one, they can be written off as doubly self-hating, both as women and as Jews. This approach, however, has led to wasted opportunities. The first feminist articles published, some of them admittedly shrill and polemical, called forth from the educated, articulate, and (not unexpectedly) male leadership of American Jewry a stream of apologetic writing in defense of the faith. Instead of being considered a provocative challenge and an opportunity for examination of the tradition in a new light, the feminist critique of Judaism has evoked responses which distort the role of women in Judaism as radically as the sharpest feminist attack. What is most striking, though, is their insensitivity to the basic premise of feminist analysis.

Jewish feminists have not rejected Judaism; we are struggling with it in our desire to find a way to fulfill ourselves as Jews and as women. Had we rejected Judaism, we would hardly be spending so much of our time living, studying, discussing and thinking about it. Which is not to say that we do not find much of Jewish tradition problematic, hardly a new situation for the modern Jew of either sex. It is amusing and ironic that an eminent Reform rabbi like Roland B. Gittelsohn could not acknowledge in his recent article on Women's Liberation and Judaism that our "Jewish problem" bears many similarities to that which generated and continues to sustain Reform Judaism as well as other non-Orthodox positions.[1] While he admits that there are elements in the attitude of traditional Judaism to women which he, and presumably many other enlightened males, would find distasteful, he ultimately falls back upon the arguments of tokenism, separate but equal, and women on the pedestal (subjects to which I shall return).

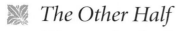

The central point of the feminist critique of Judaism, as of all other patriarchal cultures, is traditional sex-role differentiation. In patriarchal cultures virtually all social roles and most character traits are ascribed according to sex, with the positions of highest status and the most highly prized characteristics, such as intelligence, initiative, emotional strength, reserved for men. While men are allowed to define themselves through a wide spectrum of activity in the world (and in Judaism, in the synagogue as well), women are defined in socio-biological terms as wife and mother, and relegated almost exclusively to home and family life. The only qualities considered "feminine" (and hence approved in women) are those useful in the serving, nurturing, and home-making roles which are the woman's preserve. One need not assume a male conspiracy to explain this social configuration. Obviously biological factors, chiefly the exigencies of child-bearing, were critical. However, the biological underpinnings of patriarchal culture have been eroded—child-bearing, after all, occupies relatively little of modern woman's time—and the role differentiation which they generated serves only to perpetuate inequality and to deny freedom of choice to men and women alike. [. . .]

SPIRITUAL INEQUALITY

The Jewish woman, we are told, is responsible for the moral development of the family, being endowed with an exceptional capacity for moral persuasion. At the same time, however, the female in Judaism is regarded as inherently close to the physical, material world, while the Jewish male is immersed in the spiritual. Thus, conveniently, the male-female role division is perceived in the Jewish tradition as a most natural one, based as it is on the fundamental polarity of the male and female characters. The Jewish woman, therefore, is not spiritually deprived by her virtual exclusion from synagogue and study, for her spiritual capacity is inferior to the man's. Better for her to supply his and his children's needs, while he supplied her spiritual wants. A most efficient division of labor! And one which explains the tendency which existed among Eastern European Jewry to relinquish responsibility for the physical support of the family to wives, while the husbands withdrew to the *beit midrash* to study and acquire spiritual merit for the entire family.

These imposed definitions of male and female, however, seem constraining today, when men and women alike seek to uncover and express both their common humanity and their individual uniqueness. It can be argued that there are few halakhic barriers to women taking upon themselves an ever greater role in Jewish religious life. Girls can, and do, study much the same curriculum as boys in institutions of Jewish learning, except for rabbinical schools. There is no halakhic rule barring women from laying *tefillin*. Yet the psychological effects of tradition and upbringing are difficult to overcome. A woman who has, throughout her life, come in contact with a synagogue whose ritual is reserved for men gets the message: she is not needed there. Quite literally, she does not count. And if she chances or chooses to be there, she must not disturb the proceedings but merely observe them. Even should she begin to feel the first stirrings of discontent, there is no easy way for her to chart her own course. Within the synagogue she has few role models, and mechanisms for change do not lie within her hands. Thus, the most educated and progressive Jewish woman—who knows full well that her mastery of Hebrew and Jewish knowledge exceed that of the vast majority of Jewish men—feels ill-at-ease the first time she has an *aliya*. If the synagogue is to be open to men and women on a basis of equality, then women must take a regular, rather than occasional, part in services as laymen as well as rabbis and cantors, and their participation must ultimately become both normal and normative. Only then will women truly have the freedom to choose, as men do, to participate or not.

LAWS OF FAMILY PURITY

Much has been made of the fact, and rightly so, that the Jewish tradition respects female sexuality and accords the right to sexual fulfillment to male and female alike.[11] While it is well to distinguish the Jewish attitude to sexuality from the negative Christian attitude with which it is often wrongly identified, it is precisely in this area that the second-class status of women within Judaism is highlighted.

Jewish attitudes to sexual relations and to female biology were formulated early in the development of Judaism. The fact that Judaic culture was polygamous for much of its history has, as Dr. Trude Weiss-Rosmarin has noted, profoundly affected the Jewish legal concept of adultery.[12] A married woman commits adultery when she has sexual relations with any man other than her husband, while a married man is legally an adulterer only when he becomes sexually involved with another man's wife! The attitude of the Jewish tradition to the menstruating woman—despite the modern rationalizations that the laws of Family Purity serve to safeguard the woman's health, to prevent sexual desire from becoming sexual license, or to keep marriage a perpetual honeymoon—reflects a primitive taboo.[13] According to halakhic prescriptions, the menstruating woman, or *niddah,* is to have no physical contact whatsoever with a man. Like the person suffering from a gonorrheal discharge, she is impure. Contact with her is permitted only after she has been free of her "discharge" for seven days and has undergone ritual purification in a *mikvah*. During her period of impurity anything she touches becomes impure. While this state of impurity is a legal rather than a hygienic concept and, according to rabbinic authorities, does not imply that the *niddah* is physically unclean or repugnant, it is not clear that simple Jewish men and women throughout the ages have interpreted the laws of Family Purity in such a disinterested manner. Even the mere fact of legal impurity for two weeks of every month has involved many disabilities for a woman. And the psychological impact of the institution, especially in its strictest interpretation, upon a woman's self-esteem and attitude to her own body would seem to be harmful.

Although irrelevant and even totally unknown to the vast majority of young Jews, the laws of Family Purity remain fundamental to Orthodox Judaism. In Israel, where the Orthodox rabbinate enjoys a monopoly, each prospective bride receives a booklet instructing her in the importance of Family Purity and admonishing her that, according to a midrash, death in childbirth is a punishment for the abandonment of the laws of *niddah*.[14] Anonymous medical opinion is invoked to testify that women need to be preserved from any and all disturbance during this two-week period of frailty. To the modern woman, who knows that she is indisposed, at most, for a few hours a month, this type of reasoning is not only inaccurate but also offensive.

At the very least, leaders of Orthodox and Conservative Judaism should be willing to confront openly the issue raised by feminists regarding the laws of Family Purity. If within traditional Judaism, the essential separation of the *niddah* cannot be totally eliminated, based as it is on injunctions in the Torah, still, the more restrictive "fences around the Torah" should be lowered. Finally, the rationales for Family Purity should exploit neither medical fantasy nor sexual mythology.

What Jewish feminists are seeking, then, is not more apologetics but change, based on acknowledgement of the ways in which the Jewish tradition has excluded women from entire spheres of Jewish experience and has considered them intellectually and spiritually inferior to men. Realizing the historical, social, and biological factors which contributed in all generations to Jewish attitudes towards women, we must try to examine the Jewish tradition within its own context and refrain from pointlessly blaming our ancestors for lacking our own insights. But until we all recognize that a problem exists—that the conflict between the objective reality of women's lives, self-concept, and education and their position within Jewish tradition is a most significant one for all of Judaism—we cannot begin to take steps to attain equality for women, both in Jewish law and in Jewish attitudes.

Much of the strength of the Jewish tradition has derived from its flexibility and responsiveness to the successive challenges of the environments in which it has been destined to live. In an age when the alienation of young Jews from Judaism is of major concern to the Jewish community, we can hardly afford to ignore fully one-half of young Jews. Thus, the challenge of feminism, if answered, and not dismissed as the whining of a few misguided malcontents, can only strengthen Judaism.

NOTES

Notes two through ten are for material not included in this edition.

1. Roland B. Gittelsohn, "Women's Lib and Judaism," *Midstream,* XVII, 8, Oct. 1971, pp. 51–58.

11. For a discussion of the Jewish attitude towards sexuality, see David M. Feldman, *Birth Control in Jewish Law,* New York 1968.

12. Trude Weiss-Rosmarin, "The Seventh Commandment," *Jewish Spectator,* XXXVI:8, Oct. 1971, pp. 2–5,

13. The basic laws of the *niddah* are to be found in Leviticus XV:19–31 and in the tractate *Niddah.*

14. For a translation of this booklet, written by Chief Rabbi Unterman, see *Israel Magazine,* IV:1, Jan. 1972.

Jewish Women Call for Change

EZRAT NASHIM

The Jewish tradition regarding women, once far ahead of other cultures, has now fallen disgracefully behind in failing to come to terms with developments of the past century.

Accepting the age-old concept of role differentiation on the basis of sex, Judaism saw woman's role as that of wife, mother, and home-maker. Her ritual obligations were domestic and familial: *nerot, challah,* and *taharat hamishpachah.* Although the woman was extolled for her domestic achievements, and respected as the foundation of the Jewish family, she was never permitted an active role in the synagogue, court, or house of study. These limitations on the life-patterns open to women, appropriate or even progressive for the rabbinic and medieval periods, are entirely unacceptable to us today.

The social position and self-image of women have changed radically in recent years. It is now universally accepted that women are equal to men in intellectual capacity, leadership ability and spiritual depth. The Conservative movement has tacitly acknowledged this fact by demanding that their female children be educated alongside the males—up to the level of rabbinical school. To educate women and deny them the opportunity to act from this knowledge is an affront to their intelligence, talents and integrity.

As products of Conservative congregations, religious schools, the Ramah Camps, LTF [Leaders Training Fellowship], USY [United Synagogue Youth], and the [Jewish Theological] Seminary, we feel this tension acutely. We are deeply committed to Judaism, but cannot find adequate expression for our total needs and concerns in existing women's social and charitable organizations, such as Sisterhood, Hadassah, etc. Furthermore, the single woman—a new reality in Jewish life—is almost totally excluded from the organized Jewish community, which views women solely as daughters, wives, and mothers. The educational institutions of the Conservative movement have helped women recognize their intellectual, social and spiritual potential. If the movement then denies women opportunities to demonstrate these capacities as adults, it will force them to turn from the synagogue, and to find fulfillment elsewhere.

It is not enough to say that Judaism views women as separate but equal, nor to point to Judaism's past superiority over other cultures in its treatment of women. We've had enough of apologetics: enough of Bruria, Dvorah, and Esther; enough of *eshet hayil.*

It is time that:

women be granted membership in synagogues
women be counted in the minyan
women be allowed full participation in religious observances—*aliyot, baalot keriah, shelihot zibbur*
women be recognized as witnesses before Jewish law
women be allowed to initiate divorce
women be permitted and encouraged to attend Rabbinical and Cantorial schools, and to perform Rabbinical and Cantorial functions in synagogues
women be encouraged to join decision-making bodies, and to assume professional leadership roles, in synagogues and in the general Jewish community
women be considered as bound to fulfill all *mitzvot* equally with men

For three thousand years, one-half the Jewish people have been excluded from full participation in Jewish communal life. We call for an end to the second-class status of women in Jewish life.

The Population Panic

SHIRLEY FRANK

For just about as long as anyone can remember, Jewish speakers, leaders, thinkers, writers, and general semi-professional groaners and hand-wringers have been overwhelmingly concerned with the question known as "Jewish survival." Although we have survived for over 3,000 years, we do not take that survival for granted; in fact, we seem to regard it as an inexplicable anomaly, and our mind-set is one of perpetual vigilance against threats to our continued existence. In the past, of course, and in other parts of the world, the threats have been obvious physical ones: wars, pogroms, persecutions, forced conversions, political repression, the Holocaust. Here in America, we have long recognized and identified the greater danger as deriving from more subtle causes, such as assimilation, ignorance, apathy and intermarriage. But now a new threat has been spied on our bleak horizon, and it is spreading over us rapidly like a malignant black fallout cloud. This new danger is an insidious three-initialed foe more to be feared than the KGB, the PLO, or the KKK—namely, the ZPG, or Zero Population Growth movement. Young Jewish people, it seems, ever concerned about all the problems of humanity, have thoughtfully, though misguidedly, taken it upon themselves to volunteer en masse to do their share in not adding to the world's "population explosion." The result is a "demographic crisis," according to our many commentators on the subject. They point out that our birth rate is lower than that of the rest of the American—not to speak of the world—population, that it is declining, that we have not yet recovered our pre–World War II numbers, that we are barely reproducing ourselves even now, and that, at this rate, given the large numbers of defectors we have to account for, we are dooming ourselves to imminent extinction unless something is done immediately to turn this pernicious trend around.

To this end, a large number of Jewish periodicals and newspapers have published at least one article on this "hot" subject, many rabbis have sermonized about it from their pulpits, and in February 1976 a Conference on Jewish Fertility was held in New York at which scholars read papers exploring the problem from various historical and sociological perspectives. Moreover, as is usual in Jewish life, an organization has been formed to tackle the problem at hand: "PRU"—for Jewish "Population Regeneration Union," punning on the Hebrew commandment "*p'ru ur'vu*" ("be fruitful and multiply")—founded in New York by Rabbi William Berman, a recent graduate of the Jewish Theological Seminary. Among other things, "PRU" disseminates question-and-answer leaflets urging us to save ourselves before it is "too late."

As we Jews know only too well, an idea that is hammered out continually in an alarmist or propagandistic manner by very sincere and devoted, sometimes fanatic, people, can begin to take hold, regardless of its relationship to truth. That a serious and even critical Jewish demographical problem exists is gradually coming to be taken for granted. Even such a hip new publication as *The Second Jewish Catalog*, for example, in its opening chapter on "Birth," alludes in passing to "the fact that Jews as a people have a lot of catching up to do." Leaders of organizations obviously feel called upon to issue statements not on whether or not the problem exists—for this is already considered a given—but on what is to be done about it.

- On January 24, 1974, *The New York Times* reported that Rabbi Sol Roth, newly-elected president of the New York Board of Rabbis, stated "that Jewish families should have at least three children and asserted that the frequently projected goal of zero population growth 'should find no application in the Jewish community.'"
- On July 14, 1975, *Time* magazine published a brief article called "The Disappearing Jews," including an already much-publicized recommendation by Orthodox Rabbi Norman Lamm—now president of Yeshiva University—that "each Jewish couple should have four or five children" because "Jews are a disappearing species."
- At its annual convention, in June 1977, the Reform Movement's Central Conference of American Rabbis (CCAR), an organization known for its liberal stands on most issues, released a statement scarcely differing from those of the Orthodox rabbis, urging Jewish couples "to have at least two or three children." Their reason? "Because there are simply not enough of us to be assured of survival in succeeding generations."

Clearly the idea has "caught on"—with all the power of an idea whose time has come.

But why, we might naturally ask, has the time for this idea come just now? Has our "fertility" been attacked by some previously unknown disease and taken a sudden downward plunge? Is it because no one thought of it before—because, as one of Rabbi Berman's "PRU" leaflets puts it, "until recently the most immediate threat to our survival has been unaccountably ignored"? Would the other problems to which Rabbi Berman alludes—"Jewish illiteracy, secularism, materialism, and of course persecution"—miraculously disappear if only we could dispatch this "most immediate threat"? Are we, in fact, in imminent danger of going the way of the dodo bird and the sabre-toothed tiger? Or are there other reasons for this preoccupation just now?

And finally, what does it mean for the Jewish woman, just beginning to seek an identity for herself beyond the old familiar role of "Jewish mother," to be urged to have a family of at least two or three, or four or five children? Does it not seem a strange, if not a perverse, coincidence that, after all these centuries of Jewish history, just in the very decade when Jewish women are demanding greater and more meaningful participation in Jewish religious and communal life, beyond and even, in some cases, outside of motherhood—in the very decade when, for instance, women are finally being ordained as rabbis—certain segments of the Jewish community are loudly hitting the old "barefoot and pregnant" motif as if our very lives depended on it?

Perhaps the most basic question—the one that must be dealt with first—is: How much *do* our lives depend on increasing our birth rate? Why are the prospects for our survival deemed to be so precarious—and why now?

Nearly always mentioned is the fact that we lost six million of our people in the Holocaust and that we have not yet numerically replaced them. A recent CCAR position paper notes "a touch of irony" in the fact that some people are choosing to have no children at all just when "the need to replenish the Jewish people has never been greater." But is this true? It seems, on the contrary, that, despite God's promise to Abraham, the Jews have never been a particularly numerous people. As we know from our long history of wanderings and persecutions, and from our liturgy itself, we have long been "a small remnant," "a saving remnant." As recently as the year 1650, there were only about 675,000 Jews in the entire world. Despite relatively poor medical conditions, the arrival of the Enlightenment, which led to rapid assimilation in western Europe, and semi-medieval persecutions and pogroms which continued in eastern Europe, we did not die out as a people. If we did not die out then, why should we die out now, when, even after the Holocaust, we are 14,000,000 strong? Moreover, inasmuch as the Holocaust ended over thirty years ago, the allusions to it do not in themselves explain why we are hearing this frantic call to action just at this particular time.

Another explanation offered is that we have had our eyes newly opened by the most authoritative Jewish population survey ever to have been undertaken, the 1970 National Jewish Population Survey, the results of which are being released gradually in the *American Jewish Year Book*. This survey confirms that our birth rate is indeed relatively low.

But even this information should come as a surprise to no one. As far back as 1889, a study of over 10,000 Jewish families in the United States revealed that the Jewish birth rate was lower than the non-Jewish. Similar findings were noted in 1905, and even during the heyday of what we remember as the mammary-gland fifties, when a house in the suburbs and a family of 3.7

children were supposed to be every girl's dream, a study showed that in 1955 the average family size of Catholic and Protestant couples was 2.1, compared to an average of only 1.7 for Jewish couples. Several studies cited through the sixties reveal similar proportions. Thus, the survey does not actually seem to indicate that the 1970's are any more critical a period in Jewish history than earlier decades.

It is, as I suggested above, largely due to the malign influence of ZPG that the various doomsayers attribute our latest "danger" and against which they raise their heaviest artillery. ZPG, according to the rather frenzied and much-repeated argument, though fine and even important for the rest of the world, must not apply to the Jews. It is only *other* people whom we should expect to exercise self-restraint, reproducing, as it were, on the quota system.

This view reflects another popular argument for reversing the current trend towards a low Jewish birth rate—namely, that Jews are special people. According to this argument, it is the highly talented, intelligent young people who are limiting their families, and in some cases choosing not to procreate at all. Nevertheless, the remarkable attainments of American Jews and their admirable contributions to society have frequently been noted as a strong reason why we owe it to society to continue to produce and raise as many of these prodigies as possible. "The Jewish people," as one of the "PRU" leaflets puts it, "have made great contributions to civilization and 'cooperating' themselves out of existence would be a disservice to 'humanity' as well as to themselves." The fact remains, however, that the survival of even so "special" a people as the Jews cannot be guaranteed unless the human race—of which, after all, we are a part—survives.

One might justifiably wonder, nonetheless, how many couples actually base their childbearing decisions on concern about the survival of the human race, or, for that matter, how many would base their decisions on concern about the survival of the Jewish people. It may well be that the whole ZPG argument simply provides an additional rationalization for couples who have already made up their minds for other, more personal reasons, and even the doomsayers would do better to turn their attention to the more likely reasons.

Running at a distance behind the ZPG movement as another reason for our current "plight"—but perhaps closer to the mark—is the matter of values and priorities—the high value placed, as one advocate for Jewish fertility puts it, on a "lifestyle of hedonism and unimpeded mobility" or "the arbitrary purpose of pursuing a hedonistic lifestyle." In addition, of course, there is also the growing number of people who are divorced or whose marriages are so unstable that they hesitate to bring a child or another child into a world that might involve a stressful single-parent situation or a complicated, even nasty, custody case.

It may seem strange, but in most of the discussions of this burning issue of Jewish "fertility," there is little or no direct reference to the effects of the women's movement, even though it should be obvious that the number of children a woman chooses to have or not to have is likely to be related to her aspirations and her achievements in other areas of life. One might conclude, from reading the various articles, that most couples consult world population charts before deciding whether or not to have a baby, rather than consider who will be responsible for taking care of the child. In most of the articles and speeches, feminism, when it is mentioned at all, is passed over quickly, as though it were another faddish trend like hedonism or a swinging lifestyle. Despite the fact that attempting to raise the birth rate above its present levels means, for the most part, urging the diminishing number of people who are in stable marital situations to have three or four children, there is little mention of the woman who must decide, not whether to have a child or a Cadillac, but whether to have that third or fourth child or to take advantage of newly expanded opportunities and seek a much-delayed education or career. Passed over rather lightly is the fact that additional childbearing and childrearing are likely to be at the expense of women's emergence and self-fulfillment, precisely at a time when, as we noted earlier, Jewish women are beginning to assert rightful claims for a life and an identity of their own, apart from their roles as wives and mothers.

One might have supposed, offhand, that the women's movement, far from being ignored, would be attacked head-on as the principal culprit responsible for the diminished Jewish birth rate, but, as we have seen, this is not the case. It is, indeed, this absence of a feminist awareness, this evident inability to come to terms with the feminist implications of the issue, that renders the current panic about Jewish "fertility" somewhat suspect and strongly suggests that its emergence so close on the heels of the emergence of Jewish feminism is something more than a coincidence.

This suspicion is intensified when we consider that most of the speakers and writers of articles and position papers urging Jews to have more babies are male—a notable exception being Blu Greenberg, who deplores the fact that "many Jewish women continue to put off having children until their middle thirties so they can pursue careers," and whose husband Irving Greenberg's name is listed among the "supporters" of "PRU." Interestingly, all the other people whose names appear on the PRU letterhead are also male. This is perhaps not entirely inappropriate, inasmuch as the commandment to be fruitful and multiply is considered by the traditional-minded to apply, like nearly all commandments, to men only. It is rather a pity, indeed, that they cannot fulfill it by themselves—but, in the present state of technology, women are necessary.

Even this fact is not always to be taken for granted. At the end of one of the first popular treatments of this subject—what one might call the seminal piece—written for *Commentary* in September 1961, Milton Himmelfarb inquired: "Where does a Jew's obligations lie? Should he absent him from paternity awhile, for the good of the human race? Or should he be of good courage, and play the man for his people?" One hardly dares to wonder what "play the man" means in this context. It seems clear, however, that man is making decisions about his paternity quite as if he were a self-fertilizing flower. Not surprisingly, perhaps, Mr. Himmelfarb's name also appears on "PRU"'s stationery.

One still can hardly avoid the possibility that this latest panic is a kind of gut response to the rapid changes that are everywhere taking place as a result of the women's movement—changes that are obviously taking place too rapidly for many people, especially for many men.

There is little to be gained, however, from pretending that the women's movement does not exist, or that its influence is trivial. Only by being aware, for example, that family size is related to women's aspirations for themselves, can we truly understand the dynamics of population growth and make effective decisions about what, if anything, needs to be done.

For lack of a feminist perspective, the causes cited by the various doomsayers for the alleged demographic crisis here in America tend to miss the mark and therefore not to lend themselves to appropriate solutions. If couples are refusing to procreate for such reasons of hedonism and materialism, we may as well admit that these people are already lost to Judaism through assimilation, not sterility. But is the pursuit of pleasure and material goods really the motive for postponing parenthood? From a feminist point of view, the allusions to hedonism and materialism may be explained partly as code language recalling the days when women's income was considered mere "pin money," and women were often urged to stay home and give their children the love and attention that they needed more than the "little luxuries" a housewife's outside income might procure for the family. Couples who delayed having children while the wife continued to work were thought to be saving up their money for the purchase of a home or to indulge in trips and other extravagances.

This point of view, besides failing to take into consideration a real economic world in which a woman's income usually goes to buy necessities, not luxuries, ignores the possibility that women, like men, work for reasons other than money—to utilize their talents, for example, to meet people, to contribute something to society, to maintain dignity and self-respect. These complex motivations are lost when the head of the Rabbinical Council of America, Rabbi Walter S. Wurzburger, bemoans the fact that "the pursuit of personal careers and other indulgences are taking precedence over the traditional joy of family life and the transmission of the Jewish heritage to the next generation." He is clearly suggesting that a career is an "indulgence," not a necessity; but since we all know that a career of some sort is a necessity for a man, we might conclude that he was speaking in a disguised way about women.

It seems unwise, to say the least, for responsible spokespersons of the Jewish community to be thus suggesting, however implicitly, that a woman's career is unimportant, or, its obvious corollary, that a woman's place is in the home. Those who point with such pride to the remarkable achievements attained by American Jews as a reason why we should raise our birth rate should recognize that this high achievement level has been reached almost entirely by Jewish men, and not by Jewish women. Quite conceivably, not one of these men interrupted his career to spend several years diapering babies. Since Jewish women presumably inherit the same genes as Jewish men—the genes that our doomsayers urge us to pass along to a multitudinous next generation—we can only conclude that a great deal of talent is being lost somewhere along the line—perhaps in the diaper pail; for Jewish women, in stark contrast to Jewish men, have been underachievers in virtually every field, or, at best, the mothers of overachievers. Unless the continued production of Jewish male prodigies is our only goal, we must wonder what appeal this argument could possibly have for the modern woman who may no longer be content to experience her achievements vicariously—in the time-honored, but much-maligned, Jewish-mother manner—through her children? And what sort of a future is envisioned for the larger number of girls who would doubtless also be born—would they, too, be seen primarily as the breeders and nurturers of future Jewish male prodigies?

The Holocaust argument, too, must be understood in a different perspective. This argument in all likelihood owes its effectiveness to the fact that survivors of the Holocaust feel a certain guilt at having survived—and, in one way or another, we are all survivors. Whether deliberately or unconsciously, it seems for the purpose of nurturing such guilt feelings that the present downward trend in population growth is constantly associated with the Holocaust—as if those who are failing to reproduce in sufficient numbers are somehow collaborating with Hitler. Commentators quote Emil Fackenheim's powerful statement, "Jews are forbidden to grant posthumous victories to Hitler." And, to reinforce the point still more strongly, the term "genocide" is used with abandon to describe what we are supposedly doing to ourselves. No one, however, should be more sensitive than Jews to the loss of meaning implied in the watering-down of the term" genocide" to mean anything less than the wholesale murder of human beings as practiced by the Nazis during World War II.

The fact remains that we cannot replace the Holocaust victims, and any attempt to equate the unborn with Jews who were murdered is an insult to the martyrs' memories—for surely we define those six million Jewish lives in terms more significant than their numbers alone. Moreover, those who urge women to breed more babies for the sake of increasing the Jewish population are strangely, indeed shockingly, echoing Hitler's exhortation of German women to breed more babies for the Fatherland.

If, on the other hand, we really seek to perpetuate the memory of the Holocaust victims and to render their lives and perhaps even their deaths somehow meaningful, it may well be that a person who studies Jewish history, researches *shtetl* life, or teaches Yiddish is doing more to effect these goals than a person who stays at home producing a large number of babies. As Rabbi Rebecca Trachtenberg Alpert put it in the *Reconstructionist* (April 1977), "whether or not one chooses to become a biological parent, by a commitment to enhancing the life of the Jewish people, a person can exert an influence, can be a spiritual ancestor to future generations."

At this point, of course, one would expect any doomsayer to retort that one can hardly be a spiritual ancestor to future generations if there are no future generations. "Sociologists maintain," according to Rabbi Berman, "that if the present birth-intermarriage rates continue indefinitely, American Jewry will be reduced to a remnant within four generations." Rabbi Jonathan M. Brown of the Reform movement asks "How many Jews will there be in 2073, when our movement will celebrate its two hundredth anniversary? There is an increasing awareness of the *possibility* [his italics] that only a few Jews will remain; all the others will have disappeared, victims of assimilation, mixed marriage, indifference, and a low birth rate."

But inasmuch as the low birth rate is only *one* of several factors affecting Jewish prospects for survival, it follows that there is indeed room for the "spiritual ancestor," the Jewish woman, for example, who makes a commitment to tackling one or more of the other problems and who hands down a meaningful Jewish heritage to a niece or nephew, a neighbor's child, a student, a YWHA "little sister," an adopted child, or even a perfect stranger—perhaps even a future convert. There are more ways of enhancing the chances of Jewish survival, and even of increasing the number of Jews, than just making a number of trips to the local lying-in hospital.

It also follows that we can ill afford to alienate young Jewish women by promoting a primitive pronatalism that is almost insulting, in its implication that Judaism wants their wombs more than it wants their minds. [. . .]

And indeed, I find that this is what depresses me most about the current debate concerning Jewish population. I find that the urging of Jewish women to become, as Mary Gendler put it, "baby machines," in order to save the Jewish people from extinction depresses and disgusts me—not so much because I am a feminist, but because I am a Jew. I am deeply ashamed at the idea of Judaism sinking to a level where we are scrounging around for every warm body we can get. It was for this reason, I thought, that we Jews rarely engaged in proselytizing or missionary work—because we were never unduly concerned with numbers, with quantity rather than quality.

Ultimately it is not appealing to be told that one must raise additional numbers of children, not only to make sure there are enough of us left after any possible future disaster, but to make sure there are enough of us left after taking into consideration those who intermarry, convert to various other religions and cults, or are hopelessly lost through assimilation. To assert that our major problem is now our low birth rate does not make these other problems go away; nor does it make them less severe. There is still a desperate need to ensure Jewish survival by making Judaism and Jewish life clearly meaningful and necessary.

13

Selections from The First Jewish Catalog

In 1973, the Jewish Publication Society of America published *The First Jewish Catalog: A Do-It-Yourself Kit,* compiled and edited by Richard Siegel, Michael Strassfeld, and Sharon Strassfeld. "How do you bake your own hallah?" asked the description on the book's back cover. "How does the Jewish calendar work? Are there rules and procedures for death and burial? How do you plan your own wedding?" And it continued: "For anyone who has ever wondered about how to make wine, crochet a kippah, locate a Jewish film, start a Jewish library, bring the Messiah, where to study, and many more aspects of the Jewish experience, this is the book you've been waiting for."

As it happened, many American Jews were indeed waiting for *The First Jewish Catalog.* A product of the *havurah* youth movement, the "catalog" self-consciously recapitulated the ethos of the Jewish counterculture for both its own benefit as well as the benefit of a mainstream Jewish audience. As the subtitle suggests, this was a book meant to serve primarily as a reference work, but one with a slight tongue-in-cheek antiauthoritarian twist. It did not presume to prescribe how readers should celebrate or recognize their own Jewishness. It did presume to offer a kind of Jewish potpourri, full of unexpected surprises and hidden delights. And it was a runaway Jewish best seller.

Taken together, the three editions of the *Jewish Catalog* sold more than half a million copies. It was the most successful book (with the exception of the Bible) ever published by the Jewish Publication Society in its century-long history. The catalog not only reflected a deeply felt need for a renewal of faith among many American Jews; it also fueled and directed many of the unfocused impulses relating to that need. In short, the catalog was a singular event that marked both the end of a truly radical and alternative Jewish counterculture—and the beginning of a new, more inward-looking era, when alternative values (at times associated with New Age spiritualism) began fully to be integrated into the mainstream of American Jewish life.

The selections reprinted here from the *First Jewish Catalog* offer a good introduction to the book's double project. On the one hand, the editors and their many collaborators sought to introduce (or reintroduce) a more earnest and heartfelt religiosity into everyday American Jewish life. There was a distinct impression among many young Jews that spirituality and religious observance had fallen into severe disrepair precisely—and however paradoxically—due to the fact that most established synagogues placed such a low priority on these concerns.

On the other hand, and less well remembered, several of the catalog's contributors were devoted especially to the task of politicizing the meanings of Jewish rites and rituals in the United States. They themselves had found their way back to a meaningful Judaism as a result of their engagement with social issues (both domestic and international). And they felt powerfully that this commitment to political action and social change were among Judaism's most pressing obligations.

It is not possible to know how *The First Jewish Catalog* was read by its hundreds of thousands of readers. But it may be fair to conclude that the link between social change and religious identity may not have been foremost on their mind. In other words, as the 1970s proceeded and the American Jewish community—like Americans more generally—moved steadily away from the radical impulses of the 1960s, the call to political action and the explicit links between New Left politics and a revitalized Judaism may well not have been the major lessons gleaned from the catalog. Instead, and as the copywriters for the Jewish Publication Society appear to have recognized, readers wanted most to learn how to bake good hallah bread.

The three contributors whose work appears here after the catalog introduction have each been significant voices calling for Jewish renewal. Rabbi Burt Jacobson of Berkeley's Kehilla Community Synagogue contributes to the essay on how to start a *havurah*. Zalman Schachter, who became a rabbi through Chabad (Lubavitch), a branch of Hasidic Judaism, offers his reflections on devotion. And Arthur I. Waskow, a political activist turned activist rebbe, suggests to his early 1970s readers how to bring the Messiah to this world.

Introduction

RICHARD SIEGEL, MICHAEL STRASSFELD, AND SHARON STRASSFELD

Perhaps the most difficult question we have been asked in the course of compiling this catalog has been, "What exactly is it?" Having realized quite early that there are no preexisting categories which would adequately satisfy this compulsion for definition, our rather vague response was generally, "It's a compendium of tools and resources for use in Jewish education and Jewish living in the fullest sense of these terms." Traditional Jewish compilations did not seem overly concerned with definitional precision or rigidity. To the extent that they were records and guides to life, they were wide-ranging and multifaceted. Thus, the Talmud interweaves stories and anecdotes with legalistic debate; the Rambam's commentary on the Mishnah includes a recipe for haroset; the *Shulhan Arukh* lists customs, variations, and kavvanot (intentions) along with ritual and legal prescriptions; and the *Siddur Kol Bo* ("the prayer book with everything in it") has alphabets, diagrams for tying tefillin, calendars, and even pictures of fruit juxtaposed with the traditional order of prayers. Not to be presumptuous, this catalog takes these earlier texts as models for its breadth, variations, uncategorizability, and necessary incompleteness.

A detailed analysis of the origin and development of this project is not crucial to the use of the catalog; however, a short summary may be appropriate. This can be seen largely as an outgrowth of the countercultural activity of the late 1960s—both in the secular and Jewish worlds. The move toward communal living, returning to the land, relearning the abilities and joys of "making it yourself," voicing social and political concern which characterized the general counterculture (see *The Making of a Counter Culture* by Theodore Roszak, Doubleday, 1969) was paralleled (a few years later, of course) by the development of a "Jewish counterculture" (see "The Making of a Jewish Counter-Culture" by Bill Novak, *Response* 4, no. 1 [Spring-Summer 1970]). What *The Whole Earth Catalog* (Portola Institute/Random House, 1969–71) was to the former, i.e., an access to tools and resources, this catalog was envisioned to be for the latter.

As the project developed, however, it became apparent that what was needed was not so much a cataloging of already existing resources but a guide or manual to the range of contemporary Jewish life—i.e., a resource in itself.

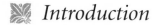

The present volume thus represents an amalgam of the resource-retrieval catalog and the guide to Jewish life. (For a more complete description of the origins of the catalog, the attitude toward halakhah expressed in it, the traditional and contemporary models for it, and a rationale for the subject matter included and the audiences addressed, see "The Jewish Whole Earth Catalogue: Theory and Development," a master's thesis by George Savran and Richard Siegel—contact editors.)

Basically our intentions are (1) to give enough information to be immediately useful; (2) to direct those interested to additional resources; (3) to present the traditional dimensions of the subjects covered; and (4) to open options for personal creativity and contemporary utilization of these directives. We make no claim to be a repository of the whole past of Jewish ritual, law, folklore, crafts, and so on. This is a nonexhaustive selection of materials which offer the possibility for immediate application and integration into one's personal environment. (Hopefully, the needs of the community and the availability of other material will spur further investigation, increased communications, and additional compilations.) The orientation is to move away from the prefabricated, spoon-fed, nearsighted Judaism into the stream of possibilities for personal responsibility and physical participation. This entails a returning of the control of the Jewish environment to the hands of the individual—through accessible knowledge of the what, where, who, and how of contemporary Judaism. [. . .]

You can plug in wherever you want. Some people may be drawn to the halakhah and various types of halakhic observance within a mitzvah system. Others will be more concerned with the underlying psychological, mythical, spiritual levels and the vehicles which have developed within Judaism to express these. Still others will find the possibilities for physical expression within traditional forms—openings for the artist and craftsman. There is no need to be reductionist about this; many other orientations and needs can find expression within this work. The hope, in fact, is that the catalog will facilitate the development of a "repertoire of responses" so that a person can accommodate himself to the rapid pace of societal and environmental change—as well as to his own personal, emotional, and spiritual flux.

There are two potential drawbacks to this diversity, however.

1. The book reads unevenly. Solution: do not read it all at once.

2. An orientation to which you may respond in one section may not be evident in another. Solution: draw your own transference. If this book opens you to an awareness that there are manifold ways of approaching the facets of Judaism, it will have fulfilled an important function. It is up to you, however, to build on these flexibilities and extend them according to your own creativity.

Ultimately, however, our intentions or hopes for this book are irrelevant. You will or will not respond to what is included for reasons which are beyond our anticipation or our abilities to effect.

May this book serve to fulfill the intention of:

זֶה אֵלִי וְאַנְוֵהוּ

"This is my God and I will beautify Him."

Blueprint for a Havurah

RABBI BURT JACOBSON AND THE EDITORS

INTRODUCTION

Many of us are lonely and hunger for meaning beyond our limited selves. We seek genuine fellowship and joy with others, the excitement of encounter with the Transcendent, and the discovery of our roots in the past.

One answer to our quest seems to be emerging from the youth culture—the creation of a new form of extended family: communes, co-ops, and, in the Jewish counterculture, the havurah.

A havurah is a core community of individuals who care for one another personally, and strive to attain a shared human and Jewish consciousness through shared activities and experiences. In this way a community structure is gradually built, and the havurah becomes a meaningful center in the lives of its haverim.

The task of creating a havurah is most difficult, given the individualistic and institutional conditioning that is at the root of American living patterns. A havurah cannot be built overnight. A group that wishes to become an interdependent community must accept the fact that this will require change in both the outer and inner patterns of living. And such change—if it is to become genuine change—can only come about over a prolonged period of time, and possibly with a great deal of the tension that comes with growth.

Such a community can only develop through compromise. But compromise and consensus should not be attained through the mere repression of individual conscience. We should attempt to create a structure that retains the polarity of individual and community, rather than merely seeking a framework in which the individual escapes from his autonomy and becomes dependent upon the will of the group.

THE COMPONENTS OF HAVURAH

The following articulation of elements that might go into building a core community is based primarily, though not exclusively, on the experiences of Havurat Shalom during 1969–71. A number of the ideas discussed are adapted or quoted from a pamphlet called *Making Communities* written by an anonymous Canadian commune.

1. You begin with a shared dissent from existing Jewish institutions and their modes of participation, and a group decision to initiate an alternative model.
2. You must have a personal compatibility of members, or at least an initial agreement to work together in areas of mutual concern. It is difficult to measure in advance how well people will get along once the havurah becomes more intensive. Yet one of the goals of the community should be the development of a sense of generosity, care, and responsibility toward one another. For only through a sense of giving can you put another's interest before your own, which is so necessary to community-building. From the very beginning members should have mutual respect, a sense of humor, and the ability to compromise. The size of the havurah should be limited so that superficial relationships can become truly genuine, and so that every member bears some active responsibility toward the community.
3. Haverim should make responsible personal commitments to the new community for a set period of time (perhaps two years) despite the problems and tensions that might occur.
4. If at all possible, the group should have a committed Jewish learned leader
   a. whose leadership role is accepted;
   b. who fosters leadership potential among other members so as to eventually minimize or eliminate the need for his own leadership role;
   c. who does not have a holier-than-thou attitude toward other members and is thus open to criticism.

   Such a leader may be found among Jewish professionals in the city, or may be found in a nearby city. This leader should work directly with
   a. aiding work-group chairmen;
   b. changing community coordinators;
   c. teaching the entire community.

   As a teacher he should give members a sense of the geography of Jewish values as embodied in the tradition, as well as methods of access and inquiry into Jewish source material. Thus some members can eventually become teachers themselves. The length and times of work-group leadership roles should be short in duration—perhaps four or six months—giving everyone a chance to lead different work groups and coordinate communal activities. All members should serve in at least one work-group.
5. Every healthy individual has a conscious set of goals and values that give him a set of wholeness. In like manner, a community must slowly develop a shared consciousness—shared values, attitudes, and ideas, and a vision of the goals of the havurah. But such a communal consensus can only be built where individual goals and values overlap. Such a consensus will widen slowly as members get to know each other, and learn from one another through shared experiences. At the very beginning, each haver should examine his

own life and try to determine which values and goals are most important to him. The members can share these things with one another and find out where their individual goals overlap.

6. The havurah should be involved in a step-by-step development of exciting shared experiences and activities which will implement the specific community goals.

   The creative power that the community exerts upon personal and interpersonal development will stem, to a great extent, from the amount of willingness that the members have toward sharing, in terms of time and energy. In this fashion the community can develop bonds of love and responsibility and become a true center. These experiences can lead to a true community structure and discipline.

   The following is a list of the kinds of experiences and activities which might become part of the havurah structure. Each area would be planned by one work group and the community as a whole would accept or modify the work group's proposals. The following structure is quite full and detailed, and again it must be stressed that such a structure will be developed slowly over a period of years. A new havurah will create its own order of priorities out of a large number of possibilities.

a. *Education*

(1) Shared day care for the children.

(2) Classes for youngsters—formal or free; taught by the Jewishly learned leader and/or other willing and capable haverim. (If this is impossible, the havurah will have to seek help from the "outside" community.) Classes may be developed by age bracket, interest, etc. The "little red schoolhouse" approach might be used when the ages of youngsters differ, and older students can help teach younger students. The youngster-teacher relationship should be emphasized. Kids should be involved in at least 2–3 hours of classes a week.

(3) Classes for parents/adults. Parents should study some of the same areas of subject matter which their youngsters are learning, perhaps together with their youngsters at times. In this connection, parents should study with their children's teacher. Possible areas of study might include traditional and modern sources on the following: Who Is Man?; Man and His Fellowman; Experiences and Ideas of God; Social Justice; The Basis and Nature of Jewish Tradition; Family Relationships; Eretz Yisrael; Myth and Ritual in Religion; Particular Rituals (the Sabbath, kashrut, traditional life-style).

   The community could also study the history and literature of a particular period of time, e.g., the biblical period, the rabbinic period, etc. Also, traditional commentaries on the portion of the week. Other areas of study might include Comparative Religion; Religion, Science and Technology; Religion and Politics; Yiddish and Hebrew Literature; Conversational Hebrew; The Thought of Modern Jewish Thinkers. The number of study areas for each semester or year will depend on the resources of the community.

(4) In line with this, the community should develop a communal library of Jewish and other books and records. If the community has its own building, the library could be located there. If not, a listing of books and records from each member's home could be compiled by a havurah librarian and this list given to each member. The havurah should also purchase books which can be of benefit to all members, such as the new *Encyclopaedia Judaica.*

b. *Celebration* The havurah should experiment with traditional religious observances and rites of passage, as well as create its own new forms of celebration and commemoration. The havurah can compile its own loose-leaf prayer book. Shared times of celebration could include:

(1) The Sabbath: Friday night services and a communal meal; Saturday morning services, Kiddush or luncheon; the third meal and Havdalah.

(2) Holy day celebrations: a community Seder, an all-night Tikkun on Shavuot, a havurah sukkah, Rosh Hodesh celebrations.

(3) Midweek communal meals with singing, storytelling, guest speakers. These meals could be potluck or elegantly planned.

(4) Weekend retreats of celebration and study at nearby Jewish camps, Christian retreat houses.

(5) Forms of meditation.

c. *Social and political justice* A haver could research a particular problem in the Jewish or general community at large, and a specific work group could explore various tactics to deal with the problem. One area that should be considered is the development of ongoing personal programs for Jewish old-age homes. The havurah should consider strategies for taking over positions of power on the federation, synagogue, center boards, and city council. Professionals in the havurah—doctors, lawyers—could donate their services and time to youth-culture centers, free clinics, and halfway houses.

d. *Encounter* Encounter sessions are times when members can confront one another openly and honestly on a feeling level. This can be very important, especially for haverim working so closely together, since tensions often build up. Encounter means the lowering of the defense mechanisms, the airing of gripes and criticism; but it also means mutual encouragement and complement. Encounters can take place as frequently as members feel the need for this activity. There should also be times set aside when members can share with the community what they are doing and experiencing on an individual level.

e. *Meetings* Meetings should be held only when there are issues and problems that the havurah as a whole must resolve. They should never last longer than two hours. Every thirty minutes or so, haverim should stand up and laugh.

f. *Fun* Socializing, open house, plays, dancing, choir, sports, picnics, Jewish and other crafts, Jewish cooking, creating magazines, theater parties, etc.

g. *Economy* The havurah should consider having, in some sense, a shared economic base, which can also add to its solidarity. Such economic sharing can be of various kinds: a food-buying co-op, shared group insurance, shared Israeli bonds, a community treasury fund for members in need, shared income, communal philanthropy, shared stockholding. (If all members own stocks in a particular corporation, they may wield greater control over company policies through combining their proxies and getting other stockholders in the company to do the same.)

7. A decision regarding the special needs of the havurah: whether homes and apartments can suffice, or whether a special building is necessary. If the community has enough funds for a building, it should consider one that is located in a semirural area (perhaps an old farm) which could offer a greater seclusion and closeness to nature. It could also be used for retreats and as a campsite—during the summer and during holy day vacations—for a havurah family camp. Eventually the farm could possibly become a Jewish retreat center for other havurot (which are now developing as a result of your activity!) and for local synagogues (and the havurah will be the host!). Some of the farm acreage could actually be used to grow vegetables, and families might come out on weekends to work on the garden. The farmhouse and the property would probably need a good deal of work to be put in shape, and this work should be done by the members themselves.
8. The havurah should develop a policy of relations to the Jewish and general community, a visitor's policy, and a policy of new admissions—including a set of criteria for membership.
9. Do not be frightened by the magnitude of the task. Every act that brings the community closer to realizing its vision—no matter how seemingly insignificant—is real and important. No community has yet become the Ultimate Utopia. And a community that feels secure because it has truly achieved its vision begins to stagnate. For man cannot be man without some insecurity, and without creating problems to knock his head against. The constant revolutionary process of growth is perhaps more important than the goals that have been achieved.

A First Step A Devotional Guide

RABBI ZALMAN SCHACHTER

INTRODUCTION

Much of Judaism concerns relationships, especially the relationship between God and human beings. The Bible contains so many descriptions of human and divine encounters, of God seeking out a person or of a person seeking God. Our traditional liturgy seems to assume that God and any and all Jews have a relationship. When we speak the words of the prayer book, we often find ourselves saying things to God, telling God: You are praised, You are holy. Sometimes the words of the prayer book seem to describe particular ways we are supposed to relate to God; for example, we are told that we should love God. Modern (and not so modern) Jewish theologians provide us with a variety of opinions on the matter of relating to God. But reading Bible, liturgy, and theology can lead to a real sense of conspiracy; all those sources conspire to tell us that we ought to relate to God, and none seems to tell us how or where to begin.

Jewish mystics (kabbalistic and Hasidic) have always tried to address "how-to" questions. Sometimes they preferred to deal with these questions in face-to-face meetings with their students, but sometimes they or their students wrote books. Texts which concern such questions as how to experience the Divine Presence, how to love and fear God, how to worship, how to enter into a relationship with God do exist. The problem is that these texts exist in Hebrew and Aramaic; relatively few of them have been translated into English.

A First Step by Zalman Schachter is not a translation. It was first written in English. It is a contemporary attempt to make accessible spiritual and devotional techniques from classic, Jewish sources, sources on which the pamphlet was based. We reprint part of it here for you in the hope that it may prove useful.

TO WHOM THIS MAY CONCERN:

This guide intends to give you practical information in the area of spiritual discipline and resources. I imagine you, the reader, in the following way. You are a "seeker." This means (to me) that you are trying to find a *way* to express some spiritual stirrings in yourself and to develop that holy source within you, so that it may begin to flow freely. You have for sometime searched for the *way*. You have read some Jewish books, which have succeeded only in increasing your need for this search. You have also read some non-Jewish material. You have become further convinced that somewhere, somehow, there is a greater reality, and you have from time to time made efforts in the direction of finding it. I take it that these efforts proved disappointing to some degree, that you have many times cast this search aside, only after some time to take it up again. This cycle has repeated itself. You are perhaps now looking for a practical way, which will show you some measure of advance. I also take it that you are concerned enough to spend some time and effort at working with discipline and resources.

You need not have a clearly crystallized philosophy. All you need is a willingness to test some of your already held beliefs, and those which you wish to hold, in the laboratory of your experience.

All this I take for granted. You will consider it only fair if you are required to spend at least a half hour each day, and an additional two hours each week, at this work. You will have to be honest with yourself. You cannot do this work alone. You need a trusted friend with whom you can work together and with whom you can freely discuss your work. Spiritual work in loneliness, without the possibility of sharing and comparing, can be harmful. Be prepared to let the work affect you fully, and take you into its own direction. Be prepared to have your mode of living profoundly changed in all its aspects. Read this manual time and time again. Do not proceed with a new exercise before you have the previous one under full control and can *at will* duplicate it any time you desire.

If any of the above does not apply to you, you need not read further. It will only be a waste of time. This guide takes your motivation for granted, and also the fact that you do follow and apply it.

This is not an inspirational text, nor does it contain anything new. It is deliberately dry. To add a number of very charming illustrations and stories might divert you from *working*.

But even if you do follow this guide honestly and conscientiously, it will not take you *all* the way. It will only introduce you to some *elementary techniques* of the spiritual laboratory. When you will have reached the last of the exercises in your own practical experience, and when you can "control" your actions as outlined here, you will need a *teacher* and *guide* to prescribe the specific and very personal other steps for you. Let me assure you that there *are* teachers who can take you further. Further steps cannot be given to you in a manual, since it cannot speak to your own specific differences from other people. Your own very individual further development will need individual guidance.

This primer is the result of experience with a limited group; but for you your own progress will be the decisive factor. You will soon come to realize that, in order to make progress in this work, a certain levelheaded sobriety is immensely necessary. Anyone thinking that rapture awaits him instead of hard work will soon be disappointed.

Let me explain to you the function of kavvanah. Kavvanah means intention. Our intention is always free. There is nothing that can obstruct your intending. Even if the whole world coerces you into a pattern of actions, you can always "intend" whatever you want. For instance, you sit in the dentist's chair. He drills and you feel a sting of pain, but you can "intend" this pain as an offering of love. You offer to God the moment of pain, intending to suffer it for Him. You might put it in somewhat this way: "Ribbono Shel Olam!—You are good and Your universe is good. The All is filled with Your mercy and goodness, as is the pain I feel. I cannot bring You any other sacrifice. Please accept this moment of pain as a love offering from me." Or you work in your day-by-day endeavor. You do whatever you must do, and you intend: "God of law and order, You have ordained work for man. In doing, I intend to do Your will, I wish to cleave to You in this action." Or you travel and time is taken up by it. You lean back and wink at Him in your mind as if to say, "Sweet Father, I enjoy Your presence! The rhythm of the wheels, the fleeting scenery, we are all nothing but You. You contain me and my vehicle. I will be careful in travel, for this is Your will. Guard my going out and my coming back. I am secure in You."

You see, these "arrows of awareness" are rather simple to practice. You will soon find that placing yourself in His presence will come with some practice.

Especially when engaged in doing a mitzvah, you will want to put your intention to use. On the Sabbath, when eating, you can intend, "Likhvod ha-Shabbat—May I eat this food and enjoy it for Your sake, for this is the mitzvah of the Shabbat."

When putting on the tefillin,or lighting the candles, you can intend: "Lovely Lord, take my body as an instrument of Your will. My limbs are prepared, and are at Your disposal. Use them!" And then you say the blessing.

It is helpful to have a visual image in the kavvanah. You picture the will of God flowing into your body and soul, becoming united with the limbs, organs, senses, brain, and nerves, and moving—make sure at this point to feel them moving by His will—to execute the mitzvah. This should become very familiar to you. Do not go on to the next point until the practice of kavvanah has become firmly established in your habit pattern.

On the examination of one's conscience and going to sleep

Deliberateness and watchfulness over your actions and motives now becomes important. You will find yourself failing persistently. At this point study the *Mesillath Yesharim* by M. L. Luzzatto (Jewish Publication Society, 1948). For encouragement, also read Rabbi Milton Steinberg's Yom Kippur sermon entitled, "Our Persistent Failures," in *The Believing Jew* (pp. 213–28).

You will then have come across Rabbi Levi Yitzhak's Heshbon ha-Nephesh—Reckoning of the Soul—before going to sleep. This is what we will begin to work on now.

Before going to sleep start out by fully and completely forgiving anyone who wronged or hurt you, and pray for the welfare of that person. Continue by affirming the Oneness of God, and your longing to love Him, and then read the Shema.

Finally, take a short tally of your actions during the day. Begin with the first thought upon awakening. (This thought is of tremendous power, it exerts influence on the rest of the day. Make sure to think a good first thought and last thought every day.) Don't spend more than five minutes on this tally to begin with. Just check through your actions to see if they are as you planned them. If you are sure that you did not do the right thing, hold the thought, word or action up to God and, with a short arrow prayer, ask Him to remove this kind of thing from your life. Again, much will depend on the sobriety and tenacity you show every night.

Once a week (Thursday night might be best) you must set aside more time than usual. Do this when you are still fresh. If you leave this until you are too worn out, you cannot expect to succeed. Therefore, plan the evening accordingly. Let us say you are now alone and not too tired. At first, you slip into the "life" meditation, and then, when you come to feel His presence in your being, you begin to judge yourself in His sight, not harshly, not carelessly, but justly. Do this in great detail; look at your motivations in great detail; don't condemn or convict yourself, but visualize yourself before God, and listen to His judgment.

This does not mean that you will not get anywhere. It *does* mean that your *real effort* will be rewarded.

This manual is intended as a laboratory guide, to help you on your way. In order to keep you from confusion, it is suggested that, for the time being, you stop any further outside reading in this area. Later on, when you will have some real experience behind you, further reading will prove to be a joy instead of a hindrance. The many states described will be familiar to you, and serve as a further validation of the rightness of your own experience. But until you gain positive experience, refrain from further reading, in order to find the way.

On the other hand, inspirational (instead of *how-to-do-it*) reading is of immense importance. You will find a bibliography in the back. Choose one of those books but do not read it in one sitting. Rather, find time (it need not be very much—in this you suit yourself to your own schedule and inclination) and hold on to this time as something very precious. Address God and ask Him that your reading may inspire your *continued effort*. Then read for a while. Before you put the book away, close it and think back to fasten what you have read in your memory. You need a *model* to sustain you in this work. Your reading ought to give *this* to you. Anything describing the thoughts and lives of tzaddikim makes, therefore, very necessary reading. However, do not, at this point, look for functional aspects of that literature. You must work quite a bit before some of the formulas shown there will apply to you. A certain amount of responsibility for your progress can be taken by the compiler of this guide, only if you see fit to trust it from the outset. If you make up your mind to do so, this manual will be of help to you. (Scholarly documentation of sources can be supplied. For your practical work this is not necessary, and at this point would only be intrusive.)

The approach used here is that of classical Jewish mysticism, as refined by Hasidism and, in particular, by the Habad school.

This approach seeks to get you to work on yourself and to help you achieve something.

Many prayers have been offered for your success.

How to Bring Mashiah

ARTHUR WASKOW

1. "If you're planting a tree and you hear Mashiah has come, first finish planting and then run to the city gates to tell him Shalom" (Yochanan Ben Zakkai).

THEREFORE: Plant a tree somewhere as a small tikkun olam—fixing up the world—wherever the olam most needs it. Plant a tree in Vietnam in a defoliated former forest. *Go there to plant it* if possible (even if difficult); if not send money to:

Abraham Heschel Memorial Forest
Trees and Life for Vietnam
Glengary Road
Croton on Hudson, N.Y. 10520

Plant a tree in Appalachia where the strip mines have poisoned the forests. *Go there to plant it; start a kibbutz there and grow more trees.* Plant a tree in Brooklyn where the asphalt has buried the forest. *Go back there to plant it* and live with some of the old Jews who still live there. If policemen come to save the asphalt, keep planting. Offer everybody a turn with the shovel.

2. "Mashiah will come when the whole Jewish People keeps/remembers Shabbat twice in a row" (Talmud, Shabbat 118b).

THEREFORE: Forget about all the things you *mustn't* do on Shabbat, and instead think of all the things you would most *like* to do on Shabbat (and forever). Do them. Read Torah with some friends and talk about it; walk on grass barefoot; look very carefully at a flower without picking it; give somebody something precious and beautiful without asking him to pay you; give love. Since it's not enough to do this alone (see the prediction), pick out a few Jews on the street, tell them it's Shabbat, and dance a horah with them (or the kazatsky, if you're into Yiddish).

3. "The nations . . . shall beat their swords into plowshares. . . . They shall never again know war" (Isaiah 2:4).

THEREFORE: Get together a minyan and travel up to West Point. Take along ten swords and a small forge. Put the small forge in the main entrance, start it glowing, and beat the swords into something like a digging tool. Dig holes for ten trees, and plant the trees in the roadway. Meanwhile, sing "Lo yisah goy" and "Ain't Gonna Study War No More" alternately, and if any West Pointers stop to see what's going down, offer them a reworked sword to dig with.

4. "Mashiah will come when one generation is either wholly innocent or wholly guilty" (Talmud, Sanhedrin 98a).

THEREFORE: Analyze the tax system of the United States, and publish a detailed answer to these two questions: (a) Are United States taxes used largely for purposes prohibited by Torah (e.g., oppressing the poor, destroying trees, etc.)? (b) Are any Jews in the United States successfully avoiding payment of all taxes? If the answer to (a) is "Yes" and to (b) is "No," proclaim that the entire generation is guilty *in fact*, regardless of their personal opinions. Ask all shuls to include the proclamation in their Shabbat prayers with strong kavvanah: "HaShem, we are at last *all* guilty: send him!"

5. "And a woman shall conceive and bear in the same day [i.e., without pain]" (Midrash on Jeremiah). "See whether a man doth travail with child; wherefore do I see every man with his hands on his loins, as a woman in travail . . . Alas! for that day is great, so that none is like it" (Jeremiah 30:6–7).

THEREFORE: If you're a man, practice having a baby. Whether you're a man or woman, take a class in the Lamaze method of trained, fully awake childbirth. Learn and practice the exercises. If you're an expectant father, take as much time off from work as your wife/lover does (before and after the birth), and try to experience fully what giving birth and baby care mean.

6. "For the Lord hath created a new thing in the earth: a woman [nekevah] shall court a man [warrior]" (Jeremiah 31:22).

THEREFORE: If you're a woman, surround the nearest warrior type with a ring of laughing, singing women. If he threatens you with a gun, ask seventeen of your sisters to join you in taking it away from him—gently. But more important, whether you're a man or a woman, let the female *within you* encompass the warrior *within you*. Let that soul of yours which is open, receptive, enveloping, envelop that soul of yours which is angry, threatening, thrusting.

7. "In that day shall the Lord [Adonai] be one [Ehad], and His name one" (Zechariah 14:9).

THEREFORE: When you pray and come to "Adonai" in the prayer, either *think* "Ehad" with full kavvanah at the same time you are saying "Adonai," or *say* "Ehad" while you think "Adonai."

8. Rabbi Joshua ben Levi found Elijah the prophet, disguised as a leper, begging at the gates of Rome. "When will you come to proclaim the Mashiah?" he asked. "'*Today, . . . if you will hear his voice,*'" replied Elijah (Talmud Babli, Sanhedrin 98a).

THEREFORE: Hear his voice. Open yourself to hear it. Practice saying, "Hineni"—"Here I am"—in a sense of total openness.

9. "In the days to come . . . instruction shall come forth from Zion" (Isaiah 2:1–3). Not out of Sinai. "Behold, the days come, saith the Lord, that I will make a new covenant with the house of Israel, . . . not according to the covenant that I made with their fathers in the day that I [led] them out of . . . Egypt. . . . [Instead,] I will put My law [Torah] in their inward parts, and in their hearts will I write it. . . . They shall teach no more every man his neighbor and every man his brother, saying: 'Know the Lord'; for they shall all know Me" (Jeremiah 31:31–34).

THEREFORE: Stop teaching. Listen inward, inward to your own heart, for the new covenant: the covenant of the Torah from Zion. Listen especially for what is new about it.

10. Said a poor tailor one Yom Kippur, "I have committed only minor offenses; but You, O lord, have committed grievous sins: You have taken away babies from their mothers, and mothers from their babies. Let us be quits: may You forgive me, and I will forgive You." Said Reb Levi Yitzhak of Berditchev to the tailor, "Why did you let Him off so easily? You might have forced Him to redeem all of Israel!"

THEREFORE: Do not let God off so easily. Hear His/Her voice, but challenge His/Her answer. Wrestle mightily; like Yaakov, you may win. *Keep on wrestling!*

ACKNOWLEDGMENTS

1. GOING SOUTH

Michael Walzer, "A Cup of Coffee and a Seat": Reprinted with permission. Originally appeared in *Dissent,* vol. 7 (Spring 1960), pp. 111–120.

Betty Alschuler, "Notes from the American Revolution—1962": Reprinted with permission. Originally appeared in *The Reconstructionist* (Dec. 28, 1962).

Albert Vorspan, "The Freedom Rides": Reprinted with permission. Originally appeared in *Jewish Frontier,* vol. 29 (Apr. 1962).

Richard L. Rubenstein, "The Rabbis Visit Birmingham": Reprinted with permission. Originally appeared in *The Reconstructionist* (May 31, 1963).

Seymour Siegel, "Pilgrimage to Selma": Reprinted with permission from *Congress Bi-Weekly,* volume 32, # 7, pp. 5–6. © 1965, American Jewish Congress.

2. AT HOME (ALMOST) IN AMERICA

Shad Polier, "Kennedy's Impact on American Freedom": Reprinted with permission from *Congress Bi-Weekly,* volume 30, # 18, pp. 6–8. © 1963, American Jewish Congress.

Jewish Frontier, "The Pity of It: An Editorial": Reprinted with permission. Originally appeared in *Jewish Frontier,* vol. 30 (Dec. 1963).

Arthur Hertzberg, "America is Galut": Reprinted with permission. Originally appeared in *Jewish Frontier,* vol. 31 (July 1964).

American Jewish Congress, "The Fourth Dialogue in Israel: The Challenge of Jewish Youth": Excerpts from the Fourth Dialogue in Israel (The Challenge of Jewish Youth), reprinted with permission from *Congress Bi-Weekly,* volume 32, # 13. © 1965, American Jewish Congress.

Detroit Jewish News, "Sandy Koufax, an American Hero": Reprinted with permission. Originally appeared in *Detroit Jewish News* (Oct. 22, 1965), p. 4.

3. LIVING WITH THE HOLOCAUST

Lucy S. Dawidowicz, "Boy Meets Girl in Warsaw Ghetto": Reprinted with permission. Originally appeared in *Midstream,* vol. 6 (Summer 1960), pp. 109–112.

Marie Syrkin, "Hannah Arendt: The Clothes of the Empress": Reprinted with permission. Originally appeared in *Dissent,* vol. 10 (Autumn 1963), pp. 344–352.

Steven S. Schwarzschild, Emil L. Fackenheim, and George Steiner, "Jewish Values in the Post-Holocaust Future: A Symposium": Reprinted with permission from *Judaism,* vol. 16 (Summer 1967). © 1967, American Jewish Congress.

Abraham Joshua Heschel, "Disaster": Originally appeared in Abraham Joshua Heschel, *Israel: An Echo of Eternity* (1967), pp. 111–115. Reprinted with permission of Susannah Heschel.

Alfred Kazin, "Living with the Holocaust": Reprinted with permission. Originally appeared in *Midstream,* vol. 16 (June/July 1970), pp. 3–7.

4. BLACK-JEWISH RELATIONS

Joachim Prinz, "'America Must Not Remain Silent . . .'": Reprinted with permission from *Congress Bi-Weekly,* volume 30, # 13, p. 3. © 1963, American Jewish Congress.

Myron M. Fenster, "The Princeton Plan Comes to Jackson Heights": Reprinted with permission. Originally appeared in *Midstream,* vol. 10 (Summer 1964), pp. 76–83.

Albert Vorspan, "Ten Ways Out for Tired Liberals": Reprinted with permission. Originally appeared in *American Judaism,* vol. 14 (Fall 1964).

Abraham Joshua Heschel, "Religion and Race": Reprinted from Abraham Joshua Heschel, *The Insecurity of Freedom* (1966), pp. 85–100, with the permission of Susannah Heschel.

Leslie A. Fiedler, Arthur Hertzberg, and Paul Jacobs, "Negro-Jewish Relations in America: A Symposium": Reprinted with permission. Originally appeared in *Midstream,* vol. 12 (Dec. 1966).

Irving Howe, "In This Moment of Grief": Reprinted with permission. Originally appeared in *Dissent,* vol. 15 (May–June 1968), p. 197.

Rabbi Bernard Weinberger, "The Negro and the (Orthodox) Jew": Reprinted with permission. Originally appeared in *The Jewish Observer,* vol. 5 (Sept. 1968), pp. 11–14.

5. THE STRUGGLE FOR SOVIET JEWRY

Judd L. Teller, "American Jews and Soviet Anti-Semitism": Reprinted with permission. Originally appeared in *Jewish Frontier,* vol. 32 (Apr. 1965).

Elie Wiesel, "Fear and Heroism: A Visit with Russian Jews": Originally appeared in *S.O.S. Soviet Jewry,* vol. 2, no. 5 (Jan.–Feb. 1966). Courtesy of the Labadie Collection, the University of Michigan.

Erich Goldhagen, "Soviet Jewry: Range of Repression": Reprinted with permission from *Congress Bi-Weekly,* volume 33, # 9. © 1966, American Jewish Congress.

Student Struggle for Soviet Jewry, "I Am My Brother's Keeper": Originally appeared in *S.O.S. Soviet Jewry,* vol. 3, no. 1 (Sept.–Oct. 1966), and *S.O.S. Soviet Jewry,* vol. 3, no. 3 (Jan.–Feb. 1967). Courtesy of the Labadie Collection, the University of Michigan.

6. THE JEWISH STAKE IN VIETNAM

Albert Vorspan, "Vietnam and the Jewish Conscience": Reprinted with permission. Originally appeared in *American Judaism,* vol. 15 (Passover 1966).

Arthur J. Lelyveld, "Peace: Jewish Imperatives": Reprinted with permission from *Congress Bi-Weekly,* volume 33, # 6, pp. 8–10. © 1966, American Jewish Congress.

Michael Wyschogrod, "Peace: The Real Imperatives: A Letter to Arthur J. Lelyveld": Reprinted with permission from *Congress Bi-Weekly,* volume 33, # 7, pp. 7–8. © 1966, American Jewish Congress.

Meir Kahane, "The Jewish Stake in Vietnam": Reprinted with permission. Originally appeared in *Jewish Press,* June 9, 1967.

Mike Masch, "Anti-War Marchers Turn Out En Masse in Washington": Originally appeared in *Jewish Exponent,* Nov. 21, 1969. Reprinted with permission by the *Jewish Exponent.* Permission granted in 2003.

"Jewish People's Peace Treaty": Reprinted from *Brooklyn Bridge*, vol. 1, no. 3 (May 1971). Courtesy of the Labadie Collection, the University of Michigan.

Balfour Brickner, "Vietnam and the Jewish Community": Reprinted with permission. Originally appeared in *Christian Century*, vol. 87 (Apr. 29, 1970).

7. AFTER THE SIX-DAY WAR

M. Jay Rosenberg, "My Evolution as a Jew": Reprinted with permission. Originally appeared in *Midstream*, vol. 16 (Aug./Sept. 1970), pp. 50–53.

Steven S. Schwarzschild, "On the Theology of Jewish Survival": Reprinted with permission. Originally appeared in *CCAR Journal* (Oct. 1968), pp. 2–21.

Sharon Rose, "Zionism in the Middle East": Reprinted from *The Great Speckled Bird*, Oct. 26, 1970. Courtesy of the Labadie Collection, the University of Michigan.

Balfour Brickner, "My Zionist Dilemmas": Reprinted with permission. Originally appeared in *Sh'ma*, vol. 1, no. 1 (Nov. 9, 1970).

8. HOW JEWISH IS IT?

Norman Mailer, "A Program for the Nation": Reprinted with permission. Originally appeared in *Dissent*, vol. 7 (Winter 1960), pp. 67–70.

Philip Roth, "Writing about Jews": Reprinted from COMMENTARY, December 1963, by permission; all rights reserved.

Leslie Fiedler, "The Jewish Intellectual and Jewish Identity": Originally appeared as Address by Leslie Fiedler and following discussion, from the Second Dialogue in Israel. Reprinted with permission from *Congress Bi-Weekly*, volume 30, # 12, pp. 51–59. © 1963, American Jewish Congress.

Susan Sontag, "What's Happening to America": © 1967 by Susan Sontag. Reprinted with permission of The Wylie Agency, Inc.

Allen Ginsberg, "Witness for the Defense at the Chicago Conspiracy Trial": Excerpted from the trial transcript in the case of *United States of America v. David T. Dellinger, et al.*, No. 69 CR-180 (Northern District of Illinois, Dec. 1969).

9. ON JEWISH RADICALS AND RADICAL JEWS

M. Jay Rosenberg, "To Jewish Uncle Toms": Reprinted with permission. Originally appeared in *Jewish Frontier*, vol. 36 (Feb. 1969).

Jewish Liberation Project, "Editorial": Originally appeared in *Jewish Liberation Journal*, vol. 1, no. 1 (May 1969).

David Weissman, "Radicals Invade Federation, Glue 200 Mezuzahs to Doors": Reprinted with permission. Originally appeared in *Jewish Post and Opinion*, Nov. 14, 1969, p. 4.

Abbie Hoffman et al., "At the Chicago Conspiracy Trial": Excerpted from the trial transcript in the case of *United States of America v. David T. Dellinger et al.*, No. 69 CR-180 (Northern District of Illinois, Dec. 1969, Feb. 1970).

"Radical Zionist Manifesto": Originally appeared in *Genesis 2*, vol. 1, no. 3 (Apr. 1970).

Aviva Cantor Zuckoff, "Oppression of Amerika's Jews": Reprinted from *Rat*, Feb. 3, 1971. Courtesy of the Labadie Collection, the University of Michigan.

Jonathan Goldin and Morris U. Schappes, "Dialogue with a Radical Jewish Student": Reprinted with permission. Originally appeared in *Jewish Currents*, vol. 24 (July–Aug. 1970), pp. 26–30.

Brooklyn Bridge Collective, "We Are Coming Home": Originally appeared in *Brooklyn Bridge,* vol. 1, no. 1 (Feb. 1971).
Zvi Lowenthal and Jonathan Braun, "An Interview with Meir Kahane": Originally appeared in *The Flame* (Winter 1971).
Steve Cohen, "The JDL: Politics of Jewish Experience": Originally appeared in *ACIID,* vol. 2, no. 4 (Apr. 1971).

10. THE MAKING OF A JEWISH COUNTERCULTURE
Balfour Brickner, "Notes on a Freedom Seder": Reprinted with permission. Originally appeared in *The Reconstructionist* (June 13, 1969).
Bill Novak, "The Making of a Jewish Counter Culture": Reprinted with permission. Originally appeared in *CCAR Journal,* vol. 17 (June 1970), pp. 16–27.
Stephen C. Lerner, "Ramah and Its Critics": Reprinted with permission from *Conservative Judaism,* pp. 1–28, Summer 1971, © The Rabbinical Assembly.
Jerry D. Barach, "The Chavura: Blend of Chaos, Tranquility": Reprinted with permission. Originally appeared in *Cleveland Jewish News,* May 12, 1972, p. 15.
Mike Tabor, "Young Jews Discover Their True Forebears": Reprinted with permission. Originally appeared in *Jewish Post and Opinion,* June 18, 1971, p. 2.

11. THE SEXUAL REVOLUTION
"Rabbi Conducts Jewish Gay Service": Originally appeared in *Gay,* vol. 2, no. 40 (Dec. 21, 1970). Courtesy of the Labadie Collection, the University of Michigan.
Martha Shelley, "Gay is Good": Originally appeared in *Brooklyn Bridge,* vol. 1, no. 3 (May 1971). Courtesy of the Labadie Collection, the University of Michigan.
Jewish Post and Opinion, "Rabbi Bans Hot Pants, See-Through Blouses": Reprinted with permission. Originally appeared in *Jewish Post and Opinion,* July 20, 1971, p. 1.
Dr. Morris Mandel, "Problems in Human Emotions": Reprinted with permission. Originally appeared in *Jewish Press,* Oct. 8, 1971.
Jewish Post and Opinion, "Fun in the Bedroom Is the Jewish View": Reprinted with permission. Originally appeared in *Jewish Post and Opinion,* Apr. 13, 1973, p. 3.
Helen Cohen, "The Games Singles Play": Reprinted with permission. Originally appeared in *Jewish Post and Opinion,* Aug. 24, 1973, p. 10.

12. JEWISH WOMEN AND FEMINISM
Betty Friedan, "A Comfortable Concentration Camp": Reprinted with permission. Originally appeared in Betty Friedan, *The Feminine Mystique (1963).*
Brooklyn Bridge Collective, "Jewish Women: Life Force of a Culture?": Originally appeared in *Brooklyn Bridge,* vol. 1, no. 1 (Feb. 1971).
Rachel Adler, "The Jew Who Wasn't There: Halacha and the Jewish Woman": Reprinted with permission. Originally appeared in *Davka,* vol. 1, no. 4 (Summer 1971).
Paula E. Hyman, "The Other Half: Women in the Jewish Tradition": Reprinted with permission. Originally appeared in *Conservative Judaism* 26 (Summer 1972), pp. 14–21.
Ezrat Nashim, "Jewish Women Call for Change": Reprinted with permission. Originally distributed in 1972. From Jacob R. Marcus, *The American Jewish Woman* (1981), pp. 894–896.

Shirley Frank, "The Population Panic": Reprinted with permission. Originally appeared in *Lilith,* vol. 1, no. 4 (Fall/Winter 1977–78).

13. SELECTIONS FROM *THE FIRST JEWISH CATALOG*

Richard Siegel, Michael Strassfeld, and Sharon Strassfeld, "Introduction"; Rabbi Burt Jacobson and the Editors, "Blueprint for a Havurah"; Rabbi Zalman Schachter, "A First Step: A Devotional Guide"; Arthur Waskow, "How to Bring Mashiah": All reprinted from **The First Jewish Catalog,** © 1973, *Michael Strassfeld, Sharon Strassfeld, and Richard Siegel,* The Jewish Publication Society with the permission of the publisher, The Jewish Publication Society.